May 2022

# Learning Diplomacy

For Hawle,
with admiration
and respect.

The Association for Diplomatic Studies and Training
Foreign Affairs Oral History Project

# Learning Diplomacy

## *An Oral History*

## AMBASSADOR LUIGI R. EINAUDI

*Interviewed by: Charles Stuart Kennedy
and Robin Matthewman
Initial interview date: May 17, 2013*

**To order additional copies of this book, contact:**
Xlibris
844-714-8691
www.Xlibris.com
Orders@Xlibris.com
542252

# FOREWORD

For over 235 years extraordinary diplomats have served the United States at home and abroad with courage and dedication. Yet their accomplishments in promoting and protecting American interests often remain little known to their compatriots.

ADST (adst.org) is an independent, nonprofit organization committed to capturing, preserving, and sharing the experiences of America's diplomats. Founded in 1986, we have the world's largest collection of U.S. diplomatic oral history—available on our website and through the Library of Congress. This rich resource is available without charge to scholars, practicing diplomats, journalists, and ordinary citizens all around the world. But that is not all we do. We support the training of foreign affairs personnel at the State Department's Foreign Service Institute. We also conduct educational outreach, produce podcasts and videos, and have an active social media program. And we have facilitated the publication of over 100 books by members of the Foreign Service and others.

Thank you for your interest in American diplomacy. We urge you to visit us at adst.org and make a donation to support this important and fascinating work. Because diplomacy matters.

*Susan R. Johnson*
*President*
*Association for Diplomatic Studies & Training*

# PREFACE

This account begins with family and education, then focuses on my diplomatic career. As in other ADST interviews, the discussion proceeds chronologically. My family background in the search for knowledge and public service was followed by the discovery of Latin America through student politics and an apprenticeship in the relations of knowledge to power at RAND. This led to a quarter century at the State Department, followed later by five years at the Organization of American States. My State Department career began and ended with tours on the Secretary of State's Policy Planning Staff, the first under Republican Presidents, the second under a Democratic one. Highlights included working under Henry Kissinger, revolution and counterrevolution in Central America, and ending the war between Ecuador and Peru. At the Organization of American States, first as the U.S. Ambassador, and later as an elected Assistant Secretary General and a year as interim Secretary General, I sought to strengthen regional support for democracy, helped resolve boundary disputes in Central America and had a speaking role in the tragedy of Haiti.

My interviewers and I discuss the workings of government, its people, and the complexities of theorizing about politics. Our dialogue brings out internal stresses within administrations, the difficulties of rendering foreign policy coherent, both domestically and multilaterally, and the pains and infrequent joys of conflict resolution and peace-making. A variety of U.S., Latin American and Caribbean leaders and governing experiences give life to the tale.

The concluding "Afterwords" try to bring together elements of what is needed to advance U.S. interests in today's world, which calls simultaneously for rootedness to defend our interests and empathy to prevent others' problems from engulfing us as well. Our unparalleled strength is limited by our difficulties in listening, in respecting the sovereignty of others, and in working for democracy among countries -- not just within them. These blind spots hamper our ability to complement our national power by engaging multilaterally – a tool essential to dealing with an increasingly complicated world.

The events described here also make evident the damages caused by lack of resources for diplomacy and inadequate career support for the Foreign Service, particularly as compared to the training and promotion policies of the Department of Defense.

These dialogues began in 2013 in a series of interviews conducted by Charles Stewart Kennedy. After further questions by Robin Matthewman, I edited the transcript with materials gleaned from piles of contemporary notes and documents, some of which appear as appendices. None of this makes up for all I have forgotten! But if the account omits a great deal, the text occasionally touches on things I did not know at the time. I can at least say that it is accurate to the absolute best of my abilities.

# ACKNOWLEDGEMENTS

Those who sustained me along the way are part of me: my wife Carol and our children, Maria, Elisabeth, Mario and Peter, all of whom were affected by my many obsessions. I also owe much to the entire Einaudi, Michels and Urban clans.

Great is the debt to my two Foreign Service interviewers, Stu Kennedy and Robin Matthewman. Other ADST stalwarts were Susan Johnson, Lisa Terry, Margery Thompson, and Heather Ashe. Aubrey Molitor and Sophia Reitich helped me overcome the hurdles of permissions and refinement. At the Columbus Memorial Library of the Organization of American States, Stella Villagrán and Rocio Suarez provided constant encouragement along with documentary support.

Those who shared in the events and their telling include Leo Rios, Lynn Sicade, Matt Evangelista, Caesar Sereseres, Francisco Villagrán, David Randolph, Stephen McFarland, Mary Ellen Gilroy, David Spencer, Ciro de Falco, Clement Moore Henry, James Michel, Todd Greentree, Paul Spencer, Fernando Andrade, and Michael Shifter. Their recollections provided both fun and perspective.

I was also spurred on in various ways by Amalia de Luigi, Eamonn Gearon, Joan Affleck and Nepier Smith, David Greenwood, Sandra Honoré, Frank Mora, Jay Cope, Robert Maguire, Ed and Ellen Casey, Michele Manatt, Johanna Mendelson, Beatrice Rangel, Paolo Soddu, Hugo de Zela, Francesco Tuccari, Roberto Marchionatti, Hirokazu Miyazaki, Paolo Silvestri, Jean Michel Arrighi, and Abe Lowenthal.

I am grateful to them all. I hope you, the reader, will benefit from our efforts.

# TABLE OF CONTENTS

Research on the third world—Africa, Asia, and Latin America
Teaching political science at UCLA
Researching Peruvian military in Lima, Peru 1964-1965
Head of Social Science research on Latin America
Worked with Pentagon, Air Force, and NSC
Identifying Foreign Trends
"The 'System' does not work"
Negotiated RAND's first contract with State Department
U.S.-Peruvian relations after 1968 military coup

Washington, D.C.— Foreign Service Reserve Officer on the
Secretary's Policy Planning Staff 1974–1977
    Winston Lord, Director of S/P
    Henry Kissinger, Secretary of State
    Rise and fall of Chile's President Allende
    Pinochet Coup and U.S.
    Launch of Global Outlook Program (GLOP)
    U.S.-Latin America relations
    Speech writing for Kissinger
    Marcona expropriation in Peru
    Travels with Kissinger
    Transition, Panama Canal review and first Country Reports
    on Human Rights

Washington, D.C.—Director of the Inter-American Bureau's
Office of Policy Planning and Coordination 1977–1989
    Tour of Caribbean Basin with Andrew Young
    Terence Todman and Human rights (see also Appendix Three)
    Argentine Dirty War
    Viron Peter Vaky and interagency coordination

# ILLUSTRATIONS

Front cover: Flags of OAS member states, courtesy of LR Einaudi
Back cover: Carol P. and Luigi R. Einaudi, courtesy of Paula Ferris
Einaudi

# APPENDICES

## Reference

Bibliography, library, papers, collected speeches at CML http://www.oas.org/en/columbus/amb_einaudi.asp

# Family Background

*Q: Today is the 17ᵗʰ of May 2013 and this is an interview with Luigi R. Einaudi. What does the R stand for?*

EINAUDI: Roberto, after my mother's father, Roberto Michels. I use the middle initial to differentiate myself from my father's father, Luigi Einaudi, who never used a middle initial.

*Q: Well, let's start at the beginning, when and where were you born?*

EINAUDI: March 1, 1936 in Cambridge, Massachusetts.

*Q: Alright, it is certainly a distinguished name. I googled you on the internet and the first thing I came to was the president of Italy and I felt this is a little bit above my pay grade but—*

EINAUDI: It was above mine too.

*Q: But anyway, could you talk about the Einaudis. Can you talk about their history and then we will move to your mother's side, but could you talk about them?*

EINAUDI: Yes, of course. The Einaudis come originally from what is still today the poorest valley of the Italian Alps, the Val Maira, up against France. They were classic mountain folk:

herdsmen, woodsmen, and peasant farmers. The first to leave was my great grandfather Lorenzo. He came down into the valleys of Piedmont and settled in Carrù, a small cattle trading center where he won a competition to collect taxes. He died in 1888, when my grandfather Luigi was fourteen. His widow closed out the tax year then moved with her children to Dogliani, another small town nearby where she had family. Dogliani is in the middle of Piedmont's Langhe, one of the great wine-growing regions of Italy. In the second half of the nineteenth century, the vine plague known as phylloxera and the opening of production in the Americas left many local farmers bankrupt. My grandfather wrote of the tears of relatives as they lost their land.

Grandfather Luigi won scholarships for secondary school in Genoa and studied economics at the University of Turin. In 1897, at the age of 23, he went into debt to buy San Giacomo, an old estate outside Dogliani. It was beautiful but falling apart. Over the years he replanted the vineyard devastated by phylloxera and restored and expanded the house. San Giacomo remains the family headquarters; in fact, now that I am largely retired, my wife and I live there several months a year. I have always thought of my grandfather as an Italian Horatio Alger, up from nowhere on the basis of merit and enterprise. He was what the French call "polyfacetic": farmer, technical innovator, teacher, economic theoretician, journalist, businessman and politician. Above all, he was a prolific writer. His bibliography when he died in 1961 had almost 4,000 entries. His politics were classic Liberal, but always grounded in local realities. Named senator in 1919, he was rumored for one of the first Mussolini cabinets in 1922 but was ultimately not chosen because of his anti-monopoly views. For thirty years, starting in 1895, he published an article a day in Italian newspapers. After Mussolini abolished freedom of the press in 1925, he stopped, and wrote only for the London Economist, whose "Italian Correspondent" he remained until World War II. As he got into more and more trouble with the Fascist regime, he limited his activities to teaching at the University of Turin, to working his beloved vineyards, and to acting as Italian representative for the Carnegie and Rockefeller foundations. He had developed the Rockefeller tie after a 1927 trip to the United States paid for by Laura Spelman Rockefeller. It was that relationship that enabled him to organize what became in the 1930s something of an underground railway -- getting young Italian scholars out of Italy so that they could work free of Fascist conformity.

His oldest son, my father Mario, joined that outflow in 1933 after he refused to sign an oath of allegiance to Mussolini or join the Fascist party, both of which were required for a university career. In 1918, grandfather organized Woodrow Wilson's appearance at the University of Turin and my father listened to Wilson firsthand at the age of fourteen. When he needed a democratic alternative to Italy under fascism, the United States was the obvious choice. My brothers and I were all born here and grew up with decidedly mixed influences. We spoke Italian at home. In grade school I couldn't go out and play on Saturdays until I'd written to my grandparents. Sometimes it was a bit much. Then in December 1944 grandfather flew back to Rome from exile in Switzerland in an American Flying Fortress, to become part of the first postwar government as governor of the Central Bank. In 1946, he voted Monarchist in the referendum that replaced the monarchy with a republic, then was elected to the Constituent Assembly with the most votes in the history of Dogliani. In quick succession he became Minister of Finance, Minister of the Budget, and Deputy Prime Minister. In 1948 he became the first duly elected president of the new Italian Republic.

*Q: That's quite a progression. How did it affect you?*

EINAUDI: We were Americans by then. But I was also Luigi Einaudi's first grandchild, the eldest son of the eldest son, and I was named Luigi like him. He did not have much time for youthful vagaries but paid me special attention. While President, he had my grandmother retype the first letter I sent them from prep school and sent it back to me, marked up in yellow pencil, with my Italian corrected for both grammar and style. Grandfather was always interested in education. He wrote newspaper op-eds called *Prediche inutili* (Useless Sermons), focused on how to reason correctly. To this day, if you google "Conoscere per deliberare," [roughly, "think before acting"], the phrase he coined to stress that you need to know before you can decide, you will be plunged into his "useless sermon" on why you need to know what you are doing -- particularly if you are in government and can affect the lives of others.

I described ten lessons he tried to teach me in an essay that the Turin newspaper *La Stampa* published on its front page on October 31, 2011, the fiftieth anniversary of his death:

- *You must set the good example.*
- *Do the right thing even if you will never be thanked.*
- *A printed page must please the eye as well as the mind.*
- *Solutions would often be simple were it not for politics.*
- *Never underestimate the common man.*
- *The English are not the only ones who know how to count.*
- *Things are not always what they seem.*
- *Time is precious.*
- *If you repeat a lie often enough, people will believe it.*

- *You should never say anything today that you will be ashamed of tomorrow or ten years from now or even twenty years after saying it.*

Grandfather Einaudi had a great influence on me. But I was American in a very deep psychological sense. We used to say that at the end of the war my father found himself with three American sons, all born and raised in the States. In 1947, during our first post-war visit to Italy, I was repelled by the sense of class that I found there. The farmer who worked the land at San Giacomo pulled his forelock when he met me, bowed, and called me *Padrone* (owner, or boss). I was eleven years old. I cringed. My formal education was entirely American. I married an American. I served in the U.S. Army. Those are all life-defining experiences.

To finish the Einaudis as a topic, my father finally landed a tenure-track position as professor of government, at Cornell, in 1944.

*Q: Could you tell me where your father went to university? And what was his scholastic background?*

EINAUDI: He studied law at the University of Turin in Italy and then was an early beneficiary of a Rockefeller fellowship to travel for post-graduate work. In 1927, he studied in Berlin, then at the London School of Economics under Graham Wallas and Harold Laski before completing his foreign tour in the United States. At the Harvard Law School, he began what would become his first book, _The Physiocratic Doctrine of Judicial Control_, the physiocrats being an early school of economists. In 1933, when he felt he could not in conscience remain in Italy under Mussolini, his contacts at Harvard enabled him to go there as an instructor in the old Department of History, Government and Economics.

*Q: Before we move on, I've got other questions of your early years but on your mother's side, where are they from and what's her background?*

EINAUDI: Well, if the Einaudis represented the upward-striving Italian bourgeoisie, the Michels represented the declining would-be nobility of Cologne, Germany. My mother's father, Roberto Michels, was a political sociologist and cultural interpreter who lived most of his adult life in Italy and Switzerland. One of the pressures on me as a young man was that both of my grandfathers had biographies in the <u>International Encyclopedia of the Social Sciences.</u> I felt that I had an awful lot to live up to.

The Michels were a moneyed business family with Bonapartist ties. In the back and forth of Cologne between the French and German wars and occupations, some of my grandfather's forebears had been French citizens. He became an officer in the Prussian Army but resigned his commission and went to the University of Halle where he wrote a thesis on Louis XIV. Growing up, he felt neither German—certainly not Prussian—nor French. He became an internationally minded socialist and embraced a radical revolutionary syndicalism that transcended national boundaries. His socialist activism marked his life in many ways. First, it denied him the ability to teach in Germany. He was strongly supported by Max Weber, but even so spent five years living in Marburg hoping for an appointment at the University which never came through. The second was that his experience led him to conclude that if his left-wing Socialists, who in theory were the ultimate expression of pure democracy, were in fact run by just a handful of leaders, then there wasn't much hope for democracy.

In his widely translated book, *Political Parties* (1912-14), Roberto Michels formulated what he called the "Iron Law of Oligarchy".

He was in effect saying that society is incapable of being as liberal as desired by Luigi Einaudi, who advocated free trade, freedom of expression and a free press. In contrast, Michels argued that the ideals of democracy are unattainable, and that society cannot escape being ruled by leadership elites. He had been teaching in Turin (where my parents met as children). He renounced his German citizenship to protest World War I but was denied Italian citizenship and wound up in Switzerland from 1914 to 1928, when he returned to Italy. In some ways he lived in permanent intellectual exile, with a complicated life that left him yearning for a cosmopolitan internationalism that could not exist in Europe between the wars. Michels was caught not only in the collision between socialism and democracy but later in the rise of fascism and of various illiberal movements in Europe. He died at 60 in 1936, two months after I was born. I never met him, but his influence on me through my mother and his writings was almost as strong as that of Luigi Einaudi, with whom I did live and study.

My personal values are deeply rooted in the idea that the United States, to some extent personified by Franklin Roosevelt and the New Deal, but also by its culture and civilization, has provided a foundation to maximize individual rights and freedoms in the face of the pressures of industrialization and in opposition to both communism and fascism. I once opened a lecture by identifying myself simply as an American born in this New World of parents who had come here in search of freedom.

*Q: Where did your mother go to school?*

EINAUDI: Art schools in Turin and Paris. Manon Michels was a very good artist. She won a scholarship to Poland in the 1920s, exhibited her paintings and lived the life. She was an exceptionally good portraitist. She used to say that the only paintings she sold were portraits whose subjects bought them so she could not put their warts on public display by exhibiting them. When very young she served as her father's secretary and became multilingual, but she never had formal academic training outside the arts. She never went to university.

*Q: That's very true of the period. I mean you could move into the art field or something like that, but there was no particular need to have a sort of obligatory university chop.*

EINAUDI: That's true.

*Q: Before we leave family entirely, I have heard that a cousin was nuncio in Cuba and that you have family in Argentina.*

EINAUDI: Giulio Einaudi, a distant cousin, is a Jesuit who served in the Vatican diplomatic Corps in Washington, and became Papal Nuncio in Cuba, Chile, and later Croatia. My father's middle brother, Roberto Einaudi, was an engineer and partner in a multinational steel firm based in Argentina where his son and two other cousins work. In fact, my entire family is heavily engaged internationally. My father's youngest brother, also named Giulio Einaudi, founded a publishing house that translated both American and Russian literature into Italian. An Italian-born cousin, Franco Einaudi, earned a PhD in Physics at Cornell, became a US citizen and retired as head of NASA's Earth Sciences Division. His brother, Giorgio Einaudi, was for years Italy's scientific attaché here in Washington. My brothers both work internationally, Roberto as an architect, and Marco as a geologist. My grandfather's excellent red wine is now exported around the world by cousins who own the Poderi Luigi Einaudi. Musician cousin Ludovico Einaudi tours from Europe and Russia to the United States, Japan and China. All of us stay in touch and all of us trace back to great-grandfather Lorenzo's flight 150 years ago from his hardscrabble mountain life.

Q: *Did all this make a difference in your work as a U.S. diplomat?*

EINAUDI: My family sensitized me to the existence and views of different cultures, gave me confidence, and occasionally provided invaluable foreign contacts. I generally avoided working on Italy to avoid conflicts of interest, but my name still gave me an advantage, particularly in Latin America. Grandfather Luigi's book on public finance was translated into Spanish in 1948 and for the next twenty years was the basic economics text in many Latin American law schools. While I was at State, at least ten presidents and ministers in Central and South America asked me to autograph their copy. This name recognition helped my effectiveness, but also created resentments among some of my colleagues in the Department. On one occasion Bernie Aronson came back from a trip to South America as Assistant Secretary, gave me the names of persons who had asked him to say hello to me, then said "This is the last time I will ever transmit a greeting to you." Years later, when we were both out of government service, Aronson told me "When I was talking to you, I never knew whether I was talking to one of us or one of them." My mentor Pete Vaky told me it was best simply never to mention my foreign connections.

At a more general level, my family made me aware there were different ways of looking at things. As a way of ensuring perspective, my father always insisted on including the United States in his courses on comparative government. He felt focusing only on foreign institutions made it harder for students to appreciate different ways of doing things. Father was a bit of a contrarian. With his colleague, the physicist Hans Bethe, he founded a discussion group they called "the vicious circle" in contrast to "the circle," an established Cornell faculty club. And he thumbtacked a poem by W.H. Auden to his office closet door. Its ending, "Thou shalt not sit with statisticians nor commit a social science," expressed perfectly why Mario Einaudi always taught "government" rather than "political science." He believed politics was not quantifiable, that it was art and history more than numbers. On the other hand, he also believed the jet plane would shorten not just physical distances but also those of culture and distrust. My mother was never sure. The impact of the internet has prolonged the uncertainty for me.

To go back to grandfather Einaudi, one simple way he helped prepare me for a diplomatic career was that he had me write my first cable. In the summer of 1954, I was in Italy with him when an Italian expedition made the first successful ascent of the world's second tallest mountain, K2 in the Karakoram. The American Alpine Club, which had failed in a major attempt the year before, sent Italy a telegram of congratulations. Grandfather knew of my interest in mountaineering, and knew that at Exeter I had met Robert Bates, since 1938 the key figure in U.S. efforts to climb K2. Grandfather gave me the incoming telegram, saying "Here, you're an American, these are your people, you draft an answer." I do not remember what I wrote, I don't even remember seeing the final text, but the pressure of having the President of Italy ask me to compose that cable was like having one side of me write to another side of myself. It was an extraordinary experience.

*Q: Alright, as a kid did you grow up in Cambridge?*

EINAUDI: No. We moved around a lot. That was the Depression, there was no permanent academic hiring; life was difficult. When his five years at Harvard were up, they were up. Father went to Fordham University in New York. I was two. When the war came, we became very aware of the risks of bombing in urban areas. The silhouettes of the German planes my father looked out for as a warden from the roof of our apartment building in the Riverdale section of New York City are among my earliest memories. In 1941 we moved to Chappaqua, far enough outside the city to feel safe. Then in 1944 we moved to Ithaca and Cornell. What I mainly remember is sports. Playing softball and failing to make the transition to hardball because I couldn't see the ball well enough. Playing football and having my mother tell me she didn't want to have me ruined and killed in that violent game.

# Schooling

*Q: Okay, well let's talk a little bit about Ithaca. How old were you when you were there?*

EINAUDI: I was there from the age of eight to the age of fourteen.

*Q: All right, well let's talk about schooling; how were you as a student?*

EINAUDI: In grade school I could do well but would get bored. My father tired of my fights with the Ithaca schools and also with my uppityness; I had come to the conclusion that my parents were as dumb as could be -- the usual adolescent rebellion, if you will. In fact, Father had been extraordinarily supportive of me. From the age of twelve on I was doing filing and simple research projects for him at Cornell, the kind of stuff we now ask interns to do. I had a lot of lively spirits. I skipped the eighth grade, but after the ninth grade Father concluded that it would be best for my education and our relations if I were to go off for a while. My parents sent me to Phillips Exeter Academy in New Hampshire where I remained for three years. The first term was a disaster. My grades were Ds and Cs and an occasional B. But in the end I graduated cum laude and won prizes, even in mathematics which is not exactly my strong point. One of my former roommates reminded me recently during our 60th class reunion that he and others had been very offended that I won the French language prize and the fifth-year national prize in French after studying French only one year. My mother, who had become multilingual by absorption in her teens as her father's secretary and traveling companion, refused to give me any credit, saying I should know French almost instinctively. She told me also that with every new language I learned, I would lose the purity of knowing precisely what words meant in their own culture.

*Q: Were you much of a reader?*

EINAUDI: I read all the time, sometimes at night with a flashlight under the blankets when I was supposed to be sleeping.

*Q: Do you recall any books you read and the ones you particularly liked or were influential?*

EINAUDI: I loved a prolific author unknown in the United States even though he wrote mostly about the Wild West and the pirates of the Caribbean. This was an Italian named Emilio Salgari. He wrote roughly between 1890 and 1910, but his books were still being reprinted in paperback after World War II. I could read his stuff forever. My grandfather got very annoyed and said, "You are right to read and that is the most important thing, but on the other hand you should read stuff by people who have something to say."

*Q: Sounds familiar.*

EINAUDI: Yeah, oh boy. Jules Verne influenced me enormously. Novels like his <u>Mysterious Island</u> or <u>Voyage to the Bottom of the Sea</u> still assumed that an educated man should and could know everything. It was like the mentality of the French Encyclopedia, the last great Encyclopedia, published between 1751 and 1780 as France was getting into the Revolution; it was based on the idea that all human knowledge could be fitted into a single set of volumes. Verne's heroes were men who were able to calculate their position on the earth, who understood how to build a water system, who did all kinds of technical things as well as deal with the human and animal world around them. Daniel Defoe's Robinson Crusoe, to shift to an English-language author, had the same kind of sense of adventure.

*Q: I reread it not too long ago and it is a tremendous book on how to survive on an island. It lays out what you do to survive by yourself and by God you have to take care of yourself. It's a great how-to manual.*

EINAUDI: The edition that I still have has the most incredible detailed drawings of the ship and its contents before it was wrecked. It is also shockingly racist.

These readings had a profound influence: If you respect your individual abilities as a human being to face whatever world into which you are thrust, then what you are looking for is a free society where you can continue to follow your intelligence and grow in freedom. And that is the meaning of America.

Later, and from a more professional standpoint, two books I read with my grandfather stand out. The Georgics of Virgil in the original Latin when I was 16 demonstrated continuities in agrarian life since Roman times. Reading Tocqueville in French on the French Revolution when I was 18 taught me that bad government can be a bigger stimulus to revolution than poverty.

*Luigi Einaudi teaching Latin and agriculture to his grandson Luigi R. in 1952 by reading Virgil's Georgics in the original Latin. (Photograph courtesy of LR Einaudi.)*

*Q: Given your family background and then the Second World War with both Italy and Germany, were you getting visitors who were refugees from there and a lot of conversations where you were the kid sitting underneath the table listening?*

EINAUDI: My father was close to Luigi Sturzo, the progressive priest who in 1919 founded Italy's reformist Popular Party, but whose opposition to Mussolini led to tensions with the Vatican. When Sturzo was exiled in 1940-44 to then isolated Jacksonville, Florida, Father helped him with everything from his finances and publications to contacts in New York City. But our family had little to do with the organized Italian community here in the United States, partly because many immigrants here were pro-fascist. My mother never liked her German roots. German was spoken in our house only when my parents wanted to communicate without the children understanding them. We spoke Italian at home to maintain the language. And we were very aware of our foreignness. My mother was particularly sensitive because of her father's lengthy statelessness. During the War she had a rule that when others were present we should speak only English. My mother would say "Be careful. Never speak Italian in the presence of strangers." The United States was at war with Italy and "we don't want to give the impression that we are foreign."

*Q: I would think this would be difficult with a name that wasn't Smith or Brown.*

EINAUDI: It was difficult. In fact, there is an element here of stubborn family pride. To this day there is only one friend I allow to call me "Lou" instead of Luigi. I think that Father's decision not to return to Italy after the War came as a burst of the same kind of rebellion I later expressed against him. His father was becoming powerful and well known and he, by Jove, was not going to go back to Italy to become his father's son. He was an independent man and had become an American; very proudly so.

*Q: Well, family is important. I may come back to other parts but let's talk about Exeter. I went four years to a somewhat similar prep school called Kent and actually I spent one summer at Andover to study physics; this is before the War ended. But I would think these schools were so terribly Waspish, White Anglo-Saxon Protestant and all. Did you find that all of a sudden a Luigi in the middle of this would seem to be kind of an alien flower blooming in this particular garden?*

EINAUDI: Actually, I think I never felt any more foreign than I was. That's perhaps a strange formulation, but I mean that what resistance there was came more from within me than from them.

I felt at home at Exeter. I felt there was space in its civilization for me. Had I been Jewish, had I been Black—

*Q: Oh yes.*

EINAUDI: —had I been Native American I might have felt differently.

*Q: Yes, when I'm saying White Anglo-Saxon Protestant, I mean this was still a pretty biased era.*

EINAUDI: It was all of that, yet I actually wound up very happy at Exeter. I believe Exeter contributed more to my intellectual growth and formation than did Harvard. I don't know how Kent was when you were there but our class at Exeter had a Navajo scholarship student, a handful of Blacks, and quite a few Jewish students. The most dramatic change since is that today there are girls. But Exeter is also now nine percent Black and seven percent Hispanic. Those of my classmates who adjusted to Exeter only with difficulty included many of Jewish origin. Some later told me that the daily chapel sessions and Sunday Services—all of which were obligatory and called nondenominational—had a Protestant spirit they could not escape.

*Q: Well when I started there Kent was run by Episcopalian monks so there was no doubt about this. There were no Blacks, I can't think of an Asian, there may have been some Hispanics, a few Jewish students and they had some problems there. I am older than you are—I was born in 1928—and anti-Semitism was still, you might say, the prevailing spirit in the power classes of the United States. Not virulent but it was there.*

EINAUDI: Of course. I have always felt that the United States has a Protestant soul. Today there has been a general decline in religiosity and the country has opened up in many ways. Nationally we are not yet integrated racially like Berkeley or any major Eastern city, but Jack Armstrong the All-American Boy is no longer the national model.

Q: I would like just for the record to note that Jack Armstrong, All-American Boy was a radio serial whose lead was very obviously a White protestant blond.

EINAUDI: Exactly. I feel today's ethnic and racial openings are very positive.

Q: Question: Coming from Italy was your family Catholic?

EINAUDI: Yes.

Q: How Catholic was it? I mean your nuclear family.

EINAUDI: My father's side could be described as standard Italian Catholic: grandfather and grandmother generally attended Sunday mass. Even so, grandfather was a believer on his own terms. In Dogliani when I was a child, mass would be said by a visiting priest in the restored chapel at San Giacomo. Grandfather would force the priest to read the mass out of an old seventeenth-century Bible. The priest would invariably get lost looking for particular texts and grandfather would sit there chuckling. Once I asked him after the service why he had guffawed, and he said it was a hoot to see that the eternal Church was always changing its eternal truths to the point they could not be found. Grandfather was hard to pigeonhole, but could be described as a lay Catholic, supportive of the church as a social institution, but opposed to Church attempts to control daily life, such as political preaching from the pulpit. He used to say that the Italian Communist Party had learned well from the Church, that if you repeat a lie often enough people will believe it.

My mother had a quite different approach to religion. She converted to Catholicism as a teenager with her family while in Switzerland. But her stateless experience led her to conclude that you should belong to the religion that is in the majority wherever you were living. Hers was a non-confrontational approach. I myself took a rather hands-off approach, that if push came to shove you should, like Pascal, bet on the existence of God because you wouldn't want to be wrong, and also that if any religion were to be valid it would probably be Catholicism. But I was not observant, nor was Carol, though she was Protestant, and had been a Rainbow Girl when in school. When we married, she and I agreed to differ, but we also agreed that in our common life religion should not be used to divide, as too often has happened throughout history. I think we were able to instill a sense of morality in our children (we have four, with ten grandchildren). Our children vote and they take their children with them to learn civic rituals, like voting. But to the extent that religion is part of our cultural heritage, we have not transmitted that in full. In the increasingly secular world in which we now live, that is cultural impoverishment.

*Q: Where did your family fall in American terms politically, on your father and mother's side?*

EINAUDI: Democrats. Father saw Roosevelt and the New Deal as providing a modern answer to the survival of democratic civilization in the industrial age. If you add that my father left Italy refusing to sign a loyalty oath to Mussolini, then you can imagine his reaction to the agitation to require loyalty oaths during the McCarthy period in the United States.

In 1953, as a freshman at Harvard, I helped organize petitions against McCarthy. I remember sitting at a table outside the dining hall and having some of my fellow students refuse to sign, not because they liked McCarthy, but because they feared that someday their signatures would turn up in a government file and they would be denied employment. One of the things that brought my future wife and I together was that we were both instinctively anti-McCarthy. Her Massachusetts family, incidentally, also had immigrant roots – Polish and Scotch-English – but what counted most was her father's trade unionism.

Culturally, I tended to equate the Democratic Party with greater freedom, greater openness and also greater internationalism. I am a registered Democrat and have usually so voted. So it is an irony that I wound up being named ambassador by a Republican president and that afterwards the incoming Democrats looked at me with skepticism.

In my professional life, I have always sought to support nonpartisan national interests. I mean by that that I sought to go beyond personal, particular, or partisan interests to incorporate the needs of community.[1] As Ambassador, I had a political appointee on my staff, Roger Noriega, who said that, unlike me, he was not going to pretend he was above politics. At noon January 20, 1993, the moment of transition from George H.W. Bush to Bill Clinton, he resigned without being asked. He was being correct. And he was also correct in thinking that I never thought of myself as political.

---

[1] Exeter's motto "NON SIBI" links a good life to "selflessness." I tried to articulate its meaning for public service in a talk I gave to the Exeter student body in 2006 that is reproduced below as Appendix Four.

I thought of myself as serving national interests and sought to implement policies as effectively as possible. When I disagreed, when I felt certain policies violated proper diplomacy and even national interests, I would argue against them internally, and when I failed, look for ways to limit the damage, or find other things to do. But I felt that, not having run for office, I did not have the right to substitute my policy preferences for those of our elected leaders. I am still uncomfortable sometimes when some of our retired colleagues sign petitions on current foreign policy events.

*Q: Yes, I remember this and I was a bit disturbed. I think this was against George W. Bush, in his first term.*

EINAUDI: I had two major Foreign Service mentors, one of whom was a Democrat with a capital D, Viron Peter Vaky. I suspect that had Dukakis won the Presidency in 1988, Pete would have hoped to become Ambassador to the OAS, the position to which I was later appointed as the Bush Administration sought to work its way out of the Central American conflicts. But even as a convinced Democrat, Pete never would have engaged in partisan political activities while on active duty. My other mentor, Bill Bowdler, was also an exemplary professional who defined his responsibility as being to national interests rather than partisan politics. His fate was demoralizing. Bill had served on the NSC, been Ambassador to South Africa where he had distinguished the United States by visiting Steve Biko's family after Biko died in police custody and then attended his funeral to the outrage of the Afrikaner government. When he returned, he became assistant secretary for Intelligence and Research (INR). In 1979, he accepted becoming assistant secretary for Inter-American Affairs at a time when it was obvious that major hell was going to be paid because of U.S. domestic politics over Central America. And he worked himself to the bone. I still remember doctors coming to his office in the Department to treat his blood pressure because he had been working so hard that he was in physical crisis. Bill was born in Argentina. I felt kinship because he had early Argentine roots the way I had had early Italian roots, even though I was born in the States. I really respected his professionalism. In 1974, we had traveled together to Brasilia. An officer in a God forsaken post in Brazil's northeast cabled asking whether we could stop on our way back to Washington. I remember seeing that cable and thinking it was totally out of the question, totally out of the blue, out of everything. It was after midnight and Bill and I were both exhausted. We finished our immediate task and Bill said, "Now we have to answer that cable." He was a former Ambassador, then serving as Deputy Assistant Secretary of State, but instead of arrogance, he acted with total selflessness. And this man was not protected by the Foreign Service when he was treated with partisan cruelty over Central America.

*Q: The treatment of William Bowdler by the Reagan administration was disgusting. Many people have commented on this in these oral histories about how this really stunk.*

EINAUDI: So true. Bill is one of the mildest men, he does not hold grudges. He is a builder and does not like to criticize.

*Q: Where is he now?*

EINAUDI: He lives in Sharps, Virginia, in the house that originally belonged to his wife Peggy's father who was the minister there. Bill was born in 1924, and can no longer drive or climb the stairs to the second floor, but he and Peggy still live surrounded by their Cuban art with a daughter-in-law nearby and helpful neighbors.

[Note: William Garton Bowdler died January 19, 2016 at the age of 91. I wrote an obituary note for DACOR.]

*Q: I was just interviewing by phone a man who is now blind up in Amherst, Mass, Monteagle Stearns.*

EINAUDI: I remember the name.

*Q: He is in his '90s. It is said that when Dulles came in as Secretary of State he said, "Now we are all together here what I want is positive loyalty." This is well remembered but not with pleasure because it implied that somehow the Foreign Service was disloyal. "Positive loyalty" became something of a dirty expression during the whole of the Dulles administration.*

*How about returning to your dining room table as a young kid. What did you hear during the War about Mussolini? Did they talk much about him? Was it "that man in Rome?"*

EINAUDI: There was no love lost for Mussolini among the Einaudis, who were anti-fascist to the core. On the Michels side, it was different. Because of his disillusionment with democracy, Roberto Michels was less hostile, and is sometimes classed as a supporter of Mussolini because of his focus on leadership. And it is true that his contacts with Mussolini helped him finally become an Italian citizen and return to Italy from Switzerland in the late 1920s. But Michels died demoralized in 1936 before the racial laws and before the culmination of Mussolini's bad decisions and the War. In France, Switzerland and Germany, Michels sought to explain Italy under Fascism. His biggest problem probably had to do with the distinction between explain and defend. It is sometimes very hard to explain situations without appearing to defend them.

*Q: I know it.*

EINAUDI: And that's a particular difficulty for a Foreign Service officer. Speaking to young people thinking of joining the Service I put it this way, "Look, you've got to be prepared to be crushed and ground to dust between U.S. nationalism and foreign nationalism." Because Americans have a horrible tendency to see people in the Foreign Service as people who are somehow too close to foreigners, even to the point of being ready to betray America's secrets. This is the diametrical opposite of their vision of the U.S. military, who are there to win America's wars. What's left for the Foreign Service except be namby-pamby explainers and defenders of the foreigners who are obviously out to get us? At the same time, foreigners see the Foreign Service and American diplomats as instruments of American intervention, economic interests and imperialism.

*Q: Going back to Exeter, did you get involved in any extracurricular activities?*

EINAUDI: Not outside school. We were very isolated. No girls. In school, I joined a debating club named for Daniel Webster, an early alumnus, and the mountaineering club. But the extracurricular activity I loved most was cross country in the fall and track and field in the winter and spring. I ran the thousand yards in the winter and the mile and the two mile in the spring. One Christmas vacation in Ithaca, I slipped on a bicycle on an icy hill and broke my leg; a standard sharp ankle break. I spent that spring on crutches and became the manager of the track team. Track as a whole had become an important part of my life. The coach, Ralph Lovshin, was one of the half-dozen teachers at Exeter I most liked. When I went to Harvard and reported to Bill McCurdy, the track coach there, he asked me what my best times were. I told him, he responded "Well, we won't hold that against you." I decided I had better things to do.

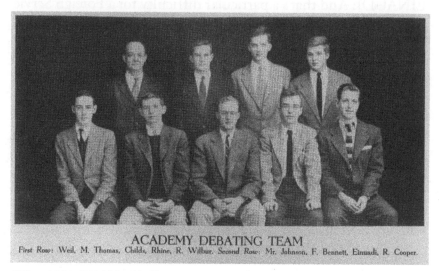

ACADEMY DEBATING TEAM
First Row: Weil, M. Thomas, Childs, Rhine, R. Wilbur. Second Row: Mr. Johnson, F. Bennett, Einaudi, R. Cooper.

*(The 1953 PEAN, Phillips Exeter Academy [Exeter, New Hampshire, 1953], p. 111. (Reproduced with permission from Phillips Exeter Academy.)*

*Q: Yeah. Well, okay you graduated from Exeter when?*

EINAUDI: 1953.

*Q: So you went to Harvard. Was this sort of fore-ordained or how did you pick Harvard?*

EINAUDI: It was fore-ordained. Those were, of course, other times. Of the 200 of us who graduated from Exeter in 1953, about 80 went to Harvard. I won a Harvard honorary prize fellowship. I think my parents had sent me to Exeter partly wishing to ensure that I would go to Harvard; Harvard is after all where my father had taught, and Cambridge was where I was born. Rupert Emerson, a professor of government who became one of my mentors in college, had literally carried me out of the hospital after I was born. His Russian-born wife Alla knitted a blanket for Carol's and my first child Maria just as she had for me twenty-three years before. In the economics department there were professors who had worked with my grandfather. So being at Harvard was all very natural.

*Q: So you went there in '53 and graduated in '57. What was Harvard like when you arrived there? I mean how would you describe it?*

EINAUDI: For me, after Exeter, it was a great disappointment. Because there were all these people whom we knew, it was part of our family lore. I went there with very high expectations and wound up very unhappy. All of us Exeter kids were so well prepared that we were easily bored. Overall, we were not any better than the high school guys; in fact, I would say that, if you compare us to the public-school kids, by the time the four years had passed the Exeter people may even have done slightly worse than the best public-school kids.

*Q: I've heard it said the first two years the prep school kids did far better because they were prepared for writing and all this but in the end there is a much better distribution.*

EINAUDI: Indeed so. Part of the problem was that many Exeter students felt Harvard was beneath them. There was no advanced placement yet. As a freshman I found myself forced to repeat required distribution courses in the natural sciences, for example, covering basic materials that I had already studied, already knew and wasn't interested in. That was bad enough, but my Harvard experience was also greatly affected by something else; my recruitment into the U.S. National Student Association (NSA). I spent early summer of 1955 in Cambridge at something called the International Student Relations Seminar. I took my first trip to Latin America later that summer and wound up on Harvard's disciplinary probation for having come back late for classes. I did not really care. I found more scope in international student politics than I did in my Harvard undergraduate training.

Q: *What was your basic course concentration at Harvard?*

EINAUDI: I was a government major. One of the reasons I wound up becoming a specialist on Latin America was to avoid being stereotyped. My grandfather was still president of Italy during my freshman and sophomore years and since I was known for family reasons to some professors, there was more than one occasion on which during a government class lecture the professor would stop and ask me to speak -- as though I was supposed to know everything because I had this background. Let me tell you it really upset me.

Q: *I can imagine.*

EINAUDI: Remember that I said that my father stayed in the States after the War partly because he didn't want to be his father's son? I think both my brothers chose their life work in part to differentiate themselves – Roberto became an architect because he liked to draw, and Marco became a geologist so he wouldn't have to sit around in offices. Well, I didn't want to be either my father's or my grandfathers' son – but my ambition was still a life in public service, like my father and grandfathers.

I found the perfect solution to this dilemma when by chance I was sent by the NSA to Chile in 1955. We talked earlier about the Protestant and White nature of dominant American society in those days. There was of course a concomitant lack of cultural diversity. The NSA was invited to attend a meeting of the Congress for Cultural Freedom in Chile. The letter was filed unread because it was in Spanish. Then came a wire asking, "What are the names of your delegates so we can issue the tickets?" Chaos. A free trip! "We need to find somebody who can speak Spanish!" And it is a fact, unbelievable in today's world, that in 1955 the NSA International Commission, in Cambridge, Massachusetts, could find no one who could speak Spanish. Then somebody said, "Well, let's send Einaudi, at least he can speak Italian."

That trip took me to Argentina and Uruguay as well as Chile. It even had an element of drama related to Italy and family. When the plane from Santiago arrived at the gate in Buenos Aires, there was a sudden hubbub as someone boarded and called out "Luigi Einaudi." I stood up and went forward amidst mounting confusion. They were expecting the short 81-year-old president of Italy arriving without fanfare; they found a 19-year-old student with an American passport. Even so, in Latin America I found an escape from family and Europe both. I could prove myself on a battlefield in which no one in my immediate family had previously ventured. And I could do so without losing the advantages of my cultural background. Argentina had so many Italians that Peron once considered making Italian a second official language. Chile in 1955 had political parties that were very reminiscent of the parties of France and Italy at the time. The main parties were Conservative, Christian Democratic, Liberal, Socialist and Communist; there even was a Radical Party, a small centrist group with minimal support just like the Italian Radicals and Liberals.

*Delegates from Argentina, Chile, and the United States at a 1955 meeting of the Congress for Cultural Freedom in Santiago de Chile. Pedro Guglielmetti of Chile is in the front row, second from left, Abel Alexis Latendorff of Argentina is second from right. In the second row, Mariano Grondona of Argentina is second and Luigi R. Einaudi third. Diarmuid O'Scannlain of USNSA is in the middle of the last row.* (Courtesy of LR Einaudi, personal photo).

Suddenly I realized that there was an interesting other world out there that I had not known existed, one where my cultural background was useful. And I would be on my own. The only drawback was that Spanish came so easily it hobbled my Italian.

Returning from that first trip I published my first article, a special supplement to the November 1955 edition of the *USNSA News* on an investigation in which I had participated of Peron's secret police intelligence organization. Cards were kept on university students, 70,000 of which had entries referring to personal folders on individual political beliefs and organizational activities, and on which depended their university attendance, visa eligibility, and employment.

A personal experience on that 1955 trip influenced my future career. I found myself—a representative of the U.S. National Student Association, hence of the United States—set up in the Aula Magna of the Faculty of Law of University of Chile, the major national university of Chile, to debate the American intervention in Guatemala in 1954. I knew nothing about it. My opponent in the debate was Juan José Arevalo, who had from 1945-1950 been the president of Guatemala and whose successor Jacobo Arbenz was the one who had been thrown out in the 1954 coup. Arevalo was a former teacher and had been in exile in Argentina in the '30s and '40s, so he was a man with some capacity and international scope. He wasn't limited to a provincial view of the world from one country, and he just went off like a rocket. He wrote a book which is probably still one of the best-selling radical denunciations of U.S. imperialism ever written, _The Shark and the Sardines_.

_Q: I remember that and I have often seen it quoted._

EINAUDI: The image was certainly arresting. It was pure Latin American nationalism expressing itself in the form of anti-imperialist rhetoric. The biggest analytical mistake of much U.S. reporting in this period, so heavily influenced by the Cold War, was to see anti-imperialist rhetoric as proof of Communist sympathies. In any case, here I was, at the age of 19, without any background in Central America (I don't think I'd even heard of the United Fruit Company), never having dealt with any of this, set up in a formal debate against a formidable and literate former President. Arevalo shredded me, took me apart. I was full of myself, proud of being both American and European, and I wound up being publicly humiliated in a head-to-header in the country's most important university. To some extent the next years became a reaffirmation of my need to defend my own dignity and to explore ideas and principles that would include space for these unknown Latin Americans.

The next year, the summer of 1956, I led a five-person NSA delegation to South America. In Panama, our first stop was at the new university campus, which was attracting upper-class students who would previously have gone abroad, but were now participating in the forging of a nascent Panamanian national consciousness. In Colombia, the university world was still dominated by the Catholic Church and its student organ, Pax Romana. In Ecuador, the national student federation FEUE was in the hands of Communists with whom we had to go toe to toe in sharp debates. In Peru, we had to walk by tanks to enter the University of San Marcos, where the students were on strike against the Odría government. In Bolivia, Oscar Zamora, who later became general secretary of the Prague-based but Soviet-run International Union of Students, and was then the head of the FUB, the Bolivian student federation, taunted a black member of my delegation, Marian McReynolds, telling her he was a free man even though he was from the south of Bolivia.

On landing in Paraguay, we had to wait a long time on the tarmac. The Pan Am pilot finally came on the intercom and said in his best Chuck Yeager drawl "Sorry for the delay, folks. President Stroessner is on board, and he's checking to see if he is still in power before deplaning." As our delegation was leaving Asunción for Montevideo, we crossed paths with my friend from Fordham, Ralph Della Cava, who was investigating torture under Stroessner as part of a RIC (Research and Investigations Commission of the International Student Conference). Ralph gave me a package that contained affidavits and other proofs of torture, including castration, by the regime. By the time the Paraguayan police searched Ralph, I had successfully mailed the documents from Montevideo to ISC headquarters in Leiden, the Netherlands. Ralph was released, but when my delegation and I arrived from Montevideo at the hydro port in Buenos Aires, we were stopped and the police went through our baggage with a fine-tooth comb. They released us only after leaders of FUA, the Argentine student federation, who had come to meet us threatened a ruckus. The next day, I brought my delegation to the U.S. embassy to lodge a protest. A consular officer dismissed us with a lecture: "stay out of politics." The Italian embassy was more forthcoming. They told me that old Peronists in the Argentine police had been asked to detain us as dangerous Communist agitators.

In the course of these adventures and as a delegate to the International Student Conference in Ceylon that fall, I met a lot of student leaders who later made a mark. Two such acquaintances paid with their lives. One was José Antonio Echeverria, the leader of the Cuban Student Federation, whom I had met in Chile. He was killed in 1957 during an attempt to lead a revolution against Batista. Another was the Nicaraguan Silvio Mayorga, later a founder of the Sandinista Front for National Liberation, who was killed in the mid-1960s by Somoza's national guard. Several others, from Central as well as South America, remained friends for life, and will appear in these pages, part of a personal political network that proved invaluable in my State Department years.

*The NSA delegation at the 1956 International Student Conference in Peradeniya, Ceylon. From the left, Clive Gray, Luigi Einaudi, Jim Edwards, Bruce Larkin and Stan Glass. Standing with papers in the right background is Jose Antonio Echeverria, President of Cuba's Federación de Estudiantes Universitarios (FEU), killed the next year in an abortive coup attempt against Cuba's dictator, Fulgencio Batista. (Photograph courtesy of LR Einaudi, personal photo).*

The tension between my political activism and my studies was attenuated by the fact that two of my instructors in Government had ties to the NSA. Paul Sigmund had been NSA International Affairs Vice President, and Helen Jean Rogers had been Secretary-Treasurer when still a student at Mundelein College in 1948. Both taught political theory at Harvard. In Section one day, instructor Rogers asked undergraduate Einaudi "would you say Machiavelli was the first Protestant?" It took me a while to realize the very Catholic Helen Jean was referring to Machiavelli's concept of virtue as a possible link to the Protestant ethic.

*Q: Let me give you a chance to talk about the study of government. Today everyone talks about political science and I find myself extremely skeptical. When I look at things written by political scientists for the most part I find them completely unreadable and absolutely unuseful for a practicing Foreign Service person. When I went to Williams, the study of government was basically how governments work and not abstract formulae. How was it being taught at Harvard?*

EINAUDI: The Harvard Government Department was not monolithic. The primary intellectual influence in the Department was that of Carl Joachim Friedrich, a German of my father's generation. Friedrich had adapted his European background to the quantitative American tradition that comes out of Bentley and was very much a believer in systematic accumulation of knowledge to generate scientific laws. That approach was coming to dominate American political science. Nowadays there are few departments of "government" around. Harvard is still "government" at the undergraduate level but "political science" at the graduate level. Cornell is also government, but most universities have switched to political science. To think of political science as science is to miss the art and problems of government. I share your view that this has led to abstraction and illegibility. A reaction is needed to consider more of the art, culture and political sociology of government and the importance of institutional structures, history, etc.

A lot of academic economists have also become pretty useless to the daily policy practitioner. The highest rewards in academic economics have tended to go to the mathematicians. So you don't get answers to practical questions. I was actually depressed when Tom Schelling got the Nobel Prize in economics. I had met him when we were both at RAND. His position was that history is simply of no interest. Well, the conspicuous failures of U.S.

military actions in Iraq and Afghanistan because of our inability to get beyond what could be achieved by the use of force suggest that our political leadership has sometimes sent people into battle without understanding the importance of history and culture.

*Q: In any case, you obviously were able to get through the government phase of your training without being infected by the virus of mathematics.*

EINAUDI: Precisely. More common perhaps was a virus that might be called "profound skepticism." Stanley Hoffmann stood out as a subtle and powerful intellect, but I remember mostly that he lectured that international law does not exist in the face of power. Most important to me among the professors of Government was Rupert Emerson, whom I mentioned earlier as a friend and mentor, His best-known book, <u>Nationalism, From Empire to Nation,</u> was a study set in the dissolution of European empires in Africa and Asia. It stressed non quantifiable factors, like history and culture, to explain what constitutes a nation and the relationship between a people and state boundaries. I wrote my undergraduate honors thesis on the Bolivian Revolution of 1952; Victor Paz Estenssoro, the major leader of that revolution and later twice President of Bolivia, became a friend during his exiles in Lima and Washington. But my undergraduate thesis was inspired by Bolivian exiles I had met in Chile in my NSA activities, and their discussions of revolution and social struggle, including the Leninists' defeat of the Moscow-line Communists for control of the COB, Bolivia's tin miner union. That thesis, basically a descriptive history, helped me graduate *Cum Laude* despite my activist absenteeism.

*Q: While you were there particularly in the government department was Marxism, not Soviet Marxism, but was Marxism as a theory a darling of the department?*

EINAUDI: No, not at all. H. Stuart Hughes was I think open to Marxist thought, but he was not in the Government Department. Some Government Department professors, William Yandell Elliott comes to mind even before Henry Kissinger, had long consulted with Washington, including probably the CIA. The dominant ideology, developed initially by Friedrich and then taken up by his student Zbigniew Brzezinski, was built around the concept of totalitarianism. They were very committed to the idea that we had seen the emergence of a new system of government, a system they defined, in both its Nazi Fascist version and its Soviet Communist version, as capable of reaching into all aspects of life, hence "totalitarian." One of their key teachings was that its totalitarian nature meant that it could not be overthrown internally or domestically. That was the ideological posture that ran through a great deal of analysis that was being taught in those days. Later, in a 1979 *Commentary* article, Jeane Kirkpatrick popularized this analysis into the doctrine that led some of the Reagan people to argue that it was alright to support dictatorships because they were not totalitarian. Dictators that were friendly and anti-Communist were okay. Not being totalitarian, they could always be changed later.

*Q: Well McCarthyism is in full flower at the time. Tell me how the Soviet Union was treated at Harvard when you were there to study in government?*

EINAUDI: My Russian language teacher was an aging lady from St. Petersburg who insisted on teaching us "cultured" pre-1917 pronunciation. I start my answer this way to emphasize that Harvard was full of swirling currents. The Government Department projected both very traditional and very radical views. Merle Fainsod started as an expert in the U.S. government, then wrote the classic *How Russia is Ruled*, which became a basic text far beyond Harvard. His factual and institutionally based analyses contrasted with the Friedrich-Brzezinski school of totalitarianism which was so anti-Soviet that it also had elements of being anti-Russian. Rupert Emerson's wife Alla, herself of White Russian origins, used to complain that anti-Soviet views were so strong they made Russia and Russian culture disappear.

Life is very complicated, and I keep reminding the people I work with to use plural forms because most situations involve many elements and not just one. Like Washington sometimes, people at Harvard often think of themselves as the center of the universe. I have long been skeptical about simple total explanations of everything. Kissinger's last words to me as he left the State Department were "Well, I am sure that in my absence we will have a very humane and Peru-centered policy," a parting shot at issues on which we had had differences. At another stage a State Department colleague labeled me "Dr. Democracy." But I am totally opposed to single issue politics. I don't think anybody has ever suggested that I am hostile to human rights, but I cannot accept making human rights the only consideration in policy toward any particular country as some did under President Carter. Assessments of complicated issues need to be protected from grand oversimplifications, whether of the right or the left.

*Q: While you were at Harvard what about race relations in the United States? I don't mean how many African Americans were there but was this a topic of consideration or not?*

EINAUDI: This was not a hot-button issue, neither for me nor I think for many of my classmates. We greeted Supreme Court decisions as Supreme Court decisions, not as calls to arms.

Q: *Brown vs. The Board of Education was 1954.*

EINAUDI: Yes, my point is that the Warren Court decisions were seen more as part of a progressive flow of history, not as conflicts calling for mobilization. Our perspective was something of an automatic reflex rooted in a Northern ethic denouncing what we saw rather passively as those racist Southerners. I was such an innocent that in Chicago in 1956 when I was turned away from an empty restaurant because I was with Marian McReynolds, a black fellow delegate, I did not realize what was happening until after she had taken my arm and gently steered me into the street to avoid a scene. As I remember, race became a big issue for me only after I had left Harvard and was teaching at Wesleyan in 1961-2, when some of my students got involved with the Freedom Riders in Mississippi.

Let me add that the lack of social consciousness in the Harvard of the 1950s extended to gender as well: Gloria Steinem was known not as a feminist or role breaker but as the Ice Queen among her many envious would-be suitors – even as she was organizing the U.S. presence at the Helsinki world youth conference.

# U.S. Army Draftee

*Q: Today is the 6th of June, D Day, 2013, with Luigi Einaudi. Luigi we've reached the time that you are getting out of Harvard and the military is breathing down your neck. Did you enter the military immediately after graduating from Harvard?*

EINAUDI: I graduated in June and my date of entry into the Army was September 11. My draft board had let me know over the summer.

*Q: That was 1957. Did you have a military commitment, any ROTC or something or who was after you?*

EINAUDI: Not at all. In those days those who went to university were exempted from the draft. But I had decided not to go directly to graduate school after graduating from college. I was going to take a couple years off to do student politics. My involvement in Latin America through the National Student Association was more interesting than the idea of graduate school. Unfortunately, my draft board in Ithaca, New York, decided that here was this guy no longer eligible for an exemption, perfect bait and I got my notice almost immediately. By September I was on my way to induction at Fort Dix and then on to Fort Knox Kentucky for basic training, where I was assigned to Company C, 13ᵗʰ Battalion, United States Army Training Center, Armor.

*Q: You were how old when you went to basic training?*

EINAUDI: 21.

*Q: How did you find basic training?*

EINAUDI: It was an extraordinarily positive experience. Military training was a corrective to the privileged life I had led at both Philips Exeter Academy and Harvard College. Both schools had tried for diversity. But what they attained was certainly not America in the broad sense. As a draftee in basic training, I came into contact with so much that I had not known previously. Only four out of some two hundred recruits in my basic training company had college degrees. The four of us were immediately named platoon leaders. In my platoon I had one young man who was illiterate. Illiterates were not supposed to be drafted. I would sit on his bunk at night and compose letters to his family and read the letters he was getting back. I also did the paperwork to get him released. Finally, they came through and he was released. But for a month I had a close relationship with somebody that I never would have known before.

*Q: Were there African-Americans in your platoon?*

EINAUDI: Yes. At Exeter and Harvard, minorities and ordinary people had been few and far between. In my platoon I had an inner-city Black kid from Cleveland with attitudes and life experiences totally unknown to me previously. There was also my great savior, a young white kid from rural Kentucky, a racoon hunter named Bobby Coffee; I've often wished I knew what happened to him.

When you have to lead on maneuvers you very rapidly learn that you are no stronger than your weakest link. As a young man I had fetal nuclear cataracts and couldn't see very well; in basic training it took me a lot of time and effort to qualify with a rifle. But Coffee had great eyes. So when my platoon went on night maneuvers I put him on point because he could see where we were going and I couldn't. We had another chap who, as the expression goes, had twelve feet and four fingers and couldn't do anything right. If we were ever to be in combat, he was the one who was going to get us killed, so we had to figure out to use him in ways that would not expose us to risk -- just as we had Coffee see where to go when I couldn't see. So I learned a great deal, not just about my society but also about the importance of teamwork. The Army tried to convince me to go to Officer Candidate School, but I did not want to extend my time in service.

There was one other notable experience from the army. When basic training was over, my orders assigned me to Fort Lewis Washington for onward assignment to U.S. Army Alaska where, presumably (with my weak eyes!) I would have been given an M1 and told to watch out for Russians coming across the Bering Strait.

*Private Einaudi in the snow at Fort Knox, 1958. (US Army photograph, reproduced courtesy of Fort Knox)*

*Q: An M1 is a rifle.*

EINAUDI: Yes, the M1 was still the standard issue rifle in our day. It wasn't a bad rifle and we all learned to take it apart and reassemble it. I did not before and have never since had a firearm in my house, so learning to handle the M1 rifle and qualifying with my bad eyes was my only experience other than one time shooting at cans with a .22 at a friend's house over a New England Thanksgiving. My youngest brother Marco has good eyes, and as a teenager in Ithaca owned a Winchester lever action 22, a

Remington 30-06 deer rifle, and a Luger. I don't think, however, that either he or our middle brother Roberto now owns a gun. None of my four children have ever had firearms in their homes.

*Q: You were assigned to Fort Lewis Washington.*

EINAUDI: Yes. The public relations folks even put out a release saying I was "Alaska bound". But I rebelled. I said, "I am not going to be sent off to Alaska to rot waiting for the Russians." My background was in Europe -- I had fluent Italian and French and pretty good Spanish – far better than the Russian I had picked up after two years at Harvard. So I simply started to raise a ruckus, the kind of thing that can get you in trouble in an institution like the Army. I wrote to my senator who at that point was Jacob Javits of New York and he sent a letter supporting me. Fort Knox is near Louisville, and one of the Binghams who owned the Louisville Courier Journal had been one of my classmates. They wrote a little editorial about personnel mismanagement in the Army, sending off to Alaska somebody whose skills would make him useful in Europe, et cetera. Finally, I was called in and told, "Your orders have been rescinded and you are being assigned to U.S. Army Europe. But we must point out to you that this new assignment is not due to all of this unacceptable pressure that you have brought upon us but to the fact that we are resuscitating an old Army tradition that he who graduates first in his class gets to choose his assignment. You graduated first in your class in basic training, so we are allowing you to choose to go to Europe. Unfortunately, the next shipment of soldiers headed for Europe doesn't go out for a month and since you engaged in all of these unfortunate activities outside the chain of command you are assigned to permanent KP, kitchen police, until then." The next month I spent cleaning kitchens and repairing lockers. I experienced the horrors of the lowly subject to arbitrary authority. One day I organized our little kitchen crew to clean up things fast so we could get some time off and go to town. The sergeant came along with a bucket of slop and spread it all over the floor and said "There, now, clean that up. Teach you to be uppity."

The military experience made me a better American, probably a better person. After I got to HQ USAREUR (U.S. Army Europe, in Heidelberg Germany), I was able to get married. I ironed my own uniforms to save money; I was being paid $93 a month as a private, but I managed to save a fair bit of that waiting for Carol to come over.

*Q: What was the background of your wife?*

EINAUDI: Carol Peacock was beautiful and smart; what more need I say? My parents had come to the United States as political refugees from Italian Fascism in the 1930s. Her mother's father, Edmund Urbankiewicz, had come to the United States in 1905-06 as a political refugee from Poland under the Russians. By profession he was a skilled tool and dye man and got good work at the old GE plant in Lynn, Massachusetts. His wife Paulina was an interpreter/translator and dressmaker. Paulina brought Carol's mother Mary with her from Poland and later had five more children in the United States. Paulina's sister emigrated to Curitiba, Brazil about the same time she came to the United States, but they lost touch after the first world war. Paulina did keep in touch with her many family members in Poland, especially five nephews. All fought in World War II. One died, one chose exile in England, and the other three emerged a teacher, a playwright, and the minister of culture in the first post-war Communist government. Carol's widowed mother Mary visited Poland to see them in 1967. She found conditions different from what she had expected. The culture was not particularly socialist. Many in the younger generation were wearing blue jeans, listening to the Beatles, and pulling for the U.S. in Vietnam. She was amazed.

Francis Franciscan Peacock, Carol's father, was of Scotch-English origin, He was a draftsman and a union man, also at GE in Lynn. One of the things that brought Carol and I together in addition to her brains and beauty was politics. Like mine, her family were Democrats, committed Roosevelt New Dealers. Her father had been a leader of the American Federation of Technical Engineers, Local 142, which belonged to the International Union of Electrical Workers. He had never been a Communist, but the IUE was one of the unions accused of having Communist ties and he had gotten pressure from the House Un-American Activities subcommittee. That experience made Carol anti-McCarthy, just as I was anti-McCarthy because of my father's experience with the Mussolini loyalty oaths and the renewed pressures in that vein during the McCarthy period. We hit it off automatically in our political self-identification and interests. Other than that, she is very different. She was a biology major in college and later in life became an intellectual property lawyer. We were not the same, but we certainly matched up.

*Q: How did you meet?*

At the 1956 NSA national conference in Chicago, Carol represented Simmons College. Her mother Mary had graduated from there in 1928, and Simmons was strong in the natural sciences, in which Carol was interested. Boston is not far from Cambridge. We saw each other again at a conference at MIT and things took off from there.

*Q: Let's talk about your experiences in Europe, where did you go, where did you serve?*

EINAUDI: From Fort Knox I flew to Frankfurt, Germany, for onward assignment. I flew Military Air Transport, was formed up and marched in uniform through the streets of Frankfurt to barracks. The next day, I was offered three assignments. The first was as a driver with the U.S. Mission to Potsdam. I was told "you will have to be prepared to drive fast because there will be occasions when we want to get away from the Russians, and as a driver it will be your responsibility—" I interrupted, "No, I'm a lousy driver." In a car chase I would have gotten everyone killed. As I've already said I couldn't see at all well then; I see much better now only because laser techniques developed after my retirement enabled removal of my fetal cataracts. The second choice was a unit in Leghorn, Italy. Having just marched through the streets of Frankfurt in full uniform almost as an occupying soldier, I thought I'm just not going to do that in Italy. My wife-to-be, my American education, and my experience in the Army had all turned me fully into an American. But my name and life always held the possibility of my being seriously involved with Italy. I did not want the personal conflict. So again, I said no. That left a third option, the Adjutant General's Office at Headquarters United States Army Europe in Heidelberg. The job was to proofread circulars and publications. It was a desk job in a headquarters, not in a unit out in the middle of nowhere. I accepted and quickly also became a lecturer on the Uniform Code of Military Justice and how to behave if you were ever captured by the enemy. This freed me from having to participate in maneuvers.

So suddenly there I was, in an ideal situation. I could bring Carol over and we could marry. In that assignment I also learned something that proved critical to my later work in the State Department. I had been taught by my grandfather that no matter how nice, a theory that can't explain the facts it purports to cover isn't a good theory. But at Harvard I had always focused on the theory more than the facts. And now I learned to pay attention to detail, to really master the facts. Once I proved a competent proofreader, I didn't get much supervision. My assistant proofreader was a fellow draftee, also from Harvard. He and I simply ran things on our own, happy as larks. Until one day the U.S. Army Europe Circular on the Shipment of Household Goods, which we had proofed without supervision, was printed and distributed all over Europe. The title of the circular came out reading "on the Shipment of Household Gods."

Q: *Appropriate in Japan but maybe not—*

EINAUDI: Exactly. Funny, even, but certainly inappropriate. It was then that I learned that if you do not focus properly, the eye naturally leaps over the title to the text. You cannot afford that if you are a proofreader. Complacency kills.

Q: *Just to get a feel for it this is 1958ish, am I right?*

EINAUDI: Yes.

Q: *What was the attitude around you about the, I'd say, "Soviet menace"?*

EINAUDI: Distant. It was the basis of planning and of operations and maneuvers but it was not particularly real, I think, for any of us. As soldiers, we were remarkably isolated and had little news about current events. The moment of greatest potential for actual conflict while I was on active duty was President Eisenhower's decision to land Marines in Lebanon. Being stationed in Germany, our local Army-town relations were still dominated by memories of WWII – and there was a strong sense that we were almost an occupation force. Our Master Sergeant had been reduced from a wartime rank of Colonel; he and some of our older career cadre hated the Germans and didn't bother to hide it. In the classes I gave on the Code of Conduct ("name, rank and serial number is all you are authorized to give out under questioning if captured") there was no doubt that the captors, if that were to happen, were going to be the Russians. They were the enemy. But I don't remember any blood and guts to it.

My two years as a draftee taught me not to be frightened of the military. I don't see them as a hostile body, I see them as a collection of people whose behavior, morale, and attitudes depend very heavily on their leadership, their organization, and the missions they are given by their civilian leaders.

*Q: Later during the Vietnam War, particularly towards the end, our military sort of fell apart but the military was a pretty cohesive group at that time, wasn't it? In other words, you didn't have a lot of soldiers going off and smoking hashish or taking drugs, not being very disciplined or not. How would you say you found it?*

EINAUDI: My experience fits the more positive pre-Vietnam pattern you describe. After my wife and I married, we were authorized to "live on the economy." We rented a room on Rohrbacher Strasse, lived in our own honeymoon world and did not share life at Patton Barracks. And I never served in Vietnam. But, yes, the levels of morale and respect for our leaders were very different from what ultimately proved to be the case in Vietnam.

I have always been and am today more than ever a supporter of the draft or some form of mandatory national service. In pushing for the reinstitution of the military draft, I have never found any support from officer friends. The commander in chief of the U.S. Southern Command, who played a key role during the Peru-Ecuador conflict, was a much-decorated four-star general named Barry McCaffrey who later became drug czar under President Clinton. McCaffrey just would not hear of reinstating the draft. Barry said there had been too many cases in Vietnam, not just of drugs, not just of breakdowns of unit discipline, but of American soldiers simply shooting American officers in the back. His generation of officers simply would not hear of going back to the draft. I personally think that is a great mistake, because basic training is a socializing and nationally unifying experience everyone should have—and which our country increasingly needs, even if only on a non-military, national service basis.

*Q: Yes. My personal feeling, however, is that reinstituting the draft would cause many problems. Anyway, did your exposure to Germany at all change your international focus? What part of the world particularly interested you besides the United States?*

EINAUDI: Carol and I used our leave time to go from Germany to Italy; we honeymooned in the Italian Alps in places I knew as a young man. Christmas 1958 we spent in Rome with my grandfather and grandmother. Later, Germany became very important to me and to the United States again in ways that have not, I think, been generally appreciated. After the defeat of Hitler, denazification was a key objective of the Allied Military Governments in Germany. This in turn led to a focus on political parties and their educational as well as representative functions. I don't know at what stage of German constitutional development this came about, but the practice developed of public funding for the international as well as domestic activities of political parties. My exposure to Germany helped me later to connect with the party Stiftungen, the German Party foundations run by the Christian Democrats, the Socialists and the Liberals that supported international political movements. But my central focus remained on Latin America.

*Q: Okay you came back, got out of the military, when, in '59?*

EINAUDI: Yes, September '57 to September '59 are my service dates. My experience in the army confirmed a lesson I had learned from my family: the world is difficult and changeable, so it is important to keep your feet firmly planted on the ground. Having roots, knowing who you are, matters. Score one for Grandfather Einaudi over Grandfather Michels.

# Graduate School

Q: *Then what?*

EINAUDI: Back to Harvard for a PhD. Easily said now, very difficult then. Our first child, my oldest daughter Maria, had been born in an Army hospital in Heidelberg.

Q: *My daughter was born in a military hospital in Frankfurt.*

EINAUDI: You probably paid about $10 or less; I paid something like $6 or $7, all for the food my wife consumed while she was in the hospital. That was all I paid for the birth of my daughter; talk about cradle to grave socialism, but that's another matter. We came back with this small child and I still needed to finish my education. A logical thing in today's world would be that under that kind of pressure the wife would work. Later, in her forties, Carol did go to work and became a very successful lawyer. But back then it wasn't easy dealing with my father, and I was worse. My father was paying the bills and I was culturally limited. My smart wife had majored in biology at Simmons and quickly found an exciting job with the first DNA lab at MIT. My father simply said, "You can't do that. I'm paying the bills and the money you will make as a lab assistant at MIT is not even going to pay for the babysitter you will need to hire to take care of my granddaughter.

In the meantime, my son needs to complete his education." So Carol resigned a job she really wanted and would have enjoyed. I made some money by taking a teaching position as a Teaching Fellow and translating a book by Raymond Aron from French into English for the Harvard University Press, then took my first job out as fast as I could. In the fall of 1961, I accepted an instructorship in government at Wesleyan University. I had the illusion that at Wesleyan I could recreate my happy Exeter experience, but I went mainly because I needed the money. We were thinking of a second child and my grandfather was writing "That's all very nice but you should not be an economic burden on your father, you better get out there and work."

*Q: You also had the GI bill, didn't you?*

EINAUDI: I did not serve during wartime so I didn't have any support of that kind. I left Harvard having completed almost all the requirements for the PhD but not having actually written the thesis, which I only returned to complete in the spring of 1966.

*Q: I want to stay with your graduate school years before we move on. The Kennedy election in 1960, between Kennedy and Nixon, is sometimes treated as a watershed election. How did you feel about it? Were you engaged or not?*

EINAUDI: That's a very relevant question. I was very engaged and rapidly becoming very alienated. I thought you were going to lead laser-like to the Kennedy-Nixon debates in which they took turns posturing and out-demagoguing each other on Cuba. As a life-long Democrat I was instinctively pro-Kennedy. I had spent the summer of 1950 in Los Angeles when my father had taught at UCLA and had been exposed then to Nixon, not very favorably. But in the debate Kennedy and Nixon outdid each other in talking about how you had to get rid of Castro and take care of things. Nothing they said showed awareness of the complexities of the Cuban situation. So I became very concerned. My partisan feelings didn't blind me to the fact that, for whatever reason, Kennedy was heading toward disaster on Cuba.

*Q: You were at this point working on your PhD—?*

EINAUDI: Yes. I was at Harvard as a second-year graduate student and teaching fellow.

*Q: What was the subject of your dissertation?*

EINAUDI: It was titled *Marxism in Latin America, from Aprismo to Fidelismo*. My thesis was something of an intellectual history of the twentieth century political left in Latin America leading up to the Cuban revolution. The analysis was linked closely to the insights I had gained from experiences with Latin American students in the 1950s, the years *Fidelismo* was brewing.

I completed my PhD thesis in 1966 on leave from RAND. We went to live with my wife's mother, Mary, in Stoneham, Massachusetts. Carol did all the typing. I had been very struck by the importance of language in communication. For example, C. Wright Mills' book *Listen Yankee*, reads very radical in English, but in Spanish it reads like much normal political discourse.

*Q: C. Wright Mills was very well received…*

I became interested in the idea that you have to look behind the language to understand what is being said. Different cultures express things differently. I asked Harvard Professor Adam Ulam to be my thesis advisor. Ulam was an expert in the Soviet

Union and Marxism. He had written a very interesting and to me inspirational book entitled *The Unfinished Revolution*, which explored language and Marxism as an expression tied to certain stressful political and social moments in history, like the industrial revolution. Those insights I applied to the emergence of a left-nationalist political movement, *Aprismo,* the doctrine of the Peruvian Victor Raul Haya de la Torre. Haya's influence began in Peru in the '20s and spread through much of Latin America. My thesis was about the parallels between *Aprismo* and *Fidelismo,* the movement that emerged in the late '50s out of the Castro experience in Cuba.

One of the experiences that radicalized many young Latin Americans had been American support for a coup in Guatemala in 1954. The thesis laid out how *fidelismo* was partly a response, both tactically as well as strategically, to events in Guatemala.

*Q: You are referring to the coup against Arbenz.*

EINAUDI: Precisely. After that, to quote Che Guevara in one of his less known but critical quotes "They may get us for being Communists but they won't get us for being stupid." Guevara had actually been in Guatemala in 1954. After the Cuban revolution, he and others expected something like the Bay of Pigs because of what had been done against Arbenz. To prepare for that, Castro's Cubans decided to turn to the Russians for help. The Americans will make trouble, but we are going to get the resources that will enable us to beat them. I wrote this up in my thesis and then was happy to see it buried in the vaults of Widener Library. I still wasn't through figuring out what was going on, I also feared publication might damage my chances of a government career; my thesis was very critical of U.S. policies.

*Q: How was Cuba playing at Harvard?*

EINAUDI: In 1956, as a Harvard undergraduate, I had been a member of the U.S. delegation to the International Student Conference which took place in Peradeniya, in what was then Ceylon, now Sri Lanka. The head of the Cuban delegation at that conference was a chap named José Antonio Echeverria, the president of the Student Federation of the University of Havana; I had met him earlier in Chile. In the spring of 1957, he attempted to pull a coup against Batista. He and his followers seized the radio station but José Antonio was shot and killed by Batista's soldiers. I still have the text of a talk I gave on Cuba then at the Philips Brooks House. My basic position was that if you said Castro was crazy, I could accept that, but I would not accept that he was a Communist. The wellsprings of Castro's actions were Cuban nationalism, ignorance of the outside world, and narcissism – certainly not obedience to a foreign totalitarianism.

Tying this back to my PhD thesis, in it I explored how language can make something sound Marxist even when it isn't. You have to be very careful in making judgments about people and about what they really believe or do. Castro himself pointed out that during the revolution against Batista the Communists were "hiding under the bed;" they weren't out there dying or leading things the way Echeverria did, even though José Antonio was a rival to Castro. Trying to beat Castro to the punch was one of the reasons Echeverria tried his coup when he did. But I don't think that anybody at Harvard gave much of a damn.

Then, in the fall of 1960, I started to receive warnings from friends in Latin America that the Eisenhower administration was cooking up what later became the Bay of Pigs. Fernando Andrade, a Guatemalan student movement friend, visited me at Harvard and told me, "You know, there's all kinds of funny stuff going on with unmarked planes ferrying people who aren't Guatemalans in and out of this big private estate in Retalhuleu. Looks like something is being planned to invade Cuba." Forewarned, I was able to pick up a lot of information and rumors. As often happens when the U.S. government tries to do something external to itself in secret, the government can successfully keep it secret from most of its own employees and sometimes from the American public but not from people who really are capable of watching and following carefully. In those days the government had the advantage that it succeeded in getting leading papers to self-censor: on request of the White House, the <u>New York Times</u> did not publish material that was being published openly in Latin America and even in a regular academic newsletter at Stanford.

In January of '61 I heard that my Harvard Dean, McGeorge Bundy, who also taught U.S. foreign policy, was about to head off to Washington to be President Kennedy's National Security Adviser. I sought him out to tell him what I knew about what was being planned and to warn him that this just wasn't going to work. Most people don't know that McGeorge Bundy had actually started out in life wanting to be a historian, focusing on Colombia and Latin America; he thought he knew something about the region and its people. As a teaching fellow I was very junior; and he was not only my Dean, but an intimidating chap with a high dome facilitated by receding hair and a good cranial structure. I told him what I had heard and he said, "Well I don't know anything about it but if I were in their position I'd be doing the same thing." I said, "Well look, let's discuss it." At that point he decided to cut things short. He broke in and he said, "We are on the verge of a civil war in Cuba." I didn't think that was quite in the cards, but there had been some conflict in the Escambray so I let it pass, thinking that if there was going to be a civil war in Cuba, what business was it for the U.S. to get involved? Then he unleashed the sentence that destroyed me. He said, "Yes, it's going to be a civil war between the Communists and the liberals." While I was mentally picking myself up off the floor he added "They know on which side their bread is buttered." I was thinking "Where are the Cubans?" Cuba did have a Communist Party. It had never come close to power, and had played little if any role in the revolution against Batista, but it did have some labor base and maybe the capacity to rally fifteen percent of the vote on a good day. But who were the liberals? Aside from some cosmopolitan individuals, Cuba's liberals could probably be counted on the fingers of two hands. But it was the Cuban people who were missing in Bundy's assertion. Where were all the supporters of General Batista? Where were all the supporters of Fidel Castro and Fidelismo? What about Cuban nationalism? Bundy's assertion was so far removed from the realities on the ground that I was speechless. Here was a full professor, my dean, a man whose imposing forehead made him look like the personification of authoritative intelligence—and he was speaking nonsense.

That spring at Harvard brought another tough experience related to Cuba. As a Teaching Fellow, I was assisting Government 113, a course on Latin American politics taught by Assistant Professor John Plank. The semester had barely begun, when John suddenly disappeared. It turned out that he had gone to Washington to help develop the program of the "Cuban Revolutionary Council" that was meant to take over Cuba's government after Castro was thrown out by Brigade 2506, the exile invasion force that landed at the Bay of Pigs. I took over his course, and had to prepare and deliver some thirteen lectures. It was a good class, several of whom were to have careers centered on Latin America -- Alec Watson, Abe Lowenthal, David Spencer, Joe Love, and others whose names now escape me. Being thrown into lecturing without notice or help did not improve my views of university life or the wisdom of our leaders.

These experiences really shook me. I felt from then on that I had to train myself to have comebacks that my superiors could understand in spite of their ignorance. I used to call it learning to slam doors on policymakers, meaning that I had to learn ways to communicate with them in ways that they could no longer escape the realities of what they were dealing with.

*Q: How did you go about training yourself to do that?*

I left academia to go to the RAND Corporation. I knew that the U.S. government had done some very stupid things but I didn't know why. A professor is in a position of authority over young people and can teach them all kinds of things. College students are not dumb, but still I felt that if I was trying to teach them materials without knowing why what was happening was happening, then I would be using my students as cannon fodder for unproven theories or for my own preferences. I had to learn before I could teach.

*Q: Did you go directly from Harvard to RAND?*

EINAUDI: No, I spent the 1961-62 academic year in Middletown Connecticut, as an instructor in government at Wesleyan University. I had been brought there by E.E. Schattschneider, Sigmund Neumann (both of whom studied political parties in the tradition of my grandfather Michels) and Joe Palamountain. Clem Vose and Nelson Polsby were colleagues. It was an outstanding group that treated me well, though I was asked to teach a seminar on African independence, which I knew nothing about. I also had some excellent students, among them Rick Tuttle and Joel Johnson, with whom I would stay in touch later in life. But I felt cramped and cut off from the real world.

# Rand

*Q: How long did you work for RAND?*

EINAUDI: Eleven years, from the summer of 1962 to the end of 1973.

*Q: What were you hired to do and what did you do?*

EINAUDI: I was brought to RAND to work on the "Third World" which is a catchall misnomer. Africa, Asia and Latin America don't have much in common except for their marginality in the perceptions of Western outsiders. At RAND, it turned out that Africa did not exist, and that Asia meant Vietnam, where the colonial war was becoming ever more consuming. I wound up focusing mainly on Latin America and, on the side, teaching political science at UCLA.

When I accepted its job offer, RAND was still in its glory years, "back when you RAND guys still wore white hats" as Senator Al Gore, Senior, the father of the future Vice President, put it when I called on him with regard to a Spanish bases project just after Dan Ellsberg leaked the Vietnam papers. The RAND Corporation had been founded after World War II to serve the U.S. Air Force which was the most technological but also the youngest and least established of the military services. To provide independent thinking that would strengthen Air Force capabilities, Hap Arnold, the Air Force commander at the end of World War II, decided to create RAND, meaning "Research And No Development," an entity he hoped would strengthen the Air Force by hiring smart people at better than government or university salaries and getting them clearances to enable access to U.S. government documents without the restrictions of being government employees. For me, RAND seemed like a perfect half-way house between academia and government, one that would enable me to learn about how decisions were made without losing my autonomy and freedom.

*Q: Did it turn out to be the half-way house you hoped for?*

EINAUDI: Ultimately, yes. But RAND didn't have an easy time fitting me in its programs. And at first I had a very hard time personally. At one stage I was under so much pressure that I actually began to stutter. Albert Wohlstetter, in whose honor a hall was later named at the Heritage Foundation, called me a fellow traveler. I called him a cold warrior. He looked at me and said, "You mean you want the cold war to be hot?" He was a nuclear strategist working to ensure a nuclear standoff. He saw the world in terms of a real risk of hot war, and his political views were shaped by his anti-Communism. I was watching the nibbling at the world periphery, and seeing that many people I knew were being misrepresented and twisted, becoming casualties of this war whether it was cold or hot or whatever it was. Years later, it was a career Foreign Service officer, one of the very few career Foreign Service officers ever to become Secretary of State, Larry Eagleburger, who in 1991 at the OAS General Assembly in Chile actually apologized in the name of the United States for having accused progressive and nationalist movements of being Communist when they were not. Wohlstetter tended to see Communists everywhere. I was protected in RAND by several senior scholars, notably the sociologist Herbert Goldhamer and the Chairs of the Social Science Department, Fred Iklé and Joe Goldsen. Another strong supporter was USAF Colonel William Stewart, a JCS Intelligence briefer who had been reassigned to RAND after visiting Cuba in 1960 and returning with a skeptical view about U.S. reporting on Castro. I did not have an axe to grind. As I said earlier, I didn't like what we had done in Guatemala in 1954 or at the Bay of Pigs in 1961, but I also didn't know why we had done it. I was still looking for answers, still learning.

Fortunately for me, RAND in those days was able to charge the U.S. government so much overhead for tasked research that they had money left over for self-tasked research on matters of policy interest but for which we did not have a specific government client. In July 1962, just as I was starting at RAND, a military coup in Peru against a civilian president greatly upset the Kennedy White House. The questions it raised made military assistance and military politics of general interest. So I was able to convince RAND to use non-contract funds to send me to Peru to do research on the Peruvian military. Carol and I lived in the Miraflores district of Lima for almost a year with our two little daughters in 1964-65.

I got a great deal out of that research on Peru. My major professional regret is that I never finished putting all the materials I collected into a good book. I have donated those files, which include more than thirty interviews with important Peruvian figures from Eudocio Ravines, the Communist leader and author of *The Yenan Way*, to Conservative Prime Minister Pedro Beltrán and several Presidents, tables on military sociology, and a full-length book draft, to the Columbus Memorial Library. Fortunately, some of the findings were used by my friend, retired Peruvian Army Major Victor Villanueva, as the basis of his book *100 Años del Ejército Peruano: frustraciones y cambios.*

*Q: You did of course turn your Peru research into several reports and Congressional testimony, but I gather that books were not RAND's chief focus.*

EINAUDI: Quite right. RAND's focus was on policy. Books were sometimes a by-product of our research, but they were not what our clients wanted. What *was* all-consuming in those years—in time, energy, and divisiveness, was Vietnam. My brother Marco, who had been in the ROTC at Cornell, was called up to Vietnam as a French-speaking intelligence officer. I saw him off, glad not to have been asked to participate in what I saw as something of a colonial residue. I recorded my views in a 1968 Adlai Stevenson Institute book called *No More Vietnams? The War and the Future of U.S. Foreign Policy.* A RAND social gathering in 1969 got particularly heated. Guy Pauker suggested that President Nixon would cut U.S. troop strength in Vietnam substantially over the next year. Dan Ellsberg – this was before the Pentagon Papers, but Dan was already rather alienated -- disagreed. They wound up betting $100. The atmosphere was so charged, they decided they needed a witness. I was not working directly on Vietnam, so I was chosen. When the year passed, Pauker easily won, but Ellsberg did not pay up. So I did my duty and went to collect. Dan made out a check, and gave it to me to give to Guy. He had written on it "For sale of military secrets." Guy told me he would frame it.

RAND proved an invaluable training ground. When Ellsberg leaked the Pentagon papers, my social science colleague Herb

Goldhamer, who was the closest thing to a mentor I had at RAND, observed that Ellsberg might not have needed to leak the Pentagon papers had he been a more effective writer. Goldhamer, whose own work on the Panmunjom negotiations of the 1950s had been heavily censored, showed me how you could learn to communicate almost anything if you choose your words carefully. From Bob Komer, returning from his stint as Vietnam coordinator at the NSC, I learned that when visiting government offices I should "always leave something behind." To do that, I learned to write one-page descriptions of research findings that set up potential new studies. I was learning about power through writing, doing an apprenticeship for my later work in government, writing policy papers and the speeches of others.

*Q: Well then back to RAND. You were there for about eleven years? Did you end up being **the** Latin American specialist?*

EINAUDI: Yes. At RAND I ultimately headed a group within the Social Science Department focused on Latin American issues. My immediate team was made up of Richard Maullin, David Ronfeldt, and Alfred Stepan; depending on the project and availabilities, I would draw on other RAND researchers, particularly Goldhamer and the economist Bob Slighton. For a while Constantine Menges was part of the team. My main consultants were Shane Hunt, Caesar Sereseres, Ed Gonzalez, and Michael Fleet. Maullin, Fleet and Sereseres had all obtained their PhDs as my students in the University of California system. At any one point we were being supported by several contracts with different government agencies. In most cases, unfortunately, those agencies were more interested in buying my time than the time of my colleagues. It was not a stable situation. And I had to work like a dog just to keep things going.

*Q: Was there general direction in RAND or was somebody saying Luigi I think you are a little off base on this or was anybody monitoring you? You and others were hired by the State Department, the Air Force, the Army...*

EINAUDI: The Advanced Research Projects Agency (ARPA) was an important sponsor, as well as those you mention. After a few years, I developed excellent relations with NSC, State and OSD/ISA, and the U.S. Air Force. My major supporters were DASD Bill Lang of OSD/ISA, USAF Major General George Keegan, ACS Intelligence, and Everett J. "Buck" Burlando, a civilian who had served in Brazil during World War II. Unfortunately, my key audiences, the NSC and State, were consumers more than funders – very interested in my research, but without the funds to pay for it.

*Q: Was anyone looking at your results and saying I think you are off or you are getting a wrong approach or what?*

EINAUDI: I was trying to convey that the major Latin American countries were developing rather more than U.S. stereotypes implied, and more than the number of military regimes emerging in response to the Cuban revolutionary challenge seemed to confirm. I argued that the growing complexity of Latin American societies was making them difficult to rule by caudillos, even when backed by military force. This analysis led me to develop a series of studies I entitled "Latin American Institutional Development" followed in each case by the particular topic: "Changing Military Perspectives in Peru and Brazil" or "The Changing Catholic Church" in the wake of Vatican Council II.

Charlie Meyer, the Sears, Roebuck and Company executive who served as Richard Nixon's Assistant Secretary for the Western

Hemisphere from 1969 to 1973, told me later that he always thought my use of the phrase "Institutional Development" was "codeword for socialism." But overall, reactions were very positive. Our studies provided depth and context unavailable otherwise.

My work on Peru was particularly well received in the intelligence community and the Pentagon. After a second and this time openly radical coup in 1968, I was called to testify before the Senate Foreign Relations Committee. Senator Fulbright was in the chair. The testimony went very well until Fulbright said Peru did not need jet fighters. I answered that it was perfectly rational for Peru to want to have aircraft capable of intercepting the local Pan Am flight if necessary. He held his ground. I held Peru's. He was dismissive. Mindful that Fulbright had written a book entitled "The Arrogance of Power," I told him that for an outsider to tell a sovereign country what it could or could not do was arrogant. The Senator excused himself and walked out. The hearing transcript omits the exchange on arrogance.

*Q: They do say history depends on who writes it.*

EINAUDI: My work on Peru research also led to some fun moments. Carol and I loved Madame Wu's Garden restaurant in Santa Monica. According to KCET radio, the elegant owner, Sylvia Chen, *"often traveled with Cary Grant and his family, and drove around in a Silver Cloud Rolls-Royce, with a license plate that read "MME WU." Princess Grace of Monaco, Paul Newman, Elizabeth Taylor, Ronald Reagan, Robert Redford, Jane Fonda, and Mae West (who loved the bird's nest soup -- supposedly an aphrodisiac) were all fans."* Chen's grandfather had emigrated from China to Peru in the late nineteenth century, and she knew all about Peru's great Chinese *chifa* food tradition. One evening, my wife and I invited

General Arturo Cavero Calixto and the entire CAEM (Peruvian war college) class, which was visiting the United States, to have dinner at Madame Wu's with some RAND and UCLA colleagues. A good time was had by all. 54 people drank 53 bottles of wine. The U.S. Army escort officer paid the bill without flinching.

When that same CAEM class visited the State Department, Alan Flanigan, then the Peru Desk Officer, asked me to give the lecture on US policy toward Peru and Latin America. I felt the State Department was trying to dodge controversy, but I accepted. Then the morning of my talk the prospect of squaring U.S. and Peruvian perceptions made me so nervous that I cut myself shaving.

*Q: Were you right to worry?*

EINAUDI: No. Everyone was so relieved that everyone was getting along that no one paid attention to what I said.

My first serious institutional contacts with the State Department were with INR, the Bureau of Intelligence and Research. Notable figures there were G. Harvey Summ and Elizabeth Hyman, a pre-war Harvard PhD known as the "Keeper of the Latin American military museum" from whom I learned that a single donated U.S. 1940 Sherman tank had become a symbol of Paraguay's Stroessner and his power. In 1969 I negotiated RAND's first-ever contract with the State Department; it was on the politics of the changing Catholic Church. It was followed by several others, including a contract to organize a conference at Airlie House for INR on Trends in Latin America.

I was also learning about the bureaucracy and its complexities. RAND had started as an Air Force project. After the election of Jack Kennedy, his Administration formed what some called their own little State Department within the Defense Department. This was OSD/ISA, International Security Affairs, under John McNaughton, which was heavily involved in Vietnam. You asked what was I hired to do, and I answered "study the third world." But you also asked "What did you really do?" Well, at one point in those early '60s one of the things I did was carry secrets from one office in the Pentagon down two floors to another office in the Pentagon. Secrets that Air Force intelligence had, secrets that ISA wanted but didn't have.

*Q: These are offices in the Pentagon?*

EINAUDI: Yes. But, you know, offices in competition marked by mistrust, distrust.

*Q: Were you doing this unauthorized or were you doing this because the people around you wanted you to do this?*

EINAUDI: Oh, this was essentially authorized. I think that ISA was paying RAND in part because the administration civilians knew that RAND could get certain things out of the military side of the Pentagon that it could not. The people that RAND was getting it from trusted RAND so it was alright if RAND had it. If RAND then passed it along, it created an information exchange at arm's length but with everybody knowing what was happening.

*Q: Was this kind of information disconnect typical?*

EINAUDI: Unfortunately, yes. And sometimes it can be quite dangerous to U.S. interests.

*Q: Do you have an example in mind?*

EINAUDI: My research in Peru brought out multiple disconnects related to information.

The Peruvian military, like a lot of military institutions, considers its data very secret, doesn't want it known. One consequence is that their office of public information is a division of Army counterintelligence. My attempts to penetrate Peru's military information defenses met with very limited success, so I went to our embassy and asked whether they could provide an in for me to the military to at least make it clear that I had a U.S. security clearance. That I might be thought of by some to be some sort of subversive madman was not an absurd thought. Our DCM, Ernest Siracusa, had warned me when I first arrived in Lima to keep my distance from the crazy leftists in the Peace Corps. Fortunately, when I asked for help, Ambassador Wesley Jones decided the research was worth supporting, and instructed the commander of the U.S. Military Group to introduce me to the Peruvians. What happened next was absolutely fascinating. Before doing what his ambassador had instructed him to do, the Mil Group Commander went to the Peruvians to ask permission to do it. So here we had a U.S. Colonel asking his Peruvian military hosts for their approval to do what the U.S. Ambassador had instructed. He perceived himself as wearing two hats and therefore as needing authorization from both chains of command. His most honorable position taught me that sometimes life is more complicated in practice than it may seem on the organizational charts. By the way, after that, the Peruvians made sure to smile when they saw me, but provided no additional information.

Then in 1968 Peru's military overthrew an elected civilian government. The coup broke all the traditional molds. The new military government nationalized the Standard Oil of New Jersey subsidiary and did a lot of other things that caused tensions with the United States. U.S. Congressional reactions included accusations that the Peruvian leaders had Communist sympathies and assertions that President Velasco was mentally deranged by a brain tumor. By the spring of 1969, as the clock was ticking toward the six-month deadline for compensation set by the Hickenlooper amendment, the Peruvians suddenly declared our station chief, the head of the CIA contingent in Peru, *persona non grata*, and expelled him together with a number of other agency personnel. In Washington, inside the executive branch, the CIA reported that Peru's actions were unprovoked. This seemed to confirm the view that we were dealing with an anti-United States conspiracy.

My contacts in Peru told a different story. A close friend, General Arturo Cavero, had become head of the new presidential advisory council (COAP) created after the 1968 coup to "fill the back rooms" that had been occupied by right-wing politicians after General Odría's 1948 coup. Cavero told me they had realized that their Ministers were being followed. Shadowing the shadowers, they learned they worked for a firm called "Plant Protection" which they determined on further investigation was run by the CIA. Afraid that this meant the U.S. was preparing to intervene, they had expelled CIA personnel in preemptive self-defense.

I reported this to Pete Vaky, who had moved from the policy planning staff to the NSC. Vaky checked this allegation with Agency representatives at the NSC, but was stonewalled. Unsatisfied, he said to me, "Look, if you have such good Peruvian contacts, why don't you see if they can provide you with the forms on which Plant Protection was keeping the data that it was gathering." I got them and gave them to Vaky. They were Agency biographic forms. The question of who was conspiring against whom suddenly became muddled. U.S.-Peruvian relations remained rocky, and many of the military regime's illiberal domestic moves proved counterproductive, but this particular crisis was averted. But the Washington lesson was clear. Without an NSC functioning as honest broker, U.S. policy could be held hostage to the stubborn self-protection of individual government agencies.

A second lesson was beginning also to form in my mind. And it was the beginnings of the answer to the question of how and why U.S. policy was made.

*Q: What was that?*

EINAUDI: That specific government actions might often prove to be the result not of a master plan, but of lack of one, with different interests and institutional concerns predominating at different times on different issues. That the real trick might be to learn how to make things happen, how to make government work better. Not so much a question of preventing mistakes, but of how to make government work, or at least work less badly.

In 1972 I put my growing understandings of both the United States and Latin America together in a lecture in Lima in Spanish at the Institute of Peruvian Studies. The main debate on the Latin American left in those days was how to find cracks in *"El Sistema"* -- what many Latin Americans saw as an all-encompassing American imperialist "system." The debate focused on how to identify the line that, if crossed, would bring down U.S. intervention on them. In a take-off on their fear, I entitled the talk *"El sistema no funciona,"* [The System does not work.] Using a blackboard and chalk, I diagrammed an organizational chart of the various offices dealing with Latin America in different U.S. government agencies with their respective chains of command. I then argued that the system had grown so complicated it could not work predictably. There was no functioning system, and therefore there was no predictable line to be crossed. After the lecture, José Matos Mar, a sociologist whose brilliant book *Desborde popular* described the pressures internal migration put on Peruvian institutions, drove me back to my hotel. As he dropped me off, he said, "Luigi, I am sure you told us many great truths tonight. But I also think that if you keep working hard enough and long enough you will find a little office somewhere with a little man in it pulling all the strings to make it work."

*Q: Well then after this time at RAND, where were you going and when?*

EINAUDI: I joined the State Department, and tried to work hard enough and long enough to try to become that little man in that little office. My most interesting set of relationships in Washington were with Foreign Service officers on the policy planning staff and at the NSC. Pete Vaky and I first met in 1967. He was ten years my senior, an eminent professional fresh from being DCM in Guatemala. I was at RAND, fresh from Peru and quizzical about U.S. policy. Pete was intelligent, tolerant of the views of others, a responsive listener, willing to share views on how to get things done. Pete became a mentor and a life-long friend. His sure sense of authority, organizational skill and conceptual insights always made him bigger than whatever position he happened to hold at any particular time. I learned from Pete that an effective NSC is essential to good policy, and that your subordinates have to "know who to salute." There was more to come, more to learn.

In August 1973, I published an opinion piece in the *Los Angeles Times* on "South America, the revolution behind the scenes" in which I argued the problem was not guerrilla warfare but the strains of development. Ironically, I was analyzing myself out of support from RAND's major sponsors, who were interested in military matters, not development. That spring, my report to RAND management indicated that our Latin American programs were running a deficit. We were proposing many projects: training for military attachés, comparative military education, MAP training programs, arms transfers, reducing Latin American military expenditures, national security doctrines, as well as a few broader studies on economic nationalism, oil politics, expropriations, Cuba, the Panama Canal. But we had nothing assured, and nothing in the pipeline. I suggested I might be able to generate more support if I moved to Washington. By year's end, I did move, not to RAND's Washington office, but to take the position in the State Department office of Policy Planning that Vaky had held when we first met. Pete by then had moved on, first to the NSC, then to be Ambassador to Colombia.

What created the actual opening for me at the State Department was Henry Kissinger's move from national security adviser to Secretary of State. That was a crazy time. Chile had fallen apart over the summer just as Kissinger was moving from the White House to the State Department. Nixon was still in office but coming under heat for Watergate. There was an extraordinary sense that the country was at risk. We had had what was essentially the forced resignation of Lyndon Johnson over Vietnam, the assassination of Bobby Kennedy, the assassination of Martin Luther King and then the Watergate scandal. President Kennedy had been assassinated just ten years before. The United States was looking very strange.

One of the fascinating things about our time now—2013—is that the United States generally seems to be doing okay even in the middle of disasters, some of which it has helped to generate. In the 1970s, there were also contrasts. How could the country that could devise the incredible technological displays of Disneyland be caught up in the human mess of Vietnam? It was an extraordinarily complicated period, one that ultimately led to the election of Jimmy Carter and a renewed focus on human rights. How human rights concerns emerged in part as a counter to the United States somehow combining great technological capacity with great human incapacity is a totally different chapter. But the story of human rights comes later, in my time in ARA/PPC, particularly with regard to Terence Todman. It was also the focus of the lecture that is reproduced in Appendix Three.

# State Policy Planning

*Q: Today is June the 10ᵗʰ, 2013, with Luigi Einaudi. What had you heard about the policy planning office (also called S/P and policy planning staff) before you went there? How did the staff rank in your estimation as far as being an instrument?*

EINAUDI: I entered the State Department in January of 1974 as a class 2 Foreign Service Reserve officer under the then Foreign Service Act. The Washington atmosphere was very strange. Kissinger had had a very smart group of people around him at the NSC. A couple of them broke at various points over the secret bombing in Cambodia but generally the group was very cohesive and felt that they were holding the country together in a very difficult time. Winston Lord, the new S/P director, had been one of the people most intimately associated with Kissinger. I actually don't know how Winston Lord and Kissinger got to know each other. Peter Rodman had been Kissinger's graduate student and then followed Kissinger into what ultimately became a very important government career. A career Foreign Service officer then on S/P, Klaus Ruser, suggested I should be brought in. Kissinger and I had not dealt personally at Harvard but each was aware of the other.

David Biltchik was a special assistant in S/P, and he helped introduce me. He and I had been together from kindergarten to third grade in Chappaqua, New York. We had met again at Harvard, but he was by then a year behind me as I had skipped the eighth grade in Ithaca. But we became close again when I started commuting to Washington from California for RAND and frequently stayed with him and his wife Jane. David had joined the Foreign Service, but then came the irony. As I came in, he went out. He said he did "not want to do the same things my second 20 years that I had done the first 20." He went into business consulting and as the years passed we lost track of each other again.

*Q: How did you feel about joining the Policy Planning Staff?*

EINAUDI: I was very proud. Going to S/P ended my fears that I wouldn't measure up to what my father or my grandfather had expected of me. I had an enormous respect for the State Department, for the importance of American diplomacy, and within that for the Policy Planning Staff which I associated with George Kennan and beyond that with Dean Acheson.

*Q: And George Marshall.*

EINAUDI: Absolutely. George Catlett Marshall, who actually founded the Policy Planning Staff when he became Secretary of State.

I was also proud because I felt I was needed. It was less than ten years since Lyndon Johnson had complained that he was not getting transcripts of what McGeorge Bundy was saying in the Dominican Republic after our 1965 intervention. J. Edgar Hoover had answered that the FBI was not set up to interpret what Bundy was saying in Spanish. The United States was changing, but not in knowledge of our neighbors to the south. Scotty Reston of the New York Times had written that "Americans will do anything for Latin America except read about it." And most members of the American establishment I knew confirmed that. Neither Arthur Schlesinger nor Zbigniew Brzezinski knew much about Latin America. In fact, Walter Mondale pretty much summed up the situation later when he said "All I know about Latin America is Pete Vaky's telephone number."

I also felt comfortable because S/P had been one of my clients when I was at RAND. I felt I had support from both the career service and the incoming Secretary of State. I rapidly developed a good relationship with Winston Lord, the new Director, who was close to Kissinger. I was extremely happy.

*Q: You have told us why you were interested in the Department. Why was the Department interested in you?*

EINAUDI: I think I was seen as a counterweight to the prevailing focus on current events. Under contract to the State Department's Office of External Research, my RAND team and I had put together a retreat at the Airlie House conference center in Warrenton, Virginia, in May 1972 on "Trends in Latin America." In preparation, we circulated a collection of papers we had written on evolving patterns of politics, economics and security in the region, mainly South America and Mexico. These papers later became the basis of *Beyond Cuba: Latin America Takes Charge of Its Future* (New York, Crane Russak, 1974) pp. xiv, 250, of which I was the editor and principal author. The analyses were well received, and provoked much discussion. They became the substantive key to my invitation to join S/P.

*Q: What did you figure the policy planning staff was doing?*

EINAUDI: Not as much as it might have. The office's bureaucratic designation had actually become S/PC. The letter C stood for Coordination, and was added by our predecessors in the hope that even if they were not consulted, the label coordination might at least lead them to receive a few papers after they were done. Under Kissinger, we knew we were not marginal. We changed it back to the original designation, S/P, for the Secretary's Office, Planning.

*Q: I wondered if you had understood the importance of that point.*

EINAUDI: Yes, information and coordination are both critical. A policy planning staff exists in part to correct for one of the characteristics of modern bureaucracy: overspecialization. Offices charged with particular responsibilities send forward policy recommendations based primarily if not solely on their specialty. Information and policy recommendations shot upward for decision without lateral coordination is known as "stovepiping." The risk is that all interests are not fully and fairly represented. Good policy requires that offices with other specializations that also bear on the issue also have an input. Ensuring that happens is critical to a sound policy process. But coordination means more complications and more work, so it is often disregarded.

*Q: Disregarded, okay, but don't some people want to be disregarded?*

EINAUDI: Bingo! That is a great observation. Before joining S/P I had consulted for John Richardson, the Assistant Secretary for Cultural Affairs (CU). Kissinger found culture a useful instrument, so I drew upon Richardson and CU's programs more than once. After a few months, Richardson summoned me to his office. "Luigi," he said, "Until you showed up, I saw the Secretary maybe once or at most twice a year. *I like it that way.*" Richardson was unusually competent, but the message was clear, he did not want the extra work and troubles that might come if I kept steering things his way.

Still, I was optimistic. I did not have some of the reservations about Kissinger that others had, not because I approved of everything he did or was said to have done, but because I've learned to try to learn for myself what is happening rather than act on hearsay. In fact, that was one of the reasons that I wanted to come into the staff. I was still on the search to figure out why U.S. policies were so often counterproductive. I thought that if I could not serve as a brakeman, at least I would be high enough in the hierarchy that I would not only understand a bit more about the what's and why's of policy, but perhaps even learn to help shape it.

*Q: What did you think you were brought in to do?*

EINAUDI: On one of the few occasions when Kissinger met with the S/P staff as a group, he told us what he wanted. "Most of the people I deal with spend their time criticizing me about the mistakes I made last week or telling me what I must do next week. I want you to tell me about the issues we will have to face two or even six months from now."

This was not an easy challenge. Governing is generally a business of surviving today. The best I could do was to try to put today's particular problems into a broader context, historically, and globally. During that first tour on S/P, I wrote pieces on Brazil, Mexico, and Peru in which I tried to put Kissinger's upcoming visits to those countries into a strategic context, keeping in mind both their immediate histories and the global context. Needless to say, most of our work was not forward-looking like that.

*Q: Was Latin America your specific beat?*

EINAUDI: Absolutely. I always tried to think in global terms, but I was brought in to cover Latin America.

*Q: Okay, give me a tour of how you saw Latin America in 1974.*

EINAUDI: Well, the big issue on everybody's mind, including as it turned out the incoming Secretary of State, was Chile; I had kept in touch with Chilean friends since my original trip there in 1955, but the Pinochet coup of September 1973 had brought Chile to the headlines everywhere.

In 1972, while still at RAND, I had visited Chile, invited by Pedro Guglielmetti, a friend from 1955 then at the trade union federation of Chile, the CUT, which was a major backbone of the Allende government. I did not meet with Allende but I met with his defense minister, José Tohà, and many Chileans across a broad spectrum as well as our embassy. In 1970, after Allende's election, our military people had been instructed (in the case of our army attaché, very much against his sense of propriety) to keep Allende from taking office. This had been a major U.S. intervention in Chilean politics. And it failed. Allende took office anyway, and then things started to go downhill domestically. Chilean politics became polarized. But while internal troubles grew in Chile, the United States started losing interest. Chile obviously was not going to become a Soviet satellite, so it was not going to have much importance. U.S. policy remained hostile, but unseating Allende was no longer on the front burner. Word was that the CIA was instructed to (simply!) ensure that Allende would be defeated in the next election.

When in 1973 the Pinochet coup took place, the response was relatively passive in most official circles outside Chile, but popular anger and anti-Americanism in much of Latin America and Europe was sharp. Chile had had a long democratic tradition, its Communist Party was only part of the "Popular Unity" government, and Allende himself was a Socialist doctor with longstanding democratic credentials. The sharpness of the controversies and the riot of accusations against the United States, made it evident that something was rotting in hemispheric relations. Kissinger decided to try to see if something could be done to remedy matters.

*Q: This was Henry Kissinger?*

EINAUDI: Yes. Kissinger cooked up with Mexican Foreign Minister Emilio Rabasa a process he called the New Dialogue. Its unstated purpose was to reset relations in wake of the coup in Chile. My task was to work with the Inter-American bureau (then known as ARA) to make it happen. Foreign ministers from the entire hemisphere were invited to the Mexican Foreign Ministry in Tlatelolco to review our relations. The discussions were to be informal and outside all existing structures. The OAS Secretary General was invited only in a personal capacity. The idea was to start over, to see what was happening, to identify what was wrong and see what could be done to improve things. The meeting took place in Mexico City, at the Mexican Foreign Ministry in Tlatelolco, in February of '74, just about two months after I had joined S/P.

*Q: When you got there what were the members of the policy planning, ARA, and others talking about? Obviously Chile was at the top of the agenda and it was controversial. Were they feeling that we were on the right course, the wrong course? What was, you might say, the professionals' viewpoint of this?*

EINAUDI: I think most professionals felt trapped in an extremely difficult situation. Vaky had described to me some of the pressure at the NSC. Private U.S. companies like ITT and anti-Allende Chileans like the Edwards family of *El Mercurio* had gotten through to President Nixon. In the name of anti-Communism, the U.S. was being dragged into what was by then a mostly internal Chilean affair. Most of the career people didn't know the details but they were aware that things were not well. One of the first lessons that I learned even before I joined the State Department was to be very careful of some of the other agencies. The CIA had a tendency to be less than fully open about their activities, even inside the government. On Chile in 1974 I think our diplomats were in trouble. It was not of their own doing. As Foreign Service officers in Latin America they were serving in an area where the Secretary of State believed we were in trouble and we didn't know what we were doing. So it started negative for them and then got worse. At the Tlatelolco meeting a number of events happened that led Kissinger to call in the ARA Assistant Secretary Jack Kubisch and really ream him out. When we got back to Washington from Mexico that was the launching pad for GLOP.

*Q: Global Outlook Program.*

EINAUDI: That's right. Kissinger basically said that he saw in Mexico that our diplomats did not have the respect of the foreigners with whom they were dealing. Paraphrasing, his argument was *"If you can't understand the foreigners, the very least you can do is understand us, understand U.S. policy and what I am trying to do. If you can't handle the locals, at least you should understand our global outlook. As it is now, Foreign Service Officers are going native without benefits for us. I want them moved around. People have to be moved out of the geographic area in which they are serving, NOW."* It all happened very fast and to a lot of persons. By June or July a very major shakeup had begun that left a very bad taste in a lot of mouths. Kubisch came to me. He had been rewarded the way purged senior people often are in the State Department, with an embassy; he was told that he was being sent to Greece as ambassador. The military junta in Greece had been accused of numerous abuses. Kubisch came to me and asked "Does Kissinger really hate me that much that he wants to have me killed?" I cite the incident purely to show that GLOP created some truly absurd reactions.

*Q: I've heard the basic thing again and again. Kissinger went to Mexico and was terribly disappointed. Do you have any idea of some of the examples of what went on there? I can understand people maybe not having the same world view that he had but was it egregious? Did you get any feel for this?*

EINAUDI: Well you know we Americans tend to throw our weight around even when we think we are not. Most of our neighbors are very small countries. Even Mexico or Brazil (and for that matter even major European countries like Italy) deal with us in an asymmetrical power context. We have so much more than they do and generally speaking so many more resources. At Tlatelolco, Kissinger was still imbued with the Nixonian view of the "special relationship" with Latin America and tried to clothe it in a call for "Community." Our neighbors just reared up and engaged in what we could call the "trade unionism of the weak"; they were 34 countries to our one and they were in no mood to be run over. A Peruvian delegate friend of mine commented "strange how roles have shifted. In the Alliance for Progress days, you guys were all statistics and we were all dreams. Now we are the ones looking for facts and you are the ones proposing dreams." The basic tone in Mexico City was set by the Foreign Minister of Guyana, Sir Shridath Ramphal, "Sonny" Ramphal, who later became Secretary General of the British Commonwealth. He took the floor as spokesman for the English-speaking Caribbean and answered Kissinger head-on. He said, "You are talking about a need to rebuild trust and confidence and create a community. But allow me to remind you that Aristotle said that community among unequals is impossible. We are not your equals and under these circumstances, Sir, community is just a lot of hot air, even if coming from you." Well, there wasn't a briefing book in sight that had prepared Kissinger for having Aristotle thrown at him. Or for a challenge expressed in the political theory that was supposed to be Kissinger's and Harvard's personal monopoly. Or from the English-speaking Caribbean that was thought would be with us against the Latins. Then Jack and some of his—

Q: *Jack Kubisch.*

EINAUDI: Jack Kubisch and some of his team were not given much visible respect by the foreign ministers. So Kissinger was now faced with a diplomatic rebellion by our neighbors on top of all the other problems in the hemisphere. I mean we had at that point the coup in Chile, a radical military government in Peru, we had the Brazilians who were feeling their oats and becoming difficult, Argentina was in turmoil as usual. Then the Caribbeans, English speaking and considered a safe dozen votes, stood up and rebelled in the name of Aristotle. It just created an extremely difficult environment. Kissinger didn't trust anyone. After three days, a long time for him to spend on any one thing, particularly something not of central interest, he had to leave. He left me behind as his representative to settle the final communiqué he had finally drafted with the ministers. His instructions to me were very simple; "you are not authorized to change one comma" and that was the end of that. The communiqué did not mention "Community," but Kissinger quotes me approvingly in his memoirs as summing up its contents as an "American program and Peruvian principles set into a Mexican framework." Many did not realize it at the time, but Tlatelolco was the end of the "special relationship" in U.S.-Latin American relations. President Nixon had attempted to revive the concept, with Kissinger as his National Security Advisor. The idea of a special relationship had been something of a fail-safe. But no longer.

Later that month of February 1974, we had a follow up meeting in Brasilia on technology transfer. Bill Bowdler, at that point ARA's principal deputy assistant secretary, headed a top flight delegation that included Richard Roberts, the Director of the National Bureau of Standards, plus Mark Finnegan, one of our country's leading intellectual property lawyers. I represented the Secretary. We had a positive approach. We were ready to at least discuss everything: patents, royalties, production, research. The Brazilians asked us, "Why does your position here differ from the position that your people are taking *right now* in Geneva in the global talks?" We asked Washington for instructions. We got a Kissingerian/Nixonian answer: "We are prepared to do more in this hemisphere than we are globally because we have a special relationship." The Brazilians ended the negotiation, "Thank you very much, we are not interested in preferential treatment." They did not want a special relationship. They wanted equal global standing.

*Q: Did you sense that the State Department principals had shown a lack of policy sense at this meeting? Or was this Kissinger trying to make a point?*

EINAUDI: On GLOP, Kissinger was trying to make a point, but he was also hitting a nerve. The career Foreign Service is just that, it's a Foreign Service; many of its people spend several years abroad. I think there was then a limit of eight consecutive years abroad. It is marvelous to serve abroad and most officers serve U.S. interests very well. But looked at from Kissinger's standpoint they were not attuned to the politics of the United States and to the many changes taking place in the United States. So as is typical of what happens to the Foreign Service and the State Department generally in our society, instead of defending the Department, instead of investing in the people of the Foreign Service and strengthening institutions like the Foreign Service Institute to provide serious education beyond language training, instead you just criticize and shake up the personnel system again. There are obviously different ways and perspectives for looking at this. I don't feel that GLOP [the Global Outlook Program] was a particularly good technique, but I also worry about a system that puts too much attention to assignments and not enough attention to history and preparation and cultural background. I wouldn't throw out Kissinger any more than I would throw out the Foreign Service. What is needed is mutual interpretation. There just were not enough of us who could even try to serve as go-betweens. And that is just a small part of a much bigger problem: the gulf between the government and the country.

*Q: I served in Yugoslavia as chief of George Kennan's consular section. I had a feeling this man really doesn't know the United States very well. But he knew his area very well, he knew the Soviet Union, he knew the Russians. My feeling is that it's much better to have somebody who knows his field than one who is really attuned to the United States or to the Secretary of State.*

EINAUDI: Yes and no. Many years later Elliott Abrams, who was then Assistant Secretary for ARA, came to me and asked, "Why can't I find a single expert on Mexico here in our bureau?" I said, "Well, you might ask Henry Kissinger why he put in GLOP." The tension between culture and diplomacy is longstanding. The Foreign Service considers its members generalists as opposed to specialists; I was for the most part considered a specialist. In fact, a colleague has pointed out that because I knew Latin America so well I was in many ways an argument against GLOP. A generalist is somebody who knows the whole of diplomacy and is able to take on tasks in very different circumstance with a minimal amount of preparation. Among Foreign Service Officers that perspective also arises from bitter experience, with a political system that puts them into situations for which they have not been prepared and will not be educated, situations in which they must promote policies on which they have not been consulted, and in the implementation of which they will be faulted rather than defended. Therefore, the best thing to do is learn to be very quick on your feet, learn how to operate and not worry about big grand ideas which from the standpoint of a public servant are really the responsibility of elected officials.

*Q: Did you ever get a sense from Kissinger that he felt political pressures?*

EINAUDI: I did not have that kind of relationship with him. But I do recall one moment that was revealing of his view of himself. In April 1974, the OAS General Assembly was held in Atlanta,

Georgia. The New Dialogue had already lost steam. Watergate was unraveling. Jimmy Carter participated in the opening ceremonies as governor of Georgia, the first time I had seen him. It was also the first (and perhaps only) time I ever found myself sharing a cab alone with Henry Kissinger. The cab driver recognized him and as we got out, he said "Mr. Kissinger, have you ever thought of running for President? The country needs someone like you." Kissinger, startled, grunted without answering in words. Then, walking away, he turned to me and said "would you ever have imagined the United States in such turmoil that people would look to a fat Jewish German boy for leadership?" During the General Assembly, Miguel Angel De la Flor, the Air Force General who was Peru's Foreign Minister, took the floor in full uniform and invited Kissinger, who as host was presiding, to "join us at the head of the legion fighting the greater battle facing mankind, the struggle against poverty and underdevelopment."

*Q: Yeah. Well it's a puzzlement is it not? A friend of mine, Warren Zimmerman, had been with the policy planning staff and he found himself writing speeches; the secretary was the one before Kissinger.*

EINAUDI: Bill Rogers. William A. Rogers, not William D, who was Kissinger's lawyer and later Assistant Secretary for Inter-American Affairs and Under Secretary for Economic Affairs.

*Q: And Bill Rogers says I don't want you to put me on the front page of the newspaper which, of course, is the antithesis of Henry Kissinger.*

EINAUDI: That's right.

*Q: But I mean it had become a place for word-smithing and not for policy planning.*

EINAUDI: That may have some truth to it – for that time and under that Secretary -- but in fact word-smithing can be at the heart of policy. Certainly, Kissinger saw it that way. Kissinger thought that speeches were an important way to find formulations that would help move policy forward. Many people were either cynical about Kissinger's motives or believed that speeches are just hot air and don't count, or even just propaganda. In that regard there is a big difference between State and Defense. Foreign Service officers know that speeches often slide over a lot of stuff and have to be purposely ambiguous, so they tend not to pay too much attention. Military officers are accustomed to rules of engagement and manuals, so they tend to look at speeches as sources of guidance.

In any case, I suffered a great deal writing speeches. The S/P speechwriting team was terrific. It was headed personally by Winston Lord. The full-time writers were FSOs Charlie Hill and Mark Palmer, plus for a while Townie Friedman held over from the previous S/P. They were supported on substance by the whole staff. A typical Kissinger speech would take a dozen or more drafts. It was a wearing process even when it did not involve a midnight call at home telling me I had to have a revision on Kissinger's desk at seven the next morning. Once, during one of many painful speech-writing sessions Kissinger said in exasperation "Why does it always take fifteen drafts?" Lord answered, deadpan, "It would help if you read the first fourteen."

Q: *Funny, but obviously speechifying was a chore.*

EINAUDI: Indeed. And for me that grew to include translations. In Mexico, I realized that many of our carefully prepared policy nuances were being missed in the Spanish. One night, I went to check on the translation of a Kissinger text being prepared for the next day. The elegant Spanish republican exile translator took my changes well at first, then finally exploded, "You are making him sound just like an ordinary Mexican politician." I was pleased. My efforts to get Kissinger across in plain Spanish were working.

*Q: It is said that being able to write well is key to virtually any career.*

EINAUDI: Words convey meaning. A good policy paper is a work of art. Its elements are clarity, brevity and the presentation of real options with pros and cons for each of them. Grandfather Einaudi's lesson that a printed page must please the eye as well as the mind helped me enormously. Sometimes I had to rewrite memorandums intended for the Secretary from bureaus so eager to include every fact and nuance that their pages seemed black, so dense was the print. In my undergraduate days, I had poked fun in a public debate at President Eisenhower's reported refusal to read memos longer than one page. Now I was becoming a specialist in one-pagers.

Another example of the importance of words is the memorandum of conversation, known colloquially as a memcon, in which a note taker summarizes for the record the gist of a conversation. Kissinger thought the memcons he was receiving were often inaccurate. He thought the summaries sometimes had him saying things he had not said. As he said with his characteristic generosity, he didn't want people "attempting to summarize what they had not understood in the first place." He wanted verbatim accounts of what everybody had said. Unless you are a trained stenographer that is hardly an easy thing to do. But I soon found that I could reproduce a half hour meeting almost in its entirety on the basis of the notes I took during that half hour if I was then able to spend the next two hours recreating them and writing them up. I learned to do that and found it a very useful way to get access to important meetings. The importance of accuracy was made clear years later when the memcon I had written of a conversation with the Argentine admiral who was then foreign minister was declassified. The conversation had taken place in Chile in June 1976, early in Argentina's military dictatorship and before human rights was the red flag it later became under Carter and Patt Derian. But it became public when people were looking for a smoking gun to prove that Kissinger had approved repression in Argentina. I had faithfully recorded exactly what was said. The Argentines had repeatedly brought up terrorism; equally insistently, Kissinger had attempted to turn the discussion toward other matters, saying "we can't help much on the terrorist front," questioning the effectiveness of military governments, and noting that "you cannot succeed if you focus on terrorism and ignore its causes." Finally, however, faced with Admiral Guzzetti's insistence, he said "If there are things that have to be done, you should do them quickly. But you must get back quickly to normal procedures." None of the buzzwords of later debates -- let alone Operation Condor, which was still unknown to us -- were spoken, and the indiscriminate disappearances were still in the future, but that phrase was enough to fuel the accusation that Kissinger had given the green light to the Junta's abuses.

That Kissinger did not challenge Guzzetti directly was I think partly a matter of personal style. I found when writing for him that Kissinger frequently wanted to formulate policy in a way that avoided his own voice; it's almost as though he was trying to be a professor laying out principles rather than taking personal positions. But he could be very forceful about personal positions when he did take them. One of my first troubles with him came in Mexico City at Tlatelolco when he instructed me to take a position I thought unwise from one negotiating group to another. I stopped and was starting open my mouth to object; he looked at me and said, "This is not a seminar at Harvard. Get moving."

*Q: Well let's take the crisis with Chile. How did this play out from your perspective and our involvement?*

EINAUDI: As I noted earlier, in 1970 the United States intervened covertly in an effort to prevent Allende from taking office, but failed. Clamorously. By 1973, when Pinochet moved against Allende, we were in a largely reactive role, much less involved than is generally thought. The idea that it was the United States that overthrew Allende is a case of the public imagination being unreliable because based on the presumption that the United States is the center of the universe and has all kinds of power that in practice it does not have. Exaggerating U.S. power also disregards local events, many of which we don't know and are out of external control.

How did Chile play out? In many different and complicated ways. People everywhere remember Chile 1973 simply as a U.S. mistake. In academic and political literature, Chile generally stands simply as a black eye for the United States, even though it was primarily a Chilean affair. Then local repression was mixed with economic growth some of which followed policy lines originating among American economists. Time and the excesses of the military regime weakened Pinochet as they did most of the military regimes that emerged in Latin America in the years of anti-Castro reaction. Meanwhile, Chileans who were forced into exile wound up all over the Western world, in Mexico, Italy, the United States -- and they learned about the functioning of open societies that they never would have learned if they had stayed home. In the end, Chile came to symbolize profound political change: in 1973, OAS member states and the OAS Secretary General were all silent when the Pinochet coup took place; in 1991, Chile was where the OAS adopted Resolution 1080 calling for an immediate collective response to any interruption of the functioning of a democratic government. That formula avoided using the word coup but the rejection of military coups was very clear.

For the United States government also, Chile played out in complicated ways. The U.S. was not the primary mover of the initial coup but some Americans, both official and private, favored Pinochet, while others did not. And the U.S. government did ultimately support a return to democracy. Harry Barnes and a number of other Foreign Service officers played a positive role in creating the conditions that helped lead to the restoration of a democratic government in Chile.

One of my initiatives on the policy planning staff was to encourage the holding of policy dialogues with our counterparts in key Latin American countries. In Chile, an S/P delegation led by deputy director Sam Lewis was exchanging views with military leaders. Pinochet came in unannounced. After sitting down, his first words were "I have been a better friend of the United States than the United States has of Chile." Then Pinochet asked us to turn around, and as he spoke, the curtain behind the conference table was drawn back and we found ourselves staring into the muzzles of machine guns and rifles. They were pointed at us. No human being was holding them. They were all mounted, just on display. But they were trained on us. Pinochet broke the startled silence. He said, "These are all weapons we seized from Allende and his Cuban friends. If we had not acted you would have been in greater trouble than you are now." We were far from convinced, but the drama made the point: Pinochet saw himself as fighting on our side in the global Cold War. His coup had stopped the Communists. Why were we being critical? He had been our friend. We were not behaving like his friends.

The ideological tensions in and over Chile were a harbinger of what happened with Central America a few years later. That's when the blood flowed in the region and symbolically tore apart both U.S. policy and the U.S. diplomats attempting to implement it. The 10 years between 1973 and 1983 saw eight Assistant Secretaries for Inter-American Affairs, from Jack Kubisch to Tony Motley, with Rogers, Shlaudeman, Todman, Vaky, Bowdler and Enders all in between. In other words, rotating assistant secretaries each lasting little more than a year, nearly all done in by domestic political tensions, most of them over Central America.

*Q: Yeah.*

EINAUDI: It was extraordinary – and humanly destructive.

*Q: Before moving on I'd like to ask what was your take on these accusations that during the overthrow of Allende, American citizens were killed and mistreated. The missing were the subject of a book and a movie . . . I'm a consular officer and problems like that seem so outlandish. What was your view as an insider?*

EINAUDI: The Chileans did disappear or execute a lot of people. Interestingly enough, many fewer than in Argentina next door. Chile is a country with a substantial body of education, law and tradition and some institutional continuity. When they had their bloodletting, some Americans were indeed caught up in it. Outlandish and horrible. Movies and popular mythology have a tendency to portray this as something the U.S. government wanted to happen, basically on the assumption that the U.S. was behind the coup. As I said earlier, the U.S. did attempt – and failed -- to prevent Allende from taking office when he was first elected in 1970. But the coup by Pinochet was mainly a domestic Chilean disaster.

*Q: That is the second time you have said that. What do you mean?*

EINAUDI: Allow me to go back to May of 1973. I was still at RAND. There was an abortive anti-Allende uprising by some tank commanders; it had no chance and was quickly put down. But while the coup attempt was going on, the Allende governing coalition asked workers to occupy factories as an act of protest and to keep the coup from succeeding. After the uprising failed, the Chilean Communist Party ordered its people to evacuate the factories, arguing that the crisis was over and it was time to get back to normal. The Chilean Communist Party was a serious party with a long tradition in the copper industry going back to before World War I, a genuine working-class movement which I am sure had all kinds of ties to the various internationals and received subsidies from the Soviet bloc. The Movement of the Revolutionary Left, a group of young folks inspired by Castro and other Latin American radical experiences, refused. "We've occupied the factories and by Jove the revolution is on." When that happened, by then it was June, I commented to anybody who would listen (no one was particularly interested), that "A coup is going to take place in Chile because the military commanders will not stand for utter chaos in the country." In fact, by August, Pinochet as commander of the Army said publicly something to the effect of "Come on you politicians, pull yourselves together and fix this. If the military has to move, the military is good at only one thing and that is killing people." And that is what then happened in September. And when the coup finally took place, the repercussions went far beyond Chile. The line became "The U.S. did it," without anyone asking what had changed since the U.S. had tried and failed three years earlier.

Some have also sought to link the United States to a secret cabal among various South American military groups and intelligence services, called Operation Condor, created to assassinate leftist politicians in exile. In September 1976 Operation Condor struck the United States when a former Chilean defense minister, Orlando Letelier and Ronnie Moffitt, an American citizen riding in the car with him, were killed by a bomb planted by Chilean intelligence agents right here in Washington.

*Q: Yeah. I remember…at Sheridan Circle.*

EINAUDI: That's right. Assassinations are bad business and our hands have not always been clean. Pete Vaky had been DCM in Guatemala and I believe recorded concerns in a memo I have never seen. Guatemala was a country in which after 1954 the CIA station chief was sometimes probably more important than the U.S. ambassador. There, death squads were operated by locals who were on a covert U.S. government payroll and thought they were doing the right anti-Communist thing with our blessing. I don't think any U.S. officials were involved in anything like that in Chile. I am not in a position to evaluate more recent reports that the CIA had access to the encryption system used in Operation Condor. What I do know is that the Chileans I knew – particularly those who knowingly accepted support from the CIA – felt they were using the CIA, rather than the reverse.

*Q: Did the example of Chile have a significant effect on you in later parts of your career dealing with Latin America? Were you always keeping in mind the pitfalls of Chile?*

EINAUDI: I had of course worried about the pitfalls of U.S. over-extension and interventionism long before Chile, in fact ever since I had become conscious of what happened in Guatemala in 1954. In Chile, in addition to the ill-fated efforts with the military against Allende we have already discussed, U.S. government agencies intervened politically throughout the 1960s, often supporting Christian Democrats against parties to their left. Personally, however, I never suffered one way or another. My approach was never partisan – even less abroad than at home.

*Q: In what other areas were you particularly active while in S/P?*

EINAUDI: I argued successfully for policy planning consultations with leading Latin American countries. S/P Deputy Director Sam Lewis, who had served in Brazil, led them, just as did the one to Chile I mentioned earlier. On another occasion, in 1975, I met alone with Brazil's Foreign Minister Azeredo da Silveira to explore whether Brazil might, with its highly professional diplomacy, be prepared to take on broader responsibilities appropriate to a regional power. Silveira's answer was that an activist foreign policy would inevitably encounter "acidentes de percurso": accidents along the way. The United States had the wealth and power to absorb such accidents, he said; Brazil did not. His wisdom and caution were later abandoned to Brazil's discomfort during the Lula presidency, when global ambitions led Brazil into an ill-fated nuclear deal with Iran and a general overextension in foreign policy.

One of my key tasks was accompanying Kissinger on his travels to the region. Latin America wasn't seen as particularly serious.

Kissinger's travels there gave Winston Lord a chance to get some rest so I became the lead person other than the Latin America bureau itself. Winston knew that I was smart and that Kissinger respected me. In addition to the 1974 trip to Mexico for the New Dialogue, I accompanied Kissinger on two trips in 1976. The first to six countries in February and then in June on a trip to the Dominican Republic and Bolivia on the way to the OAS General Assembly in Chile. The scene in Santiago was impressive. It was not quite three years after the coup. The streets were lined with silent people. It felt as though the government was hosting this meeting in an attempt to get legitimacy. Many people were not happy with the government but the government also had a lot of support. The environment was surreal.

I had a terrible fight with Kissinger when the first 1976 trip began in Venezuela. At the opening reception, Kissinger discarded a draft I had written for him and gave a toast he invented off the top of his head. When we were all back in control room in the hotel Kissinger asked me how I thought it had gone. I said, "Well I won't tell you what I think. I'll quote one of the leading Venezuelans there who came to me afterwards and said 'My God what incredible pressures must Kissinger be under to say trash like that.'" There was some consternation in the U.S. delegation at my directness. Bill Rogers, Kissinger's friend and lawyer who had succeeded Jack Kubisch as assistant secretary, said when he saw me the next morning, "I thought you would be found floating headless in the river." Instead, on the rest of the trip, Kissinger used everything I wrote for him. When we got back to Washington, we had the speeches published in a nice 28-page pamphlet with a green cover. [*Major Statements On Latin America by Secretary of States Henry A. Kissinger Made During His Visits To Venezuela, Peru, Brazil, Colombia and Costa Rica, February 1976.*] Needless to say, that opening toast in Venezuela was not among them. It almost made up for the fact that we had spent four nights in a luxury hotel on the beach in Rio, during which I had to work so hard I never once felt sand between my toes.

*Q: What was the Venezuela toast? What was the gist of it?*

EINAUDI: The gist of what Kissinger said after discarding what I had written was the "special relationship." Latin Americans interpret language about special relationships as meaning we think they are inferior little brown people that need to be protected. They did not want to be in a colonial relationship with the United States. Venezuela at the time was very much in the lead in supporting on the global scale the various United Nations organizations like UNCTAD, they were pushing for the expansion of OPEC. They were leading something called SELA, the Latin American economic system; these are all early harbingers of the positions later promoted in extreme forms by Hugo Chávez. It made absolutely no sense to go down and speak as though they should be good little colonial children. But that was how Kissinger had spoken. The Venezuelans thought that the United Fruit Company, the oil companies, and the rest of the Empire must have been holding a gun to Kissinger's head to force him to speak such drivel.

*Q: After that? How did Kissinger react?*

EINAUDI: After that, he basically used the drafts I prepared for him. He even joined in a little experiment in Peru, where our relations with the radical military government were still tense. Expropriations, nationalist posturing, and other factors would have made any normal diplomatic formulations sound hollow or hypocritical. But the edge was off, and both sides wanted the visit to succeed. So I suggested to Kissinger that a formula for his arrival statement that would convey the right positive ambiguity would be to copy de Gaulle's "je vous ai compris" [I have understood you] statement in Algeria in 1958, saying without entering into any detail that we understood what Peru had been going through. The next day, the Lima headlines were "Kissinger: The United States understands." Even Kissinger was impressed.

*Q: Did foreign governments understand our policy processes?*

Everyone was constantly looking for "*interlocutores valables*," the Spanish phrase for persons with whom it is worth negotiating because they can deliver. A senior Brazilian diplomat, speaking in the pre-Lula days before Itamaraty itself was emasculated, once told me that the U.S. officials concerned with Latin America had such little power that none of them was worth talking to. Once Kissinger invited former minister Azeredo da Silveira, who had just come to Washington as Brazil's Ambassador, to lunch at the State Department. As always Kissinger came in late and last. Silveira noticed that when Kissinger arrived, he did not recognize the Country Director for Brazil. He had never met him before. Silveira archly said, "Well Mr. Secretary I see that I know your Country Director better than you do." The annoyed perception that most U.S. officials are not close to the Secretary and the President, nor to relevant U.S. domestic constituencies, leads many foreigners to think that if they could get high enough in the U.S. government, the Secretary of State or the President would reverse decisions taken at lower levels without reference to what the foreigners think are the strategic interests of the United States. In practice, that is an illusion. In my experience the concrete merits of specific issues are rarely overridden on the basis of some sort of grand strategy.

Silveira's predecessor as Brazil's ambassador to Washington, João Augusto Araujo Castro reached a somewhat different conclusion about us as a result of his experience presenting credentials to President Nixon. After a brief chit-chat, Araujo noticed Nixon was getting antsy, so he asked "Who are you seeing next?" Nixon said "I don't know, let me look." He consulted the papers on his desk, then said "The new ambassador of France." Araujo took great delight in telling me this. He concluded that because Richard Nixon could not remember he was about to see the Ambassador of a country as important as France meant that American leaders see foreigners as all the same -- irrelevant. Not incidentally, Araujo was the author of an influential "freezing of power" theory of international relations, according to which the United States sought to freeze the system to exclude others.

*Q: I gather you also dealt with the Marcona expropriation in Peru?*

EINAUDI: Indeed. That was a fascinating assignment. I still had my S/P duties, but wound up making ten trips to Lima in a dozen months. The Marcona corporation was an innovative and highly profitable multinational operation that mined iron ore in Peru, transforming it first into pellets and then slurry for shipment to Japan in large ships designed for the purpose and operated independently. What made things particularly complicated was that Marcona's founding genius, Charles W. Robinson, was Undersecretary of State for Economic Affairs, soon to become Deputy Secretary.

*Q: How was that conflict of interest handled?*

EINAUDI: As far as I know, very well. Robinson's pride and I know not what else was very hurt by the expropriation, but unlike some Marcona executives outside government, he did not suggest sending the marines, sought only fair compensation, and did not interfere in our efforts to obtain it.

*Q: What was your role?*

EINAUDI: Being in S/P, having the Secretary's confidence, and also knowing the Peruvians, I was in a position to play something of a coordinating role among the parties. The U.S. team included our Ambassador in Lima, Bob Dean, and a Deputy Assistant Secretary from ARA, the economist Albert Fishlow, but I was the glue, both in Washington and with the Peruvians. The discussions were prolonged and difficult. At a particularly unhappy point, when Peru was in effect being confiscatory, Fishlow and I went to see the Foreign Minister in his office in the beautiful colonial Torre Tagle Palace. General de le Flor greeted us with a conventional "How are you?" to which Fishlow and I responded in chorus "Terrible." Taken aback, De la Flor turned away. With his foot he nervously pushed the hidden button in the floor to summon coffee. Then, suddenly, he looked up with a smile. "Oh. For a minute I forgot. Neither of you is a professional diplomat."

*Q: Did you get a settlement?*

EINAUDI: Once the stage was set for a final negotiation, I recommended our side be headed by Carlyle Maw. Maw had been Kissinger's lawyer and had followed him to State first as the Legal Advisor and then as Undersecretary for International Security. Then in his mid-seventies, he found government more interesting and fun than his New York legal practice. Maw was precisely the kind of older gentleman of undisputed authority that inspired respect. In Lima, when our little cavalcade let us off for our negotiations at the old Ministry of War on Avenida Arequipa, passing cars honked impatiently. Maw turned, still standing in the street, and bowed to them, smiling. Maw obtained a substantial compensation for the assets Peru had seized. Marcona executives told me the amount was grossly inadequate for the losses they had sustained from the disruption of the whole; they preferred the old days, when we might have sent in the marines. When Maw left the Department, he gave me his files on Marcona. They were among the documents I left in ARA when I retired. I hope they were retired properly. They were no longer there when I went to look for them a few years later.

*Q: Did Cuba come up at all while you were in S/P?*

EINAUDI: Only marginally. Several Latin American countries, led by Costa Rica's Foreign Minister, Gonzalo Facio, wanted to be freed of the trade embargo that had been imposed under the aegis of the OAS in the early sixties. They argued that if the collective embargo was lifted, the U.S. could keep its embargo, but other countries would be free to do as they wished. In 1976, at Facio's pleading, and with the concurrence of Bill Mailliard, our Ambassador to the OAS, a special ministerial meeting was held in Ecuador for the sole purpose of revoking the collective sanctions. But the votes proved not to be there. I spent a miserable night trying to draft a closing statement for the U.S. delegation. Try as I might, I could not find a formula to reconcile the contradictions in our positions. Ultimately, I failed, and Deputy Secretary Ingersoll, who had headed our delegation in Kissinger's absence, did not speak. My lesson from that fiasco was that I should at least have drafted a statement showing appreciation for the host government and its efforts. It was the Quito taxi driver who took me to the airport who drove home the mistake. Said he: "You must really dislike us." Even if we had nothing to say, he added, we could at least have said that we liked the host city and its beauty. Kissinger's only comment when I reported back was that we had learned the hard way that Gonzalo Facio did not know how to count.

*Q: Did your travels with Kissinger produce similar learning moments?*

EINAUDI: One lesson might be that the wiles of authoritarians should not be underestimated. Joaquin Balaguer was a civilian and a poet as well as the three-time President of the Dominican Republic after Trujillo. At lunch, discarding the usual seating protocols, Balaguer sat Kissinger and the other visiting Americans at his side two deep, moving his own people toward the end of the table instead of keeping them near him. As the junior member of the American delegation, I found myself next to the Foreign Minister. I was of course delighted to have him to myself. He told me our seating arrangement was typical. Balaguer maximized his power by monopolizing powerful visitors and excluding his own people.

Hugo Banzer was a military man who served twice as President of Bolivia. The first time he led a coup, the second time, twenty years later, he was elected as a civilian. He was a man of rural origins, with a strong sense of nationhood and dignity. At breakfast, Kissinger told him about our arrival in Cochabamba at dusk the evening before. The motorcade from the airport had had a fairy tale quality. A beautiful soft twilight sunset illuminated streets thronged by friendly crowds. It could not have been nicer. Banzer replied, "I know. I was there. As President, I could not for protocolary reasons greet you myself. But I was not going to miss the first time a Foreign Minister of the United States visited Bolivia. I was on the sidewalk, part of the crowd."

Kissinger was interested in Banzer's concerns over Bolivia's lack of an outlet to the sea. It was 1976, and with elections coming up in the United States, he told me domestic political entanglements meant there was little he could do in the Middle East. He asked, would helping Bolivia be a potential opening for his energies? On the flight from La Paz to Santiago, I summarized the history of the War of the Pacific and the complexities of a negotiation with Bolivia, Peru and Chile. We never returned to the subject again.

*Q: What about Central America? Did it come across your scope at all?*

EINAUDI: Until I joined S/P, I had always flown over Central America, stopping in Panama on the way down to South America. One of S/P's duties was to handle the Dissent Channel. Jim Cheek, a political officer in Managua, used Dissent cables to object to the way our political ambassador was minimizing embassy reporting of domestic criticism of the Somoza regime. From a bureaucratic standpoint, being in S/P was to represent the regional bureau to the Secretary, quite as much as the Secretary to the bureau. In July 1975 I accepted a U.S. Information Agency invitation to lecture in Mexico, Colombia and five Central American countries. For the first time I began to learn how unique each Central American country was. They were immediate neighbors, but each was very different. In some respects, they inhabited different universes.

My visit to Nicaragua under Somoza was particularly interesting. Nicaragua didn't get many visits from Washington at a relatively senior State Department level. Somoza received me in his bunker and treated me very nicely but with a little bit of trepidation. To complete the program, the embassy held a reception attended by prominent Nicaraguans, not all of whom were in the government. I was told years later by one of them, Edmundo Jarquín, that my visit had been taken as a signal that Somoza's relations with Washington were no longer cast in stone. Kissinger, who was later to be very critical about the destabilizing impacts of human rights policies in Central America, would not have been happy.

*Q: Let me ask a question. Had this been planned or was this their interpretation?*

EINAUDI: This was their interpretation. We are not always very good at understanding the consequences of what we do. I was behaving, if I may say so, quite normally as an American. Americans are inherently open and pluralistic. Obviously when we are representing our government we do not deal with terrorists or people who are our committed enemies. But we tend to deal with pretty much everybody else. I met with Somoza, and I met with other Nicaraguans invited by our embassy to a cocktail party, among whom some were critics of the regime. And it was just that element of normalcy to my behavior that seemed novel in Somoza's Nicaragua.

*Q: I have to just add here that in Yugoslavia, a new ambassador arrived who remarked to me, "You know I am reading where they interpreted my coming here as a hard line to Yugoslavia. It is just a normal appointment." Outsiders tend to see what they want to see.*

EINAUDI: That is exactly right. Politics and culture determine perceptions. And that is true in the United States as well. Both of my primary mentors in the Foreign Service, Pete Vaky and Bill Bowdler, were victimized after becoming Assistant Secretary by domestic political reactions to the Sandinistas. Central America in the 1980s offered countless proofs of the risks of stereotypes and misperceptions in heated political times.

*Q: Did you ever regret coming to the State Department?*

EINAUDI: Sometimes, particularly during the Central American times in the 1980s. But governing can be exhausting even in good times. No one in S/P had time to read or learn. Kissinger said that being in public office was to draw down intellectual capital. And there was certainly a life style problem. After keeping many a warmed-over dinner for me, my wife Carol went to work in self-defense against my absenteeism as much as to avoid our impoverishment by our daughters' college expenses. And my body suffered from massive disuse, particularly compared to our life in California, where I would run to and from work three or four days a week, a distance of just over five miles each way. In the State Department, I never had time for myself, never the time to be bored.

*Q: Well, how about the transition? Policy Planning positions are notoriously vulnerable, particularly at times of a change of party.*

EINAUDI: The transition to the Carter administration was deceptively simple for me. One reason is that I was innocent enough to believe that as a lifelong Democrat I was unlikely to be removed just because a Democratic administration was taking over. Another is that I was asked by the transition team and the incoming NSC to begin work on the Carter Administration's first Presidential Review Memorandum, PRM-1, to set the parameters for the Panama Canal negotiations. I became its principal drafter, beginning a full week or even two before the Administration took office on January 20. Transitions are usually a tense downtime, but this one for me was very busy. I had also taken on the largely self-imposed task of organizing the drafting of the first-ever *Country Reports of Human Rights Practices*. Responding to Congressional requirements and certifications was an increasingly important bureaucratic burden during the 1970s and 80s. I wanted to ensure that the growing emphasis on human rights issues recognized their legal setting in each country, so I sacrificed my Christmas-New Year's holiday of 1976-7 making sure that the format for each country report began with the relevant local constitutional context. You could say that this institutional focus was a relic of the approach of Russell Fitzgibbon, the UCLA political scientist who was the dean of US Latin Americanists in the 1940s and 50s but is now largely forgotten. Most importantly, it reflected my concern that US diplomacy take the law, history, and differing national perspectives into consideration.

The final and most important reason the transition proved all right for me is that in April 1977, when the axe threatened to come down on me so that the new administration could bring its own person to S/P, career Foreign Service officers saved me by offering me the directorship of the Policy Planning office of the Inter-American Bureau.

# ARA/PPC

*Q: Today is 5 February 2014 with Luigi Einaudi. Luigi you were moving on to be head of policy planning in ARA. When did you take on these responsibilities and how long were you doing it?*

EINAUDI: I became Director of the Inter-American Bureau's Office of Policy Planning and Coordination (ARA/PPC) in early 1977 and stayed until I became ambassador to the OAS in late 1989. More than twelve years.

*Q: That is certainly an unusually long time for one assignment! What accounts for it? What were some of the highlights of your tenure?*

EINAUDI: Let me take an early highlight, a tour of the Caribbean Basin in the summer of 1977 with Andrew Young. It helps explain why I survived: I enjoyed what I was doing, did it well, and was able to earn and keep the respect of people with different political views. By the time twelve years passed, I had almost become part of the bureau furniture, and was considered its institutional memory.

*Q: Andrew Young was then Carter's Ambassador to the UN?*

EINAUDI: Yes. I was asked to be his escort because I was considered broadly knowledgeable, politically savvy and able to back him up in whatever he might need. Traveling with an official plane, the delegation actually hit 13 countries in 12 days. From Mexico to Venezuela, with stops in Haiti, the Dominican Republic and Suriname, but with a primary focus on the many countries of the English-speaking Caribbean. Our objective was to encourage ratification of the American Convention on Human Rights (which Carter signed, but which the United States has, to this day, not ratified).

Young brought his wife along, but really threw himself into the task. In Haiti, he got so carried away in his positive extemporaneous remarks it seemed as though he wanted to reelect Baby Doc on the spot. In Trinidad and Tobago, the legendary and reclusive Prime Minister Eric Williams agreed to receive Young -- at a large table in his kitchen at home. Young opened the meeting by saying that he was sorry to have arrived at Howard University just after Williams had left teaching there. Suspecting that Young was trying to butter him up, Williams raised his open hand high over his head and brought it down so hard on the wooden table that the room resounded with what sounded like a cannon shot. We all jumped. "It was a good thing," Williams exploded, "I would have flunked you." Williams' authority established, the encounter went quite well after that. In Suriname, our schedule was so packed that I wound up meeting civil society leaders by myself, alone, after midnight, in a downtown Paramaribo law office.

The Caribbean we found was a far cry from the swashbuckling hub it had been back in the time of European discovery and conquest, the trading route of the colonial Americas, or even the pathbreaker of black freedom it had been with Haiti and then again with the independence of the former British West Indies. Proud yet fragmented, its small, often tiny countries were moving toward the lament articulated later by St. Lucia's Julian Hunte "The world no longer needs small island states." Except, some from the United States and Europe might say, for sailing and recreational tourism.

But it was learning about the meaning of the Caribbean to our civil rights movement that made the most impact on me. Young told me that after the death of Martin Luther King he and other Black Americans had gone to Barbados to recover. Everyone there was Black, from the garbageman to the prime minister. "It made it possible to be normal. To forget about the pain of being Black in America." To Young, the English-speaking Caribbean was not just our third border, it was virtually part of the United States.

At the end of the trip, Young thanked me for my support and blurted "I don't know how you could have survived" in the previous Administration.

*Q: O.K., what were some of the key issues when you first arrived in ARA?*

EINAUDI: The Carter years were marked by the introduction of human rights policy, the Panama Canal treaties, and the burgeoning crisis in Central America, particularly Nicaragua and El Salvador. My office was the Assistant Secretary's primary source of substantive support and coordination. Importantly, my role as speech writer on Latin American matters for the Secretary followed me down from S/P and stayed with me throughout.

*Q: What do you mean?*

Speechwriting was a major skill I had developed in my period on the Policy Planning staff. George Shultz later said that I was a genius at knowing both *what* to say and *how* to say it. That bit of hyperbole hides the fact that, while leaders are called upon often to speak, their staffs don't usually volunteer to write speeches and are often cynical about their content. I had learned from Kissinger that words count. Words can be used, not just to articulate policy, but to develop and sometimes stretch policy, to blunt criticism and to seek or even create consensus. I was always trying to teach that lesson to my staff.

*Q: Was there at this time an effective overall policy planning organization in the State Department?*

EINAUDI: The short answer is no. There was in the bureau an about-to-be-abandoned bureaucratic process for economic assistance, called the CASP, Country Analysis and Strategy Papers. I remember the CASP, prepared with AID, chiefly for what I considered its overweening interventionism, like setting the number of condoms to be used annually by aid-receiving countries. But there was no process involving the regional bureaus on major policy questions. The culture at State has not changed much on planning, since the days when George Marshall, coming out of a military background, noted with amazement that the Department had no planning function and founded the secretary's policy planning staff. What Marshall didn't perhaps appreciate is that the primacy of domestic politics and the can-do attitude of newly elected national leaders arriving in Washington make a mockery of most attempts to plan foreign affairs. Political dynamics force the State Department to continually adjust to new demands, some of them irrational, and most of the time without much concern for international realities. You have to be nimble to survive at the policy level in the Foreign Service. I think our national interests would be better served if everyone had more of a grounding in foreign affairs. I am a strong proponent of expanding the Foreign Service Institute and the training given to Foreign Service officers. There are many budgetary and other limitations to overcome, but the A-100 course simply bears no relationship to the difficult problems diplomats must face.

*Q: A-100 being the junior officer course.*

EINAUDI: That is right, the entry-level course for new officers. And at last reading I don't think we even have the Senior Seminar any more.

*Q: No, we don't.*

EINAUDI: As usual the State Department has no resources while the Defense Department has so many it is sometimes hard to keep track of them. On the positive side, flag officers in the military spend half their careers in training and education. At best, and if they're lucky, senior Foreign Service folks are sent to a university as Ambassadors in residence. And even then, it is not as part of career development, but more as a holding pattern or a way station to retirement.

In fact, one of our colleagues felt even the A-100 course was largely a holding bay, preparing FSO's for administrative issues of life abroad while the personnel system figured out where to send them. The lack of diplomatic training is partially a matter of funding, but the problem goes much deeper -- to lack of sufficient personnel to fill all operating positions. Not having enough Foreign Service officers means that to assign personnel to training or educational slots means not filling front-line positions. Personnel shortages already lead to sometimes extensive gaps between assignments, gaps that prevent the passage of contacts and knowledge from one officer to another. Some would even question the usefulness of training people who will in any case be forced to deal primarily with immediate problems and short-term issues and not be around for the long-term consequences. The daily pressures of government life are such that they leave little time for reflection, thus leading to a constant process of intellectual disinvestment, with little opportunity for reassessment and recharging. I strongly believe the Foreign Service needs a mid-career course analogous to the Army's Command and General Staff College.

*Q: You were also executive secretary, weren't you?*

EINAUDI: Yes, for a few years, but Executive Secretary of the ARA–NSC IG, which was the Interagency Group for Inter-American Affairs in the National Security Council system. I was NOT, of course, executive director of the Bureau. I had no administrative role or personnel role. Indeed, in the twelve years I was PPC director, I always had trouble getting the FSOs I wanted. I kept asking for up and coming officers, saying that they would learn a lot because I was in many ways a teacher. But I had a hard time convincing people that policy papers and speech writing were important skills that offered multiple career benefits. Being on a regional planning staff was not considered a good career track. It wasn't like being a desk officer or a country director that puts you in the geographical chain of command and therefore potentially on an ambassadorial track. Even so at least nine officers who served with me in PPC later became ambassadors: John Hamilton, Bismarck Myrick, Phyllis Oakley, Mike Skol, Joe Sullivan, Bill Wood, Mike McKinley, Mike Fitzpatrick and Geoff Pyatt. I also wound up with other very good officers in PPC who did not become ambassadors: Vittorio Brod, Suzanne Butcher, Terry Kleinkauf, Bob Morley, Shaw Smith, Richard Harrington, Dennis Skocz, Fay Armstrong, Jim Swigert and I'm sure several others I do not immediately recall. Still, it was not as easy as it should have been to get good personnel.

*Q: Certainly, I gather you were not immune to bringing in political appointees.*

EINAUDI: I was always overworked, always in need of help. At the height of the Central American troubles PPC simply had too many demands to fill with the staff we had. Elliott Abrams got tired of my kvetching and authorized me to bring in two Schedule Cs of my choice. White House Personnel sent me 40 CV's. Half were young kids who thought they deserved a job just because they had participated in a campaign. But twenty or so merited interviews, and I met with all of them. The two I ultimately chose, Dan Fisk and Phil Peters, had both been staffers at the House of Representatives, Fisk with the Republican Policy Committee and Peters with Jim Courter (R-NJ); both proved outstanding.

In a non-political vein, in 1985 I brought in on a formal two-year loan from the University of California a former PhD student of mine, Caesar Sereseres. Sereseres consulted in PPC and the Office of Nicaraguan Affairs for several more years. He was in the Contra camps in Yamales before and during the February 1990 election of Chamorro, and was at San Pedro de Lovago when the Contra's grassroot fighters turned in most of their arms. He supported Santiago Murray and the OAS-CIAV in Nicaragua from late 1990 to late 1993. Throughout this period, he also followed the wars in Guatemala and El Salvador and maintained excellent operational ties with DOD and SOUTHCOM. I was also always glad to accept officers on detail from the Department of Defense. Army Col. Bob McGarity had been a Mil Group commander; he worked to coordinate our military assistance, called MAP. USAF Lt. Col. Curt Morris, Jr. became Mil Group commander in Uruguay when his tour in PPC was up.

These outsiders all brought contacts and experience that strengthened the Department's hand in both policy formulation and execution. This was particularly necessary throughout the Reagan years, when military and paramilitary activities in Central America made just staying informed a problem. Even within the Bureau, PPC had to coordinate with officers that SOUTHCOM Commanders, starting with General Galvin, assigned to keep tabs on Department policies. These special "Military Advisors" typically worked with the Office of Central American Affairs and various Nicaragua task forces as well as PPC, sometimes advising the Assistant Secretary directly. Army Lt. Col. Jerry Clark, was to die in a car accident in Panama in 1989, stood out for his experience in Honduras, and his knowledge of the Contras, the Honduran military, the Agency, and of course the Defense Department and its various components. Sereseres spent a lot of time with him in Honduras, the Contra camps and our embassy.

*Q: Let's get back to policy. You said you had started drafting a policy review memo on Panama before the new Administration had even been inaugurated and before you came to ARA. How did that happen?*

EINAUDI: I knew the people associated with the newly created think tank called the Inter-American Dialogue, including Sol Linowitz, Abe Lowenthal, Bob Pastor and others. They had convinced Carter to make it a priority to end what had come to be seen as an unsustainable colonial relationship with Panama.

Ellsworth Bunker, who joined Linowitz to negotiate what came to be known as the Torrijos-Carter treaties, had been our Ambassador to Italy when my grandfather was president and made sure in his courtly way that I knew it. Prior experiences in Panama had convinced me that the essentially colonial status of the Canal had become a festering sore that was damaging U.S. interests. In January 1964, I was visiting General O'Meara and U.S. Southern Command, when Panamanian students attempted to raise a Panamanian flag outside Balboa High School in the Canal Zone. In a scuffle with American students, the Panamanian flag was torn. The riots that followed cost more than a dozen lives and millions in damages. The Canal Zone shut down. I was staying in Panama City rather than in the Canal Zone, so I was caught up in the reactions among Panamanians. With a Panamanian friend from student days, I went to a bar near the burned-out Pan American Airways building. The bar was filled with young Panamanians. Their debates were heated and dominated by nationalist anger: raw, primitive and authentic. A Communist politician, experienced and internationally aware, tried to speak, but was quickly reduced to being an onlooker. The rage we saw that night reminded me of pre-Castro Cubans.

*Q: Did you play a role in the negotiations after that?*

EINAUDI: Not directly. I did meet with General Torrijos in Panama once, but all I recall is that he had me follow him into a bathroom and opened all the water faucets, saying that would make it harder to bug what we said. There is little doubt that distrust played a key part in the negotiation. At key points, the Presidents of Panama's neighbors, Costa Rica, Venezuela and Colombia—Daniel Oduber, Carlos Andrés Pérez and Alfonso Lopez Michelsen—played a major role as go-betweens, supporting

Torrijos and giving him confidence that he could trust us. In a final effort to inspire confidence, the treaties, once completed, were signed at OAS headquarters in the Hall of the Americas. The hemisphere's heads of state and government were present as witnesses. All concerned, large countries and small, believed this multilateral dimension increased the likelihood of compliance, by everyone concerned, big and small. One example of the rampant and stereotyped hypotheticals making the rounds was that we needed to make sure that some Panamanian Colonel could not shut the Canal to hold a birthday party for his daughter in one of the locks.

*Q: Did your office play a role in the ratification process?*

EINAUDI: ARA's congressional relations fell under my purview as Director of PPC. In fact, the C in PPC when I took it over stood for "Congressional Affairs" rather than "Coordination." Phyllis Oakley headed that part of the office and we all worked hard on the often-uphill public diplomacy efforts that the Panama treaties required.

Ratification was a close call. Opposition to "giving away" the Panama Canal helped propel Ronald Reagan to the presidency in 1980. In 1977, when the Carter-Torrijos treaties were negotiated and signed, the Central American wars were still a couple of years down the road, but can you imagine the position the United States would have been in if the Canal issue had not been resolved by the time Nicaragua and El Salvador blew up? PPC was in effect commandeered to work on obtaining ratification. We had a wall map of U.S. states, votes, and speeches to be made. I made several domestic trips to make presentations supporting the treaties. One of them was to Cincinnati. We were self-conscious about trying to influence domestic opinion, worried such a role was outside our mandate. Later, under President Reagan, a whole separate Public Diplomacy office was created with political leadership to promote U.S. Central America policy domestically, and such scruples were left in the rear-view mirror.

*Q: What about Argentina? You mentioned human rights, but the dirty war, the disappearances and all were going on in this time.*

EINAUDI: I was not much involved personally on Argentine matters, either in S/P, or even when in ARA. The major exception was the 1982 Falklands/Malvinas war and its aftermath. When Harry Shlaudeman was ambassador to Argentina, he invited me down as part of an effort to reopen contacts with the military. Otherwise, I was not directly involved with Argentina until 1995 and the Peru-Ecuador war.

In general terms, of course, you are quite right, Argentina's dirty war permeated regional politics. The extreme bitterness it created was revealed again recently with the naming of the new Pope, Pope Francis. Some claimed that as the senior Jesuit in Argentina at the time Francis was responsible for the arrest of two Jesuits he should have protected. I've looked at this recently and discussed it with a friend who followed Latin America for the U.S. Conference of Catholic Bishops. It is perfectly clear that in the atmosphere in Argentina at the time, he could not keep them from being arrested. But he almost certainly kept them from being killed. The accusation wound up without legs.

The Argentine repression was so pervasive it was out of control. In one of my rare visits to Buenos Aires in that period I went to see Mariano Grondona, a conservative writer I had first met in 1955. As we were leaving his apartment, he saw an unmarked Ford Falcon parked across the street and *right away* he said, "Who are those people?" and I said, "Well they are the people who are assigned to protect me." He said, "All right" and dropped it. For a well-connected Argentine who had written favorably about Somoza to react with fear just to see an unmarked car parked in the street should convey what an incredibly bad scene it was. People tend to forget that, unlike Central America, where one could argue that social conditions justified rebellion, Argentina's years of terror began as almost an intellectual game. In May 1970, no more than a dozen educated bourgeois youth led by twenty-two-year-old Mario Firmenich and Norma Arrostito planned and kidnapped retired General and former President Pedro Eugenio Aramburu and executed him in cold blood after a three-day secret mock trial. It was the first act of the *Montoneros* proclaimed people's struggle against imperialism and its lackeys. After that, there were killings on both sides, but once the relatively few terrorists were captured or wiped out, the government kept murdering their presumed allies and relatives, mostly on suspicion and without legal process. It was a very, very bad period. Argentina will never fully recover.

*Q: I have accounts that Terry Todman was trying to play this down and Tex Harris was a relatively junior officer going out and collecting accounts. We seem to have been a disunited embassy at the time of how to deal with Argentina.*

EINAUDI: I have a different take. Not on Tex Harris, who was in Buenos Aires as a political officer and later was President of AFSA. He did a great service with his reporting at the height of the dirty war in 1977-79. Tex did indeed have problems in the embassy. His ambassador did not like Tex's reporting -- but that ambassador was NOT Terry Todman. Terry Todman only became Ambassador to Argentina more than ten years later, in 1989.

Terry Todman was President Carter's first Assistant Secretary for the Western Hemisphere, and as such the first human rights era Assistant Secretary. I worked intimately with Terry throughout his time as Assistant Secretary and remained in touch with him afterwards, even getting him to help me and the OAS in Haiti in 2003. Todman was a black man from the U.S. Virgin Islands. As far as he was concerned, he personified human rights. He had made it into the U.S. Army and served in Japan. He had made it to the Foreign Service and done more than survive. He had done well. When he was named assistant secretary, he had already been an ambassador multiple times, to Chad, Guinea and Costa Rica. All assignments, of course, outside Washington. So here was a classic "outside man" suddenly brought back to Washington and plunged as Assistant Secretary into the middle of ideological and bureaucratic dogfights. He was to deal with Latin America – a part of the world not considered important enough to warrant informed consistent front-line attention from higher ups – and thus easily disrupted by militant human rights advocates newly placed strategically within the Administration. These included Patt Derian, the political appointee assistant secretary for HA, the new bureau for human rights, and Bob Pastor, just 29 years old when he came from Harvard to become Carter's main Latin America advisor at the NSC.

Terry felt that human rights were so much part of his persona, upbringing and tradition that he didn't need to be told how to conduct a policy that was respectful of human rights. But he immediately came under direct pressure from Derian and Pastor. Pastor, in particular, defined his NSC role as pushing the president's human rights agenda, and had developed a strong relationship with Deputy Secretary Warren Christopher. Christopher chaired what came to be called the Christopher Committee, whose purpose was to mediate internal disputes between the human rights advocates and those who did not feel that human rights should be the single-issue criterion on which to determine our relations. There was so much smoke in the fights between HA, the NSC, and ARA that the Christopher Committee became the symbol of human rights activism unchecked.

Years later, when Christopher returned as Secretary of State, he asked me to look at the Committee's record, arguing that he had exercised enormous restraint. And he was right. Loans and other relations were in fact rarely blocked solely over human rights issues. And let me be clear: Derian did great service, exemplified, among other things, by her visit to Argentina with the Inter-American Commission on Human Rights. But with a president like Jimmy Carter and a national security advisor like Brzezinski, neither of whom knew anything about Latin America, the young and inexperienced Pastor wielded a lot of unsupervised influence. It was a very complicated period. Groundbreaking and positive in key ways, but still very difficult.

To get away from all these headaches, Todman spent much of his time as assistant secretary traveling. The tea leaves were clear: when he was out of Washington, he didn't have to deal with bureaucratic infighting and these terrible time-consuming and backstabbing conflicts. He didn't have to worry about Pastor; he didn't have to worry about Derian. He didn't have to worry about being undercut with the Deputy Secretary or even the Secretary of State, both of whom disliked adjectives and gave the impression of viewing displays of emotion with distaste.

*Terry Todman and Secretary Vance meet with a Peruvian delegation, February 10, 1977. At the far left are the outstanding Peruvian diplomat Carlos Garcia Bedoya and former Senator Gale McGee, then Ambassador to the OAS. I am in the middle rear, between Peruvian foreign minister de la Puente and Todman. Both sides asked me how to approach the other before meeting. (US State Department photograph, 1977).*

*Q: How did tensions come to a head?*

EINAUDI: Terry was invited to speak at the Center for Inter-American Relations in New York, now the Americas Society. He asked me to draft the speech and instructed me to emphasize the mistakes made by human rights advocates and those who would subordinate relations to the single issue of human rights. He had a set of things that had gotten under his craw and felt some in the administration did not realize that progress in such matters is always "slow as molasses." Terry and I fought over this speech like cats and dogs. I kept telling him he should bow more to Administration policy and moderate his language, and worked hard to remove or soften harsh formulations. But he insisted. The final text outlined a set of mistakes to avoid. I was so focused on moderating his most explosive language that I did not realize that the final text actually contained ten points.

For the record, here is that part of the speech, which he gave February 14, 1978:

*"Our experiences over the past year have shown clearly that we must be careful in the actions we select if we are truly to help and not hinder the cause of promoting human rights and alleviating human suffering.*

- *We must avoid speaking out before learning all the facts, or without calculating the likely reaction and responses to our initiatives.*
- *We must avoid expecting other governments to achieve overnight fundamental changes in their societies and practices in response to our bidding and without regard to historical circumstances.*
- *We must avoid assuming that we can deal with one issue in isolation without considering the consequences for other aspects of our relationships.*
- *We must avoid believing that only the opposition speaks the truth, the whole truth, and nothing but the truth, about conditions in their country.*
- *We must avoid presuming to know so much more about another society than its own citizens that we can prescribe actions for them without bearing any responsibility for their consequences.*

- *We must avoid punishing the poor and the already victimized by denying them assistance to show our dissatisfaction with their governments.*
- *We must avoid pointing to some and not to others. Selective morality is a contradiction in terms.*
- *We must avoid condemning an entire government for every negative act by one of its officials.*
- *We must avoid holding entire countries up to public ridicule and embarrassment, trampling on their national dignity and pride.*
- *Finally, we must avoid being so concerned with the rightness of our course that we lose sight of our true objective – to alleviate individual suffering."*

Todman followed this litany by saying immediately that *"While taking care to avoid such mistakes, we will not by any means retreat into silence or indifference"* and listed five positive steps to advance human rights.

But the die was cast: the speech was received as the Ten Commandments against Administration policy. A few weeks later Terry was relieved from the position of Assistant Secretary and sent off as Ambassador to Spain.

So if I hear that Terry was not as strong or as sharp against violations in Argentina as with hindsight he might have been, I can understand the view. But I am not prepared to condemn him. Terry was given an impossible job without political support in the middle of a bureaucratic guerrilla war in Washington for which his prior experience as a representative of the United States abroad had left him totally unprepared.

*Q: What happened next?*

EINAUDI: To replace Todman, Secretary Vance asked Pete Vaky to cut short his posting as Ambassador to Venezuela and come to Washington as Assistant Secretary for Inter-American Affairs. Trying to reduce internal disarray and bring order out of the previous chaos, Pete asked Vance to activate the NSC-ARA Interagency Group and make him Chairman. The new IG could not alter the NSC's strategic access to the President, or end internal differences within State, but it did provide a new measure of authority and coordination. Then Pete made me the IG's Executive Secretary, adding that to my duties as the Bureau's planning director. Interagency coordination was one of the recurring themes of my career in the State Department.

*Q: How did the IG work?*

EINAUDI: It meant a lot of extra work. We had to have meetings. Meetings had to be staffed. Decisions had to be prepared and followed up. You had to do all kinds of things. Vaky knew I didn't have the staff to do this, so he found the money for me to hire someone who could administer the IG. One of the smartest personnel decisions I made in my life was to hire Pat Chatten. Pat was the wife of Bob Chatten who was a senior USIA officer and a very good one. Like so many wives, she was underutilized and unappreciated professionally. Pat did a wonderful job.

As long as Vaky was the Assistant Secretary the Interagency Group for Inter-American Affairs worked. Jimmy Carter had a very bad visit to Mexico in 1978 and when he came back he mandated a government-wide policy review. In his administration, policy reviews were called PRMs, Presidential Review Memoranda. Vaky had me call a government wide meeting to lay the groundwork for the review. It was absolutely fascinating. 82 or 83 agency representatives showed up. Every office in town thought it had a role in Mexico -- and did in many ways. Mexico is our immediate neighbor. We share almost two thousand miles of border. The review showed how hard it is to develop and implement a coordinated policy. One of the findings of Presidential Review Memorandum 32 was that every issue had to be dealt with on its own merits. You could not, for example, say we need oil from Mexico, therefore, we will be soft on migration from Mexico. For the longer term, however, we found that relations with Mexico could be shaped differently, depending on whether they followed a globalist approach or a more neighborly one that could lead to an "economic community" along European lines. I laid out that choice in a talk I gave at the Johnson Foundation in Wisconsin in 1979. Despite the development of NAFTA fifteen years later, tensions between those two visions influence policy to this day.

*Former Senator Gale McGee, our Ambassador to the OAS and a strong proponent of the Carter-Torrijos Treaties, thanks me for my support for the*

*treaties, November 20, 1978. Ambassador to Mexico John Jova (previously Ambassador to the OAS) is to our left. (US State Department photograph, 1978, courtesy of Gale McGee)*

*Q: OK, let's get back to the nuts and bolts of PPC.*

EINAUDI: As 1978 turned into 1979, Mexico, and even human rights controversies, gave way to concerns over stability in Nicaragua and Central America generally. In the spring of 1979, Pete convened a Chiefs of Mission meeting in Costa Rica. Unbeknownst to us, even while we were meeting, our local Costa Rican government hosts and the Venezuelan government were facilitating military assistance to the Sandinista rebellion against the Somoza dynasty. The ruler at the time, Anastasio "Tachito" Somoza, was a son of Anastasio "Tacho" Somoza, who had come to power in the 1930s exploiting his association with the U.S. Marines; "Tachito" ["little Tacho"] was a graduate of West Point and a General in the Nicaraguan National Guard. His oldest son, Anastasio "Tachitito" ["little little Tacho"] Somoza, had attended Harvard and Sandhurst, was a Colonel in the National Guard and the heir apparent. It was widely known there was unrest, but though Nicaragua was "in our back yard" we didn't have a clue what was really going on.

*Q: Really?*

EINAUDI: Nobody was telling us anything. It was partly that we did not know where to look. We were operating blind at a moment things were coming unglued and we were not particularly liked. Somoza was intransigent in the face of mounting opposition. The U.S. government was divided: The State Department saw the handwriting on the wall, but the other foreign affairs agencies were waking up but slowly and belatedly. The White House was tentative, for global reasons. Selflessly, two of our finest career officers, first Bill Bowdler, then the assistant secretary of our intelligence bureau, and after him Larry Pezzullo, our ambassador to Nicaragua, had accepted to try to negotiate Somoza's departure even though they were without clear instructions. Opportunities for a managed transition were lost while Somoza resisted with help from Congressmen Jack Murphy and Charlie Wilson. Pete sadly quoted Emerson to me "When you strike at a king, you must kill him." We had sent Bowdler and Pezzullo to war with flyswatters.

*Q: I gather that after Somoza fell people feared a domino effect and that El Salvador was thought to be next?*

EINAUDI: Absolutely. On July 17, 1979, Somoza fled telling his commanders that he was sacrificing himself so the U.S. could send in the troops to stop the Communists. His National Guard, essentially a pretorian force, immediately fell apart. On July 19, the Sandinistas took over a Nicaragua in which they were the only organized armed force. I was told President Carter wanted to avoid a similar situation in El Salvador, but said he did not want us to be backing the wrong horse. On July 24, Pete Vaky left for El Salvador on a fact-finding mission. He took me along. What we found in El Salvador was utterly dispiriting. The President was Colonel Carlos Humberto Romero. He turned out to be the most illiterate and unimaginative person I have ever met in high office. Romero received us with his staff officers. Everyone was tense. The discussion was incoherent. Toward the end of the meeting, Pete and Romero went alone into the next room and spoke privately for a few minutes. Some later alleged that he asked Romero to resign, but Pete told me he only stressed the need for initiatives to keep the situation from deteriorating further. El Salvador had been growing exponentially since the mid-1950s, and its emerging professional and middle classes were pressuring the traditional elite, which had used the military to prevent change and repress a Christian Democratic electoral victory in 1972. Unfortunately, Romero had neither the imagination nor the capacity to go beyond the role of warden. That night, I was so depressed at his lack of redeeming qualities that I started jotting down the names of all the presidents I had ever met. Immediately Romero went to the bottom of the list. The more names I added the lower he fell, until he fell to number 40, where he remained only because I could not think of anyone else. Romero was overthrown that fall, and El Salvador entered a maelstrom of uncertainty and violence.

William D. Rogers once observed that Washington and overseas calendars seldom coincide. By the time of our 1980 presidential election, the Sandinistas were in power in Nicaragua, posing the issue of how to deal with a radical government that was also supporting revolution beyond its borders. During the transition to the new Reagan administration, El Salvador faced a sudden escalation of guerrilla warfare. From retirement Pete Vaky wrote in *Foreign Affairs* that "El Salvador had . . . become a symbolic battleground for policy arguments within the United States." Talk of "losing" El Salvador recalled "losing" China years before.

*Q: OK, well then, staying with El Salvador. What was going on there?*

EINAUDI: In the summer of 1954, after grandfather and I read Tocqueville's *L'Ancien Régime et la Révolution,* he had me read the English agronomist Arthur Young, who had travelled in France in the years before the revolution, recording social and economic conditions. From those readings, emerged a conclusion: bad government, more than misery as such, was the source of revolution. This lesson helped me greatly at the time of the political and social explosion that shook El Salvador. Most outside observers attributed what happened to the consequences of misery in a traditional society, when in fact the spark was bad government in the form of the repression of a new bourgeoisie emerging from two decades of uninterrupted economic boom and population growth.

El Salvador was in many ways the real birthplace of the Central American revolution. The fact that the Sandinistas won in Nicaragua first was in some ways an aberration brought about by the relative weakness of Somoza from a political, military and geographic standpoint. El Salvador was where nuclei of active, radicalized, members of the middle class and of the aspirant middle class came to see in revolution the solution to their problems, turned to force, and found external support. El Salvador had a particularly extensive violent history. In El Salvador, following the upsets of the Great Depression, a peasant uprising was repressed with such violence that it stood out even on a global scale. Appropriately remembered as "*La Matanza*," The Killing, of 1932, a count of 30,000 was the common estimate of the dead. It saw one of the first cases of the use of airplanes against civilians. General Maximiliano Hernandez Martinez then ruled until 1944 with a pretorian military.

In the relatively peaceful times after WWII, El Salvador began to grow enormously. El Salvador has roughly the same population as Nicaragua crammed into one sixth the territory, with many different centers of activity and an entrepreneurially gifted population. By the 1960s and early 1970s growing new social groups—doctors, merchants, lawyers, professionals—had developed. Using a European framework, one might have called them provincial notables. The Salvadoran landed elite was always joked about as being 14 extended families. I don't know what that number was based on, but land ownership was certainly concentrated and the owners felt threatened by the emergence of these new voices. In 1972, a Notre Dame-educated engineer named Napoleón Duarte won the elections for president. The landed elite turned to the military and Duarte was imprisoned, tortured and thrown out of the country. From 1972 onward, the presidency was occupied by a succession of colonels. In effect El Salvador's wealthy imposed their will by military force on a society that could no longer be contained that way. In the universities all the young people could think about was revolution. The discussion was how do we change this damned place? An incredible number of factions developed. University life is generally that way, but this time they would sometimes fight among each other and kill each other off. Still the military government remained deaf and mute and the elite thought this, too, could be controlled. Meanwhile the lack of change was radicalizing the opposition. Nobody knew how to get out of this violent cycle.

Mauricio Borgonovo, a friend from the 50's when he was at MIT and I at Harvard, became El Salvador's foreign minister in 1972. He was actually one of the reasons I made that trip to Central America in 1975 when I was in S/P. He told me I should come down and see for myself what was going on. That was the trip when I also met Somoza. In April 1977, Borgonovo was kidnapped by one of these small university-based groups. The instant I learned of his kidnapping I knew he would not survive. Borgonovo was, as the name suggests, of Italian origin. When I asked how he and his family had managed to become prominent in El Salvador, he answered "In the land of the blind, the one eyed is king." That arrogance likely did him no favors. His body was found in May with three bullets to the head. The FPL, or Popular Forces of Liberation, issued a statement saying he had been "executed as part of the prolonged war the F.P.L. is continuing until it achieves a final popular revolution toward socialism." In explicit response, a clandestine organization calling itself the *Mano Blanca* (*White Hand* or White Warriors Union) denounced "Jesuits and other Communist priests" for Borgonovo's death. On the day of Mauricio's funeral, a priest conducting a Catholic Youth meeting was machine gunned to death.

A month earlier, Rutilio Grande, a Jesuit priest inspired by liberation theology and Vatican Council II, had been shot and killed while traveling in a car with parishioners in an area where he had been engaged in a pastoral mission advocating social change. I talked earlier about radicalism often being local and not necessarily communist, even if it was sometimes Communist supported. Another truth is that much militant radicalism originated with the Jesuits. After years of following a doctrine of trying to teach the children of the elite about social justice, many Jesuit leaders had said to themselves, "here we are, we have been attempting to create social consciousness in the elites for 20-30 years, for generations, and where are we? Nowhere! It is time to break the mold." Nowhere was this religious radicalization more evident than in Central America and particularly in El Salvador.

The 1977 assassinations of Rutilio Grande and Mauricio Borgonovo marked the transition from intermittent violence to what in a couple of years would become an all-out civil war. It was a horrendous spiral. Looking back, I have felt and still feel very deep sadness. It was a tragedy. I don't think the U.S. had much to do with it beyond being trapped in relationships and histories and external politics. I will come to that. But the civil war itself was truly vicious. I lost friends on both sides, or, better, all sides, because even when things are polarized there are always nuances. In addition to Borgonovo, those assassinated in that fratricidal conflict that I knew personally included Francisco "Chachi" Guerrero, a conservative Supreme Court justice, Napoleón Romero, who fought as a guerrilla under the name "Miguel Castellanos," and Ignacio Ellacuría.

Ellacuría was a Spanish-born theologian, one of the original radicalized Jesuits. In the late 80s, he told me about how time and events had changed attitudes, including his own. In the 1970s, university students could talk about nothing but revolution and how to make revolution. After a decade of civil war, he said, university students were talking only about peace. How do we get peace? Ellacuría was expressing his own evolution. After preaching change, he had dedicated himself to working for peace, trying hard to draw the violence out of this horrible situation. It was then, in 1989, that a military squad entered his compound and assassinated him, several other priests and their housekeeper. This was the kind of bloodletting that was going on, the kind of counterproductive insanity that characterized the period.

*Q: Did you feel pressure from U.S. political movements using Latin America as their star case that whatever we were doing was wrong. Did you feel that?*

EINAUDI: Of course. It was a perfect storm. The Central American revolutions had begun, showcasing heroes and villains enough for everyone, regardless of ideology. American conservatives saw wild-eyed Marxists serving as fronts for the Soviet Union, which was using them as tools to pay us back for Afghanistan. American liberals, many of them already radicalized by protests against the Vietnam war, saw starving peasant women and children being murdered by military death squads in the service of rapacious oligarchs supported by the CIA and a dissembling State Department. Both visions contained enough elements of truth to enable their believers to deny other views. Everyone was screaming and demonizing those who disagreed with them. No one was listening. If that was not bad enough, the conflicts on the ground boiled up during the transition from Jimmy Carter to Ronald Reagan. And to top it off in El Salvador the rebel coalition, the Farabundo Marti National Liberation Front (FMLN)—whose components had as much or more history as the Nicaraguan Sandinistas who had already come to power, decided "oh my God, Ronald Reagan has been elected president; we've got to act before he sends in the U.S. Army." Wanting to preempt Reagan, they launched what they named with characteristic hubris their "final offensive" to take down the government. This happened during the transition from Carter to Reagan, creating an extraordinary problem for those of us in government. The Carter administration was winding down, the new Reagan team had criticized Carter policy, but was not yet in office. Few in the Washington policy elite had believed the situation was really critical until the intelligence reports started coming in about intensifying fighting and external flows of weapons from the Soviet bloc. We were caught between intense conflicts in the region and sharply polarized American politics. Those were bitter, bitter times for everybody concerned.

During the run-up to the U.S. election, an additional criticism had emerged from American conservatives. Henry Kissinger was quoted as saying that Jimmy Carter had unleashed human rights policies onto the world not knowing on what shores they would wash up and with what consequences. This suggested that the Sandinistas were a result of woolly-headed liberal subversion of perfectly normal social orders in Central America. The Iran hostage crisis and the failed rescue effort generalized the unease. A change in administration was in the air. I thought some policy continuity would be critical to containing the Sandinistas in Nicaragua and building a democratic center in El Salvador.

Normally an office director level government official does not have much public voice, but in May 1980, the Konrad Adenauer Foundation asked me to give the keynote speech at a conference on Central America they organized here in Washington with the American Enterprise Institute. I was worried about potential policy discontinuities between Carter and Reagan, so I accepted and consciously attempted to stake out positions acceptable to both sides and to reconcile human rights policies and realpolitik. I argued that in dynamic situations where there is a lot of change, sometimes the way to maintain stability is to go with the flow. What we were dealing with, I said, was partly subversion, but also partly the breakdown of the traditional order, a breakdown that eroded the power of the military, the church and the landed oligarchy, all of whom faced challenges from emerging middle classes, exploding populations, and rising expectations. My presentation [the text is Appendix One] was very successful, and was even excerpted on a Sunday "For the record" in the Washington Post. It never would have happened had it not been for the Germans who invited me. Of course, true believers don't see nuances very well. A member of Nicaragua's ruling Sandinista Directorate told a Mexican newspaper that my stress on diversity showed I did not understand that the Sandinistas were the Leninist vanguard of Central America's future, thus revealing the stupidity of the Americans.

That December, after Reagan's election but before his inauguration, four American nuns were assassinated in El Salvador. By that time,

President Romero was gone, Vaky had resigned and Bill Bowdler had replaced him as Assistant Secretary. Bowdler, Bill Rogers and I went to San Salvador immediately to look into the assassination of the nuns. Rogers at that point was out of government, a lawyer with Arnold and Porter. My job was to write the report for the President. The first thing I asked when we got there was "Where is the car?" referring to the white van in which the nuns were traveling. It had been abandoned by the side of the road. Acting like a big shot from Washington, I immediately said "We ought to impound that so we can look at it for evidence." They did, and the fingerprints found later helped identify the soldiers who had actually done the killings.

During that visit, our ambassador, Bob White, was maneuvering behind Bowdler's back, looking for reconfirmation by the Reagan people as ambassador in El Salvador. It was an incredibly difficult and bad moment for everybody concerned. And it was not just an isolated case that Salvadoran soldiers had killed these American nuns. In El Salvador slaughter took place on levels even greater than what had happened in Argentina. In Argentina they kidnapped and killed people, destroyed individual families. They even threw some people out of airplanes over the South Atlantic. But they did it thinking they knew who they were killing, one victim at a time or one family at a time. In El Salvador, both the guerrillas and right-wing death squads started killing a few people at a time, but before it was over, some Salvadoran military units had pulled a series of My Lais, killing everybody in a village. It was similar to what General Rios Montt was later tried for in Guatemala -- the indiscriminate killing of local inhabitants *en masse*. In the meantime, Nicaragua was serving as a morale-building and logistical-supply link that enabled El Salvador's guerrillas to overcome errors that would have proved fatal under any other circumstances. No previous guerrilla movement in Latin American history had suffered successive defeats like the failure of the 1981 "final offensive" and the blow of the 1982 elections – and survived. Cuba, referred to as the "emerald island" in guerrilla messages and documents, was the key new factor in this survival. Thanks to Cuban advice and support, the FMLN became a well-organized guerrilla force with outside support through Nicaragua, which had become the "warehouse" for weapons from the Communist bloc. It was a vicious, vicious time. And neither left nor right was prepared to negotiate or give in.

Events in Nicaragua and El Salvador created the sense in the United States that we had blown it, that everybody in government should be fired. The public mood was not to support change, it was to stop it, to do more to defend ourselves from foreign Communist incursions close to our shores. President Reagan opened his presidency by reassuring Walter Cronkite that he was not going to send combat troops to Central America, but the word was that some in the incoming White House were proposing we should invade Cuba to cut the cancer out at the root. That was the atmosphere and it was an atmosphere made even more heated by genuine human rights violations, some of them against U.S. citizens.

*Q: Did you feel in this period that events there were (1) not in our control and (2) were dragging us in? What forces were working on us? How did Central America become such a focal point during the Reagan period?*

EINAUDI: Events were out of everyone's control, and certainly not in ours. But I'm not sure we realized it immediately. I think nobody outside of Central America has ever taken Central America very seriously. At the same time, what happened in the 1980s blew the importance of Central America quite out of proportion. I am trying to think how to explain what was happening. First of all, I think we generally were not well equipped or prepared for what was to happen or even for what was happening as it happened. Our ambassadors in Central America had included utterly unqualified political appointees. Consider Turner Shelton in Somoza's Nicaragua. But beyond that, our embassies were small and without resources. I suspect that once everything is declassified, it will also be seen that a strategic decision had been taken during the Kissinger years to focus on countries with regional projection and power. In Latin America, this meant Mexico and Brazil, cutting back our presence, including CIA activities, in smaller countries like those of Central America that seemed less important. Whatever the reasons, in Central America, we weren't ready, informed, in a position to know or with the resources and organization to do very much.

Two things happened in Central America at the same time. First, the traditional Central American triad of military, landowners and the church fell apart under pressure from the growth of the middle class. It fell apart because of changes within the Catholic Church, particularly the Jesuits, and because of social pressures that provoked extreme resistance from power-holding landed and military elites who reacted in a violent repressive fashion. Generalized opposition to the Somoza dictatorship in Nicaragua was to some extent dragging other Latin American countries into the conflict as well.

Second, and making things worse, many leaders had given up on the United States. They thought we were out of it, and most importantly, they thought it was going to be much easier to throw out the dictators, the military, and the oligarchs than it later proved to be. An undoubted friend of the United States like Carlos Andrés Pérez, President of Venezuela, was willing to provide arms and training to the opposition to Somoza without telling the U.S. He had given up on U.S. policy on Somoza. We had in his view not responded effectively or properly. Even democratic Costa Rica allowed the Sandinistas transit and support for their battle against Somoza without informing the U.S.

While this was going on, Soviet leaders were looking for something to get back at us for our support for the Mujahideen opposition to Soviet activities in Afghanistan. Central America provided a means to poke around in the soft underbelly of the United States and to show the Americans they couldn't get away with impunity with blocking Soviet actions elsewhere. The net result was a quite extensive Soviet bloc operation. North Vietnam and Cuba were the primary agents. Through them, a lot of weapons we had abandoned on the battlefields of Vietnam were funneled into Central America. The Cubans did an incredible amount of training. Central America became a cold war battlefield. The cold war coincided in a horrific fashion with the struggle for modernization and democracy. Somoza used to say that he was a West Point general defending democracy. We could not have a clearer cold war framework than that.

Then the Reagan administration came in, bringing with them a handful of academic conservatives and other policy critics. Then during the transition, in December-January, 1980-1981, suddenly all kinds of intelligence reports started coming in about violence and shipment of weapons into Central America, the FLMN launched its final offensive, *et cetera*. The Reagan team had campaigned to some extent on the stupidity of Carter policies in Central America, but at a rhetorical level, without taking it very seriously, thinking of it in ideological terms and with the attitude of "who cares about those places?" Suddenly, the reaction shifted to "oh my God, this is really happening. We have to do something."

Once and if everything is declassified, I suspect there will be indications that when the Reagan administration first came in, some of its people wanted not only to fight the Sandinistas but to attack Cuba because it was considered the point of origin, the staging ground, for subversion in Central America. There is no doubt, of course, that the Castro government was very much involved, just as there was no doubt that the Sandinistas were being euphorically intransigent and working to support the FMLN in El Salvador. There is also no doubt that some of our reactions were warped by ideology and ignorance of conditions on the ground. All kinds of things were happening. I was not on good terms with the Reagan transition team in the State Department and once Bowdler left and John Bushnell became Acting Assistant Secretary and was holding on for dear life as the new Administration was trying to organize, everything went more or less on hold for my office, PPC. There was no established policy to coordinate. I focused my efforts on trying to limit the disasters in El Salvador. In the election campaign, conservative critics had argued that Carter had done stupid things. That implied that all we had to do with a change in Administration was change our policies and everything would be well. The key was to reverse policies.

*Q: What does that mean? How do you reverse policies?*

EINAUDI: Just the point. Sounds good. Particularly in a polarized political campaign. But what does it mean? How do you define reversal? What do you reverse?

I had key advantages in defining how to reverse policies on El Salvador without adding to the chaos. My first and simplest advantage was Tom Enders, Reagan's new assistant secretary. After a series of power struggles in which I did not participate, Enders took over in May or June, as a compromise career person untainted by either politics or service in the bureau under the previous administration. He quickly discovered that I knew what I was talking about and that he could trust my loyalty and judgment.

The second great advantage stemmed from personal contacts, both in the United States and in El Salvador. My eleven years at the RAND Corporation, where many senior people came in and out in a revolving door with the U.S. government, had given me several useful connections. One of these was Fred Iklé. Fred and his wife Doris were good personal friends. Fred originally chaired the RAND Social Science Department, then left to head the Arms Control and Disarmament Agency. Under Reagan he became Undersecretary of Defense for Policy. Fred and I respected each other professionally. He also had the measure of Menges, who turned up as one of the several NSC staffers trying to take everything over.

Fred called me during the Carter-Reagan interregnum to discuss how to reverse policies in El Salvador, which, he said, was the goal of the incoming Reagan team. I was able to talk to him about what there was, what there wasn't, what should be done, what might be done, what would be horrendous to do, et cetera. An obvious opportunity to reverse policies was that if the Soviet bloc was supplying weapons and ammunition to a side that was hostile to us, then it would not make sense for us to deny weapons and ammunition to the other side that was friendly to us. That was a logical and defensible reversal. On the other hand, to reverse policies could also mean reversing social policies, like agrarian reform. This was very much on the minds of both Central American and American conservatives. Guatemalan conservatives were throwing champagne parties when Reagan was elected. But reversing agrarian reforms in El Salvador would have thrown gasoline on the fire of destabilization. It is not that the agrarian reforms put together in El Salvador had been so brilliant. They had been hastily conceived and unleashed backlashes and great uncertainty. But that, in a sense, was the point. There was a great need for predictability. To reverse course against a more open agrarian order would have been suicidal. But this is not how it was seen by some in the incoming Administration.

What emerged from discussions with Fred Iklé – is what I conveyed to Tom Enders. We could build on the Republican slogan that under Carter we had been unreliable allies. Reversing policy meant that we would become reliable instead of unreliable. To be reliable allies in El Salvador meant many things. For starters, it meant not blackballing them on governmental relationships. Under Carter, the Salvadoran military asked us formally for advice on human rights. Patt Derian had taken the position that the Salvadoran military leaders were off limits, so their letter was not answered. That kind of thing was easy to reverse, as was deciding not to deny them ammunition even while still pressing them on human rights. On the other hand, the Salvadoran government was pursing agrarian reform, so we are not going to make them reverse it. Both actions, the reversal on arms and the non-reversal on social policy, derived from the same principle: We are going to be a reliable ally. So we tried to build a center in El Salvador by combining the conservative approach predominant in the Reagan White House with elements of the more progressive orientation required by conditions on the ground. I think it was Iklé himself who first suggested that sustaining agrarian reform in El Salvador could be used to demonstrate we were reliable allies.

*Q: Did you sense a tension with Tom Enders? I've heard many people say the guy in the first place is so big, tall and all and very smart.*

EINAUDI: He was indeed.

*Q: So he was a commanding presence which in Washington, particularly if you are not of sufficient rank, is a real asset. Was it also a problem for him?*

EINAUDI: That is exactly what happened, and in that order. His commanding presence helped him take control, but it also accelerated his fall. Enders was 6'5" or 6'6". Rumor had it that he was taller than the height limit for the Service if there was one at the time he entered. In any case he was as physically imposing as he was intellectually imposing. He made short shrift of the interagency system by simply dominating it. Since he was both super bright and super imposing physically, basically everyone stood at attention and saluted when he spoke. This was fine so long as his policies seemed to be working. The FMLN's initial "final offensive" had failed badly and, with our support, the center was beginning to hold. Enders and I thought elections would further consolidate progress.

Our Ambassador to the United Nations, Jeane Kirkpatrick, had taken the position that elections and human rights were secondary in times of war. She held up Argentina as a successful counterinsurgency model, taking the position that in fighting Communism we could support anti-Communist dictators because dictators could be changed while totalitarians were incapable of change; that's an intellectual concept that I strongly disagree with and which events have since demonstrated to be wrong.

*Q: But wasn't Kirkpatrick knowledgeable about Argentina?*

EINAUDI: She had written her doctoral dissertation on Peronism, but was always more of a theorist than an empiricist or historian. During the Cold War the internal irreversibility of totalitarianism had been elevated into both an academic (cf. Brzezinski) and political mantra to justify supporting virtually anyone so long as they were anti-Communist. Kirkpatrick's contact with Argentina had left her favorable to the military government there, and she extended Franklin Roosevelt's earlier "he may be a son of a bitch but he's our son of a bitch" doctrine to argue that war was no time to hold elections. My position had been very strong that, in El Salvador, unless you find some outlet for popular participation you are not going to win, period. I wrote a speech for Enders that spelled out U.S. support for elections. When I brought it to Tom after clearing it with all the usual suspects, he asked what changes I had had to make in the course of getting the clearances. I answered "none" and Tom characteristically responded "Maybe that means we did not ask for enough." I said, "Instead of asking for more, let's use what we have to get Kirkpatrick's clearance as well." I took it to her myself. She read the draft in my presence, grimacing, as though such practical matters were trivial compared to her lofty abstractions. But she cleared it.

*Q: Why did you feel you needed Kirkpatrick's clearance? As Ambassador to the UN, she was not in your chain of command!*

EINAUDI: You are right, her clearance was not formally necessary. My desire to get it was political. Ideas and their proponents matter. Kirkpatrick had argued that elections and human rights were secondary in times of war. I was covering our backside in case things did not go well.

The elections did go well. Very well, in fact. Then in late January-early February 1983 Salvadoran guerrilla forces seized the Usulután town of Berlín and held it for several days. The FMLN seizure of Berlín turned out to have been planned and staged in Cuba, with mock-ups of the village, all very much the way U.S. special forces train for their engagements. As a parenthesis, I have long maintained that one of the reasons the Central American revolutionary movements lost out was that "our Cubans" were better than "their Cubans." By which I mean that the many veterans of the Bay of Pigs who had gone into the U.S. military or the CIA were able to best their counterparts in Cuban intelligence and related activities. The CIA's Felix Rodriguez, U.S. Army Colonels Johnny Lopez, Gil Pérez and several others whose names escape me, contributed greatly to our efforts. Let us not forget, however, that foreigners were always less important than the Central Americans who had to live, fight and die in their own—and in other's—wars.

The unexpected military defeat at Berlín cost Enders his aura of invincibility. Suddenly Enders' policies, which had seemed effective, looked as though they had been too soft. Your OH interview with Tony Gillespie refers extensively to the continual difficulties Enders faced in gaining acceptance for the negotiating principles of what was being called a two-track Central American policy of negotiations (constantly hamstrung by hardliners in Congress and the NSC) and force (support for the Contras and limited military assistance, mainly to El Salvador and Honduras). As the gods of evil chance would have it, as the news of the fall of Berlín was coming in, Enders was getting ready to go to Spain to meet with influential international Socialist leader Felipe González and to touch base with Portuguese Prime Minister Mario Soares, also a socialist, on the way back. Before he and I left, Enders sent a later partially declassified SECRET/SENSITIVE memo through the Secretary to the President suggesting we strengthen both negotiations and force. He later sheepishly apologized to me for sending it without showing it to me. He was right to apologize. His hasty drafting enabled it to be mistakenly interpreted in the White House as meaning that he was planning to make a deal with González and the Spanish Socialists that would sell freedom and America down the river. Those fears also gave a fresh opening to those who wanted Tom out for personal reasons that had nothing to do with policy. Suddenly the very dominance that had led him to control the interagency group—because half the people would shut up rather than confront him—became a fatal weakness. Because he owned the policy, he could not shuck off the Berlín failure on anyone else. He was sent as Ambassador to Spain, long misused as a graveyard for former ARA assistant Secretaries.

*Q: What happened next?*

EINAUDI: Enders' departure turned out to be the death of the interagency system. It became less and less meaningful under Enders' successor, Tony Motley, who had enough political experience not to feel wedded to bureaucracy. By the time Elliott Abrams came in, the IG still existed formally, but nothing was happening. Operationally, it was replaced by the RIG, the restricted interagency group. The designation of restricted was appropriate. Its meetings were usually just three people: Abrams,

Dewey Clarridge from the CIA and Oliver North from the NSC. I was excluded. I didn't know what went on, but I was reminded of my childhood mountain climbing days where I would fear going out on a cliff face because I did not know who on the rope might slip and fall and take us all down. I had an image of these people walking on a cliff's edge each ready to jump the other way when something bad happened. The only thing wrong with that image was that those three were all so supremely arrogant and confident that they expected to land on their feet no matter what happened.

*Q: I want to go into all that, but first let's go back to what you said about the Catholics and the Jesuits. Was the central command in the church, i.e. Rome, playing much of a role or was this pretty much at a local level?*

EINAUDI: In February 1981, I was sent to the Vatican, leading one of two teams to carry out a special European consultation on Central America. I was the Director of ARA/PPC; Hank Cohen, then a deputy assistant secretary in INR, led the other team, which included David Randolph, an FSO who had served in Nicaragua and knew Central America well. Cohen went north and I went south. I took Spain, Italy, Portugal, Austria and the Vatican. The Reagan triumph in 1980 had led Central American conservatives to think that finally the Americans are going to come and get rid of all these Communists for us. At the same time, the Reagan triumph had led the revolutionaries to get moving before the Americans got themselves organized. All hell was breaking loose in El Salvador and ricocheting everywhere else. We in the State Department wanted to explain what we saw happening to our European allies, some of whom had a finger or two in the mess.

In going to the Vatican, one of our concerns was the American Catholic church. An increasing number of American clergy and lay people were being radicalized by the way things had been developing, particularly in El Salvador, but also to some extent in Guatemala. When the Catholic nuns were murdered in El Salvador in December 1980, I had been the third member of the commission the Carter Administration sent down to investigate in its lame duck days. That I had been directly involved gave me credibility. Washington felt it was vital to talk to the Vatican because many American church people were shooting off in pro revolutionary directions without any awareness of what else was going on.

Everything was exploding and we were trying desperately trying to find a center that could hold.

Q: *You said earlier you were a Catholic?*

EINAUDI: Yes, but the classic sort of agnostic non-practicing Catholic.

Q: *A good European Catholic.*

EINAUDI: Yes, and with ties. In 1980, my cousin Giulio had become Papal Nuncio to Cuba. And Church people have over the years been among my major allies in peacemaking -- in Haiti, and in Nicaragua and Honduras. It is important to remember that conflicts that tear apart society are also likely to tear apart its institutions, including the churches. But moral authority is always important to enlist on your side. And in times of tension and turmoil, having a prophetic element or vision can provide direction and win allies.

The Vatican Cardinal I managed to see in 1981 as a representative of the U.S. government to discuss Central America put it very simply. He said, "It is your business. Don't come to us. The American Church is the American Church. It is your business." He was, of course, correct, at least in the sense that the troubles in Central America and in the United States were feeding off each other in both politics and religion.

*Q: Is there in the American Church a foreign ministry here, a group within the church or something that deals with Latin American and other affairs?*

EINAUDI: There is the U.S. Conference of Catholic Bishops. For years its senior staff person on Latin America was a lay person, Thomas Quigley. He was a marvelous and very intelligent man. I wonder what he would have to say about all of this right now if he were to join us. He is more or less our generation. He would probably point out that in all of these things the number of people who are really participating is a tiny handful.

*Q: Again, I am not a church member, and I haven't dealt with places where the Catholic Church was very important, but what about the Maryknoll group? Did they play a role?*

EINAUDI: Yes. But the Catholic Church is very complicated, with many groups and tendencies, even among those associated with liberation theology. The Maryknolls are generally associated with worker priests and the indigenous, but the only Maryknoll I have known personally is Miguel d'Escoto, who served as the Sandinista Foreign Minister. Since Vietnam the best-known Catholic resisters against U.S. military interventions abroad were the Berrigan brothers, but the Berrigans were tied to the Jesuits, not the Maryknolls. My distant cousin, the papal nuncio Giulio, was a Jesuit, and I can talk about some of their doctrinal and political views. I have to plead ignorance on the Maryknolls.

*Q: Another group that we haven't mentioned are the glitterati, pop stars, movie stars, people who gain the headlines, for example, Bianca Jagger or more recently Sean Penn. Did they play any role or were these just actors off on the side?*

EINAUDI: The glitterati in general are more capable of creating storms in teapots and getting under people's skins than playing constructive roles. I don't want to seem dismissive because any responsible government official should be careful to factor in celebrities and their views one way or another. Today of course with the general weakening of central government authority and the growth of non-governmental organizations, some believe private individuals and groups can replace governments. There are policies, even out of the State Department, that suggest diplomats are supposed to be exporters of democracy, vanguards of God-knows what political vogue. I cannot put my finger on specific cases in Central America where celebrities affected policy or events. On the other hand, I did strongly feel we needed to do more to keep in touch with public opinion.

*Q: But you did have the Reagan administration where the president himself is saying, as he did in a March 1986 press event pushing for contra aid, "It'd mean consolidation of a privileged sanctuary for terrorists and subversives just two days' driving time from Harlingen, Texas." You could see the arrows on the maps in the newspapers pointing from Nicaragua or El Salvador up to Texas. I mean it was a peculiar period.*

EINAUDI: Oh, it was a terrible period. Indeed, we in the State Department contributed some of those maps. Clearly these places were close to the United States. Clearly there was a danger of contagion and spill over. The maps tried to make the point. My bigger problems were with analyses that were ideologically determined, or disregarded facts, historical accuracy or foreign policy sense. I had endless battles with Robert Kagan and Otto Reich of the Office of Public Diplomacy, created under Reagan to influence public opinion. My feeling was that anti-communism lasted as a single-issue policy until New York state apple growers decided they would not pay taxes to support activities in Central America when they were having a hard time making ends meet.

Being surrounded by the contradictory demands of irreconcilable superiors, hostile movements, and uncompromising creeds was thoroughly demoralizing, to me and to my staff. I instructed them to keep their heads high, and hold on to their ideals, lest they drown in the mud of the trenches or perish in the freezing gales. I told them to think like Occam and reject conspiracy theories if a straight forward explanation or plain incompetence would explain, and to remember, like Buridan's medieval ass, that it was important to keep going, even if the choices were difficult. And just as my father had kept WH Auden tacked to his office closet door, I tacked on the inside of my office door a poem, *Exiles* by the Nicaraguan Pablo Antonio Cuadra.

EXILES

(Dedicated to Stefan Baciu)

When the cock crows I get up and see the sunrise in my
country,
lovely and radiant. And my heart is a king receiving
his throne.
No. I will not leave the land of my birth. Here, I
will die.
But the sun sets and my eyes go back to the country of
my dreams
and all the world's ashes drift down to cover its face.
Then I wish I were a foreigner
so I could return to my country.
Then I hear the cheerful murmur of cities not my own.
I hear the night crowded with exiles.
I ought to leave, I tell myself,
and my dream journeys on with stars as its guardians

until the cock crows
and dawn once again takes command of my song.
No. I will not leave. And I go back
to raising the wall with fallen stones.

*Pablo Antonio Cuadra found this poem tacked to my office door when he visited me during his exile, so he happily signed it for me. When Violeta Chamorro won the election in 1990, Cuadra returned to Nicaragua and his job at La Prensa. (Pablo Antonio Cuadra, 1985, reproduced courtesy of LR Einaudi).*

Those were demoralizing times. Latin America had a long tradition of exile. The Peruvian politician Victor Raul Haya de la Torre spent six years in the Colombian embassy in Lima after the 1948 coup. That experience had led to one of my definitions for "development:" having a place to hide when you're not in power. Those of us in the State Department were on the front lines with no place to hide. My daughter Maria had named one of her paintings "There will still be heroes when the world finally ends." I hung it on my office wall. None of us felt like a hero, but we fought to keep the world from ending.

*Q: What did you really do?*

EINAUDI: I worked harder than ever. And when Henry Kissinger accepted to Chair the National Bipartisan Commission on Central America in 1983 to try to shore up economic support for El Salvador and the Contras, I made sure his report declared that the U.S. government realized that support for dictatorship was not a formula for stability. Page 11 of the final report reads: "Experience has destroyed the argument of the old dictators that a strong hand is essential to avoid anarchy and communism, and that order and progress can be achieved only through authoritarianism."

Whenever Americans use force there will be other Americans who say, "Oh my gosh you shouldn't militarize things" or "There should be bigger economic and political dimensions to what we are doing." This happened in Central America as well as more recently in the post-9/11 world. The Reagan administration responded with the Caribbean Basin Initiative or CBI. The CBI was extended not just to Central America but to all the independent countries of the Caribbean Basin. It was a combination of trade and aid. The greater market access to the United States granted by the

CBI was later weakened with the spread of the rules of the World Trade Organization, but for a while it did extraordinarily well. I am a free trader in the sense that I believe that increased economic activity that follows rules is likely to raise all ships. I am less sure that the rules that have gone along with free trade are always the right ones. A trade agreement will always result in winning and losing sectors in all countries involved. Sometimes adjustment policies should be used to offset losses in transition, similar to Friedrich List's defense of infant industries against Adam Smith's stress on free trade. A consideration for "Community Adjustment and Investment" was belatedly included in NAFTA, but I do not believe it was taken seriously.

*Q: Considering the overheated politics and all the upwards and downwards, how did you survive particularly with Central America and all that? Bill Bowdler was kicked out with six hours' notice. I would have thought you'd be prime meat also.*

EINAUDI: The Reagan transition team asked for my letter of resignation. Expecting that would happen, I had applied for and obtained a fellowship at the Woodrow Wilson International Institute for Scholars at the Smithsonian. I delayed leaving while policy toward El Salvador remained in flux, then left in September 1981, taking all the leave I had been working too hard to take since joining the Department, a total of nearly four months. In January 1982 I was told that my letter of resignation had been lost, that I didn't need to submit a new one, and that I was needed back to help put together the Caribbean Basin Initiative and articulate it for President Reagan (which I did, writing the President's Caribbean Basin Initiative speech with Dana Rohrabacher and a little help from the White House fact checkers). So I survived that transition partially by getting out of the heat but being ready to come back.

Later, when Elliott Abrams became Assistant Secretary, Jeane
Kirkpatrick told him that the first thing he should do was "get
rid of the WOP down the hall" meaning me. Abrams did not.
In the Carter days, I had been asked if I wanted to be a deputy
assistant secretary and I said, "No, I'm going to keep myself under
the radar." I liked the work; I liked the people I was working
with and I thought I was making a difference, particularly on El
Salvador. I had seen a lot of things, helped a lot of people, trained
a lot of people and with all the bloodletting they needed at least
one person who had an institutional memory and who knew what
was going on. So I survived – partly by temporarily leaving.

*Q: Not everyone did—*

EINAUDI: You are absolutely right. Central America for several
years was a really bad scene for everyone working on it. But I
think it is important to realize that the State Department and
the Foreign Service and many other colleagues in the U.S.
government did an enormous amount of good work, and that
without them, the human costs of the conflicts would have been
greater and today's prospects for decency and dignity would be
less. And they certainly paid a price. The Reagan period was
extraordinarily difficult. It was horrible for the career people,
many who wound up losing their jobs and getting purged. It was
far worse than when Todman's position was sacrificed by internal
warfare over human rights policy. Pete Vaky and Bill Bowdler were
sacrificed over the consequences of Nicaragua and the instability
and uncertainty about what to do about El Salvador. El Salvador
ended Tom Enders' term as Assistant Secretary. Deputy Assistant
Secretaries (DASs) were also affected by the turmoil. Jim Cheek
was booed as a reactionary when he tried to speak on Nicaragua
at the Latin American Studies Association (LASA) under Carter.

But after Reagan came in, he went from being an ARA Deputy Assistant Secretary to virtual exile in Kathmandu. Another FSO, the talented and funny Myles Frechette who always thought of himself as engaged in "high impact ops," put a sign on the door of the DAS office he was never allowed to occupy formally that read "DEFENESTRATED." And it was a very difficult time, not just for those in the career (or semi-career as myself). Even the new political appointees fought among themselves. At the NSC, Menges and North could not get along. People didn't trust each other. There were tensions and problems everywhere. And, of course, a few folks, even in the Foreign Service, played politics and profited.

*Q: Speaking of turmoil, how do you evaluate our response to human rights issues in El Salvador? Some have argued that we were complicit.*

EINAUDI: There were certainly problems, but they were not generally our policies as such. The El Salvador of those years, particularly 1979-82, was a near feudal fratricidal maelstrom that sucked regional and international forces and people into it.

Our ambassadors initially were Frank Devine, a sweet man who was in over his head and knew it, and, from the spring of 1980 to the spring of 1981, Bob White, a progressive who never quite found his footing. Then, from the summer of 1981 to 1985, we had Deane Hinton and Tom Pickering, two of our best career diplomats who each played critical roles in terrible situations. And because Central America had become a center of attention, bright and ambitious officers were attracted to serve there. In El Salvador, I am thinking, among others, of Carl Gettinger, whom I never met personally, and Todd Greentree, whom I helped entice into the Service, and who gave you an oral history. And in

Washington, I would add Joe Sullivan, who coordinated support for the 1982 election while working in my office. I have great praise for their work and that of the Foreign Service in general. During the Central American crises, they worked better, harder and longer than anyone had a right to expect and certainly far more than they were given credit for.

Later, out of the maelstrom, in 1993, when I was back in S/P, I identified what I thought were four opportunities for practical operational improvement on human rights:

- *Greater continuity and overlap at the working level, both in the department and in the field. Gapping between assignments reduces awareness and opportunities for influence – on human rights as well as all other matters.*
- *Generalized and explicit attention to human rights matters by all agencies involved.*
- *Effective persistence on the need to remove hardcore offenders. In El Salvador, for example, Major Staben* [an officer notorious for leading death squads.]
- *A more human face to the victims and their relatives.*

This is not to suggest that there were not efforts along these lines. Ambassador Pickering and U.S. Southern Command (CINCSOUTH) General Paul Gorman consciously held joint meetings with U.S. and Salvadoran military leaders to show they were on the same page on human rights and other matters. In a meeting with the leaders of the Salvadoran government that was broadly staffed in Washington by my office among others, Vice President Bush famously named six officers we demanded be removed for participation in death squads. And Pickering kept his door open to visiting delegations even when they specialized in insulting him and the U.S. government for murdering "the Salvadoran people."

But this does not change the reality that persons and institutions that did murder innocent people had working ties to the U.S. government. Most famously, in December 1981 the Atlacatl Battalion, which had received U.S. training as a unit, killed in cold blood seven hundred or more men, women and children rounded up during a sweep in FMLN country around the village of El Mozote in Morazán. In the spring of 1980, the cashiered major Roberto D'Aubuisson, who had once taken a course at the U.S. Army's School of the Americas in Panama, had masterminded the assassination of Archbishop Oscar Romero. In both cases, the details were not immediately known, and the nature of the training and its relationship to the abuses was unclear. But the general pattern did seem clear: the United States was supporting forces that used brutal violence to defend a highly inegalitarian and repressive status quo. Compounding this impression, on the El Mozote massacre and the authorship of the Romero assassination, most U.S. officials kept silent or obfuscated, and some actually lied.

*Q: Do you justify that? Do you believe that diplomats are paid to lie for their country?*

EINAUDI: No, and those who do lie destroy their own and their country's credibility. On El Salvador in those years the silence, obfuscation and lies were motivated by many things. Ignorance. Denial. Hoping the truth would not come out. And above all, fear. Fear of guilt by association. Fear of failure. Fear of losing Congressional support for resources. Fear that the truth would play into ideological distortions or stereotypes. Fear that truth would further destabilize the situation.

*Q: You say "destabilize the situation." What situation? How would you characterize the internal scene in El Salvador?*

EINAUDI: Everyone was demonizing everyone else, refusing to listen, seeing everything in black and white. In the United States, listening to people talk about El Salvador was a bit like the old fable of the elephant and the blind man. The mental images were a starving peasant, a rich oligarch, a psychopathic killer in an army uniform. The left hand found a political prisoner, a worker priest, a university idealist, a Catholic nun, while the right hand found a mad Bishop turned Communist, a corrupt politician, a labor agitator, or an American do-gooder. Turn around, and feel another elephant, this hand found a U.S. Special Forces soldier looking for Cubans to kill, a CIA agent trying to figure out whether the Nicaraguan he saw was a Contra to be armed or a Sandinista to be shot, a lying diplomat pretending nothing was happening.

Inside El Salvador itself, however, even the bits of clarity never lasted. The maelstrom that consumed El Salvador accelerated steadily every year from 1979 to 1980 and through 1981, leveled off at still dizzying levels from 1982 to 1984, then began to slow as the center took hold and the violent extremes began to be exhausted. Let me explain.

In little more than a year, no less than three different "civilian-military" juntas in succession replaced President Romero, whom Vaky and I had found so disturbing in July 1979. The first two were headed by Colonel Adolfo Majano, the most visible of a small group of reformist officers. The first Junta, in October 1979, included civilians from the left, including the social democrat

Guillermo "Meme" Ungo, who had run for Vice-president with Duarte in the 1972 elections. It announced the dissolution of the right-wing paramilitary formation ORDEN and the intention to undertake sweeping reforms. But the Junta was indecisive, paralyzed by right-wing officers, and overwhelmed by strikes, street demonstrations and killings. Ungo resigned, and a second Junta was formed in January 1980, still with Majano at its head, but this time with Duarte and more centrist Christian Democrats. The Junta's civilian Attorney General was immediately assassinated by a right-wing death squad. In March, agrarian reform was decreed, beginning with large estates. As if in response, Archbishop Romero, who had favored the reforms, was assassinated. In April a "land to the tiller" reform gave sharecroppers title to part of the land they worked. May began with Majano having former major Roberto D'Aubuisson arrested for the killing of the archbishop, followed by a rightist coup attempt led by former President Romero. The coup failed, but Majano's authority was never the same again and D'Aubuisson was released. On May 18, several hundred peasants, women and children were killed in cold blood by the army as they tried to flee into Honduras. A general strike followed May 20 in the Capital. More peasants were massacred in the north. As 1980 wore on, the dizzying array of old and new political organizations that had sprung up began to coalesce. By October, following Cuban advice, five organizations committed to violent revolution united, merging into the FMLN, the Farabundo Marti National Liberation Front. The FDR or National Democratic Front, a group of progressive and leftwing politicians led by Ungo and Ruben Zamora (whose brother had been the assassinated Attorney General) acted as its somewhat detached political voice. On December 2, four American churchwomen were raped and killed. In December, a third Junta, was formed, dominated again by Christian Democrats but this time headed by Duarte instead of Majano. On January 10, 1981, the FMLN launched its "final offensive," believing it had to take power before Reagan could send in the marines.

Through all this, the Carter administration responded with nice-sounding reformist phrases, but without the flexibility to increase economic or security assistance to put money where its mouth was. In fact, the very idea of providing security assistance was opposed with all possible force by the new human rights bureau in the department. So concrete support to the reformers in the 1979-80 juntas was minimal, while those committed to violence took the initiative.

*Q: Let me ask here, some have suggested the United States missed the boat in Central America, that things would have turned out differently if we had supported the FDR and the FMLN in El Salvador and accepted the Sandinistas in Nicaragua.*

EINAUDI: I don't think so. I see that argument as ignoring the violent realities on the ground in both El Salvador and Nicaragua, as well as the realities of politics in the United States. In El Salvador, by the time it was created, the FDR was more a case of hasty window dressing for the FMLN than a functioning reformist coalition and was never even close to the levers of power, never supportable as a practical matter. Nicaragua is a different story. The opposition to Somoza was broadly-based, but the Sandinistas felt no need to compromise. The interim government that succeeded Somoza lasted until the Sandinistas marched into Managua two days later. The Junta of National Reconstruction that followed was broadly representative, but within a year, the Sandinistas had shed most of their reformist would-be partners, while holding tight to Cuba.

*Q: You did not believe moderation and compromise were possible?*

EINAUDI: No. Events in Central America had festered to the point that the few moderates who remained had nowhere to go, no power. It was simply too late. And as far as U.S. policy was concerned, Central America was first invisible, then seen mostly in Cold War terms. Jimmy Carter may have been elected partly out of disenchantment with Vietnam, but by the end of his term he was boycotting the Moscow Olympics and threatening the Soviet Union over Afghanistan and the Middle East. In one of its last acts, on January 14, 1981, the Carter Administration restored the military aid to El Salvador that it had suspended when the churchwomen were killed. The main lines of U.S. policy, then as most always, were set by politicians who reflected public opinion. Public knowledge, that is, the range of ideas tolerated in public discourse -- what social scientists now call the "Overton principle" -- made official U.S. acceptance of groups allied with Communists politically unthinkable.

*Q: So what happened next in El Salvador?*

EINAUDI: For the next three years, the killings and fighting continued, in a back and forth but essentially stalemated war. The FMLN "final offensive" was joined by peasants misled by middle class guerrillas who told them that revolution was inevitable, that vengeance for 1932 was finally at hand. The offensive sputtered and failed despite supplies of American M-16s smuggled in from Vietnam where they had been abandoned as the U.S. withdrew. While the new government juntas struggled over reforms in the midst of the turmoil and assassinations, the United States was struggling to support both the reforms and the country's armed forces, while adhering strictly to a 55-man limit imposed by Congress for U.S. military advisors. The FMLN assassinated national officials and local mayors, engaged in guerrilla warfare, and, as Cuban training and Nicaraguan logistical support kicked in, conducted some classic positional warfare in 1983 that scored many successes and at one point threatened to cut the country in half. The Salvadoran army, resisting pressure from the U.S. on human rights, still had officers who saw anyone living in an area where the FMLN was strong as enemies to be killed, and still included personnel who participated in death squads.

*Q: Where in all this madness was the center you were trying to support?*

EINAUDI: Sometimes it seemed not to exist. El Salvador brought W.B. Yeats World War I poem to sickening life:

*Things fall apart; the centre cannot hold;*
*Mere anarchy is loosed upon the world,*
*The blood-dimmed tide is loosed, and everywhere*
*The ceremony of innocence is drowned;*
*The best lack all conviction, while the worst*
*Are full of passionate intensity.*

A great deal of U.S. policy and effort was devoted to pulling El Salvador out of the maelstrom, politically and militarily. And it helped. Medical training and helicopters saved lives of wounded soldiers previously left to die in the fields. AID's efforts to transplant experiences in agrarian reform from Vietnam and the AFL-CIO's labor organizing that cost the lives of Michael Hammer and Mark Pearlman were criticized from both left and right, but they brought glimmers of hope in the midst of stagnation and repression. And I have already talked a bit about our ambassadors and FSOs and their multifront struggles.

What I would like to record now are the contributions of some of the Salvadorans who saved their country. People without whom nothing we did would have borne fruit.

**Álvaro Magaña** was President of El Salvador from 1982 to 1984. He was chosen by the Constituent Assembly elected in 1982, mainly, I think, because he was not Roberto D'Aubuisson, whose record and reputation would almost certainly have led to the loss of U.S. assistance. The charismatic D'Aubuisson was immediately elected President of the Assembly. Had it not been for the intercession of our ambassador, Deane Hinton, D'Aubuisson, not Magaña, would probably have been chosen President of the country. Magaña was a graduate of the University of Chicago, and had been President of the Banco Hipotecario, El Salvador's largest mortgage bank. And there ends most information about him, other than that he was personally presentable. Pickering notes Magaña's good judgment, but laments his weakness. And it is true not only that his choice as president was brokered, but his government was divided among the three parties who had gotten the most votes. These were the Christian Democrats, ARENA, and the Party of National Conciliation, what was left of the pre-1979 conservative ruling coalition.

What this description leaves out is the military, and Magaña's influence over it. Salvadoran officers were generally from the lower classes, graduates for the most part of a military academy shaped in a Germanic tradition by way of Chile, but with basically a high school education and a financially limited career pattern with minimal benefits. Ambitious officers enhanced their careers and supplemented their income by hiring themselves and their units out as enforcers to landowners and other wealthy individuals. As a banker, Magaña had founded savings and mortgage services for military families. This not only made him favorably known to the military because it gave them some recognition and dignity, but also left him informed about individual officers and their incomes, not all of which were legal. As social protest mounted in the 1970s, so did private moneys for repression. The military and the "death squads" were not identical, but in some situations were virtually indistinguishable. By 1980, when all hell was breaking loose, there were about 40 Salvadoran officers whose primary income came from wealthy business men and landowners. As President, Magaña worked to break the pattern, paying them what they lost by refusing outside employment. In effect, Magaña asked officers to transfer their allegiances to the state, through him. Álvaro Magaña made it possible for El Salvador's officers to think in modern terms and to give their allegiance to the nation at a moment in which the maelstrom was threatening to drown them all. "Death squads" operate to this day in El Salvador, but they are far fewer in number, and far less enmeshed in the national military structure. Most importantly, the military's opposition to social reform was weakened and space was gained in a process that in my RAND days I had dubbed "institutional development."

President Reagan received Magaña at the White House for a working visit in June 1983. During a social interlude, Magaña's wife asked me to reassure her that we knew he had put his and his family's lives in our hands, saying "he has invested everything in you."

Also at the White House that day, I chatted with the Defense Minister, **Eugenio Vides Casanova.** Vides had been head of the National Guard when I first met him at the time of the Carter Administration cutoff of ammunition after the murder of the nuns. I asked him "How are things now?" More than two years into the Reagan Administration, he instantly said ruefully "We are still hoarding ammo." To soften the edge, Vides later gave me a copy of the Army's new regulation on human rights. Vides was probably the most literate Salvadoran officer of his generation. As with Magaña, I am not sure that the Army would have held together behind the civilian government without him. But we still did not see each other as reliable allies.

**Gregorio Rosa Chávez**, Auxiliary Bishop of San Salvador. A man of humble origins and a close associate of Archbishop Romero, Rosa Chávez would have been the enduring symbol of the emerging social consciousness of the Church had Romero not been assassinated and put on the road to sainthood. I always found his calm in the maelstrom impressive and reassuring. Rosa Chávez served as a go-between to the FMLN during all the peace negotiations, from 1984 until their culmination in 1992. In 2017, Pope Francis made him El Salvador's first Cardinal.

**Ricardo Castaneda** was Deputy Foreign Minister with Borgonovo when I first met him. Ricardo cut his political teeth as a leader of the AGEUS, the Salvadoran national student union, then studied at the Michigan Law School before becoming a lawyer diplomat. He was his country's UN ambassador during the peace negotiations. His motto was "I am neither left nor right. I solve problems." He asked me never to forget that democracy was, and had to be, a "joint venture" between El Salvador and the United States.

**Joaquín Villalobos** started in university Catholic Action, became the key military commander of the ERP, the People's Revolutionary Army. He was so renowned as a killer that he was the only FMLN leader I identified by name in a department pamphlet, *El Salvador the Search for Peace* (September 1981). Discovering that assassinations were not midwifing utopia, he declared that change required a "broad and open political model" and turned his leadership to peacemaking. He was instrumental in the negotiations that ended the civil war. Based ever since in England, he was decorated by the Colombian government for his contributions to its 2016 peace agreement with the FARC. In 2011, he participated at my invitation at a colloquium at the National Defense University, but I failed in my efforts to obtain a multiple entry visa for him. Once you are in a U.S. national security data base for a violent offense, it is hard to escape.

**Alfredo Cristiani**, a Georgetown-educated entrepreneur, was President 1989-1994. He concluded the peace with the FMLN at Chapultepec in 1992. Demonized by some because of his membership in ARENA, the Nationalist Republican Alliance founded by Roberto D'Aubuisson (who died of cancer in 1992), Cristiani continued many of the reform programs of the Christian Democrats, but with an emphasis on free enterprise principles. His chief contribution was political, the Chapultepec peace agreements that accepted the FMLN as a legal political party.

But the key player was **José Napoleón Duarte**, Cristiani's predecessor.

*Q: How did you see Duarte?*

EINAUDI: He was the key to the consolidation of the political center. Here are excerpts from the eulogy I delivered to the OAS Permanent Council on March 15, 1990.

*"I equate Napoleón Duarte with courage. Physical courage as in 1972 when his reward for winning the presidential election was arrest,*

*beating, and deportation. Moral courage as in 1980 when this great civilian and democrat agreed to participate with military officers in an unelected Junta to guide his country to make the reforms essential to begin the democratic process.*

*The history of the world is filled with stories of men who failed at the critical moment. Napoleón Duarte knew the odds. In his biography he refers to the period of the juntas of 1979 and 1980 as "the worst of times." But he never hesitated.*

*Physical courage and moral courage came together when he was struck by liver cancer. Duarte at the height of his powers was a dominant figure. I remember him at Sesori at nine in the morning of the 20$^{th}$ of September, 1986, when as President he went to meet the leaders of the FMLN guerrilla to discuss peace. The guerrillas did not come, but the plaza of this provincial town in one of El Salvador's most conflictive zones was filled—with people and with the physical force of Napoleón Duarte and his optimism.*

*Two years later, the disease and the chemotherapy had consumed 40 pounds of weight and nearly all his hair. But his vigor and his vision were untouched. I was not present at the Christian Democratic Party Congress in September 1988 when he appeared in public for the first time after his return from treatment at Walter Reed, but I am told that all who were will never forget: the man was shockingly shrunk by physical ailment, yet he was the same giant, unchanged, the man of political struggle passing on the flag of his beloved Party to Fidel Chávez Mena, recalling the many battles he and Fidel had fought together since 1960.*

*By November of that year of 1988, Duarte had put back on almost half the lost weight and some hair. Many of us here today remember the moment, on November 14, 1988, when President Duarte addressed the inaugural session of the Eighteenth Regular Session of the OAS General Assembly in San Salvador. His speech was powerful in content and powerful in delivery. It was also short. That afternoon, a U.S. diplomat* [it was me, but I did not want to personalize what I was saying more than necessary] *said jokingly to President Duarte that his excellent speech had been almost Anglo-Saxon in its brevity. The President looked horrified. "Not at all," said he, "it was simply that this morning the pain in my stomach was too great. I could not have continued had I wanted to." His improved appearance had conspired with his indomitable spirit to project the illusion of normalcy. What we had witnessed was not normalcy; we had witnessed Napoleón Duarte's courage.*

*[Duarte] was quintessentially a man of El Salvador, but he studied in the United States, lived in exile in Venezuela, and enjoyed enormous respect in Europe. He was a Christian Democrat who took both his democratic principles and his Catholicism seriously, but he was also a man open to all views and faiths, open to all humanity. That morning at Sesori, he had promised to be there, waiting for the FMLN at 9:00 a.m. And so he was, standing on the steps in front of the Church in the town square. At 10:00, after waiting in vain an hour for the guerrillas to show up, he invited the crowd to join him in the Church to pray for peace. He started to turn, then stopped. Looking over the crowd, this President of the country named The Saviour and leader of a party whose origins are rooted in the social doctrines of the Catholic Church, this man Napoleón Duarte looked out at us and said "And remember, you do not have to be Catholic to enter the Church to pray for peace."*

*This was a man who reached into all corners of our lives, from boy scouts bursting with enthusiasm to the crippled asking nothing more than a chance. Ruth Mondschein of the United States Department of Education wrote asking that I mention today that it was President Duarte who issued a proclamation to support the "International*

*Decade of the Disabled" at the Sixth Inter-American Symposium for the Handicapped. President Duarte was, she wrote, "a tower of strength and a tower of patience."*

*And this, finally, is what I want to emphasize. In the affairs of mankind, it is important to have goals. And it is important to have the tenacity to achieve them—*

*Who changed between 1972 and the 1980's? Duarte, or the world? The safe answer is probably "Both." But I believe the better answer is that the world, including the United States, changed a lot while Duarte changed very little. Duarte remained a Christian Democrat in the tradition of what the French once called a "party of movement," a party advocating social change. The United States did not become Christian Democratic, nor did it become blindly a party of movement. But in the troubled decade that spanned the late 1970s to the present, the United States did change. The United States gave increasing emphasis to human rights and democracy. . ..*

*The Duarte my country celebrates is not Duarte the Christian Democrat; it is Duarte the democrat with a small "d," Duarte the defender of human rights, Duarte the man who never gave up. His legacy can be put as a set of challenges: How can democracy be possible without respect for the rights of others? How can negotiations be possible where human rights are not respected? How can there be confidence in a negotiated agreement, even the best of agreements, if it takes place in an atmosphere of abuse?"*

Re-reading this eulogy after these many years, Duarte and I were both overoptimistic. Cultural and institutional change take time. Fidel Chávez Mena, who lost to ARENA's Alfredo Cristiani in the 1989 presidential election, greeted me at the door of his home one morning saying "My bodyguard was killed last night." I was horrified, assuming it was the result of a political attack. "No, it was a drunken knife fight in a bar. He's my eighth bodyguard to die, all of them in barroom brawls." El Salvador and Central America's problems continue.

But Duarte never flinched. I would add, for the record, that it was George Shultz who overcame doubts among some around him and insisted on holding the elections that in 1984 brought Duarte legitimately to the Presidency he had first won in 1972 only to be denied and abused by the elite and the Colonels.

*Q: Have you been back to El Salvador?*

EINAUDI: In 2010, Carol and I attended the wedding in San Salvador of Gian Paolo Einaudi, a nephew who served in the Peace Corps there and fell in love with a Salvadoran woman. We visited where Ellacuría was murdered and grieved for him and other lost friends at the civil war memorial.

*Mauricio Borgonovo and Rutilio Grande are both remembered on the same plaque in the Monument to Memory and Truth in San Salvador, which records thousands of victims of El Salvador's civil war. (Photograph courtesy of Gian Paolo Einaudi, personal photograph).*

Gian Paolo spent 1999-2002 in Santa Marta, a canton of Ciudad Victoria in Cabañas province. Santa Marta had a population of some 3,000, "repopulated" after the war, as most of its inhabitants had been displaced by the civil war. To this day, every May 18, a hundred Santa Martans or more trek two hours on foot to mark the anniversary of the massacre at the Rio Sumpul in 1980 when villagers from the surrounding area were killed by Honduran and Salvadoran troops while trying to cross the river to safety. It was from them, Gian Paolo said, that he learned how important it is to distinguish between a people and their government. The Santa Martans associated the U.S. government with the army that killed people who were only looking for better working conditions, but they loved the American workers they met in the UN refugee camps in Honduras. Of the dozen or more rural youths Gian Paolo coached in soccer in Santa Marta, all but one are now either in Virginia or California. Perhaps El Salvador and the United States really are part of a joint venture, as Ricardo Castaneda argued long ago.

*Q: OK, let's stand back a minute and go back to Nicaragua and the start of it all. How had you felt about the Sandinistas? Did you feel they were an improvement over Somoza or the revolution was a dangerous offshoot, or what?*

EINAUDI: It is not a question of who was better than whom. The Somoza dynasty had been running out of steam for some time. The 1972 earthquake laid regime corruption and ineptitude bare for all to see. Disenchantment and ineffectiveness undermined the dynasty's image. By the 1978 assassination of newsman Pedro Joaquin Chamorro even the business elite was disenchanted. But the Somozas refused to go peacefully, and although opposition proliferated, the Sandinistas were the only ones willing to stand up and fight. Our ambassador Larry Pezzullo once found Congressman John Murphy (D-NY) sitting on Somoza's desk, dangling his legs while Somoza announced that he was a West Point graduate (which he was), and that he was a general (which he was, in the Nicaraguan army) at the head of his troops fighting Communism. Of course he was not going to change, share power with his opponents, or hold elections. In that sense Somoza was self-chosen to disappear. He was not realistic. Neither he nor the Nicaraguan elites were prepared for what happened. Nor was the United States.

What happened was that even friends of the United States, the very people who had made possible the negotiated solution to the Panama Canal crisis, the Venezuelans and the Costa Ricans, started to funnel arms to the Sandinistas. They had had it with Somoza and U.S. indecision. Attempts at negotiation had failed. Secretary Vance tried to use the OAS to ensure a controlled transition. A meeting of foreign ministers voted 17 to 2 to delegitimize Somoza, but then refused to support the creation of an Inter-American military force to manage a transition. The neighbors were convinced that Somoza's days were over and that he should be overthrown. But nobody wanted to intervene openly. And few were worried about the future.

Nicaragua's neighbors also understood something else that set them apart from us. They understood that these radicals, these revolutionaries, whatever they were, even those who had ties to the Soviet Bloc, were native grown and were responding to local conditions. Except for Somoza and his most conservative allies in Nicaragua and elsewhere, they did not see them as agents of a foreign Communist conspiracy.

I was not an innocent when it came to the way power was wielded in Nicaragua. Back in my student activist days I had made the acquaintance of Silvio Mayorga, a Nicaraguan student leader who later was one of the founders of the FSLN, took up arms against Somoza and was killed. Somewhere among my stacks of papers I have a telegram sent to me by Somoza's foreign minister when I was a student at Harvard assuring me that Mayorga had been released after an arrest at the university. These were radicals, but they were not people who -- even if they were on the Soviet payroll, and most were not -- these were not people acting on alien orders. Conservatives in Central America feared them as innocents who would serve as "*tontos utiles*," Communist pawns. In the U.S. the tendency was to lump all of these revolutionaries into one bag, and to see them in a Cold War context. I am not an expert on the Soviet Union, but there can be no doubt that Soviet bloc members sent American weapons left in Vietnam to Central American revolutionaries in part to revenge the American intervention in Afghanistan.

But people on the ground generally did not focus on the Communist aspect; some may even have thought it was a good thing that far away countries of the Soviet bloc were willing to help a local cause. My own sense was that the Communist elements could be isolated and defeated politically. In many ways that is what the elections in Nicaragua and elections generally afterwards proved. Not necessarily a great sign of anti-Communist virtue, just a sign that people with totalitarian tendencies are not likely to get majority support in an open election. Ordinary people vote for things they understand, not for abstractions.

*Q: I would have thought that with those views, you would not have been a great backer of Iran-Contra—*

EINAUDI: I wasn't. I never thought a military victory over the Sandinistas was possible. I was not even sure support for the Contras would provide negotiating leverage that would outweigh the disadvantages of providing the support. In fact, my office worked hard in the Enders period to develop a policy option to contain and ultimately defeat the Sandinistas using political, economic and diplomatic pressures. I called it the "grind them down" option. Enders' DAS for Central America, the able and Vietnam-scarred Craig Johnstone, summarized one reason my option failed. He told me "You can't wear them down: two years is the maximum time for the U.S. to follow any one policy." In the broader U.S. foreign policy setting, of course, covert support for organized resistance to the Sandinistas was more palatable than a Vietnam-like U.S, military operation in Central America or an outright invasion of Cuba, to "excise the cancer at the source." George Shultz focuses chapter 19 of his 1993 memoirs, _Turmoil and Triumph_, on his efforts in 1983-4 to negotiate with Nicaragua and the efforts of hardliners in the administration to block negotiations and challenge his authority. His is an extraordinarily detailed account of what he calls the "intensity" of internal disputes at the personal and policy level. As far as I am aware, everything he writes there is accurate, partly due to FSO Charlie Hill's unparalleled notetaking. But at the start of the Reagan Administration, Shultz was not yet Secretary of State. Alexander Haig was. Intense as was the internal heat that Shultz describes in 1983-4, the heat was even greater in 1981-2. Dangerously ignorant militant and opinionated people passed through the Reagan White House. Richard Allen comes to mind. So does Bill Casey. Not to mention Bill Clark. Roger Fontaine, the original Latin America head at the NSC, was an academic conservative without government experience. Many staffers thought that they could run the world out of the NSC. Not to mention Ollie North.

*Q: What did people expect the Nicaraguan resistance to accomplish? Was the goal "harassment" or "regime change?"*

EINAUDI: Sacrificing lives with a goal of mere "harassment" would be immoral. If by "regime change" you mean removal of those in power, that was certainly the aim of conservatives in the White House and Congress and most of the Contra leadership. I never thought that likely. However, "regime change" in the form of putting pressure on the Sandinistas to contain them, or force some change (whether unilaterally, through negotiations or elections) was a more reasonable goal. Diplomacy without anything to back it up cannot succeed. When they first came in, the Sandinistas were euphoric, and did not believe they needed to negotiate with anyone. They discarded the Nicaraguan moderates who had not participated directly in the armed struggle and gave the Carter people nothing. The hard liners in the Reagan Administration also had no interest in negotiations. Over time, Nicaragua's resistance movements and particularly their peasant base provided some of the leverage that ultimately enabled diplomacy and politics to succeed.

*Q: What about Ollie North and his operation? What did you know and when did you know it?*

EINAUDI: A great deal of government work is naturally compartmentalized, even if it is not classified with "need to know" rules. On Central America in the Reagan years, the Department was often blindsided -- kept in the dark -- on important operations. Secretary Shultz wrote in his memoirs that the decision to mine Nicaragua's harbors was made without letting him know. Different agencies within the executive all had their own separate activities, often with minimal consultation, both in Washington and in the field. And then you had Congress and Congressional staffers, the public, and various interest groups. Senator Helms' staff regularly visited Central America without touching base with our embassies.

*Meeting of Western Hemisphere Chiefs of Mission, March 1984. In the front row, from the left, are Nestor Sanchez, a CIA retiree then representing the Department of Defense, Assistant Secretary Langhorne "Tony" Motley, Ambassador to El Salvador Thomas Pickering, who acted as host, and Secretary of State George Shultz. I am at the far right. Immediately behind me to my right is my former RAND colleague Constantine Menges then representing the NSC. The other participants are all ambassadors, a mix of Foreign Service and political appointees. (US State Department photograph, 1984, courtesy of Thomas R. Pickering.)*

Nobody but North knew all North was doing. North was a complete loose cannon, even with his friends and superiors. Coordination, if any, was through the restricted interagency group in which I never participated. The basic reality was that North and some his NSC colleagues thought they represented the president and nobody else did. We were very lucky in that period to have George Shultz as Secretary of State and George Shultz was lucky in turn to have Charles Hill, an outstanding career Foreign Service officer at his right hand. We owe them a great deal. They held the crazies associated with the Reagan NSC at bay. At one stage George Shultz did not feel he could fully trust Elliott Abrams, the assistant secretary. When Shultz decided he needed different eyes, he would ask Hill to get my views, an act that in itself violated the chain of command and might lead me to contradict the views of my direct boss, who was Abrams. Life gets very complicated and very messy in these situations.

*Q: What was Ollie North up to?*

EINAUDI: I had very little to do with North. One day he and I bumped into each other in the room where there were Coke machines and other dispensers of food near the elevator outside of the ARA front office. He spotted me and said, "I want you to know I think you are a great American." Which was Oliver North to a T. He was wrapping himself up in the American flag, making himself seem important. But he didn't know what he was talking about. He was confused and thought I approved some activities he was pushing in Guatemala. I did not know what they were, told him so, and North did not reply. My friend Fernando Andrade, at that time the foreign minister of Guatemala, told me that North and Admiral Poindexter had tried to convince him at the White House to have Guatemala support U.S. military action against Nicaragua and that he had refused. Sereseres later informed me that our station chief in Guatemala had told him that North asked him to do certain things he considered illegal. The station chief told North to "Come back with a written letter signed by the president and I will do what you ask." He never saw North again.

Our national bureaucracy, certainly the Foreign Service, is inherently loyal, internally disciplined and generally speaking not subject to outside influences, whether from foreign governments, corporations or other private associations. There are always individuals, particularly noncareer people associated with a particular Administration, who have better connections with the outside world than they do in the government. North was one of these kinds of people, very self-centered and very ignorant, and for a while very powerful. Fortunately, people like that usually go for a fall.

A similar independent loose cannon was Constantine Menges. Menges worked for me at RAND, where he was unreliable and unproductive. Then he showed up on the National Security Council under Reagan, where he confirmed his nickname "Constant Menace." His book *Inside the National Security Council* is meant to reveal the betrayal of Reagan by the bureaucracy. He was more academically knowledgeable than North, but fortunately not as operationally capable.

*Q: Were there differences between the CIA, State, Pentagon, and White House before Congress voted against military aid to the Contras?*

EINAUDI: The militant believers in the Contras were concentrated in the White House and among political appointees. But there were also some among the career folks in the agencies. Otherwise, differences were less than two commonalities: first, ignorance of conditions in Central America, and second, a willingness to "go along" and figure policy was above their pay grade.

The Nicaraguans had their own goals and views, also often differing among themselves. What became known as "the Contras," the Nicaraguan Resistance, or RN for *Resistencia Nicaraguense*, was a coalition of disparate groups united mainly by their opposition to the Sandinistas. Their differences were not overcome by the fact that they got U.S. views and goals indiscriminately and differently from everyone they talked to. Menges, North and others were not telling each other what they were doing, let alone others in the rest of the government. Lewis Tambs, a conservative professor who had hoped to be Assistant Secretary at the start of the Reagan administration, and later became ambassador to Colombia and then Costa Rica, made arrangements with Sandinista military hero turned oppositionist Eden Pastora without informing the Department. No one knew what was going on, with the practical result that every militant believer was free to push their own line in a chaotic freelancer's paradise.

As the Contra cause wound down, of course, no one was left willing to talk to the Nicaraguan resistance. I remember an occasion when RN leaders wanted to get our guidance on how to approach the elections. I was OAS Ambassador by then and hosted a meeting in my office for the Nicaraguans, to which I invited Harry Shlaudeman, by then again the Ambassador at Large for Central America. To the outside world, the meeting was an impossibility, the hard line (the contras) consulting the soft (the diplomats). After two hours, Harry got up to leave without having said a word. I called out that he could not leave us like that. Surely, he had some advice. Harry stopped, turned back and said, quietly, that he did not know what could be done, but whatever it was, it should be done "*con cariño.*" With affection. And went out the door. He, at least, did not want to add to the cacophony coming from the United States.

In the end, the peasant army of the Nicaraguan resistance is an unknown and untold story that proves reliable allies are hard for the weak to find in this world. I feel no sorrow for Aristides Sanchez, Enrique Bermudez, Adolfo Calero, Arturo Cruz father and son and the other bourgeois political leaders of the Contra resistance. But the campesinos and Miskito Indians that made up the bulk of their forces are another matter. Like the ordinary Sandinistas they resembled in many ways, they probably gained some awareness of rights they previously did not know they had. Maligned, they were quickly abandoned by everyone except for the OAS' CIAV mission (*Comisión Internacional de Apoyo y Verificación*, International Commission of Support and Verification, 1990-1997) that ultimately managed their reintegration into Nicaraguan society. Without Santiago Murray, Sergio Caramagna and the members of their CIAV team, the University of California's Caesar Sereseres and a handful of others, among them a handful of committed Foreign Service officers like Tim Brown, Al Barr, and David Lindwall, their fate would have been even worse. Senator Helms and his people deserve credit for helping to secure the funding that enabled CIAV to demobilize them with a modicum of dignity.

*Q: What was going on in Guatemala in the 1980s? What was the cause of the violence against the indigenous? Did things change with the election of 1985?*

EINAUDI: I was in Bolivia, invited by Bill Stedman for consultations with future President and then planning minister, Gonzalo Sanchez de Losada, when I got word that Guatemalan Foreign Minister Fernando Andrade wanted me to come to observe the first round of the 1985 presidential elections. The altitude of La Paz had overcome my lungs destroyed by a two-pack-a-day cigarette habit and forced me to strap on an oxygen tank to attend meetings. I had walking pneumonia but had to accept Fernando's invitation. We had first met in the mid-nineteen fifties, when we were both elected officers in our respective student organizations, I as President of the backwater and virtually invisible USNSA New England Region, Fernando as President of the Law Student Federation at the University of San Carlos in Guatemala after a bitter and protracted campaign in a country dominated by racist feudalism. In 1960, Fernando had visited me at Harvard to tell me about suspicious military activities in Retalhuleu, where Cuban exiles were training with the help of Somoza and the CIA for what was to become the Bay of Pigs. In 1983, he was foreign minister of the military government led by General Mejía whose objective was to organize a transition to democracy after Guatemala's long nightmare of U.S. intervention, civil war and military rule. The election and a new constitution were the culmination of their efforts. Fernando and I flew in a small civilian helicopter to polling places all over the beautiful countryside of that tragic country. Military personnel were nowhere to be seen. Order at the polls was maintained by Boy Scouts. Fernando's 1956 student campaign manager had been Vinicio Cerezo. In the 1985 national elections, Cerezo was elected President of Guatemala.

Those were all real events. But real life is harder than a fairy tale. The Guatemalan military had supported a transition to civilian rule mainly to consolidate the defeat of the URNG (Unidad Revolucionaria Nacional Guatemalteca). The URNG was an umbrella organization of armed insurgent groups united with Cuban advice in 1982, a pattern similar to the unification of the Sandinistas in Nicaragua and the FMLN in El Salvador. In Guatemala, however, rivalries among leaders remained strong and dependence on outside support was less clear. Guerrillas in the north had access to Mexico, but the key strength of the Guerrilla Army of the Poor (EGP), the mainstay of the URNG, was a decade organizing underserved indigenous communities in Huehuetenango, Quiché and Alta Verapaz. After 1954, Guatemala's military was dominated by conservative officers whose anti-communism sometimes took racist forms. The military regimes of Generals Laugerud and Lucas adopted purely repressive tactics against the EGP. As the war escalated on all sides, General Rios Montt seized power and the military adopted a multifront *frijoles y fusiles* ("beans and rifles") strategy, arming civilian "self-defense" militias and attempting to provide government services to indigenous villages. The proposed services did not materialize, but hundreds of villages were destroyed, thousands of Mayans were killed and many multiples of that displaced. The guerrillas were decimated, but fought on. The Army's vice chief of staff, Colonel Hector Gramajo, influenced by U.S. failures in Vietnam, sought both to fight the guerrillas and to shift the allegiance of the indigenous peasantry by giving them voice through negotiations and elections. When it appeared that Rios Montt planned to consolidate power in his own hands, the military command, led by generals Oscar Humberto Mejía Víctores and Jaime Hernandez, replaced Rios Montt with Mejia in 1983 to ensure a transition to elections and civilian rule.

This was Cerezo's immediate inheritance when he became President. Guatemala's economic elites were among Central America's most conservative. They had systematically blocked attempts by military governments to raise taxes to address conditions in the countryside that allowed guerrillas to gain popular support. Their power, the social divide between the small *ladino* middle class and the people, particularly the indigenous, the pervasive corruption, and the ridiculously low tax base for public services would have hampered the best of efforts, even without the shadow of the guerrilla war. Cerezo's government succeeded in staying largely out of the broader regional wars in El Salvador and Nicaragua and created some institutional underpinnings for human rights and the rule of law. But the military could not be confined to barracks. Cerezo trusted the advice of Gramajo, by then promoted to General, on how to steer civil-military relations and made him Minister of Defense. Twice, Gramajo had to put down coup attempts by right-wing military officers backed by important business leaders. After that, however, Cerezo stopped talking about negotiations with the guerrillas and gave up on a key tax reform initiative.

Like General Vides Casanova in El Salvador, Gramajo was a key figure in moving the Guatemalan military away from being a repressive tool in the service of wealthy land owners toward being an institution in the service of its people under civilian leadership. As an intelligence officer, he opposed torture, arguing information obtained by torture could not be trusted. As field commander, he notified the families of the soldiers killed under his command, and insisted that captured guerrillas be turned over to the courts, not executed on the spot. As Minister of Defense, Gramajo told businessmen it was not the military's function to block economic reforms at their request.

Sereseres and I both knew him well. He was the first and only general officer of any nationality who came to my office with his aides and let them do most of the talking. To teach officers that national stability required respect for elections and the rule of law, he founded the Centro ESTNA (*Centro de Estudios Estrategicos para la Estabilidad Nacional*, with ESTNA an abbreviation of *ESTabilidad NAcional*). In January 1990, I gave a lecture on "Political Doctrines" to the officers in ESTNA's inaugural course. I told them that a military man who disrespected human rights disgraced his uniform.

Negotiations with the URNG began in Mexico in 1994, supported by a "Group of Friends" (Colombia, Mexico, Norway, Spain, the United States and Venezuela). In 1996, no less than ten separate agreements were signed, covering human rights, the rights of indigenous people, a truth commission, the role of the military, the legal reintegration of the URNG, conditions of a cease fire, and constitutional reforms.

President Alvaro Arzu, who was from a wealthy conservative family, was able to prevail over a reluctant business elite and to lead the army back to the barracks. The negotiations were brought to a successful conclusion by Arzu's foreign minister Eduardo Stein. John Hamilton, an FSO who had been with me in PPC, represented the United States in the "Group of Friends" and helped persuade the negotiating parties and other key sectors of Guatemalan society to accept the final settlement.

The agreements had a positive effect, but were not fully implemented. When Stein became Vice President in 2004, he knew the peace accords quite well. As Vice President he took to the U.N. a proposal for international support for the peace accords and Guatemala's justice system. In 2006, the CICIG (*Comisión Internacional contra la Impunidad en Guatemala*), the International Commission against Impunity in Guatemala, was established to support the Public Prosecutor's Office, the National Civilian Police and other state institutions in taking on cases of corruption and other abuses of power. Critically, Stein succeeded in gaining Guatemalan acceptance of CICIG's ability to conduct independent investigations. CICIG was set up by treaty in the UN system, but could just as easily have been organized though the OAS if the OAS had been provided the resources like the UN.

The key was granting an international body the independent legal authority to assist Guatemalan judicial institutions.

Andrade, Cerezo, Gramajo, and Stein were certainly not the only Guatemalans who worked to modernize and democratize their society. I would like to pay tribute to Francisco Villagrán Kramer, a lawyer and scholar who resigned as Vice President in 1980 to protest human rights abuses, and his son Francisco Villagrán de Leon, a scholar and diplomat who served Guatemala as Ambassador to the United States, Canada, Germany and the OAS, and now writes and teaches in both the United States and Guatemala. All were inspired by U.S. ideals. We had several excellent Ambassadors to Guatemala in these years, but I believe we could have done more to support institutional development.

*Q: What more could the U.S. do, specifically?*

EINAUDI: There is no single best formula. Each country, time and situation is different. When Jim Michel became the U.S. Ambassador to Guatemala in 1987, he understood the need to strengthen the institutional underpinnings of democracy and supported innovative programs for Guatemala's judicial system. This bilateral technical support through AID set an important precedent for the later development of CICIG. As a general approach, I believe international organizations of governments operating in accordance with international law are the best way for foreigners to develop and support democratic institutionality. This is a universally applicable principle, but one that is particularly important for the United States, which has many private voluntary associations, NGOs, with external reach. NGOs sometimes can be perceived as having single-issue blinders and partisanship. To take one tragic example, in June 1991, as Gramajo was graduating from

Harvard's Kennedy School, the Center for Constitutional Rights sued him under the Alien Tort Claims Act for responsibility for human rights violations that occurred under his commands. In 1995, a court in Boston found him civilly liable and assessed $47.5 million in damages. His U.S. visa was revoked. After forty years of being a friend of the United States and a committed democrat, Gramajo died in 2004 with his U.S. visa cancelled by a single U.S. court judgment that did not reflect his historical role.

*Q: But did the judgment reflect Gramajo's conduct?*

EINAUDI: The cases brought against Gramajo appeared narrow but were broadly cast, and were civil, not criminal. They were brought under what in customary international law is known as "command responsibility," which extends responsibility for crimes up the chain of command. This doctrine is far more clearly stated than consistently applied. To take a U.S. example, in the trials that followed My Lai, Lt. Calley was convicted of murder but was ultimately released. Charges of "command responsibility" were not brought against senior officers like General Westmoreland, who were in positions in the chain of command similar to that of Gramajo. Captain Medina, Calley's immediate superior, who was actually at My Lai and was charged with also participating in the killing, was explicitly acquitted of "command responsibility." Gramajo helped lead a war against guerrillas, but was never in immediate command of a unit that killed indiscriminately, and to my knowledge never killed anyone himself. Gramajo himself believed the charges brought against him in the United States were politically motivated payback for the success of the Guatemalan government and did not appear in court to contest them. Sereseres is convinced Gramajo simply became one more victim of the history of U.S. involvement in Guatemala since the early 1950s.

My own experience with Gramajo was that he consistently supported openness and inclusion as pathways to progress in very difficult times.

These tensions and ambiguities, both in law and nationality, is why I am convinced CICIG provides a basic model for how the United States, and indeed the world, should support institutional development and the rule of law. CICIG's international nature shields it to some extent from domestic partisanship. That it also operates under Guatemalan law shields it to some extent from charges of interventionism. This double legitimacy gives it the best chance to address competing narratives and tragic complexities like the Gramajo case. The spread of fake news and of international trafficking in arms, drugs, people and money by criminal networks, makes careful, non-partisan, non-ideological institutional support for the rule of law more important than ever. Applying resources directly to multilateral projects advances common interests far more effectively than is generally realized. What has been happening to Guatemala's justice system since CICIG was shut down in 2019 is an insult to all decency.

*Q: Coming back to your regular activities as Director of PPC, I remember you got quite a lot of recognition . . .*

EINAUDI: In 1987, President Reagan designated me a "Distinguished Executive," for "sustained extraordinary accomplishment." The Department's nomination read that "Dr. Einaudi has played a central role in most major policy statements on Latin America and the Caribbean by the last three Presidents, five Secretaries of State, and ten Assistant Secretaries." I had personally written the key operational parts of the president's 1982 announcement of the Caribbean Basin Initiative and his

1983 address to a joint session of Congress on Central America. In both cases, I coordinated the text within the Department and with Defense, Treasury, and other key agencies, then worked with the NSC and the White House to the moment of delivery. The White House "fact checkers" proved invaluable allies disallowing a lot of ideological junk and factual misrepresentations the political staff tried to add, and which would have robbed the statements of their balance and impact. I was also probably lucky that Dana Rohrabacher, the key Reagan speech writer assigned to the CBI text, recognized me as a fellow Californian.

In one fifteen-month period in the mid-1980s, I wrote or coordinated the Latin American portions of 12 speeches by the President, 2 by the Vice President, 11 by the Secretary of State, 5 by the Deputy Secretary, and more than 30 by Assistant Secretaries – a rate of almost one a week. The "sustained" had a consequence: I was exhausted.

On December 5, 1983, Deputy Secretary Kenneth Dam sent a note to George Shultz "Attached is a copy of the speech, drafted by Luigi Einaudi and his staff in ARA, that I delivered in Miami last week. I wanted you to see the sort of work a real speechwriter can do. All in all, I believe that this speech represents the best speechwriting I have seen in the Department."

### Luigi Einaudi, 6 Foreign Service officers win top presidential awards

Luigi R. Einaudi, a member of the Senior Executive Service at State, and six members of the Senior Foreign Service—Michael R. Armacost, Harry G. Barnes Jr., M. Charles Hill, Thomas R. Pickering, Rozanne L. Ridgway and Ronald I. Spiers—have been named winners of the $20,000 Presidential Distinguished Service Awards for 1987.

The Foreign Service winners' awards will be reduced by amounts each has already received in Department performance pay awards. They were honored for "outstanding achievement" over periods of three or more years, all ending April 15, 1986.

President Reagan also approved the selection of 8 other members of the Senior Executive Service and 37 others in the Senior Foreign Service for $10,000 Presidential Meritorious Service Awards. The Civil Service awards are for the three years August 1, 1984, to last July 31. The Foreign Service awards are for three or more years ending April 15, 1986.

Mr. Einaudi, cited for his work from August 1, 1984, to last July 31, is director of the Office of Policy Planning and Coordination in the Bureau of Inter-American Affairs. He is a former member of the Department's Policy Planning Council.

Mr. Armacost is under secretary for political affairs and a former ambassador to the Philippines. Mr. Barnes is ambassador to Chile and a former director general of the Foreign Service. Mr. Hill is executive assistant to Secretary Shultz and a former director, Office of Israel and Arab-Israeli Affairs, Bureau of Near Eastern and South Asian Affairs. Mr. Pickering, now ambassador to Israel, served as envoy to Nigeria and El Salvador. Ms. Ridgway, assistant secretary for European and Canadian affairs, is a former ambassador to Finland and East Germany and a former counselor of the Department. Mr. Spiers is under secretary for management and a former ambassador to

*President Reagan presents Presidential Distinguished Service Award to Luigi R. Einaudi. (White House photo by Mary Anne Fackelman-Miner)*

Turkey and Pakistan.

Members of the Senior Executive and Senior Foreign Services are not eligible to receive both presidential and Department performance pay awards in the same year. All of the Foreign Service awardees—those who qualified for the $20,000 and those who qualified for $10,000—have already received Department pay awards. In both cases, the amounts of the Department awards will be subtracted from the presidential award, and only the remainder will be paid. The performance pay award cycle for the Senior Foreign Service begins each year

on August 1 and ends the following July 31.

Senior Foreign Service awards for the current period, April 16, 1986, to last April 15, are not being paid, pending completion of an audit by State's inspector general. The audit is mandated in the 1987 Foreign Relations Authorization Act.

In conferring the Senior Executive Service presidential awards, Mr. Reagan said: "The awards salute a small group of men and women, committed to excellence in service to our country. These dedicated public servants deserve our congratulations."

Meritorious Service Award winners in the Senior Executive Service are listed on Page 45, in the Senior Foreign Service on Page 48. □

Mr. Einaudi

Mr. Armacost

Mr. Barnes

Mr. Hill

Mr. Pickering

Ms. Ridgway

Mr. Spiers

*(U.S. State Department Bulletin, March 1988.)*

*Q: Dam was a bit of a scholar as well as a lawyer, was he not?*

EINAUDI: Yes. I still have that note because I sent it to my parents, figuring the University of Chicago, where Dam had been provost, would give it extra weight.

I felt policy was greatly constrained by public ignorance about what was happening. For a while, I made a major effort to use contacts with the press to try to convey key information. I have a great deal of respect for reporting, for the art of establishing and conveying the facts of a developing situation. But as the Central American policy debates became heated, relations with the press became increasingly tense. Called upon one day to give a press briefing on Central America to the State Department press corps when no one of higher rank felt up to it, I opened by saying, "Good afternoon. I am someone you do not believe exists: a competent bureaucrat." I may have been responding subconsciously to Mike Wallace, who had come to record an interview for 60 Minutes with Tony Motley, and behaved throughout with the greatest of arrogance and disdain toward FSOs and career government employees. Suspicion was general. The tensions of that time broke up friendships. Karl Meyer at The New York Times regularly called me for advice on editorials, but stopped calling after we had a heated exchange that ended when I told him "Even Conservatives have rights." Karen DeYoung exploded when I suggested some of the Washington Post's reporting was so out of context as to convey the wrong impression to Americans, telling me flatly "Our job is not to educate our readers." Reporters who covered Latin America regularly and accurately, like Don Bohning, Henry Raymont, Carl Migdail, John Goshko or George Gedda generally lacked a national audience. Opinion writers like Stephen Rosenfeld or Georgie Anne Geyer were important but sporadic. At one point Tad Szulc and I discussed joining up to write a new edition of Hubert Herring's *History of Latin America* after Herring died. But that would have been a long-term project, ideally aimed at teaching American college students and high schoolers that most Brazilians do not run around naked with bows and arrows. And Szulc and I were already both over-busy as it was.

My years in PPC were a whirlwind of publications as well as policy memoranda and speeches. I worked with my colleagues in government to initiate a number of special reports, on Nicaragua, El Salvador, and the Falklands/Malvinas conflict. Like some of my RAND work, I designed them to explain complexities and gain support for neglected economic and political programs. In 1983, I spoke at Chautauqua audience of more than a thousand people, and drafted an article on Central America for *Foreign Affairs* that accurately predicted coming events in El Salvador. Winston Lord, then out of government, supported its publication, but the editor, Bill Bundy, brother of McGeorge, declined to print it on anti-Administration ideological advice from James Chase, but wrote me that "you write with a style truly exceptional in a bureaucrat." His attempt to be nice insultingly conveyed what he really thought of those of us in government.

One 1985 publication, *"Revolution Beyond Our Borders": Sandinista Intervention in Central America* (Special Report No. 132), is a unique document that remains of substantive interest to this day. Its origins were Nicaragua's suit against the United States in the World Court for supporting the Contras and mining Nicaragua's harbors. L, State's legal bureau, had drafted a legal counter brief, but it was ditched after the United States refused to participate on the grounds that the Court lacked jurisdiction. Secretary Shultz asked me to prepare in its place a paper documenting what the Sandinistas were doing.

With PPC as a base, I put together a broad interagency team. We drew heavily on Sandinista statements as well as available intelligence materials on the arming and training of guerrillas in El Salvador and Honduras and the support they were receiving from Cuba and Soviet bloc states. The booklet we produced is entitled

*This revolution goes beyond our borders*, a quote from Tomás Borge, a founder of the FSLN and the Sandinista Interior Minister, who declared on July 19, 1981 that "This revolution goes beyond our borders. Our revolution was always internationalist from the moment Sandino fought." Written in the driest possible language, the report has some 200 footnotes and 7 appendices. There is a chronology and an account of negotiating efforts. The last delivery points of U.S. manufactured AR-15/M-16 rifles captured from Salvadoran guerrillas are identified from U.S. records. Two thirds of the 1,588 U.S. rifles captured in El Salvador from the FMLN were linked to Vietnam: delivered to Vietnamese military units 581; to U.S. military units in the 1960s with probable delivery to Vietnam 237; Unknown, but probably to Vietnam 236; to the El Salvador military 433; Other 101. Of course, the war in Central America had local origins. But outsiders became much involved. A good policy, lasting conflict resolution and sound judgment should take into account as many of the dimensions of a problem as possible. The wars in Central America fused virtually every aspect of revolution and counterrevolution, idealism and cynicism, hope and brutality.

Colleen Sussman, a civil servant in Public Affairs did such outstanding work on the Bureau's publications, that I successfully nominated her for a Superior Honor Award and later managed to get her promoted to a GS-12, which equaled the grade her father retired with after more than thirty years.

*Q: Impressive work, surely. But I suspect that you did not, for example, support the mining of Nicaragua's harbors? This is an area where even the World Court decided the United States had violated international law.*

EINAUDI: U.S. intervention and "Contra aid" gave everyone concerned a black eye in both U.S. and international public opinion. And, yes, I agree with you, having the CIA mine Nicaragua's harbors was an egregious violation of international law. When I learned of the mining, I asked to see Secretary Shultz personally to register my objection. I told him I could not conceive of us flaunting international law when the United States was the principal beneficiary of a stable law-based order. He told me simply that he agreed, but that there had been nothing he could do. In his memoirs, he describes the mining as part of a Bill Clark NSC power grab he had successfully opposed earlier, but that he had failed to realize the mining had later been approved.

*Q: I am curious, you have not said anything about what was going on regarding the "peace track," the various efforts to negotiate with the Sandinistas.*

EINAUDI: I was not much involved operationally. When the Sandinistas first came to power, they were euphoric and felt no need to negotiate; the Carter administration was uncertain abroad and a lame duck under fire domestically. Conditions on the ground were unworkable. After Reagan came in, the infighting within the administration was vicious. As I already explained with regard to Tom Enders, just trying to keep a political track open was a deadly third rail. Our Foreign Service colleague David Randolph recently suggested, however, that *"it is easy to dismiss* [the peace track] *entirely, as most of the U.S. government regarded it as a feint, a ruse, mere window dressing in the campaign to get contra aid. But another way of looking at it is that, ultimately, it won. The handful of us who were working it beat the whole rest of the US government, and there was a peace deal that ended the contra war...and the war in El Salvador as well. (It even laid the foundation for the end of the war in Guatemala years later.)"* David is right. And even from those years of frustration, many lessons can be learned by studying the peace track: the need for clarity in instructions, the role of perceptions, of tensions between differing objectives, domestic and regional politics and the effects of time. Nicaragua's neighbors, led by Costa Rica, but including El Salvador and Guatemala, all played important roles in identifying the elements of a peaceful solution. So too did Mexico and their Contadora supporters. Oscar Arias, José Napoleón Duarte, Bernardo Sepúlveda, Fernando Andrade, and many others contributed, as did Phil Habib, Harry Shlaudeman, and most of all George Shultz. But the peace track is their story, not mine, and I am not going to invent what I do not know directly. I have urged Randolph to record his experiences, and I hope he will do so.

*Q: I am looking at time; this is a good place to stop. But I would like to talk about issues other than Central America. Do you want to talk about what was happening in Peru, and your take on Alan Garcia?*

EINAUDI: Let me start off by saying that in 1977, Walter Mondale gave a speech in support of the Panama Canal treaties that I thought was the best piece of pure oratory I had ever heard. But I had not yet heard Alan Garcia speak. Garcia came to Peru's presidency in 1985 as the inheritor of the APRA (*Alianza Popular Revolucionaria Americana*) myth of Victor Raul Haya de la Torre. For fifty years, Haya had been kept out of power and even persecuted for his originally radical ideas, only to become Peru's most popular and durable politician. Garcia had a degree in sociology from the Sorbonne. Professors normally bask in the triumphs of their students, but Garcia's thesis advisor, the French sociologist Francois Bourricaud, told me he worried that Alan was a great political talent and mesmerizing speaker, but unpredictable. And in fact, Garcia's first term as president was erratic, economically disastrous and politically destabilizing. Its chaos set the stage for the election of the outsider Fujimori, who came across in the campaign as a practical and simple man of the people. Garcia's second term as President, nearly twenty years later, was conventional, though marred by corruption and dark human rights practices. His later suicide, after being caught up in Peruvian aspects of the hemisphere-wide bribery scandals organized by the Brazilian construction multinational Odebrecht, marked the disintegration both of a major figure and of a political system having difficulty adjusting to the explosive socio-economic changes of the past half-century.

In 1952, Cornell University anthropologist Allan Holmberg bought an old hacienda at Vicos and, to his astonishment, "suddenly found himself owning a bunch of Indians." Since then, the tripling of population, massive urbanization, the rise of a *cholo* (mixed blood) middle class, turmoil among the indigenous, the opening of new agricultural areas and mines, the changing composition (asparagus and blueberries as well as copper and gold) and destination of exports (China), transport and relations with neighbors, particularly Brazil but also Ecuador and Chile; ties to the Pacific, a unique world-class cuisine, all testify to the pulsating dynamism of what used to be called Peru's "*pueblo cobrizo*" [copper-colored people] as it escapes from a closed traditional oligarchy to a new disorder still taking shape.

Q: *Brazil, Uruguay, others, were also starting to have elections and a return to democracy. In many cases, the incoming political parties had to promise not to prosecute the military juntas and their political puppets, but those promises didn't always hold.*

EINAUDI: True. The dominant force, however, was less the organizing power of civilians and more the receding of the *fidelista* threat and the disillusionment of military leaders at the limits of traditional military and caudillo politics in modernizing societies. Outside observers repeatedly underestimated the extent that it was senior military officers that realized that government on horseback with sabers and bayonets simply no longer worked in the modern world, even with teargas added.

*Q: Well, I was wondering whether you saw, I am not sure what the correct phrase is for this, but almost the benevolent hand of the School of the Americas. I mean our training of Latin American troops. I mean this wasn't all about contras. There was also staff work and how to run good military organizations. Did you feel that penetrated the Latin American military a sort of good military doctrine?*

EINAUDI: In 1965, after studying our counter insurgency manuals, something they did with great care in Peru, because they had major domestic insurgency problems, a Peruvian colonel looked at me and said, "You know, the interesting thing about this manual is that the people who wrote it never had to apply it in their own country."

To approach your question, I would distinguish between intelligence activities and institutional patterns. I think the U.S. has had enormous influence in the intelligence area, but that has been primarily through the CIA rather than through the military. During the Cold War there were countries in which the CIA station chief was seen as more important than the U.S. ambassador. Sometimes our field intelligence folks were involved with locals who were carrying out rather indiscriminate clandestine operations within their own countries.

Military relationships have always been different. Attempts to encourage good staff work, support an NCO corps, improve maintenance, yes. All practical matters, but not much doctrine. The School of the Americas, the whipping child of a lot of anti-military opinion in the United States, has origins that go back to the enormous amount of surplus military equipment the United States had available after WWII, didn't know what to do with and wound up transferring to Latin America. Congress wanted to see this equipment maintained and so mandated the development in the late 1940s and early 1950s of various schools whose primary purpose was maintenance -- ensuring our old equipment did not rust. In the Canal Zone, there was a school for aircraft mechanics. The School of the Americas gradually expanded from this start. They had a good jungle warfare school and even developed a command and general staff school. But Americans generally aren't very interested in doctrine. The doctrine applied to internal warfare by the major South American countries had little if anything to do with the United States. It was essentially French doctrine, the national security state developed out of the French experience in Algeria, that wound up at the core of Argentine, Chilean, to some extent Brazilian military operations. The "national security state" was never taught at the School of the Americas.

*Q: Well then, what did happen at the School of the Americas?*

EINAUDI: Practical common-sense kinds of things, all without much supervision. I was very interested in doctrine, including human rights issues -- which is where all of the mythology about the School of the Americas is rooted. In the Kennedy years, I was involved in early Peace Corps training and with the founding of the Inter-American Defense College here in Washington. Later, in 1972 and 1973, I was brought in by the Special Forces as a lecturer at Fort Benning. In 1964 or 5, when I was with the RAND Corporation, I called on the State Department political advisor to the commander of the U.S. Southern Command in Panama, FSO Max V. Krebs, later ambassador to Guyana. I asked him what was he doing; how was he supervising the doctrinal content over at the School of the Americas? He looked at me as though I had come from Mars. He pulled at his cuffs, tented his fingertips, and said he was there to provide political advice to the commanding general, to CINCSOUTH. He wasn't there to worry about the content of courses and what people were being taught. I believed then and do now that the State Department has the responsibility in these situations to at least try to exercise some control. After all foreign military training has foreign policy consequences. To this day I believe the United States military does not have a clear human rights doctrine – one way or the other. The officers who have personally complained to me about torture have more often been Latin American officers who have told me information gained through torture is often unreliable. I believe torture is neither effective nor proper. We know that in our own recent history some of our people have felt and done differently. But that was in war situations, not at school. When the School of the Americas was in Panama, we didn't teach human rights. But we did not teach torture, either. The central focus was military training, not politics.

*Q: Is that how the Latin Americans saw it?*

EINAUDI: That depends. The political histories of military leaders and institutions have varied enormously country by country and period by period. Some civilians saw their military as authoritarian puppets of the U.S. Others saw them as nation builders. Some as praetorian guards, others simply as strike breakers and anti-Communist enforcers. And at different times their militaries have been all that and everything in between. Please note, also, that the distrust can be reciprocal, as military leaders have often seen civilians as weak and corrupt, or as agents of special interests rather of national security, honor, and the constitution.

From a Latin military standpoint, the basic advantage of the School of the Americas was that it had munitions. Our neighbors' forces are typically constrained by lack of resources. One General Officer told me he didn't see why their recruits needed rifles when they could train with broomsticks. With rifles you need ammunition, and ammunition is expensive. But whenever you went for training in the Canal Zone, boy you got all the ammunition you wanted. Here is a story about mortar training I was told by a Latin American officer. The officer did just as the French had taught during World War I, one shot long, one short, the third smack on target. He turned, beaming at his success. "No," said the American sergeant, "you took so long you'd be dead by now. Here's how you do it." And the sergeant grabbed the mortar and started firing as fast as he could. It took him six shots to hit the target, but took less time than the Latin American officer.

American training also does provide some of what you implied, exposure to American organization, and American approaches to maintenance. But it has proved harder to influence internal command structures, particularly when it comes to the role of noncommissioned officers. The U.S. military depends heavily on noncommissioned officers, but most Latin armies have a minimal NCO corps. They have troops in the ranks and they have officers, but they don't have that intermediate organizational layer.

I have strongly supported the OAS' Inter-American Defense College at Fort McNair in Washington, D.C. for training leaders who know each other and can help defuse interstate tensions. I was for a while on the Board of Visitors of WHINSEC, the modern name of the School of the Americas after it left Panama to occupy the old infantry school at Fort Benning where George Marshall earned his spurs. They have done some good work there in recent years, training Colombian soldiers as part of the counter insurgency and counter drug war. But they are basically training enlisted ranks rather than officers.

A more apt criticism of U.S. military relations with Latin American militaries, which has little to do with the School of the Americas, would focus on the use of military channels for political ends, to support persons or policies more attuned to our interests, even sometimes to try to destabilize governments. This too should not be exaggerated as military channels tend to be blunt instruments politically and can easily fail, as they did in Chile in 1970. The history books don't record these situations very well. Secrecy is always the enemy of knowledge and makes it easier for facts to be replaced by stereotypes and propaganda.

One American officer who was very good at fostering political relationships with foreign militaries was Vernon Walters. Walters retired as a Lieutenant General and became director of the CIA and Ambassador to the United Nations and to Germany at the time of unification. But before that he had been an interpreter for Dwight Eisenhower and later Nixon. I first met him 50 years ago or so when I was at RAND. I was terribly impressed with his Italian until he told me he grew up on the Italian Riviera, where his father was a salesman. Nonetheless, his language skills were impressive. He boasted he once won a bet that he could sustain a five-minute conversation in Vietnamese after studying the language 24 hours. What those he bet with did not know was that every time he got stuck, he sneaked in a word or two of French, which had been the language of colonial Vietnam. He was our military attaché in Brazil at the time of the 1964 coup against President Goulart. From then on, he was generally thought to be the bearer of the news that the U.S. did or did not favor a particular action by the host military. In early 1982, as a Reagan Administration Ambassador at Large, Walters visited Argentina. Some have suggested that, when asked about the U.S. reaction to a possible Argentine invasion of the Falklands, he winked, suggesting the United States would not oppose Argentina. Did he? I never asked him, and the story may well be apocryphal. But its very existence betrays concerns about U.S. policy and who controlled it.

Latin American officers have long felt they deserve better treatment from the U.S. than they receive. I remember a group of officers asking me whether our ban on military officers as presidents extended even to one who might be smart enough to get himself elected president legitimately. I answered that no officer could be elected president without creating grave problems for U.S. support for relations with their country. It was 1986, and the officers were Salvadorans, some of whom still resented our veto of former Major D'Aubuisson. They were not put off when I argued for impartial electoral procedures. They reminded me that my own country had elected Dwight Eisenhower president. They felt the real problem was that we were against them.

Civil-Military tensions also affect deliberations within our own government. There is institutionally grounded distrust between our government agencies, particularly between the civilian Foreign

Service and the U.S. military. The Foreign Service has often been given the back of the hand by Congress. For example, military people posted abroad would have rights to sell cars and do other things that Foreign Service officers were never allowed to do. Military officers often feel anger at State Department-imposed limitations on their activities "We can help but we are not allowed." So creative officers fester, the safe ones "stay in our lane."

Tensions of this kind have been a constant in the history of U.S. policy in the hemisphere. The office of American Republics in the State Department that Nelson Rockefeller founded and ran during WWII was paid for out of the Defense Department budget. Much congressional and public opinion in the US has always had the attitude that we know what the Defense Department does, it wins America's wars. Give it more money. The State Department coddles foreigners. Take money away. Such stereotypes have a terrible effect on just about everything.

*Q: How do you see our support for democracy?*

EINAUDI: One of the effects of the State Department's system of personnel assignment rotation is that FSOs are not usually in any one position for more than two or three years. By the time outsiders have identified them and realized that if they are interested in a problem in Country X you go to the Country X desk officer or country director, he or she is likely to have changed. Well, for the 12 years I was in PPC, I was in the same place and thus eminently findable. And when I had time, I was a good listener. For insiders, for the Bureau, I was sometimes an alternate channel to the outside. Many of my contacts were not linked to normal official channels. For example, I sometimes met with supporters of the Salvadoran guerrillas. Being an office director, I was not at a senior policy level. It could always be denied. In that sense I served almost as an informal dissent channel. Sometimes I even found myself having to articulate internally official positions from Latin America, like those of the Rio Group, the eight South American countries and Mexico that created the Contadora process. Being findable, many Latin Americans came to me, treating me as I were a political person, as though I could change the views of Congress. I kept saying I'm not a politician, I'm a public servant and there is a difference. The difference is that I haven't run for office and don't intend to. I either respect those who do run for office and win, or I quit. Revolutions and coups are not possible in the United States.

I got very tired of being continually asked to personally make up for missing networking and political contacts. Every time Napoleón Duarte came to Washington, he would ask me "What progress are you making in getting the Americans to support democratic political parties and movements abroad?" I started to agitate. In my files is a paper that I and my staff put together in 1982-3 on "Inter-American Leadership Development" calling for the creation of new U.S. mechanisms to deal with parties and other groups in Latin America. This informal paper called for educational exchange programs lasting from a few days no more than six months. There were many possibilities, but the basic idea was to enable democratic political parties to nominate representatives who after their experience abroad could be readily reintegrated in activities at home to share what they had learned.

I was adapting some of what I thought I had learned in my days in student politics. By the time I joined the State Department in 1974 I had been watching international student politics since the 1950s, even though my last USNSA activity was in 1960, at the International Student Conference in Klosters, Switzerland. While the Cold War fortunately stayed largely cold in military terms, political warfare was at the core of a lot of international activity. The United States had been very much an actor after World War II, to a large extent covertly, through the CIA. For many years the CIA subsidized student, youth, and labor groups of all kinds, particularly on the non-Communist left. *Patriotic Betrayal. The Inside Story of the CIA's Secret Campaign to Enroll American Students in the Crusade against Communism* (Yale University Press, 2015) is a detailed critical account by Karen M. Paget, who was a late (from 1964-5) participant.

From an organizational perspective of political conflict and ideological warfare against Communism, covert CIA support for activities was very effective for some years. Some claimed that its covert nature was designed to free it from Congressional scrutiny, which in the McCarthy period would have prevented support for anything politically left of center, which would have meant abdicating most student, youth and labor to the Russians. But covertness also led over time to misinterpretations and mistakes. Americans thought that these programs gave them more power and control than they actually had. The foreigners who were their object often also thought we had more power than we did. Importantly, participants were sometimes morally and politically compromised. When you put people in the position of thinking they're independent when their actions are being secretly subsidized – at some stage the lie is going to blow up everyone involved. The CIA relationship to the U.S. National Student Association was blown up in 1967 with a crusading piece of journalism done by <u>Ramparts Magazine</u>. After twenty years, parts of the arrangement were known to a lot of people. After the first break, the whole dam exploded and those covert structures were totally disrupted. Of course, the world of political competition and ideological warfare didn't stop in 1967 just because the Americans took their ball and went home.

Paget concludes that the CIA's student programs did not change anyone's allegiance and had undemocratic side effects. As a witting participant in some of those activities, I find the first not a good yardstick and the second wrong. What matters is not changing allegiances (whatever that means, most of the people we dealt with were never Communists). What matters is the development of the capacity to understand and cooperate that comes through the networks of acquaintances, contacts and knowledge built over time. Think of the number of times the people I first met through student politics turn up in this oral history! Their occasional receipt of covert support brought complications, but foreign recipients of support learned ways to resist manipulation. And outside support did not alter the fact these were real people in legitimate organizations. CIA support made possible contacts and activities not possible otherwise, with positive contributions to party development and improved international relations over the long haul.

Better models are available that are not covert: for example, the German party *stiftungen*, *stiftung* in the singular. *Stiftung* means foundation In German. Post-World War II denazification efforts included the establishment of programs meant to support democratic education and organizing. All the German political parties had such programs. The main ones were the Konrad Adenauer Stiftung of the Christian Democrats, the Friedrich Ebert Stiftung of the Social Democrats, and the Friedrich Naumann Stiftung for the Liberals. After 1967 these German foundations grew in relative importance for much non-Communist and democratic politics. The Socialist International, which was fundamentally anti-Communist, was largely funded by the German state through the Ebert Foundation, the Christian Democratic International, similarly, through the Adenauer foundation. When in the late 1970s and early 80s political warfare exploded into violence and civil war in Central America, the *stiftungen* provided key networking and intellectual support for democratic activists at a moment when the covert structures of the CIA dealing with international student and intellectual affairs had been destroyed and not replaced with much of anything. Private U.S. organizations, like the Ford Foundation, were of course still active, but they were afraid of being tainted, and they sometimes saw themselves mainly as supporting alternatives to governments, not as supporting democratic institutions. You still see traces of this today. For example, look at who gets genius grants from the MacArthur Foundation; you are not going to find anybody in government service.

The Reagan White House had many activist tendencies. Some were destructive and violent, as we have noted in Central America. But the Reagan activism also had positive dimensions. Among them was the creation of the National Endowment for Democracy (NED). I finally ran into a chap on the NSC staff who also worried about support for democratic networking. His name was Walt Raymond. The informal paper on leadership development my PPC staff and I put together in 1982-3 was an arrow in his quiver as he lobbied for the creation of the National Endowment for Democracy (NED) with its four institutes, the National Democratic Institute, the International Republican Institute, plus entities for labor and a private enterprise.

I had hoped the NED would help Latin American political figures relate more effectively to American political figures. It hasn't really worked that way. Part of the problem, as reported by Michael Shifter, who directed the Latin American Program at the NED before moving to the Inter-American Dialogue, was that U.S. support for the Contras, interpreted as determination to have a military solution in Nicaragua, inescapably undermined receptivity to NED among many civil society groups in Central America. Another was that, in the United States, the Republicans and the Democrats have until recently been less ideological than parties in Europe and to an extent Latin America. The *Stiftung model*, partially imposed on Germany after World War II by the winning powers wanting to ensure Germany stayed democratic, did not prove replicable in the United States.

But while times and modalities change, and specific situations differ, I remain convinced that the best way to support democratic practices is to support institutional development at home and abroad, with a primary focus on education and training open to all. Almost certainly, the best way to insulate support for democracy from partisan and national politics is to use multilateral institutions to provide relevant training and support in a multinational environment. This insight, however, came to me later in my career, when I dealt with the Organization of American States (OAS) and learned that working multilaterally is not just speeches and consultations, but requires actually participating with others in implementation.

*Q: What other issues did PPC tend to be active on during your time there? Did PPC play a strong role in counternarcotics work? Was there an assistance unit then?*

EINAUDI: PPC had no assistance unit. We covered narcotics, but illegal drugs were not the focus in the 1980s that they became later. At one point or another PPC had a finger in just about everything except economics, which was the purview of the bureau's economic office, ECP. I have a check list from 1988 that shows PPC officers covered country issues, IMET, arms transfers and other military relationships, refugees, terrorism, human rights, UN General Assembly issues, OAS liaison, nuclear non-proliferation, and a study of Latin Americans studying in the United States in comparison to those studying in the Soviet bloc and Cuba. Congressional reports, certifications and even constituent correspondence took up inordinate time and effort in certain periods.

I personally enjoyed exchanges of views with foreign governments, something I had pushed in S/P. While in PPC, I attended several NATO experts' meetings on Latin America in Brussels. In addition to introducing me to a new set of security classifications, including the feverish COSMIC, those meetings made me very aware of the limits set on intelligence exchanges with our Latin American colleagues. We did not share political intelligence with our neighbors in the Western Hemisphere, but we routinely exchanged views about them with our European allies. I also organized consultations with Japan. In Tokyo, these proved more formal than substantive, but gave Terry Todman a chance to reminisce about his Army service as a draftee during our occupation immediately after the war.

In the late 1980s, I can't remember the years, I lectured regularly in the departmental seminar for new ambassadors, then being conducted by the former child actress and diplomat Shirley Temple Black and former assistant secretary and ambassador to Brazil Tony Motley. What I remember most was the shock of political appointee ambassadors at being told that they would represent the United States, not just the president, and that in practice their immediate boss would be not the president or even the secretary of state but the regional assistant secretary.

*Q: What can you tell us about our intervention in Grenada?*

EINAUDI: One of Tony Motley's first acts when he took over ARA as Assistant Secretary in the summer of 1983 was to assemble Bureau staff and tell us he wanted to wean us from our "obsession with Central America," which he considered small and of limited economic potential. Tony had lived in Brazil as a young man and had just served there as Ambassador. He made it a point that he wanted to shift attention to South America, which was less controversial and economically more important. Thus, it was an extraordinary irony that three months after he took office ARA was intensely focused, not on South America and its hundreds of millions, or even on the continuing Central American conflicts, but on a tiny Caribbean island of some 80,000 people.

*Q: More than an irony, wasn't Grenada something of a surprise?*

EINAUDI: Indeed. Our intervention in Grenada that October caught the Bureau almost as unprepared as it did the country and the world. But not Terry Kleinkauf. She had started her Foreign Service career as a consular officer in Haiti. She learned Creole there to go with her French and demonstrated the greatest gifts a diplomat needs: the ability to respect and understand others. When Maurice Bishop was executed on October 19 as the troubles in Grenada took the unexpectedly nasty turn that led to President Reagan's decision to act, the Bureau became totally engaged in the crisis operation. And we were also faced with huge gaps in public as well as private knowledge. And that is where Terry stepped up. Terry used her position as my Deputy Director in ARA/PPC to immediately insist that we ask the Prime Minister of Dominica, Eugenia Charles, to come to Washington to appear with President Reagan when he announced the landings in Grenada on the morning of October 25.

*Q: How did that happen? I mean, State Department bureaus aren't usually at the center of action in Washington.*

EINAUDI: Central America was a freelancer's paradise, but the Grenada emergency put ARA at the center of the action. And Tony Motley was a street fighter. He knew the military, having spent ten years in the U.S. Air Force, including an assignment in the Canal Zone, had good political instincts and connections (Senator Ted Stevens of Alaska was a good friend) and, above all, was an operator. In PPC we were crashing, putting together talking points for the President to use in announcing the landings, but we knew how utterly unprepared American audiences would be for massive U.S. military action in a country few had even heard of. The Organization of Eastern Caribbean States (OECS) was asking for our support. Eugenia Charles was its chairman. Largely unknown outside the Caribbean, she was Dominica's first woman lawyer and had been Prime Minister for three years. What Terry Kleinkauf brought to the table was the personal knowledge that Eugenia was a formidable and no-nonsense presence. And was Terry ever proved right. The lady from the Caribbean had flown in from Barbados just a few hours earlier, but she stole the show from the great communicator, even correcting the President when he referred to the action as an invasion: "Not an invasion," Eugenia Charles interrupted Ronald Reagan, "we asked for support." [The video of their joint press conference of October 25, 1983 is available on U-Tube.]

*Q: The whole episode seems almost unreal.*

EINAUDI: Well, it certainly proves that having good Foreign Service officers, both on the ground and integrated into a functioning system in Washington, can make a critical difference to how we use our power, and hence to our national wellbeing. [Therese A. Kleinkauf passed away in Maine in December 2019.]

*Q: Yes, but what about our action itself? Did you favor it?*

EINAUDI: I had gotten home from a trip to Italy on a Friday night and was called in to the Department on Saturday morning to begin drafting public statements for something that had not been definitely decided, but was likely for Monday or Tuesday. I had no prior notice, and no opportunity for judgment or influence on the basic decision. Secretary Shultz, with strong support from Tony Motley, others in the Bureau and the members of the OECS, overrode doubts from Weinberger, the Defense Department and Margaret Thatcher to convince the White House, which was happy to be able to act after the frustrations of Central America. When I later visited Grenada accompanying Shultz, I learned nothing to suggest we had made a mistake. There had been chaos, there had been Cuban and Bloc military presence, there had been U.S. students at risk. Looking back, the whole episode seems as much a unique event as it does part of a broader pattern in the Cold War, US military history, or even hemispheric or Caribbean relations. But it certainly reaffirmed belief in the Monroe Doctrine, which I consider damaging to our interests in today's world.

*Q: Just out of curiosity, were you in the Shultz motorcade when it was bombed in Bolivia?*

EINAUDI: It was Aug 8, 1988. We had just landed in La Paz and were driving down from the airport. First Shultz, the Assistant Secretary and the Ambassador, then the doctors and nurses, then us strap hangers. The blast blew out the windows of the medical van but little else. The motorcade accelerated and went in a panic to a predetermined safe-house where we were greeted by an American in civvies with an Uzi who said "Welcome to Bolivia." That is one of the few dates I remember because it was 8-8-88 and Terry Kleinkauf immortalized it by designing a deep blue T-shirt emblazoned with the date and the slogan **BOLIVIA, A DYNAMITE COUNTRY!** We ordered enough of the shirts that we sold some for a couple of years after that to the members of the Marine Security detachment at the Embassy in La Paz. I personally delivered one of them to Shultz (the delivery was reported in a front-page news summary tic on the *Wall Street Journal*, revealing the substantive relevance of what is sometimes reported as news).

*This OEA-CIAV (OAS) vehicle was hit by a rocket during the contra demobilization in 1990. I was a strong backer of CIAV but was thankfully not present when this occurred. (Organization of American States (OAS), 1990, photograph reproduced with permission of the General Secretariat of the Organization of American States.)*

In addition to 8-8-88, I was bombed or shot at three other times. Once, in Peru as in Bolivia, the blast was aimed at the person I was accompanying, that time Henry Kissinger. That bomb shattered the façade of the old American Embassy on Avenida Arequipa in Lima. The other two occasions, both in Lima in the days of *Sendero Luminoso,* were aimed at me. One was a bomb set off outside the building in which I was giving a talk to a large audience. That blast was followed by a brief exchange of fire as the security guards fired at the assailants. Inside, we heard everything, but I remembered Justice Holmes' adage that one should not shout fire in a crowded theatre, so I hesitated, then just kept talking and only a few people scattered. The second time, also in Lima, was a drive-by shooting at the American embassy during a dinner in my honor. As the bullets whizzed overhead, I dove under the table and found myself on the floor next to Javier Diez Canseco, a Peruvian intellectual and former guerrilla turned politician, in whose hand a revolver had materialized. "Have to be ready," he answered my startled gaze. I was as upset at the laxness of embassy security within as without. When I went back to my bedroom, I found bullets that had entered the window. As a footnote, a Peruvian newspaper on a later occasion printed a photo of me arriving at the presidential palace alone without a security detail with the comment, "the security crisis has obviously passed."

# USOAS

*Q: Today is 13 December 2013 with Luigi Einaudi. Luigi, I would like to turn to the OAS. How did your appointment to the OAS come about?*

EINAUDI: In 1989, Central America was falling apart, and U.S. policy was falling apart with it. The incoming administration, being Republican, had the trappings of continuity, but George H.W. Bush and Jim Baker knew that they needed to change course from the Reagan policies. They understood they needed political and diplomatic support to strengthen U.S. positions and negotiate an end to dead-end conflicts. Their first step was to name Bernie Aronson the assistant secretary for Latin America. Aronson was a Democrat with good ties to democratic organizations, the Hill, and labor. He was also a very bright and determined man.

*Carol and I with President George H.W. Bush, November 18, 1992. (David Valdez, official White House photograph, 1992.)*

This recasting meant working in bipartisan fashion domestically and at the same time trying to obtain support from other countries by taking multilateralism seriously. The OAS was an obvious choice, because the U.S. not only belonged but was its major contributor. Somebody said, well let's try Einaudi. One reason my name came up at all is that I was threatening to quit. I had for my sins over the years often been made the State Department keeper for various people of prominence when they went off to Latin America, among them Andy Young and first lady Rosalynn Carter. In this case the person that I was asked to accompany was Dan Quayle. Quayle immediately identified me with Jim Baker, whom he considered his jailer because Baker had kept him under wraps during the campaign. Then Bush won. The new administration hadn't even found their way to the bathrooms yet and they had to send somebody to the Venezuelan inauguration.

It was two or three days after the American inauguration, and the incoming president was Carlos Andrés Pérez, a man who threw a lot of weight around. He was sometimes a key U.S. ally but at the same time potentially a major troublemaker. Dan Quayle was asked to represent us and I was assigned to be his State Department keeper, just as twelve years before I had been asked to accompany Andrew Young to the Caribbean and to prepare Rosalynn Carter for her trip to Latin America (her intelligent request to me had been "teach me where the mines are so that I can avoid them").

*Q: What was Quayle's problem?*

EINAUDI: Quayle's problem was that he equated me with Jim Baker. I represented the State Department. Baker had become Secretary of State. So Quayle took out his Baker resentment on me.

*Q: Well, Quayle came across as being not the brightest bulb on the Christmas tree.*

EINAUDI: I was a good personal friend of the incoming Venezuelan president, Carlos Andrés Pérez. After the swearing in ceremony, Quayle went to call on him with me in tow. Pérez saw me and came rushing forward to give me a hug. Quayle reached across me, grabbed the door and slammed it in my face to keep me out of the meeting. I had been directing the policy planning office of the ARA bureau for 12 years, a record then and still today. Most of that time I had no career status, either as an FSO or civil servant. I liked the job and I did it to the best of my capacities. I didn't mind that the work was hard or that I had no promotion prospects. The Department leadership did what you always do when you can't reward anybody with a promotion; you give them prizes and I had more than my share. But now the Quayle indignity was too much. I came back to Washington and said to everyone I am going to get out. I am not going to accept being humiliated. I had never run for office so I had no doubt politicians had the right to do whatever they wanted to me, but I would not accept being humiliated.

That is when somebody said, "All right. It is time. Maybe you can be ambassador to the OAS and be part of this reorientation of things for Central America." Bob Zoellick later told me that someone had questioned my suitability but "we decided your Italianness should not be held against you." When Jim Baker called me in to offer the job, I raised a different objection: "When you vet me politically you are going to discover that I am a lifelong registered Democrat." Baker laughed and said, "It doesn't matter; you are the best man for the job so we are going to go ahead." Very different of course from certain other things that happened, both before and after. Then Jesse Helms put me on his "hold" list, and I had to wait nine months for a Senate hearing because Helms wouldn't allow it to be scheduled. His senior staffer, Jim Lucier, interviewed me and asked how long I had been in Washington. When I told him, he responded: "I see we have both been in Washington about 15 years. I have never met you before. That means *you* travel in the wrong circles." I survived, but it did not always feel good.

*Q: Before we get into that I want to go back a bit. You went on this trip with Dan Quayle, and Dan Quayle, particularly in the early days, was sort of an object of fun. You know, to put it politely he was considered pretty much a lightweight and a surprise for why did George Bush pick him, a senator from Indiana. What was your evaluation? What did you think about him?*

EINAUDI: I always like to try to look on the best side of people and as I said before it is not my job to challenge politicians. My job as I saw it was more to mediate between them and the professional bureaucracy. But I didn't think much of him. In my mind Quayle became the ultimate poster boy for attention deficit disorder. As you know, government meetings can be confusing: by the time you get the principal and his staff and the people that are invited in to do the briefing, it is hard to keep the meeting under ten to twelve people. He did not like that, he just couldn't stick to a topic for very long, so it was very hard to get through to him.

I found no shortage of raw intelligence. He was bright enough, but he lacked focus and cultural background. Quayle had a very low golf handicap, maybe a 2 or a 3. I don't play golf, but Tony Motley does, and he told me that nobody can maintain a handicap that low without playing golf virtually full time. I think Quayle's mind was probably on golf. I remember standing on a balcony at the American embassy in Caracas with his chief of staff. The U.S. embassy residence in Caracas is up in the hills and as we leaned on the railing looking out, a spectacular view of city skyscrapers opened out before us. The guy turns to me and says, "I never imagined there would be a modern city like this. That there would be something like this out here." In a sense Quayle and his people typified some of the weaknesses of Americans facing the rest of the world when they aren't lucky enough to have had the kind of exposure, training, and education to let them know about it. They just assume the outside world doesn't exist. And if it does exist, that it is all some horrible backward place filled with incompetents. Traveling with Quayle was a very revealing experience. Wondering why George H.W. Bush chose him is spot on.

*Q: Well one of the things that almost all of us in the Foreign Service saw in George H.W. Bush was an extremely competent foreign affairs manager. He and actually Richard Nixon. They had their problems, to say the least. But in the foreign affairs field, these are two people who are rather outstanding.*

EINAUDI: I agree with that judgment. Nixon had the good fortune of having Henry Kissinger and Bush had Jim Baker. Unfortunately, I think both Nixon and Kissinger had fundamental character flaws that undid part of their legacy and their effort. Of course, so did Clinton. The presidency is a difficult business. What was interesting about George H.W. Bush, whom I got to know a fair bit, is that he actually cared about foreign affairs and about the people and their problems. During our parting conversation at the White House when he was leaving office, he asked me what was going to happen in Haiti and what could be done. He asked with real caring and interest. Then he shrugged his shoulders and said, "well, it is the next man's problem now." But while it was his problem, he really worried about it. This is a very big difference from his son. When I met with the second President Bush at the start of his administration, W. concluded our discussion on Haiti saying he was glad dealing with Haiti was not his problem. That is a totally different attitude. I don't know why or where W. got that attitude because his parents were both caring people. I have a lot of respect for them.

*Q: Well his father later teamed up with Clinton and the two former presidents worked on Haitian relief.*

EINAUDI: That is true. Not very successfully or even intelligently in my view. I'm not sure shipping bottled water from Florida to

Haiti was a good use of resources. The money could have gone toward building a water purification and bottling plant in Haiti.

*Q: Anyway, let's go back. Was the hold on you by Jesse Helms just that you were a Democrat and or had there been policy flashes between the senator and you and the State Department?*

EINAUDI: Throughout the Reagan period Helms had sought to put his people into the department to run Latin American affairs. Equally firmly, the career people had resisted. For a dozen years, starting in the mid 70's, assistant secretaries would last just about a year. The turnover was appalling. And through it all Helms staffers led by Jim Carbaugh and Debbie De Moss wanted to come in to take senior positions in the Department and Helms was pressing to get them in. By and large he failed. The political appointees that Shultz and others did accept into the bureau as DASes (Deputy Assistant Secretaries of State) tended to be moderates, not those focused like laser beams on advancing their personal ties and partisan politics in Latin America.

With Helms himself, I ultimately wound up reaching some accommodations. He asked some basic questions. One of them was, why bother having a U.S. ambassador at the OAS when we didn't seem to be doing anything there? He was right in the sense that we had been ignoring multilateral cooperation. Therefore, why bother to send an ambassador? As a result, the Organization had been largely taken over by other members. When I was finally able to take office, I found that the OAS was being run by the Brazilian Secretary General with half-a-dozen ambassadors from the Rio Group. Helms' point was why should we subsidize an operation that we are not using and where people in charge don't follow our policy line. I agreed on that, but countered that U.S.

national interests could only be advanced proactively, not by sticking our heads in the sand.

Helms ultimately became my ally on an issue very important to the OAS. The OAS people felt like illegal aliens because the United States had never given them diplomatic status by establishing a Headquarters agreement defining their rights and duties. Most international organizations, including the IMF, World Bank and Interamerican Development Bank (IDB) in Washington were covered by a general treaty but did not have recognized rights of their own. Since the OAS is a political organization run by foreign ministries, the question of legal status really mattered. It is ironic: the United States is probably the most law-abiding country in the world, but we often don't care much about formalities. Some of the ambassadors to the OAS, the Uruguayan in particular, were legal sticklers. They felt that the lack of status was insulting and demeaning. I went to the Department's Legal Adviser, and, with the support of that office (called L for short), I asked Catherine Brown from Legal Affairs and Rich Douglas, a USOAS political officer and ex submariner who was also a lawyer, to negotiate a Headquarters agreement for the OAS.

It was complicated, but when it was finished, it was done to everybody's satisfaction. I was given the authority to sign it for the United States, and Helms actually took the lead in getting it ratified. It was the first status agreement for an international organization ratified by the Senate since the UN agreement in the 1950s. It improved the views of the Latins toward us because it demonstrated an element of taking them seriously and with respect. The OAS Secretary General, the Brazilian Baena Soares, who had kept saying that being treated like an illegal alien made him feel like one, couldn't have been happier. I was very pleased and proud.

*Q: What caused Helms to take that course?*

EINAUDI: Jesse Helms was the only U.S. senator who refused to vote to condemn the Argentines when they invaded the Falklands in 1982. Everyone else supported the British. The invasion of the Falklands was an exercise in Argentine national arrogance and misperceptions born of their isolation. But Helms had some Argentine ties. I never knew quite what they were. I probably met him more often at dinners at the Argentine embassy than I did in the Senate or anywhere else. Whatever those ties were, they led him to think in terms of the primary importance of the hemisphere. It was almost as though he was a throwback to the Fortress America people before WWII. Helms believed geography matters. He was almost like a military guy in that respect. When I point out that we owe our ability to project power around the world in part to having peaceful neighbors like Canada and Mexico, most people answer that geography doesn't matter: the jet plane is shrinking the world, transportation costs in foreign trade are going down, *et cetera*.

Helms understood that geography still matters in many ways. Among American conservatives I think there is some space for the proposition that the world out there is awfully big and has an awful lot of problems, so it may be necessary for us to count on this hemisphere, not just as our backyard as some people unfortunately call it, but also as our foundation, our base for times of trouble. There were people who felt that way at the time of Iraq. Then Mexico and Chile, the two Latin American rotating members of the UN Security Council, refused to vote Chapter VII authority to invade Iraq. Some conservatives in the second Bush administration and elsewhere felt betrayed. They had felt we would have to fall back on the Western Hemisphere if our Middle Eastern and Asian adventures proved unsuccessful, so they were really put off and angered. But what Arthur Whitaker used to call the Western Hemisphere ideal is largely dead in the world in which we now live. Helms saw the hemisphere as our strategic reservoir, and although his reasoning was often very different from that of many of our neighbors, he also had some things in common with their criticisms of the U.S. government.

*Q: OK, back to the OAS. When you took it on what did you see? How effective was this as an instrument of our projecting our influence?*

EINAUDI: I saw myself as correcting our failure to use multilateralism to advance U.S. interests. I focused my swearing in statement on creating legitimate international frameworks for U.S. policy. I asked Larry Eagleburger to swear me in; he was Deputy Secretary and thus the highest-ranking Foreign Service Officer, at least politically.

*At my swearing in as U.S. Permanent Representative to the OAS. From the left, Peter, Mary Urban Peacock, Mario, Elisabeth, Maria, Carol, Luigi, Larry Eagleburger, and my parents, Manon Michels Einaudi, Mario Einaudi. (US State Department photo, 1989.)*

I had gone to see him one Saturday to ask for his support for the OAS post. Larry looked up, saw me wearing a bright red sweater (in honor of the old State tradition that we look like undertakers on weekdays and undergraduates on weekends), and joked "I always knew you were a Communist." Amazingly, five hundred people came to my swearing in, including some forty Ambassadors, from Europe as well as the Americas, and many of these were bilateral Ambassadors to the U.S. as well as to the OAS. So many came that Secretary Baker gave a lunch ten days later for the OAS ambassadors and brought the President. The wags had it that there had been so many people in the Ben Franklin room during my swearing in that the ceiling had trembled in the Secretary's office on the floor below. A lot of people follow the election returns, as the fabled Mr. Dooley once said of the Supreme Court.

*Q: That must have been a change for the OAS!*

EINAUDI: Indeed. As I had told Baker in my nomination interview, the OAS had many people who would be happy to work with us in return for a little attention. When I first went there in 1989, our mission to the OAS had to be experienced to be believed. The Mission was physically located in the Department on the fifth floor, but it might as well have been on the moon. The Ambassador's office was the old secondary office of the secretary of state. John Foster Dulles had used it as his hideaway office. One of my predecessors, former Senator (and sometime history professor) Gale McGee, had built in bookcases. It was a very nice representational office, with its own private bathroom. But it might as well have been on Mars. My predecessor as U.S. Permanent Representative, Dick McCormack communicated with the Secretary of State by writing letters. When I first went to my new office, my wife joked that S/P had been on the Seventh Floor, ARA/PPC on the sixth, so that I had only four more floors to go to hit bottom.

When I left in 1993, Mission staff gave me a mock OAS-style resolution, numbered 8010 to mock our greatest accomplishment, Resolution 1080, about which more later. This fun caricature in words captures many elements of the atmosphere in the U.S. Mission to the OAS during my time there, 1989-1993.

# USOAS

U.S. Permanent Mission to the
Organization of American States
Department of State, ARA/USOAS
Washington, D.C. 20520
(202) 647-9376

## Mission Resolution Honors Ambassador Einaudi

### RESOLUTION 8010
(AG/Res.Doc.PC/GA/Spec., April 16, 1993)

**WHEREAS:**

It has come to our attention that one Luigi R. Einaudi, erstwhile Professor of Government at Harvard University and once an analyst at the Rand Corporation, later to find favor with a heavily-accented German fellow who invited him into the labyrinth of policy planners, whence he joined the Bureau of Inter-American Affairs to do battle with rebels and revolutionaries, with liberals and conservatives -- to say nothing of his interlocutors from other countries -- and then to be named Ambassador, Permanent Representative to the Organization of American States;

**ACKNOWLEDGING:**

That before he arrived the United States Mission was truly a backwater, an isolated outpost lacking in amenities, without any form of communication with the "front office," to which officers were only occasionally assigned and those few oft never heard from again;

**CONSIDERING:**

That in keeping with his motto "paper has no legs," legs soon appeared on all sorts of diverse functionaries, ranging from the Ambassador himself through officers and secretaries and even program assistants, charged with delivering and obtaining action on said paper;

**RECALLING:**

That during his incumbency, the United States Mission to the OAS has flowered, attaining power, prestige, new personnel, a fax machine, two flags and newly upholstered furniture;

**TAKING INTO ACCOUNT:**

That before his arrival, the OAS could only be blamed for lethargy, while now thanks to its new-found activism it can be held to account not only for failing to get Noriega out of Panama but also for not getting don Daniel out of Nicaragua, the FMLN out of El Salvador, Fujimori out of Peru, Cedras out of Haiti, Castro out of Cuba, corruption out of Venezuela, Bouterse out of Suriname, the PRI out of Mexico, amnesty out of Argentina, trade disputes out of Brazil, grapes out of Chile, Rodriguez out of Paraguay, the maritime problem out of Bolivia, Escobar out of Colombia, Quebec out of Canada, the EC banana policy out of the Caribbean, and the U.S. out of the OAS;

**THEREFORE, BE IT RESOLVED:**

To confer upon our colleague Luigi R. Einaudi the title of Itinerant Ambassador to the Hemisphere, Promoter of Democracy, Dialoguer among Civilians and the Military, Defender of Human Rights, and Conciliator between Disputants (borders or otherwise),

And to wish him well in his new endeavors.

*Presented to me by my USOAS Mission staff on my departure, 1993. (Courtesy of LR Einaudi, personal photograph.)*

*Q: OK, but how were you able to change things? Did you really make it work?*

EINAUDI: One of the reasons I was effective at the OAS was NOT that I spoke Spanish and French fluently, and could manage Portuguese, the other OAS official language, and NOT that I knew a lot about Latin America and the Caribbean, but that I knew something about how to make the U.S. government function. I wasn't just sitting around not doing anything and not producing anything for the United States or for the organization. I think our system fundamentally undervalues multilateral institutions. The State Department places a great deal of emphasis on the maximizing of U.S. power through bilateral relations. We are bigger and stronger and often better organized than any other country, so our natural inclination is to take them on one by one, bilaterally. My predecessor as Director of ARA/PPC, Richard Bloomfield, liked to say that we tend to see organizations like the OAS as the trade unions of the weak, which work like a dumbbell -- with us at one end and all the rest grouped at the other end trying to balance us out, Lilliputians banded together to try to snare old Gulliver. My own approach to life is different: it is good to be strong, but also better to be thought the underdog than the super dog. One of the ways that a superpower can show respect is to talk to people within a setting of sovereign equality. The OAS is an ideal setting for that. It is where St. Lucia or Antigua or Uruguay can speak to the United States on an equal footing and with equal rights. The OAS is in that sense an extraordinary vehicle for the United States to show respect and even interest in smaller countries. Or, as an Argentine ambassador put it to me, working at the OAS was like taking a promenade around the hemisphere because you get to learn about countries and situations that are totally different from your own and from each other.

*Q: But don't the differences mean there can never be a meaningful common denominator, that common action is impossible?*

EINAUDI: The policy objective is to achieve a broad common framework, so that implementing actions -- whether taken by a smaller subgroup of countries, bilaterally or even unilaterally -- are not intervention so long as they are seen as in accordance with that framework. We have a special record of throwing our weight around in Latin America. A powerful country like the United States should not look as if it is flaunting international law as we did in mining Nicaragua's harbors in 1983. For the new Administration to give the OAS some attention was largely symbolic at first, but symbolism and psychology matter in politics. Factoring the OAS into our diplomacy was a way of showing that we were changing our approach and orientation.

*Q: How did you do that, specifically?*

EINAUDI: I started where they were, with the endless talking. I found myself enjoying the give and take of speeches. I had learned the importance of participation. In 1975, a Meeting of Foreign Ministers in Ecuador designed to lift collective OAS sanctions on Cuba failed, and the head of our delegation never spoke. I had stayed up all night trying to craft something for the Deputy Secretary to say, but had been unable to find a formula that would reconcile our own conflicting interests. Our silence was noted as hostile. I applied that lesson when I became our man at the OAS, by trying to use the position as a bully pulpit. I would take advantage of major news events to make statements in the Permanent Council that I thought would help get our views across. I found myself quoting the formula *Panamericanismo democrático sin imperio* (democratic Pan Americanism without empire) used by the Peruvian Victor Raúl Haya de la Torre when he sought to justify supporting the United States in World War II. The personalist Latin cultural traditions made mourning deaths a natural vehicle. I gave a eulogy expressing our respect for Alberto Lleras Camargo, who had been a Secretary General of the OAS as well as President of Colombia. When I took the Council floor to eulogize Thurgood Marshall and announce the schedule for his memorial service, the Chilean Chair responded by declaring that Justice Marshall's fight for civil liberties was "in the best tradition of the OAS Charter" and called for a minute of silence, after which the representatives of St. Vincent and the Grenadines, Mexico, and Costa Rica made similar extemporaneous remarks and the session got underway with a sense of solidarity and shared purpose.

Returning to why I was named to the OAS, we were able to generate critical support through the OAS for two key issues that had bedeviled U.S. policy on Nicaragua. One was the elections that removed the Sandinistas from power; the second was peacefully demobilizing the large Contra forces the United States had been supporting against the Sandinistas. Looked at in terms of the extrication policy of the United States at the time, the OAS proved critically useful. It took an awful lot of work and patience, but debates and dialogues can be used to communicate policy, to gain acceptance for it, and in certain instances even to obtain needed operational support.

Q: *Well now, the OAS, I envision sitting around a big long table and saying OK what does Uruguay have to say; what does the United States have to say; what does Belize have to say? I mean how did that work in actual meetings and real situations?*

EINAUDI: There are two parts to the OAS. One is the Permanent Council, the long table around which the countries' representatives sit in proud sovereign equality – including deciding when and whether to speak. Then there is the General Secretariat, run by the Secretary General, which serves the Council and implements the organization's policies. The activities in Nicaragua, the election observation and the OAS-CIAV operation which demobilized the Contras, were activities undertaken by the Secretariat to implement decisions taken by the Permanent Council. The Permanent Council is exactly as you put it, a meeting among representatives of sovereign states. There are 35 member states (including Cuba, which has not participated since 1962). To emphasize sovereign equality and reduce the importance of relative size or power, the Chairmanship of the Permanent Council lasts only three months and rotates in alphabetical order. This means that virtually as soon as the Chair learns his or her job, he or she moves on. So in a sense it is a recipe for permanent institutionalized chaos.

*Luigi — Only prayer works here! Eagleburger*

*Then Deputy Secretary Eagleburger listening to the OAS Permanent Council debate U.S. charges against Panama's Noriega. "Only prayer works here" perfectly catches the reactions of many outside observers to the convoluted legalisms of OAS debates. (US State Department photo, 1989, gift of Larry Eagleburger.)*

It is possible to control that chaos—but it takes time and patience. The hemisphere breaks down naturally into geographic subregions: South America, the Caribbean, Central America, Mexico, the United States and Canada. The subregions coordinate among themselves: the Caribbeans have CARICOM, the Central Americans have SICA [the Central American Integration System]. The South Americans have called themselves different things at different times and sometimes include Mexico, sometimes not. Hashing out problems in advance within these subregional groups can simplify matters greatly. In theory, whoever is the chair of a particular group should speak for that group. Ideally, we would then have only a handful of speeches on any one subject. But even when the group agrees on a common position that will be represented by X, many of X's fellow group members take the floor and say the same thing anyway. So you can wind up with 25 speeches when five would have done. This is the side that outsiders see, and this what most outsiders find utterly uninteresting and useless -- just a talk shop.

*Q. Just the point.*

EINAUDI: Indeed. And this impression is accentuated because when there is disagreement, the Council meeting is typically suspended while the issue is resolved in private. No outsider ever hears anything of the private arguments. Council debates also tend to become sterile for other reasons. Sometimes, even if little is to be decided, everybody wants to be heard. Sometimes an ambassador has to speak for his own home press even if not for his fellows or the American press. News organizations in the United States generally make it a point to ignore OAS debates, but there can be ample coverage in other countries. Of course, the fact that it doesn't show up in the American press leads some, the Brazilians, for example, to say what is said at the OAS doesn't matter. "Unless we see it in the *New York Times* we don't take it seriously." There is nothing more maddening than sitting in the council chamber and listening to speech after repetitive speech.

*Q. But do these speeches matter, given the power of the United States?*

Actually, they matter precisely because of the power of the United States. President Menem of Argentina once referred to OAS debates as a *"caja de resonancia"*, a "sounding board" for the hemisphere. If you know how to listen, you can learn an enormity about public opinion and different national interests. And even a country as disproportionately powerful as the United States needs to consider the views of others if it expects to succeed over the long term.

But you have touched on a key issue: the power of the United States. It is far and away the hemisphere's most powerful and richest country. Even with Canada and Mexico, the rise of Brazil, and the substantial economic weight of Argentina and others -- the United States accounts for about 80% of the economic weight of the hemisphere. We used to pay two thirds of the budget of the OAS. In my time as Ambassador, I took advantage of Canada's entry to the OAS to get our share reduced to 60%, 59 point something. A bill has since been passed in Congress suggesting that our quota should go down to 50%. Nothing wrong with that. I believe everybody should bear the weight of the cost of an organization like this. The key thing is whether the organization has anything to do. What has happened over the years is that the OAS is assigned tasks known as mandates, and then given no resources with which to work on them. The most blatant example is the much-ballyhooed mandate to support democracy, after which resources for the OAS were sharply cut, making support for democracy impossible to implement, in fact making the OAS look bad.

The OAS was the vehicle through which the Alliance for Progress was agreed to and to some extent managed; the Inter-American Development Bank grew out of political decisions that were taken at the OAS. But then followed a long period of reduced U.S. interest. I was named ambassador there as part of a policy decision to disentangle the U.S. from the Central American wars with as much dignity as possible, working in tandem with the UN and other multilateral organizations. The OAS for a while became a way to deal with Haiti. But since 9/11, U.S. policy has basically been to ignore the organization; it has had no purpose for it, and therefore in a sense even the money is not particularly useful. Recently the OAS appears reduced to being just an insurance policy for a future day when we once again might decide there is a purpose there.

In Spanish, OAS is OEA, which stands for *Organización de los Estados Americanos*. Some say OEA should stand for "*Olvídate de Este Asunto*," or "Forget about this matter." And handing off a hot potato or a boring problem to the OAS or the UN so they can themselves forget about it is unfortunately a good description of the approach of some governments, including ours. This approach can elicit venom. Mario Vargas Llosa, still stung by his defeat by Alberto Fujimori in Peru's 1990 presidential election, called the OAS "*la inutilidad perniciosa*" (noxiously useless) for not reacting more strongly against irregularities in behalf of Fujimori in the 2000 election.

*Q: What about the staffing of our OAS Mission from the State Department. Was it hard to get good people there? Would they have preferred to be in a country?*

EINAUDI: Absolutely. The postings at my disposal at the OAS and PPC had one basic thing in common. They were off the individual country track. The bright stars of the Foreign Service political cone all wanted to be country desk officers and country directors, with country responsibilities that would put them in line for an ambassadorship. And the OAS Ambassadorship itself was by and large the preserve of political appointees. Ambitious FSOs did not see serving at the OAS as a useful career path. But I found some good officers already there and was able to recruit others.

These were people who enjoyed their work and were smart but weren't particularly on the ambassadorial track or were ambitious for that type of work.

One officer I really liked was already in the U.S. Mission to the OAS before I got there. He had been a Foreign Service officer until he decided that he didn't want to move from country to country anymore and transferred to the Civil Service. His name was Owen Lee. Owen took a keen interest in the OAS from a nuts-and-bolts organizational standpoint. He stabilized the OAS retirement system. It is interesting. Over the years, the U.S. has had some very good people associated with the OAS. Another such person was John Ford. John Ford was one of McCarthy's victims.

*Q: We are talking about Senator Joseph McCarthy of Wisconsin.*

EINAUDI: Joseph McCarthy of Wisconsin. He did an enormous amount of damage to the United States and to many institutions including the State Department; not just to the State Department and its people, but also to the image of America. It was worse than Abu Ghraib, worse than My Lai, and I choose two examples of the American system run terribly amuck.

*Q: A footnote here: Abu Ghraib was a scandal about an Iraqi prison and where those in authority, American Army people, abused the prisoners and My Lai was a massacre during the Vietnam War by American troops.*

EINAUDI: The reason I say McCarthy was worse than My Lai or Abu Ghraib is that people who are badly led and put into terrible and stressful situations will predictably come unglued at some point. Someone is going to snap. When that happens, it is a failure of individual leadership as well as a failure of policy. What

McCarthy did was a conscious policy failure: fanning inordinate fear of Communism for political ends to the detriment of people with other views. Foreign Service Officer John W. Ford was removed as Director of the Office of Security of the Department of State because he refused to give the McCarthy Committee access to the raw files of his office.

When I met him twenty years later, John had been exiled to the U.S. Mission to the OAS. But he was again playing key roles. John Ford coordinated the U.S. military response under the OAS flag to stop the fighting during the 1969 soccer war between El Salvador and Honduras. I was there when the final pylon marking that border was placed in 2006, with the help of the U.S. Army Mapping Agency working, again, under OAS auspices. Both the end of the fighting and the actual settlement of the underlying issue, almost forty years apart, attest to the utility of the OAS as a mechanism for conflict resolution. Regrettably, John died just as I took over the Mission. I had been looking forward to his counsel. The retiree discussion sessions held for twenty years at DACOR-Bacon House were called FLAG, the Ford Latin American Group, in his honor.

The staff I found at the Mission was a mix of Foreign Service, Civil Service, and political personnel. FSO Xenia Wilkinson proved an excellent Political Counselor, Barbara Bowie-Whitman was a politically aware economic officer, and civil servant Margarita Riva-Geoghegan, the daughter of original OAS staffers, was a knowledgeable guide to the inner workings of the Secretariat. A retired FSO working on contract, Jim Todd, acted as a universal pinch hitter. I added Dennis Skocz, who had worked with me in ARA/PPC. Dennis was one of those rarities, an officer who enjoyed abstractions, and could carry an idea from one day to the next. To give me the partisan political window and support I felt I would need, I chose the Republican Roger Noriega as my staff aide. Roger had been working with AID on Nicaragua among other things; he later moved on to a varied career, including as Ambassador to the OAS and Assistant Secretary for ARA. He did an excellent job for me at USOAS.

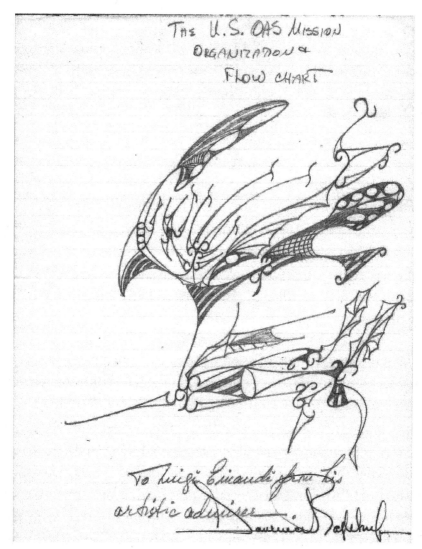

*Doodle drawn by Larry Eagleburger while listening to the OAS debate Panama, Fall 1989. (Gift of Larry Eagleburger, created for LR Einaudi, 1989)*

*Q: What about other countries' missions to the OAS?*

EINAUDI: They were rather good on the whole. Smaller countries depend on multilateralism more than we do. Being posted to Washington is an attraction. Some used the OAS as training grounds, sending promising younger diplomats on staff. And the Ambassadors themselves were often experienced career diplomats, although there were also a number of former politicians, almost never businesspeople, celebrities or former military. On the whole, their quality was good. Rarely, however, did the OAS missions get along well with their countries' missions to the White House. The Latin American ambassadors accredited to the White House generally sought to monopolize bilateral relations with the United States. This added to the isolation of the OAS, which sometimes seemed to be in Washington only by accident.

*Q: Today is 19 February 2014 with Luigi Einaudi. Luigi, we wanted to talk a bit about the difference between the Reagan and Bush administrations and their relations to the OAS and in general to Latin America.*

EINAUDI: Other than the Malvinas-Falklands war between Argentina and the UK, which probably cost Secretary of State Haig his job, relations with Latin America under Reagan were largely focused on Central America, not South America. We have spoken about El Salvador where the tensions between Tom Enders and Jeane Kirkpatrick played out most fully, with history ultimately vindicating Enders.

As the transition from Reagan to Bush took place, the Reagan policies in Central America, particularly in regard to Nicaragua and the Contras, had come to a dead end. I think Jim Baker wanted to get us out in a reasonable way as fast as possible. And this is when the OAS suddenly became part of the scene. But the first thing that happened was the confrontation with Manuel Noriega. Noriega had become the abusive dictator kingpin of Panama. Though I don't have personal knowledge of this, I believe Noriega had the kind of privileged relationship that Vladimiro Montesinos in Peru also developed with the Central Intelligence Agency. Noriega simply grew to be both too dictatorial, too big for his britches and in many ways incompetent. When elections were held in the spring of 1989 the assumption was that Noriega was going to rig them. What nobody anticipated was that he was going to be so incompetent that he would be defeated, and that he would be forced to repress the winners bloodily. The outside world was more interested in the troubles in Nicaragua and the isthmus to the north than what was happening in Panama, but Noriega's actions created international alarm.

*Q: On Panama, some have said the U.S. was determined to forcibly remove Noriega from power. Isn't that what happened?*

EINAUDI: Yes, that is what ultimately happened. But no, force was never the intent. Operation Just Cause took place only after Noriega's purposeful harassment of U.S. military personnel legally stationed in Panama turned to murder. Before that, we had made extraordinary efforts to remove him thorough negotiations, both bilateral and multilateral. I had always felt that the utility of an organization like the OAS lies mainly as a bully pulpit and creating a framework for action—sometimes by others, not necessarily acting itself. The Panama situation and our case against Noriega for drug running provided a good opportunity for the U.S. to shape regional opinion. Noriega had already been indicted in Florida. As the summer wore on, we made the drug indictment documentation and a lot of information available at a variety of

OAS meetings. The Colombians led an OAS mission to try to resolve the election impasse and get Noriega out of power. Things dragged on inconclusively. The ADST has a revealing oral history by John Bushnell about the Panama end of things.

Noriega was confident he could get away with constantly provoking and harassing our people. In the fall of 1989, while in limbo awaiting Senate confirmation to the OAS, I attended a Milgroup Commander's conference at U.S. Southern Command, then still located in the former Canal Zone. Most of us stayed in Panama City at the Hotel Intercontinental. One night there was a fire alarm. An unknown person had set off a smoke bomb in the hotel lobby. All of us visitors found ourselves in the street at 2 am in various states of undress. Standing next to me was Col. Jay Cope, who was in the process of transferring from Southcom to Washington as Bernie Aronson's military advisor. He said this was typical of the harassment from Noriega. Two months later, a U.S. officer was shot and killed along the old dividing line highway. Noriega had gone too far.

Assistant Secretary Aronson called me around midnight, December 20, an hour or so before the first paratroopers landed. He instructed me to advise the OAS Secretary General that this was happening. The OAS had been working to oust Noriega or at least resolve the electoral crisis, but our resort to unilateral military force brought out everyone's latent fears of U.S. imperialism. My job as U.S. ambassador became that of trying to soften the criticism and delay a response as long as possible, particularly since as you may remember, Noriega disappeared. We didn't find him right away. He ultimately wound up in the Nuncio's residence under diplomatic protection and had to be talked out of there. But for three or four days after our forces went in, we didn't know where he was, and we certainly did not want the OAS coming up with a critical resolution while he was still at large. I was fortunate that we had worked as hard in the course of the summer to educate people about Noriega's record and that I was able to keep postponing votes by going back over some of those materials.

The chairman of the Permanent Council was an oil man from Trinidad named Angus Khan. Khan was very able. I had presented my credentials to him little more than a month earlier. Speaking to me in private, he summed up his reaction, saying "You did the right thing, but you had no right." This of course put both the politics and the law in a nutshell. We managed to delay the vote until after Noriega was found, and happily for us the resolution "deplored" the U.S. action rather than condemning it.

The U.S. resort to military intervention was something of a surprise. Even Noriega was said to have thought nothing would happen until he actually saw the first U.S. paratroopers dropping out of the sky. Remember, there had not been a direct U.S. military action in the hemisphere since Grenada, six years before. U.S. rhetoric about Latin America since then had been pro-democracy and anti-military. Ironically, Canada had just joined the OAS precisely because they thought they no longer ran the risk of being tarred and feathered by being associated with U.S. interventionism in the hemisphere. For Canada, good bilateral relations with the U.S. are essential. They thought joining the OAS under the new circumstances would be a freebie, that they would not be embarrassed by U.S. behavior in Latin America. No sooner had they joined, than we invaded Panama. It was a very difficult moment for the Canadians.

*Q: What did the Canadian ambassador and others say to you about this?*

EINAUDI: The Canadian ambassador was in an impossible situation. The Latins wanted him to criticize us; the last thing the Canadian government wanted was to antagonize the U.S. over what for them was a secondary or even tertiary issue like Panama. Jean Paul Hubert was French Canadian, which added to his difficulty. His cultural background was one reason for his assignment, but Quebecois separatism now added to his vulnerability if he strayed from an official line. Together he and I walked a fine line. He needed to express criticism without disturbing our bilateral relations. I told the Canadian press that we in the United States were very pleased to have Canada's independent voice because it gave a broader perspective to the OAS, that we understood that they were concerned, and that we both wanted to ensure that things happened in a way that would enhance the rule of law in Panama. Hubert has since had quite a distinguished career, including as president of the Inter-American Commission of Jurists in Brazil, but Panama was a baptism of fire for both of us. He was very grateful for my support.

*Q: Well ok, let's go back to the main show, settling the Nicaraguan business. Although some things were apparently turned over to the OAS, I would think the United States would be involved more deeply. I mean we had the airplanes and the technical capability of doing all of that. We must have been involved in that, weren't we?*

EINAUDI: We provided key policy support and funding. But the U.S. was not involved operationally on the ground. The OAS Secretary General kept U.S. citizens off the OAS observation team because it was felt they would compromise its appearance of neutrality. The demobilization was largely handled by Venezuelan troops under control of OAS staff which was mainly Argentine. U.S. support for the OAS demobilization of the Contras was critical, initially in moral support and later with U.S. Congressional funding for rural human rights work to ensure fair treatment of the Contras after their demobilization. But U.S. personnel were little involved.

*Q: I am looking at time and we have to stop now. I would like to pick it up the next time at the point that the Sandinistas lost the election during your time there.*

*Q: OK, Today is 28 January 2014 with Luigi Einaudi. The Sandinistas were in power in Nicaragua; we were trying to get them out. An election was coming up, but how did we view the situation there?*

EINAUDI: By 1989, the issue for the United States was to somehow get out of the box that it had put itself in through support for the Contras and counter revolution in Nicaragua. It isn't that the Contras were untouchable mercenaries. Most Contras actually represented the popular classes and the peasants better than did the Sandinista leaders, who tended to be alienated and radicalized middle- and upper-class youths and intellectuals. But in aligning themselves with the Contras, the United States was perceived to have chosen the path of arms over the path of diplomacy, the path of force over the path of dialogue and reason. This had alienated the United States from the major Latin American countries, which had banded together in what was being called the Rio Group. Of the many fronts on which Secretary Baker organized diplomacy instead of war, the key was naming Bernard Aronson as Assistant Secretary of State. Aronson was a lifelong Democrat whose ties in Congress softened some of our domestic polarization over Central America.

My role was to help establish a multilateral framework that would gain support of the Western Hemisphere countries who felt their foreign policy principles had been violated. All of this came together in support of the elections in Nicaragua in 1990. The Sandinistas were sure they would win. It was a little like what happened to Pinochet in Chile. He thought he was going to win the referendum, allowed it, and lost—to his and to his wife's disbelief. In Nicaragua, we decided to go along with the Costa Ricans and the South Americans who felt this thing should be resolved with elections. The difference was that we were mainly looking for an exit strategy. We were faced with a growing mess. The Contras were not being defeated, but they were not winning, either, and the collateral damage was growing. I think that most Americans still do not realize that in the streets of Los Angeles among the exiles from Nicaragua and other young refugees from Central America and Mexico, tensions and gang warfare were growing and volunteers were being enlisted to go and fight on both sides in Nicaragua. So the Central American and Contra wars were poisoning aspects of U.S. life as well, although it was not widely reported or understood at the time.

We went into the Nicaraguan election thinking of it as an exit strategy. Nearly everybody thought the Sandinistas would win. A few days before the election the Sandinistas held a fantastic rally. More people participated in their rally than ultimately voted for them. Why did some people demonstrate for Ortega and the Sandinistas, and then not vote for them in the privacy of the voting booth? I don't know. But it happened. Before the election, Bernie Aronson was rather isolated in the U.S. government. In an ARA bureau staff meeting, the question was asked what do you think the outcome of this election will be? I think that Bernie and I were the only two who believed that the winner would be

Violeta Chamorro, the widow of the newspaperman who had been assassinated by Somoza's thugs in 1978.

*Q: And the OAS played a role?*

EINAUDI: Nicaragua was perhaps the first time the OAS put together an electoral observation mission that had real impact. The OAS Secretary General was Joao Clemente Baena Soares, a very experienced and canny diplomat out of the Brazilian noninterventionist school. He was not a favorite of the United States. In 1988, before my time as Ambassador, we had opposed his re-election until it became evident that we were the only ones who did; at that point we caved and voted for him. Baena didn't like the Sandinistas any more than we did. But he also knew that the big symbolic conflict had become Nicaragua versus the United States. So he said, OK, we are going to observe this election, but we are not going to involve any U.S. citizens. Our observation is going to be a professional observation done by Latin Americans.

Being, as some critics have said, a conjury of governments, the OAS has to work with the agreement of the government of whatever sovereign state in which it wishes to operate. Which in Nicaragua meant that the OAS worked so closely with the Sandinista-controlled electoral council that many thought the OAS was losing its independence and would wind up whitewashing a Sandinista victory. Separate American observers, including those associated with former President Carter, were militant and aggressive. But Baena stuck to his position that U.S. participation would undermine the credibility of the OAS with the Nicaraguans and with many others. The OAS fielded its first observers seven months before the elections, monitored the campaign throughout the country and deployed 433 persons on election day, helping to collect tally sheets from nearly all the 5,000 voting tables. As it turned out, the Sandinistas didn't get the votes, and the fact that the OAS was in the knickers of the electoral council meant that the Sandinistas had no wiggle room. Convinced they would win, the Sandinistas had allowed the OAS so much inside access they could not rig votes after the event to deny Violeta's win. Carter, being American, got a lot of credit. But the OAS was the key.

*Q: What about the disarming of the Contras? That sounds more like a job for the UN.*

EINAUDI: That is just what everyone thought. But there were several surprises. The Contras were not going to win a war, but they were still in control of territory. Honduras had become the operational base from which the Contras were organized and supported. Many Contra fighters were camped in Honduras near the Nicaraguan border, but some were also operating in rural Nicaragua where there had been a real war going on. It wasn't just an ideological war; it was also a class war. Most people have never figured out that while most of the Sandinista leaders were middle class intellectuals and professionals, the Contras were mainly peasants who didn't want to have their lives reorganized by people from the capital.

When it came time for demobilization, the general assumption was that the central job of disarming the Contras would be in Honduras, where most of them were encamped. So that job was given to the UN. The disarming in Nicaragua was given to the OAS. What happened in practice is that the Contras in Honduras went home with their arms to Nicaragua. There was no longer any fighting. They were just going home.

Miembros de la Resistencia Nicaragüense
en puntos claves para su desmovilización
Junio 6 , 1990

*Contra fighters waiting to demobilize and turn in their weapons under an OAS banner in June 1990. (Organization of American States (OAS), 1990, photograph reproduced with permission of the General Secretariat of the Organization of American States.)*

As a result, the big job of disarmament turned out to be in Nicaragua. There was no UN-OAS collaboration. The OAS is very jealous of its independent prerogatives and has always maintained a separate identity and its own chain of command and staffing. This has been notable in electoral observation and held true in Nicaragua as well. The OAS Charter contains no authority to use force like that given the UN by Chapter VII of its Charter. This limit originated in opposition to U.S. military interventions. It obviously precludes OAS actions in situations where some use of force from the international community might be required. But it does mean the OAS has genuine advantages where the main issues are political rather than military. In Nicaragua, the actual weapons collection was carried out with the help of advisors from the Venezuelan Army. But CIAV-OEA (*Comisión Internacional de Apoyo y Verificación*, International Commission of Support and Verification, 1990-1997) was an all-OAS operation, solely responsible for work inside Nicaragua, while the UN organization under Esquipulas, called ONUCA, had responsibility for Honduras. ONUCA lasted only a few months, there being nothing to do after the Contras returned to Nicaragua.

*I am in the center, in the blue CIAV-OEA shirt and cap, addressing former Contra members and families on their rights and obligations under the demobilization agreements. Quilalí, Nicaragua, September 1990.* (Alfred Barr, 1990, gift to LR Einaudi)

CIAV's outstanding work in the re-integration of the Nicaraguan peasants who had lined up with the Contras was led by two remarkable OAS staff members from Argentina, Santiago Murray and Sergio Caramagna. Senator Helms and his staff helped channel the funds to the OAS that made this possible. The role of the OAS-CIAV in pacification and support for human rights in rural areas stood the test of time and served as a model for later efforts to disarm the paramilitary groups in Colombia as part of Colombian peace efforts.

*Q: What had caused the optimism on the Sandinista side that they were going to win the election?*

EINAUDI: They controlled the standard levers of power. But most of all they were overconfident. Seeing yourself as the vanguard of history is one of the weaknesses of Leninist thinking. If you think you embody history, you think victory is inevitable, and can be blinded to the fact that how you rule also matters. The strengths of democracy and democratic procedures is that they tend to be inclusive. They are not perfect, but they give more people a chance to be heard. From the standpoint of cognitive awareness, a person raised in a pluralist and democratic tradition is much less likely to think of himself as always in the right and always expressing the will of the people. In political theory this debate goes back to J.L. Talmon and Hannah Arendt's focus on Rousseau's "popular will" as the root origin of what they call "totalitarian democracy." The Sandinistas were convinced that they were on the side of history and that they could not lose. But they did not account for the fact that they had not been able to develop the block committees and the other coercive foundations of Castro's Cuba that Chávez later copied in Venezuela.

*Q: Earlier you talked about Pinochet leaving office as a parallel to what happened in Nicaragua. Do you want to flesh that out more on what actually happened and what the U.S. position was?*

EINAUDI: What I said was that Pinochet and the Sandinistas both thought they would win. The parallel largely stops there, other than that the counting of the ballots was reasonably accurate in both countries. In Chile the vote was a referendum, Yes or No whether Pinochet should stay in office. In Nicaragua, it was an election for president. Those are two different questions in two totally different societies. Chile had a literate population, a diversified economy, and developed institutions. Nicaragua was a traditional agricultural society. Pinochet had been in power sixteen years, had grown the economy and marginalized the political far left. The Sandinistas had succeeded in displacing the Somozas and their supporters, but had been in power half that time, caught up in a deadlocked conflict with the United States, with a divided society and a ruinous economic situation. It is true that in both countries, opponents to the regime coalesced to the electoral center, thus being able to harvest support from a broad spectrum of groups. And in both cases, the opposition had considerable outside support. In Chile, U.S. policy was ambiguous. Largely supportive of Pinochet at first, it had moved toward official impartiality, allowing for both support and opposition. In Nicaragua, despite some support for the Sandinistas in progressive circles, U.S. policy was so hostile that the OAS Secretary General did not allow U.S. citizens to participate as election observers for fear of compromising the observation.

*Q: You mentioned earlier that one reason for your personal success at the OAS was that you knew how to make the U.S. government function properly. What did you mean by that?*

EINAUDI: Governing democratically has never been easy. Making governments work at all has been getting harder and harder. And just imagine what it might be like trying to make an organization work that is made up of thirty-odd governments!

The OAS is an organization of governments, and -- despite the variety of its entities and activities – of governments represented through their foreign ministries. This has important consequences. One is that the capacity of foreign ministries to represent their entire government varies greatly from country to country and issue to issue. Another is that since foreign ministries are part of the executive branch, they naturally tend to influence OAS bodies to side with executive authorities when they come into conflict with legislatures and courts. Importantly also, non-governmental actors and other civil society representatives participate in OAS activities only to the extent each member state allows.

USOAS, as the small U.S. Mission was called, had a total staff of 17, including secretaries and part-time retirees called WAEs and some accredited advisors from the departments of Defense, Commerce and Justice (but not counting links as needed to Treasury, Education and Agriculture). Our U.S. mission to the UN, by comparison, had a staff of 137. By the time I went to USOAS, Jeannie Rae Rogers, who had been with me in S/P and ARA/PPC, had moved on, but I was lucky and privileged to obtain a skilled senior secretary in Bernadette McCarron, who had both multilateral and private sector experience and was perfectly capable of fighting a multi-front war.

*Q: I thought you were a peaceful type, dedicated to negotiations. What do you mean by multifront war?*

I used to say in my staff meetings that we were fighting a two-front war, the first front against the other member countries of the OAS and their suspicions of the United States, the second front against the ARA front office, which was filled with unilateralists and bilateralists. In practice, however, it was not a war on just two fronts. We had to mobilize our government and public opinion and simultaneously deal with those of thirty-odd other countries. I had that in mind when I chose as my deputy Stephen Dachi, a strong officer who had been USIA regional director and was coming off a tour as Consul General in Sao Paolo where his early training as a dentist had played a key role in identifying the remains of Josef Mengele. Unfortunately, Dachi immediately freelanced a press interview that was interpreted as conciliatory toward Noriega and had to be replaced. His replacement was John Maisto, who had built a pro-democracy record in previous assignments in Panama and the Philippines. John was very effective and became a good friend. We needed all the help we could get. The OAS itself did not have a good reputation, and ARA was in the habit of sending U.S. positions on OAS matters directly to our Ambassadors in capitals bypassing the OAS delegations, including our own.

*Q: Sounds like a rocky start for you . . .*

EINAUDI: Yes. And the skepticism was not just on our part. The foreigners were skeptical, too. Bernardo Pericas Neto, the gifted diplomat who was then serving as Brazil's Ambassador to OAS, welcomed me by commenting after my maiden presentation to the Permanent Council that "Time will tell if he speaks as Ambassador Einaudi or Professor Einaudi." We found our footing fast. And a key element was my interagency experience.

*With President and Mrs. George H.W. Bush at an administration fourth of July barbecue, 1990. (David Valdez, official White House photograph, 1990.)*

Joseph Verner Reed Jr. presided over my swearing in ceremony. He was President Bush's Chief of Protocol and became a key ally. White House events for the Washington diplomatic corps traditionally included only Ambassadors accredited to the White House, leaving out those accredited to the OAS. This did not matter for the Caribbean ambassadors, all of whom were double-hatted, that is, accredited to the OAS as well as the White House. But the Latin American countries and Canada maintained separate missions to the OAS, hence their ambassadors were never invited. At my request, Reed changed that, even including OAS Ambassadors in the innovative substantive monthly briefings with senior Administration officials he organized at Blair House. Reed had a sure sense of protocol as being less a matter of form than of whatever advanced our interests.

Adapting form to advance interests was something I was also able to achieve on the military front. A common foreign critique of U.S. policy was that the State Department and the Defense Department were frequently at odds. Ambassadorial statements in support of democracy were often received with a wink in Latin America because many believed that the Pentagon would have the last word and that the United States would in the end always support military dictatorships. Revolution and counterrevolution in Central America made this a live issue, so at key points I would ask Major General Bernard Loeffke and/or Colonel John (Jay) Cope to accompany me to meetings in full dress uniform. Loeffke, whose mother was Colombian, was President of the Inter-American Defense Board (IADB), and had been the U.S. military attaché in both Moscow and Peking. Cope, who had served as Deputy Chief of Staff for U.S. Southern Command, was Military Advisor to Assistant Secretary Aronson. Both Bernie and Jay were personal friends and supported me and USOAS unstintingly. To support my efforts to revitalize the OAS, Bernie even offered to give up the traditional U.S. monopoly on the IADB Presidency. The offer was rebuffed by the major Latin American militaries, who found it easier to have a U.S. general as President rather than to have to accept the risk of having a presiding officer from a small country. Jay went on to found the Center for Hemispheric Defense Studies. I used to call him "the institutional memory of U.S. military relations with Latin America."

To address economic concerns, I worked to convince the Department of Commerce and USTR of the cost effectiveness of the OAS, which could provide a platform for the Administration to reach more than thirty countries at the same time. President Bush was exposed to Latin American debt problems at a summit meeting on drug trafficking in Colombia in early 1990, and wanted to develop a response in the form of trade and investment programs. The Enterprise for the Americas Initiative (EAI) announced by President Bush at the White House on June 27, 1990 was an important departure from standard bilateral approaches. The EAI's trade proposals were to be advanced through the multilateral Uruguay Round, and its lending and grant programs to support market-oriented reforms were to be administered through the Inter-American Development Bank(IDB). The Uruguayan Enrique Iglesias had recently become president of the IDB. I had introduced Henry Kissinger to him in 1976 in Chile, where Iglesias was heading the UN Economic Commission for Latin America, CEPAL. Initially a disciple of Raul Prebisch and his import-substitution model of development, by 1990 Iglesias was the right person at the right time; the EAI helped countries reduce their debt overhang and regain access to financial markets. Ciro de Falco, whom I first met when he was the U.S. Treasury attaché in Brasilia in 1974 when I went there to negotiate on technology transfer, was overseeing EAI implementation at the IDB. The U.S. was interested in conditionality; the Latins were suspicious. It was not an easy task.

*Q: But the EAI was an economic program, not a political or military one that might directly involve the OAS. What did it have to do with you?*

EINAUDI: Well, you go where the action is. I had been invited to the White House when President Bush announced the program, and had then met with de Falco and others at the IDB. The OAS General Assembly was to meet that year in Paraguay, and the Latins were sending feelers to see if a summit could be organized to coincide with it. President Bush could not go, but I learned that Carla Hills, the United States Trade Representative, might be available. The Mexican Ambassador was no longer Rafael de la Colina, the famous "Doctor NO" whose standing instruction from 1965 to 1986 had been to "just say No" to U.S. initiatives. I went to his successor, Antonio de Icaza, thinking that Mexican support would help convince the South Americans that to invite Hills to Asunción would not violate nonintervention nostrums. It turned out the timing was perfect. The Latins were as curious as we were. And Carla Hills was the perfect messenger. As she and I were leaving her hotel suite in Asunción to go to the dialogue, she stopped and went back to turn off all the lights, saying "Let's not waste energy. This is a poor country."

*Q: The Enterprise for the Americas Initiative signaled the beginning of the end of what I gather was called a lost decade for Latin America's growth. Was that your most important achievement during your time as Ambassador to the OAS?*

EINAUDI: Yes, but only as part of my broader effort to create a sense of *"engranaje,"* a meshing of gears in mutual support. As it turned out, the 1990 OAS General Assembly in Paraguay was a step toward what actually was the most important achievement, Resolution 1080 of the OAS General Assembly of 1991 in Chile. And that, in turn, was the climax of a process that had begun in Panama in 1989.

The U.S. military intervention in Panama took place in part because diplomatic efforts to deal with Noriega through the OAS had failed. This set off an extraordinary reaction by the President of Venezuela, Carlos Andrés Pérez. He and I had been introduced by Pete Vaky in 1977, when Pérez was in his first presidency of Venezuela. Also Vice President of the Socialist International, Pérez, known by his initials as CAP, did not speak English and was impatient with attempts to interpret. Once he called the ARA bureau Front Office by phone, but when he did not find someone with whom he felt he could make himself properly understood, he said brusquely "Let me talk to Einaudi" and refused to talk further until I was brought to the phone. On May 3, 1991, Carlos Andrés Pérez and I met in Caracas over breakfast at his residence. We discussed whether making the OAS more effective in advancing democracy might help avoid future U.S. military interventions like the one in Panama. The key obstacles were two: U.S. impatience and activism and Latin American doctrines about nonintervention. We agreed he would work on the South American presidents and I would work on the United States and the OAS. Pérez was about to host the South American Summit; as host, he would write the first draft of the communiqué. A lot of times the visiting presidents don't particularly look at what they are signing. Pérez decided to build on the Betancourt Doctrine, which denied diplomatic recognition to any government issuing from a coup, was named for a past Venezuelan president. On May 18, meeting in Caracas, the Andean Summit issued a communique calling for the amendment of the OAS Charter to require immediate collective suspension of diplomatic relations in case of a coup. The declaration put their foreign ministers, the curators of nonintervention doctrines, in a bad position. A foreign minister has to be careful about contradicting his president.

*President Carlos Andrés Pérez of Venezuela and I at the OAS. (Organization of American States (OAS), 1991, photograph reproduced with permission of the General Secretariat of the Organization of American States.)*

Mexico immediately made clear it would oppose any such action, citing the Estrada Doctrine that no nation has the right to judge the politics of another. In the days that followed, many foreign ministries reacted in ways that suggested the Andean Summit proposal was seen as too radical a departure to generate support. At the OAS, where missions and staff were already preparing to leave for the General Assembly in Santiago, a range of alternatives were aired informally. Most of them were procedural calls meant to avoid action by referring the issue to a formal Meeting of Foreign Ministers, an informal working group of Vice Ministers, or a Special General Assembly,

In the meantime, as Pérez and I had agreed, I was working to develop the idea that a coup would meet an automatic response, but only in the form of an OAS meeting without a predetermined outcome. We hoped this more moderate position was one the Brazilians, the Uruguayans, and the Peruvians, all of whom were noninterventionists, might be able to accept as a compromise. There was a precedent of sorts: After the "Christmas eve coup" in Suriname the previous December, the new regime had responded to international criticism by convening early elections and asking the OAS to observe them. The pressure of opinion had had some effect without resort to interventionist measures like sanctions or nonrecognition.

The General Assembly convened in Santiago without prior agreement on any particular proposal. Even the U.S. delegation, which was headed by Deputy Secretary Eagleburger, was without fixed guidance. The setting was auspicious. The new Chilean government, eager to demonstrate its post-Pinochet credentials, was billing the meeting as "the assembly of democratic renewal." That something new was afoot was evident on Sunday, June 2, when thirty heads of delegation showed up on time, at 10:15 in the morning, for their informal dialogue, which traditionally opens the Assembly. This was so unusual that Eagleburger asked me whether I was sure this was really an OAS meeting.

The day finished mixed. The good opening debate on the need for a mechanism to defend democracy was followed by a deadly afternoon in which the Chilean hosts read a draft of what they proposed be called a Santiago Declaration, about which most ministers had little prior knowledge and less interest. Meanwhile, however, small groups meeting outside the formal sessions were developing language for what was to become Resolution 1080.

Using all my skills as a spider to weave a web of agreement, I encouraged Brazil's Bernardo Pericas to propose "sudden or irregular interruption" of the democratic political institutional process as a trigger. This formula would eliminate the word "coup" and focus on political institutions. It would avoid ruffling military feathers while simultaneously suggesting that local or domestic conditions were the issue rather than outside intervention. The requirement for collective action was dropped by agreeing to preambular language that genuflected to the Estrada Doctrine by promising "due respect" to "the policies of each member country in regard to the recognition of states and governments." Brazil's move isolated Mexico, which had been the leader of the non-intervention camp and assured the support of a substantial majority of the Spanish-speaking states. But now an unfortunate characteristic of OAS meetings was exposed: the Commonwealth Caribbean felt uninformed and left out. Over next two days, the Chilean hosts, led by Ambassador Heraldo Muñoz, carefully consulted with individual Caribbean delegations. After a tense meeting with them as a group, they came on board by exacting a resolutory paragraph three that called for "a set of proposals that will serve as incentives to preserve and strengthen democratic systems, based on international solidarity and cooperation." This formula combined respect for nonintervention with the possibility of economic assistance. Small island states have always felt vulnerable and in need of support.

For the verbose OAS, the final text was a marvel of relative concision.

ORGANIZATION OF AMERICAN STATES

GENERAL ASSEMBLY

AG/RES. 1080 (XXI-O/91)

### REPRESENTATIVE DEMOCRACY

(Resolution adopted at the fifth plenary session,
held on June 5, 1991)

**WHEREAS:**

The Preamble of the Charter of the OAS establishes that representative democracy is an indispensable condition for the stability, peace, and development of the region;

Under the provisions of the Charter, one of the basic purposes of the OAS is to promote and consolidate representative democracy, with due respect for the principle of non-intervention;

Due respect must be accorded to the policies of each member country in regard to the recognition of states and governments;

In view of the widespread existence of democratic governments in the Hemisphere, the principle, enshrined in the Charter, that the solidarity of the American states and the high aims which it pursues require the political organization of those states to be based on effective exercise of representative democracy must be made operative; and

The region still faces serious political, social, and economic problems that may threaten the stability of democratic governments,

**THE GENERAL ASSEMBLY**

**RESOLVES:**

1. To instruct the Secretary General to call for the immediate convocation of a meeting of the Permanent Council in the event of any occurrences giving rise to the sudden or irregular interruption of the democratic political institutional process or of the legitimate exercise of power by the democratically elected government in any of the Organization's member states, in order, within the framework of the Charter, to examine the situation, decide on and convene an ad hoc meeting of the Ministers of Foreign Affairs, or a special session of the General Assembly, all of which must take place within a ten-day period.

2. To state that the purpose of the ad hoc meeting of Ministers of Foreign Affairs or the special session of the General Assembly shall be to look into the events collectively and adopt any decisions deemed appropriate, in accordance with the Charter and international law.

3. To instruct the Permanent Council to devise a set of proposals that will serve as incentives to preserve and strengthen democratic systems, based on international solidarity and cooperation, and to apprise the General Assembly thereof at its twenty-second regular session.

GENERAL SECRETARIAT OF THE ORGANIZATION OF AMERICAN STATES, WASHINGTON, D.C. 20006

*The original print copy of Resolution 1080. (Organization of American States (OAS), 1991, reproduced with permission of the General Secretariat of the Organization of American States.)*

The first operative paragraph opening *"To instruct the Secretary General"* gave the Secretary General no choice. He was *"instructed"* to call for *"the immediate convocation"* of the Permanent Council. This bypassed the rule that only a member state could convene a meeting of the Council and thus got around the *países limítrofes* (neighboring countries) problem, the fact that states neighboring the country where the interruption occurred might not want to complicate their bilateral relations by opening the door to criticism of a new government. Making the trigger any *"sudden or irregular interruption"* avoided finger pointing against the militaries that would have been implicit in the word "coup." Resolution 1080 therefore made the OAS response automatic, without delays, finger pointing, or need for anyone to assume responsibility.

But all the resolution did was call for a meeting. And that it was "just a meeting" created problems within our delegation. The Assistant Secretary, Bernie Aronson, had followed the negotiations at a distance, but wanted to push for the Betancourt doctrine and an immediate break in relations. I was adamant that Aronson's position would lose the emerging consensus and leave us with empty words. Aronson and I were both unhappy but neither would budge. The issue was still unresolved when Larry Eagleburger, Jim Dandridge, Bernie Aronson, John Maisto and I crammed into a tiny Foreign Ministry elevator to go down to the plenary. The elevator got stuck between floors. When we emerged a half hour later, Eagleburger had sided with me.

The next day, *El Mercurio*, Chile's leading newspaper, published a note that, to avoid what had happened to the U.S. Deputy Secretary of State, the Foreign Ministry had hired an operator to limit access to the elevator.

AG/RES 1080 (XXI-O/91), "REPRESENTATIVE DEMOCRACY" was adopted June 5, 1991 and became the basis of OAS efforts on behalf of democracy for ten years, until it was replaced by the Inter-American Democratic Charter, which is a later story.

*Q: What happened next?*

EINAUDI: The first invocation of 1080 came in September, three months after its adoption. People had expected it might be Suriname, but it was Haiti, where a more or less traditional military coup was led against President Jean-Bertrand Aristide by the Army Commander. General Cedras survived until U.S. military pressure returned Aristide to power three years later. The OAS took many measures, including missions and a collective trade embargo. I wound up chairing the Permanent Council Committee set up to enforce the trade embargo. The sanctions quickly ran into trouble, partly because we in the United States immediately made exceptions to them for ourselves, but mainly because no one else had direct practical experience in enforcement. The U.S. Treasury had been chasing Cuban assets back when terrorists were still in the shadows. But most countries had little experience in enforcing sanctions against merchants who might be violating the terms of an international agreement. Even CAP's ambassador was throwing up his hands in frustration.

President Fujimori's April 1992 suspension of Peru's congress presented a fresh challenge. Fujimori's *autogolpe*, as it was called, was not a military coup but a "self-coup" undertaken by an elected president. However, it fell squarely under the "sudden irregular interruption" language of 1080. Hemispheric reaction was negative and immediate. Fujimori boldly came in person to the General Assembly in Nassau to defend his actions, but was ultimately forced to hold new congressional elections in November. A similar attempt the next year by President Serrano of Guatemala to suspend the constitution and congress met such sharp condemnation that he resigned.

Meanwhile, the positive incentives called for in paragraph three of Resolution 1080 never developed. The Secretariat established an office, the Unit for the Promotion of Democracy, to promote democratic practices, but the unit operated with limited special funds provided by the United States, Canada and some European observers. Indeed, since the OAS was given the mandate to support democracy, resources available to it through its regular fund fell in real terms by more than 25% as inflation ate into country quotas. We should discuss this further when we come to my period as Assistant Secretary General.

*Q: What else would you like to say now about your time as the Ambassador to the OAS?*

EINAUDI: Only that I enjoyed my time there thoroughly. Carol and I had many opportunities to support music and the arts, by sponsoring exhibits and concerts at the OAS by American artists. With so many countries involved, the social circuit was a busy one. My staff thought I was overdoing things sometimes, but I never went to a cocktail party or dinner without asking for a list of issues to advance or avoid during the chit chat. And thanks to Joseph Verner Reed, Carol and I were included at the White House dinner for Italy's Prime Minister Giulio Andreotti. I have a signed photo of Reed and President Bush introducing me to Andreotti. But what I remember best from that night was when

Carol had to take a tipsy Frank Sinatra by the hand to guide him to the men's room.

As Ambassador, I was able to make a number of speeches on my own, including a Bartels lecture at Cornell, the fee for which I donated to the Research Center founded by my father. And I continued to help with the speeches of the Secretary and the President. I have a lovely note from Carolyn Cawley thanking me for my help with President Bush's speech in Brazil on December 3, 1990.

My time as ambassador coincided with the move of Spanish-language television from local origins to national free-to-air broadcasting. Univisión was blossoming just as I became ambassador. The American political system had not yet learned to take Latinos seriously as voters. So while most U.S. politicians were saying a few platitudes in badly accented Spanish, Univisión was asking me to comment on the OAS, U.S. foreign policy generally, and occasionally even on domestic matters. When I told some of the President's people that I was doing this, I was amazed that they were perfectly happy to let me keep doing so. They did little themselves. I also recorded many programs for foreign audiences through USIA and, later, CNN en español. Several dozen tapes of these programs are at the Columbus Memorial Library.

The first President Bush used the OAS as the venue to sign the first NAFTA agreement. As inevitably happens when an ambassador accompanies his president, I became something of a protocol officer, and spent much of the time escorting U.S. businessmen invited to the ceremony. I well remember two of them complaining unhappily to each other as I walked them up the grand staircase that they did not want to be limited to North America, that their interests were global. I believe that is a false choice, for all concerned. Power starts at home and builds outward. Canada and Mexico, plus Central America and the Caribbean, are so entwined with us they are in effect part of us. That closeness supports the Nixonian idea of the "special relationship" rejected by many because of its often condescending, paternalistic nature, but I believe that, if there is mutual respect, regionalism can be compatible with universalism.

*President Bush signs NAFTA at the OAS, accompanied by U.S. Trade Representative Carla Hills and Canadian and Mexican officials. Prime Minister Brian Mulroney and President Carlos Salinas signed simultaneously in their respective capitals. December 17, 1992. (David Valdez, official White House photograph, 1992.)*

Finally, I would say the OAS is a place where sometimes it is good to be able to lead from behind. President Obama was much maligned for using this phrase, but my experience is that sometimes the best way for a big country to lead is to encourage others to take the lead. Better yet, if the OAS as a whole takes a position, it becomes a regional consensus, not the position of any one country. It is far more important to obtain that consensus than to run out front trying to hog the credit. This is not an easy lesson and even harder to practice, but sometimes to take credit is to dilute the achievement.

*Q: What did you learn about diplomacy from your period as Ambassador to the OAS?*

EINAUDI: In my farewell to the Permanent Council on April 15, 1993, I identified three lessons: (1) that democracy is as important *among* nations as it is *within* nations; (2) that the best way is not necessarily the most direct or the quickest way; and (3) that history counts but so do people.

*I deliver my farewell remarks to the OAS Permanent Council, April 15, 1993. Seated behind me to the right are my DCM Sarah Horsey-Barr, Margarita Riva-Geoghegan, and Richard Douglas. (Photo courtesy of LR Einaudi, personal photo.)*

The first lesson reflects the fact that even small countries need to be respected. The second lesson reflects the fact that success in hemispheric diplomacy means everyone, particularly the powerful United States, must have the flexibility to adjust and the patience to find ways to overcome initial resistance to initiatives that challenge traditional ways of doing things. And the third underscores the fact that personal relationships are often just as important as precedent or policy.

Today I would add a fourth lesson: hemispheric asymmetries in power make the efficacy of multilateralism extremely limited without active U.S. participation. The interplay between national policies and international relations and institutions is dealt with further in appendices five through seven.

*Q: Speaking of relationships, what kind of a relationship did you have to the Secretary of State when you were Ambassador to the OAS?*

EINAUDI: I had long had an intimate relationship with Eagleburger, whose first assignment as a young foreign service officer had been to Honduras, but I will set him aside in answering this question. We have already seen that he played a key role in the adoption of Resolution 1080, but he was Secretary only a few months at the end of an Administration that was by then marking time.

I referred earlier to my close relationship to George Shultz. When Jim Baker replaced him, I told Baker's wife that I had brought all of ARA/PPC, officers and secretaries, up to the Secretary's office to say goodbye to Shultz when he left. I suggested that Baker might reach out similarly to people in State whose support he would need. She responded that her husband was "not that kind of man." It turned out that she was right. Baker kept staff at a distance. I saw more of President Bush than I did of Baker. Baker knew perfectly well who I was, but I had to take the initiative to see him.

Once, when I did ask to see him, Baker received me in his office, alone. It was some time after the fall of the Berlin wall, and I told him I was worried that our generalized use of the language "the victory of capitalism" carried with it the danger that in the rest of the world many would equate the plain word "capitalism" with the return of the robber barons. If that happened, I said, we would be throwing away our victory over Communism. I suggested looking for an adjective, any adjective, to modify "capitalism". Call it "social" or "democratic" or even just "modern" -- but find some way to differentiate from past stereotypes. Baker's reaction brought me back to McGeorge Bundy's reaction when I had gone to him on Cuba all those years before. Baker was a practical man, and did not understand what I was talking about.

Years later, at Larry Eagleburger's funeral, I told Baker I would really miss Larry and all he had contributed. Baker responded simply that he was surprised Larry had lasted so long, given how much he smoked. I certainly remembered Larry going around the Department when he was Secretary wearing a sign around his neck that read "Smoking Area." But Baker's focus at the funeral on a poor habit rather than on Larry's many accomplishments saddened me further.

Baker's organizational skills and unique closeness to George H.W. Bush enabled their Administration to field a formidable foreign policy team. In hemisphere affairs, it was unrivalled. Part of it was the people, for example, Aronson at State and Carla Hills at USTR. But it was also that no one doubted they spoke for the

Administration and the country. And to Baker's and Aronson's and the country's great credit, the Contra war finally wound down without tragedy.

*Q: Let me ask you to expand on the Shultz-Baker comparison. You seem to have preferred Shultz. Why?*

EINAUDI: Both were outstanding Secretaries of State. Both were successful Secretaries of the Treasury first. Both had the key quality of being close to their President. And both were very practical. But they were very different. I found Baker cool and diffident, whereas Shultz was warm and confident, with a sure sense of humor. When my friend Dick Bloomfield called on him on his way to Ecuador as Ambassador, Shultz asked him to point out "your country" on the globe in his office. Dick pointed to Ecuador, on the west coast of South America. Shultz smiled and put his hand on the United States. No words needed to express that moral. I was with Shultz in an airplane over South America in 1987 when we learned the Nobel Peace Prize had been awarded to Oscar Arias for his still incomplete Central American peace efforts. Without batting an eye, Shultz said "He whom the gods would have go mad they award the Nobel Prize in his forties."

*Q: Did you have a judgment on Shultz?*

We had a few important differences, but I felt at the time that, all things considered, he was the best Secretary of State with whom I worked, certainly in a class with Kissinger or Baker. Shultz was not as brilliant as Henry Kissinger, but whereas Kissinger never had his feet fully on the ground, always aware that he could not claim to be the personification of the United States, George Shultz did not have any problems about that. He was an ex-marine. He had incredible common sense. Shultz had to fight an often-lonely and sometimes unsuccessful battle during intense policy disputes within the Reagan Administration to keep the ship of state on course. He received me to hear my protest at our mining of the harbors in Nicaragua; he supported democracy and negotiation as paths to peace in Central America and kept open a direct channel to me without the knowledge of the assistant secretary to keep check on things in the days of Iran-Contra; I was with him in the air over Brazil when we got word of the bombing of the marines in Lebanon (an ex-marine himself, he had argued for sending them); and the entire country benefitted from his resistance to some of the crazies in the Administration who would have turned the cold war hot in Central America and Cuba and never let it die. Shultz was a realist. He once deleted an excellent passage from a speech I had written for him in Buenos Aires, saying, "there is no point in bringing up a problem if you can't do anything about it." No one had more common sense and greater love for America.

Much later, he invited me to the hanging of his portrait as Secretary. "The lot of a Secretary of State is not a happy one," he said as a few of us gathered on the Seventh Floor to watch the unveiling. "First they finger him when he is chosen; then they put him through the third degree by the Senate; if he survives that, they work him to death; finally, when all is done, they hang him."

# Policy Planning, Again

Q: *Your career path is full of twists. What made you return to the policy planning office, S/P, a second time, nearly twenty years after you first served there?*

EINAUDI: During the transition after the 1992 presidential election, Carol and I met the President-elect and his wife in a receiving line at Georgetown University. We had never met before, and when we were introduced, Bill Clinton was taken aback that there was an American ambassador in Washington. Hillary Clinton immediately said "Thank you for your service." The President-elect kept asking in wonderment how a U.S. Ambassador could be stationed in Washington and she repeated firmly "Thank you for your service" and moved the line along. It seemed obvious that she had already replaced me in her mind. That person turned out to be Hattie Babbitt, wife of the former Arizona Governor Bruce Babbitt, who was named Secretary of the Interior.

The Clinton transition team let me know, however, that it had evaluated me as one of the best serving ambassadors, and inquired whether I might be interested in another ambassadorial appointment, possibly to Brazil. I declined, for both personal and professional reasons. My wife Carol was on the verge of partnership in her law firm. Her career had already been derailed twice by my work requirements. A post abroad would have been one barrier too many. Moreover, the bilateral agenda with Brazil was so tough that, to be successful, our ambassador there would require allies in the White House I did not have.

Fortunately, my friend and mentor, Sam Lewis, offered me an option I could not turn down. Sam had been appointed Director of the Policy Planning Staff and suggested I join him again. I happily accepted, and sent Bryan Atwood, who was heading the Clinton transition team, a list of Democrats – Charlie Rangel, Bill Richardson, Chris Dodd, Dante Fascell – who could attest to my political bona fides.

I saw rejoining S/P as a chance to be "present at the creation," as Acheson had titled his memoir as Secretary of State. The end of the Cold War had changed the world. U.S. policy under GHW Bush and Jim Baker had been highly successful, not just in ending the fighting in Central America, but far more importantly in managing the collapse of Soviet power and reuniting Germany after the fall of the Berlin Wall. Bush had called for a "new world order," but I felt we had been "flying on empty" in policy terms and needed a new "creation." I hoped the new administration would provide an opening. Warren Christopher had called for new global precepts as he became Secretary. I wanted to contribute.

It didn't turn out that way. The key to the policy planning staff is the relationship of its director to the Secretary of State and in turn the Secretary of State's relationship to the President. It turned out that Warren Christopher thought the policy planning office had more to do with universities and intellectual outreach than actual policy, let alone planning. And Bill Clinton was his own

Secretary of State. Between Christopher and Clinton, S/P didn't have a chance.

*Q: How did that second tour on the Secretary's Policy Planning Staff differ from the first?*

EINAUDI: The utility of the policy planning staff depends on the relationship between the director of the staff and the secretary of state. If the secretary of state is interested and trusts the director, policy planning can have real meaning. Marshall had a military staffing approach that led him to create the policy planning staff and make George Kennan the original director. The situation was similar in 1974-77 with Winston Lord as the director and Henry Kissinger as secretary of state. In fact, after Nixon was gone, under President Ford, Kissinger was sometimes called the "President for Foreign Affairs."

The more common pattern is what had happened just previously, when the distinguished late Robert Bowie was director. Bowie did not have a relationship with the secretary, and the staff languished. In 1993, when Sam Lewis became director under Warren Christopher in the Clinton administration, the more usual pattern reasserted itself. When relationships are not strong between the director and the secretary of state, and if in addition the secretary of state does not have a strong relationship with the president, then the policy planning staff is marginalized. You can even see this in the evolution of the name of the staff. When it started in 1947 under Marshall and Kennan, its designation was S/P, for the Secretary's Office, Policy Planning. By 1974, when I first went there, the designation had been changed to S/PC, the C standing for coordination -- a desperate bureaucratic attempt to remind others that if they didn't want to clear their papers with the staff, at least please send along a copy afterwards. One of the first things we had done was to drop the C, becoming S/P again.

Sam Lewis had had been Deputy Director of S/P with Winston Lord when I first served there. He had more than measured up to the demanding requirements of life under Kissinger. By the time he took over S/P in the spring of 1993 and asked me to join him, he had continued his distinguished career as Ambassador to Israel. He would go on to head the United States Institute of Peace. But Sam would not last even a year as director of S/P under Warren Christopher. He told me that Christopher did not know what to do with the Planning Staff, and that when Sam told him he wanted to leave, Christopher "looked as though he was breathing a sigh of relief."

*Q: Did things improve after Lewis was replaced?*

EINAUDI: Jim Steinberg was totally different. He was very operational and practical, with a short-term focus. He acted more as a key special assistant to the Secretary, rather than as someone concerned with policy alternatives, coherence, or the long view.

*Q: Can you give me an example?*

EINAUDI: The CIA published an estimate on Cuba in 1993 that predicted that Fidel would transition power to someone else within 5 years. Believing that Clinton and his people expected to be in power for eight years, I saw this as a perfect opening for a long-term policy planning effort to prepare for something the intelligence community was predicting would happen on the Administration's watch. What might a transition in power in Cuba look like, and what implications might it have for U.S. policy? Cuba's initial efforts to transform the Andes into a new Sierra

Maestra by fomenting guerrilla foci had failed, their subsequent attempts to exploit Central America's internal revolutions had been contained, subversive opportunities elsewhere were declining, subsidies from the Soviet Union had been cut, and Cuban soldiers had returned from Africa. Privately, I called my proposed analysis "The Incredible Shrinking Fidel." Steinberg consulted someone at the White House and told me that I should forget about Cuba because "Florida believes it will not happen." When ARA Assistant Secretary Alec Watson raised a related Cuba matter with him in my presence, Steinberg's negative response was so abrupt it virtually brought tears to the eyes of Alec, a person born to smile if ever there was one.

*Q: So what did you focus on during your second time around in S/P?*

EINAUDI: Without a central focus on the Secretary and decision-making, work patterns and relationships diversified. The Deputy Secretary and the bureaus became foci as much or even more than the Secretary. Members worked on their individual strengths rather than collectively. Lewis with Dennis Ross on the Middle East. I on Latin America. Binnendijk on NATO. Steinberg on traveling with the Secretary and the crises of the moment.

The S/P routine was to open the day reviewing the overnight intelligence take and the press. We did this to get a sense of where our foreign policy issues would fit in the day's national concerns. One morning in 1993 we had in front of us Xerox copies of the front pages of six to eight major newspapers from all around the United States -- from California to Texas and Chicago to Atlanta as well as the East Coast. Suddenly Brandon Grove, Sam Lewis' calmly sound deputy, put his set down with an exasperated exclamation: "Look at these papers: not one of them has the same lead story! How can we relate to public opinion when it is so fragmented?" Brandon's insight summed up perfectly the difference between what we could call the Cronkite period, when the news was three or four major TV news programs, and the new internet era, when news sources were so many they became virtually impossible to track.

The lack of common reference points is as big a problem for national cohesion as the lack of mentors or models is for individuals. I had long been accustomed to the fact that such differences were often present in foreign affairs. For instance, who conquered yellow fever? An American will say Walter Reed. A Cuban will answer Carlos Finlay. And both will be correct. But disagreeing on a fact is less troubling than to have major historical reference points have opposite meanings. For example, I was overjoyed that becoming Ambassador to the OAS would coincide with the five hundredth anniversary of the discovery of America. My Americanness would coincide with my Italianness in the celebration of Christopher Columbus! Only to discover that the risk-taking explorer had come to be seen as a colonialist exterminator of native peoples. His statues were not yet being torn down, but the "Encounter of Two Worlds" was very subdued. Teaching at Georgetown a few years later, I referred to the Statue of Liberty as the symbol of freedom and the American dream only to have Black students in my class tell me that to them it stood for cynical oppression. I was startled and unnerved, even more shocked than I had been when I had realized that not only had my students not lived through the depression or the New Deal – most had been born since Vietnam.

S/P lost the speechwriting responsibility to Public Affairs when Christopher came in, but I nonetheless kept my hand in major speeches as I had from the start of my State Department career.

I wrote the key passages of Secretary Christopher's speeches promoting NAFTA. In May 1994, the soundbites that appeared in the press from Christopher's NAFTA speech in Mexico City, and the next day from Deputy Secretary Talbott's speech at the OAS on Haiti, were both phrases I had written. My old Secretary Jeane Rogers would have called the carpenter to widen the door frame of my office to accommodate my swelled head.

I also resumed the policy planning consultations I had initiated in 1975. In the summer of 1993, I went to Brasilia accompanied by ARA DAS Ed Casey and my new S/P colleague Harry O'Hara to have a global tour d'horizon with planners in Itamaraty, Brazil's foreign ministry. The talks covered our respective interests in the Western Hemisphere, Brazil's concerns for Africa and the United Nations, and ours in Russia, Eastern Europe and Asia. The discussions were so successful that an even more senior group of Brazilians reciprocated by coming to Washington the next summer. By that time Steinberg had replaced Lewis. When I entered Jim's office to let him know the Brazilians were outside and ask if I could bring them in, I found him coatless, with his shirt hanging out of his pants. To his great credit, when I told him the traditionalist Brazilians were very formally dressed, he tucked in and shaped up without a word. But the clash of cultures was as great as that of dress.

The big change for me under Steinberg was that he involved me in administration. Sam Lewis' two deputies both left when he did. When Steinberg came in, I became Acting Deputy Director. For five months, I took on the defense of S/P's office space, which was being threatened by a Seventh-floor restructuring and remodeling. I had a mass of personnel headaches: ending five temporary staff assignments, retiring two secretaries and reorganizing travel management, finding a new FSO staff assistant, and incorporating seven new staff members, including three new Schedule C positions and detailees from the Department of Defense and the CIA. I was particularly proud that for two of the three Foreign Service positions I was able to recruit highly competent women officers, Suzanne Butcher and Yvonne Thayer.

*Q: That sounds as though Steinberg used you as a manager rather than a senior policy advisor.*

EINAUDI: Well, I think he saw it mainly as a matter of necessity. Latin America was not high on his policy agenda, and he needed to have someone do things he did not want to take the time to do. I may not have been an FSO, but I had some rank, and after twenty consecutive years in the building, I knew the system and how to help people in it.

When Steinberg was absent, I also served as Acting Director for a total of about six weeks. I would attend the Secretary's weekly staff meeting, the Deputy Secretary's four weekly meetings with the regional assistant secretaries, and various special coordinating meetings. This brought benefits as well as obligations.

In July 1994, during one of Steinberg's absences traveling with the Secretary, Deputy Secretary Strobe Talbott asked me to prepare a paper. The official S/S-S tasking sardonically referred to it as "Think Piece: Original Sin (a Tour d'Horizon of post-Cold War problems)." It was to be sent to him five days later in Bangkok for him to read during the long plane ride back to Washington. I mobilized my S/P colleagues and pulled together the 8-page single-spaced paper reproduced as Appendix Two. Talbott later told Steinberg that it was "the best paper" he had read coming to him out of the system.

*Q: Talbott himself was an award-winning journalist on strategic issues, so that was high praise. What did the paper say?*

EINAUDI: Well, we entitled it "Sources of Conflict after the Cold War" with a subtitle that challenged the tasker, calling them "Neither Original Sin nor Passing Fancies." We argued that the major global trouble spots were all marked by dispersal of power among nations, the weakening of central governments within nations, and the erosion of traditional social relationships by technology. We identified the destabilizing factors as population growth, mass migrations, illegal narcotics, and ideological fragmentation and localisms, and argued that dealing with them would require dynamics very different from those of containing communism. The paper at Appendix Two was a collective S/P effort. It is more prescient of today's problems than of today's policies.

*Q: What happened?*

EINAUDI: Nothing. That analysis was precisely why I had wanted to join S/P. We identified approaches for future U.S. policies. But the effort ended there. We were praised, but there was no follow-up. I particularly regret the failure to follow up on international burden sharing and institution building within nations.

And here is another key difference between the two periods in which I served in S/P. In 1974-77, one of our key focuses were on policy papers for decisions. Policy papers with options and pros and cons are a question of intellectual rigor as well as format. Later, in my courses at Georgetown, I taught that style and graded my students on their ability to write policy papers that way. But the need for policy papers depends on there being decisions to be made! In S/P during 1993-1997, I don't remember a single policy paper of that kind; instead, S/P was caught up in bureaucratic infighting, like fighting the bureaus in vain efforts to prevent stovepiping to the Secretary—

*Q: What do you mean by stovepiping?*

EINAUDI: Stovepiping is the attempt of individual units in a large bureaucracy to shoot their problems and recommendations directly to the top for decision without involving other units who would also be affected by the decision. This may be justifiable for intelligence information, which needs to be protected from unnecessary dissemination, but stovepiping policy decisions can lead to not considering essential factors.

*Q: How did you try to prevent that?*

EINAUDI: Stovepiping can be controlled procedurally by an Executive Secretariat that requires certain clearances and substantively by a Planning Staff that is on distribution and seeks to ensure a comprehensive organization-wide view. But the coordination and effort this requires is not easily achieved.

Take a minor example that does not even involve policy decisions: in the spring of 1994, the Deputy Secretary instituted a system of "Megatalkers" in an attempt to improve public outreach on "the big picture dimensions of U.S. foreign policy." He assigned responsibility to S/P "working closely with the bureaus." Within a month, most of the building was alienated. One of my contacts told me her bureau was being chewed out for resubmitting language that had already been rewritten upstairs – but which the bureau had never seen and had therefore been unable to correct.

In my twelve years directing ARA/PPC I had come to realize that other offices within ARA had often seen having to clear their papers with me as unnecessary extra work. For a bureau to have to seek outside clearance with S/P for a Decision Memorandum is even more extra work. Operating officials sometimes fear that needing clearances also leads to their losing control because they provide opportunities for partisan politics, vested interests, and plain ignorance on the part of uninformed higher-ups. The most effective procedures are informal, starting with ensuring that individual planning staff members are sufficiently close to the bureaus covering the areas for which they are responsible to ensure effective coordination in the initial drafting.

*Q: How often did that happen?*

EINAUDI: It depended a great deal on the individual, the bureau and the issue.

*Q: What was your situation in that regard?*

EINAUDI: I was in a privileged position. Alec Watson became Assistant Secretary for ARA just as I moved to S/P. Amazingly, in the spring of 1961, he had been in the class at Harvard on Latin American politics that I had to teach when John Plank became involved in Bay of Pigs planning. Watson's deputies Mike Skol and Ed Casey were good friends. Skol, coming out of Venezuela had asked me in mid-1993 whether he should accept the principal DAS position in ARA. I told him he should, but should also be aware it would take another year before the U.S. government was fully organized. He took the job, then called me in, reminded me of our conversation, and said "It is now two years, and the Administration is still not organized." For ARA, this meant that having me in S/P to help them represent ARA issues to the Seventh Floor was particularly valuable.

There was of course, another variable: whether or not the issue was of interest to the Seventh Floor. In the case of ARA or USOAS, the answer was "usually not." And if the issue *was* of Seventh floor interest, ARA tended to be pushed aside. The shift would be drastic if the issue was of White House interest.

Haiti is a good example. When Watson became Assistant Secretary, Haiti was already in the hands of a Special Coordinator removed from the Office of Caribbean Affairs. Ambassador Larry Pezzullo had been brought back as Haiti Coordinator from retirement after a decade as head of Catholic Relief Services. Pezzullo's brief was to negotiate an end to the military regime that had overthrown elected President Jean-Bertrand Aristide. But just as in his prior attempt to negotiate Somoza's departure from Nicaragua in the 1970s, Larry found himself without active political support. Meanwhile, the Haitian backers of the putschists bobbed and weaved, relying on their supporters in the U.S. to neutralize Aristide's backers in the U.S. Pezzullo was forced to resign and the White House named a new Presidential Representative for Haiti, former Congressman and Black Caucus chair William Gray. The focus shifted from negotiation to restoring Aristide, unilaterally if necessary.

Operation Uphold Democracy to restore Aristide began to take shape. UN Security Council resolution 940 was obtained authorizing the use of force. The Deputy Secretary began to hold daily Haiti meetings. Steinberg disappeared to provide political direction to the Pentagon's preparations. I became Acting Director of S/P and attended Strobe Talbott's meetings. Military action was bound to be controversial, partly because Aristide was loathed and viewed as a crazed drug user by key Republicans on the Hill, and partly because military action would smack of imperial unilateralism. To defuse the latter, we encouraged Haiti's Caribbean neighbors to participate in a Multinational Force or MNF. In my days as Ambassador to the OAS, I had met Owen Arthur, the Prime Minister of Barbados who was also Chairman of CARICOM. On September 16, I went to the Willard Hotel to help him prepare his response to President Clinton the next day on behalf of the countries contributing to the MNF. Later I suggested to the Deputy Secretary that having Aristide also meet with Nelson Mandela, who was scheduled to visit Washington later that week, would improve the optics by emphasizing reconciliation. Talbott called it "a dynamite blue sky suggestion" and the meeting took place just before Aristide returned to Haiti.

*Q: Were you happy about how this developed? Did you feel you contributed?*

EINAUDI: Aristide had been legitimately elected, his overthrow was illegal, and the repression that followed was vicious. And he at least symbolized democratic yearnings. But I was not happy about the use of force and did not like the policy process that brought us to it. Policy was being determined more by U.S. domestic politics than by what would work in Haiti. I was able to kibbitz, but policy-wise I felt marginalized.

I was similarly uncomfortable about preparations for the Miami Summit of the Americas that December. I had advocated for a summit since my days at the OAS, and should have been overjoyed. But I did not like the refusal to fold in military ministerial meetings under its umbrella. I felt it was high time to routinize civilian control, but the prevailing liberal view that the militaries were pariahs and quiet resistance in military quarters combined to keep Defense ministerials separate, keeping civilian involvement definitely secondary, even for the U.S. An even worse problem arose in negotiations for a commitment to creating a Free Trade Area of the Americas. CARICOM leaders were concerned their terms of trade, already deteriorating, would weaken further in any hemisphere-wide deal. Mack McLarty, then President Clinton's Special Envoy for the Americas, agreed to meet with them to reassure them their fears were misplaced. His cleared talking points had him telling them that the U.S. would maintain certain trade preferences that I knew we had already decided to phase out in March. This was December. I was appalled. Trust is the basic coin of diplomacy. The Caribbean leaders would inevitably realize they had been deceived. McLarty agreed to see me, but deflected my concern, saying "Luigi, March is a long way off." On December 11, 1994, the Caribbean joined the call for a Free Trade Area of the Americas. The Administration had its victory. I was deflated.

The spring of 1994, during one of my Acting Director periods, I invited Sam Huntington to address S/P. A few months earlier, he had published in *Foreign Affairs* the article on "clash of civilizations" that later became the book by the same title. Huntington had been my professor in graduate school, where he gave me a poor grade because my paper on the Peruvian military did not fit his theories. He was a man who preferred his theories to the facts, rather than accepting that a theory that did not fit the facts was not a good theory. But at least he had a theory.

*Q: We did not discuss Huntington when we talked about your time at Harvard, but I thought your emphasis on institutional factors in your work at RAND might have been due to his influence, or at least to some of his writings.*

EINAUDI: No, Huntington did not influence me. I never read Huntington's *Political Order in Changing Societies*. I did read his earlier *The Soldier and the State*. It was based largely on our American experience, but it was not up to the standards of the military sociology of, for example, Morris Janowitz or my RAND colleague Herbert Goldhamer. The course I took from Huntington in 1966 was to make up for an incomplete course in my PhD residency requirement. He had left for Columbia University, but had managed a triumphant comeback to Harvard; I was on leave from RAND to finish my thesis. Focused on that, I frankly did not pay Huntington much heed. My paper for him argued that the military in Peru had become a disruptive modernizing force for a combination of historical and social reasons.[2] Huntington gave me a C+, which reminded me that some French intellectuals had rejected my father's analysis that FDR and the New Deal had made the United States more democratic: *"nous ne vous croyons pas"* [we don't believe you]. André Siegfried published his *Les États-Unis d'ajourdhui* [The United States Today] in 1950, essentially unaltered from the 1927 edition.

After the radical military-led 1968 revolution in Peru, Huntington and I had reached a truce. At my request my friend Frances Coughlin, then serving as our cultural attaché in Lima, arranged meetings for him with just about everyone who counted in Peru's military and political worlds. I still have his letter of thanks. That was why I was willing and in a position to invite him to S/P, hoping his theories would help stimulate our policy thinking.

---

[2] If I remember correctly, it was an early version of my article *"Revolution from Within? Military rule in Peru since 1968"*, Studies in Comparative International Development, Vol. VII, No. 1 (Spring 1973), pp. 71-87. Originally delivered at the 1971 Annual Meeting of the American Political Science Association, Conrad Hilton Hotel, Chicago, Illinois, September 7-11 and reprinted later in Gerald A. Dorfman, **Soldiers in Politics** (1974), pp. 160-175. Also published as Rand P-4676.

Huntington came and spoke, and the result was a disaster. His cold analysis of "creedal passions" was sound enough. But after saying that the United States needed to preserve its "Anglo-protestant culture, faith, and creed," he concluded that "Your mission as U.S. diplomats is to defend Protestantism." I was offended and told him so. We never spoke again. His ability to generalize to a universal fairtheewell from limited data reminded me of his earlier claims that carpet bombing rural Vietnam was the road to progress. I have thought of him ever since as the Protestant ayatollah.

*Q: Isn't labeling Huntington "the Protestant Ayatollah" a bit extreme?*

EINAUDI: Of course. But Huntington clearly was among those who produce general theories from little evidence as opposed to those who write from genuine experience and expertise. Clement Moore Henry, my Exeter classmate and Harvard roommate, who at one point collaborated with Huntington on a study of one-party systems, wrote me that Huntington's were sometimes *"just reflective ideas abstracted from brutal reality. Sam never did much field work or have any empathetic understanding of foreign cultures... [His were often] abstract vicious thoughts from a kindly scholar, a true counterrevolutionary with the vices of the well-meaning revolutionary despite his principal focus on political stability and institutionalization... quite a living paradox!"*

*Q: I can sense your frustration. Did you get any satisfaction from this S/P assignment?*

EINAUDI: Yes, of course. My responsibilities as Acting Deputy Director and Acting Director forced me to decline special missions for ARA to Guatemala and the Dominican Republic, but I did contribute directly on issues with Peru, Nicaragua, and Venezuela.

And some of the things Steinberg asked me to do were fun. Townsend Friedman had been a speech writer during my first period on S/P. In 1994, returning from a posting as Ambassador to Mozambique, Townie took over FSI's "Washington Tradecraft" course. He felt that over the years the course had come to convey the message that "process is everything, forget policy." Believing that officers should be encouraged to think more about policy, and in particular, to understand the policies of the people they are serving, he invited Steinberg to talk to his course. The invitation came back out of Steinberg's office marked "Luigi to do." I went, and had a great time. But not being one of the new political folks Townie had wanted, I had to speak as an interpreter.

Another internal opportunity I greatly appreciated came in September 1994 when I was asked to welcome the Department's new Civil Service employees at their swearing in ceremony. Civil Service employees swear the same oath of office as do Foreign Service officers (and the President, for that matter), but in the State Department they are generally treated as an afterthought. As a member of the Senior Executive Service and as one who had made it to Ambassador and to S/P, I think I was being paraded as something of a role model. I told them they were taking on a difficult job in difficult times, dealing with problems abroad when we had problems at home, with shrinking resources and few shared parameters. They would have to look out for themselves, but the glass ceiling could be broken. Their strengths were different from those of the Foreign Service. With the Foreign Service understaffed, undertrained, and accustomed to gapping between assignments, the Civil Service was gaining importance for the continuity essential for good policy implementation. They looked at me as though I was crazy, but I think a glimmer got through.

Deane Hinton retired after 50 years of distinguished service to the United States, mainly but not exclusively in the Foreign Service and including multiple ambassadorships. The State Department, unlike the military, had a habit of letting good people go without recognition. I had, for example, organized a farewell for the incomparable Ambassador, Assistant Secretary, and Special Envoy Harry Shlaudeman, when I learned that he was retiring without a public thank you. Hinton was a bit of a curmudgeon, but 50 years seemed unimaginable to ignore. So someone in the system decided to make a show. The ceremony was held in the Benjamin Franklin diplomatic reception rooms on the eighth floor. When it was his turn to speak, Hinton looked out over the assemblage of two hundred people, most of them Foreign Service Officers, and said, after initial throat-clearing niceties, "You are spending so much time trying to defeat women and affirmative action that you do not even know how to write a diplomatic note." The party was over.

Then, in early 1995, fighting broke out between Peru and Ecuador, and my frustrations came to an end.

*Q: Before we go there, is there anything else we should have talked about?*

EINAUDI: Perhaps two points.

I had long been aware of the limits of official Intelligence when it came to non-technical matters. I was unhappy about the cutbacks in "HumInt," the intelligence gained by human interactions as compared to "SigInt," information that could be obtained electronically. I had also learned to distinguish the products of the operations side of the Agency from the work of the analysts based in Langley, some of whom were frustrated at not being in the field and sometimes not even allowed in the field. During this tour in S/P I was visited by an Agency researcher who was quietly trying to find out which CIA products senior policy makers actually read. Intelligence products are important as common reference points for the foreign affairs community. That the intelligence community was driven to do market research on the utility of its own products struck me as positive, but also a troublesome sign of the uncertain relationship of intelligence to policy.

On this tour I set aside earlier inhibitions about dealing with Italian matters. I took a call from Foreign Minister Nino Andreatta, an old acquaintance who was an economist who had followed in my grandfather's circles. Andreatta wanted to pass on his concerns about U.S. cuts in the UN force in Somalia in which Italian troops were participating. After that, through both Sam and Jim, I encouraged the Secretary to lend a sympathetic ear to both Andreatta and Prime Minister Dini without also becoming embroiled in Italy's deepening domestic divisions.

# The Peru-Ecuador War

*Q: I want to ask today (February 2021) about the Peru-Ecuador border conflict and your role in resolving it.*

EINAUDI: Before we begin, let me say that interested readers will find documentation in my essay "The Ecuador-Peru Peace Process," in Chester A. Crocker, Fen Osler Hampson and Pamela Aal, editors, Herding Cats, Multiparty Mediation in a Complex World, United States Institute of Peace Press, Washington, D.C., 1999. I later filled in some sensitive details in a fun 2015 lecture, The End of Conventional War in Latin America: The Peru-Ecuador War and Its Impact - CornellCast. I will now give you an unvarnished version of what I still remember. No similar inside account exists.

*Q: I am sure readers will appreciate that. What was the Peru-Ecuador conflict all about?*

EINAUDI: Territory and pride forged by history into the poison of sovereignty. In 1494 a papal bull known as Tordesillas divided newly discovered lands in the Americas between Spain and Portugal along a meridian 370 leagues west of the Cape Verde Islands. But knowledge of South America's unusual geography was at best approximate. From the West, the Andes acted as a formidable barrier. From the East, the Amazon and its tributaries enabled explorers to penetrate inland relatively easily, floating inland rather than scaling mountains. While the Spaniards to the West were hindered in their Amazonian access by the Andean wall, Portuguese explorers roamed far beyond the Tordesillas line. After independence, Brazil systematically expanded its borders by applying *uti possidetis,* the doctrine that what you occupy is yours, to conclude formal treaties with all thirteen of its neighbors.

Peru and Ecuador also tried to settle their common border, but were unable to agree. An 1802 Spanish royal decree assigning duties to the Viceroyalty of Lima (to become Peru) and the Audiencia of Quito (to become Ecuador) was ambiguous as to who controlled some 120,000 square miles of inland territory (smaller than France or Spain but bigger than Italy). The conflict carried over after independence. An outside observer called it an "obscure conflict over an unoccupied wilderness." But some locals traced it all the way back to the civil wars of 1527-1532 between the brothers Atahualpa and Huáscar and between Cuzco and Quito for control of the Inca Empire, conflicts that opened the door to the Spanish conquest.

Whatever their origins, undemarcated borders are an invitation to conflict. One source counts thirty-four armed clashes between Peru and Ecuador in little more than a century. Diplomatic efforts and a request for arbitration by the King of Spain came to naught, as did a 1924 request to the United States. Bilateral talks in 1936 produced an *uti possidetis* "status quo" line based on then-existing settlements, but Ecuador did not accept it. Early in 1941 incidents between patrols near the populated coast touched off a sequence of clashes that exploded in July into war. Peru's forces were three times the size of Ecuador's, better armed, and had what may have been South America's first paratroopers. Ecuadorian resistance was overwhelmed in a few days. Peruvian forces occupied southern Ecuador. The outside world had very little patience for the conflict and less for the loser. Everyone else was dealing with WWII and the Axis. Brazil presided over peace talks. When the Ecuadorian delegation appealed to the Brazilian foreign minister that the proposed settlement violated international law, the haughty Osvaldo Aranha, who claimed friendship with FDR, is said to have responded "Ecuador, with its lack of military resistance, is not a problem for international law."

An "Act of Peace, Friendship and Boundaries between Peru and Ecuador", known thereafter as the Rio Protocol, was signed in January 1942 and ratified by both congresses a month later. Article VIII provided for a boundary, drawn by a Brazilian military geographer, Navy Captain Bras Diaz de Aguiar, that largely followed the 1936 de facto *uti possidetis* line. There were almost no population shifts. Gold mines and oil lands – the latter a reputed source of conflict between British and American companies -- remained in Ecuador. The United States, Brazil, Argentina, and Chile signed on as guarantors to provide "assistance" in case of "doubts or disagreements." Peru withdrew its forces, victorious in a foreign war for the first time in its history and in the most important military event since the disastrous War of the Pacific of 1879-84, which had led to the Chilean occupation of Lima and the loss of the territory of Tarapacá.

In 1943, a Mixed Ecuadorian-Peruvian Boundary Commission began to demarcate the border with assistance from guarantor experts. Progress was rapid in the more populated coastal area, but slowed in the less known interior. The United States supported aerial mapping, losing in the process two Army Air Force planes and 14 crew members in the fog-shrouded mountain jungles. Bras de Aguiar was called on twice to clarify his rulings. Markers formally demarcated 1,600 kilometers of the border; 95% of the Rio Protocol line was now in place. Then, with just 76 kilometers left to go, Ecuador stopped work, saying that U.S. aerial photography of December 1946 had revealed a watershed not accounted for in the Protocol's description of the boundary.

Many Ecuadorians felt the new imagery proved the Protocol had unfairly denied them access to the Amazon River, the heart of their national myth. In 1948, Ecuador declared that the Rio Protocol was *"inejecutable"* or unworkable, impossible to implement. Ecuador withdrew from the Mixed Commission.

In 1960, José Maria Velasco Ibarra was elected President of Ecuador on a nationalist platform and declared that "geographic error" made the Protocol invalid as well as unworkable. Peru continued to deny the existence of a problem, and asked that markers be set to complete the last 76 kilometers of boundary. The guarantors declared that under international law a boundary treaty could not be renounced by a single party, but otherwise did nothing. The jungle mountains of the remote Cordillera del Condor were (and to this day remain) largely unusable, but they contain the watershed of the previously unknown and certainly unnavigable Cenepa river, which had become for Ecuador a symbolic link downstream to the Amazon River.

*Looking up valley toward Tiwinza and the headwaters of the Cenepa river. (Lino Chipana, El Comercio, 1994, photograph reproduced courtesy of El Comercio, Lima, Perú.)*

Over the years that followed, Ecuadorian patrols would set up small encampments, clearing enough jungle to build a hut or two. These outposts were virtually inaccessible from the Peruvian side of the watershed, but when Peruvian patrols did discover them, they would ask the Ecuadorians to leave. In 1981, and again in 1991, the Ecuadorians did not leave, and Peru attacked to dislodge them. Peruvian officers boasted that under rocket attack the Ecuadorians always "ran like rabbits." Guarantor military attachés would confirm that hostilities had ceased, and everyone except for the Ecuadorians would forget. But the final 76 kilometers of the border remained unmarked, open for mischief.

In December 1994, while the first Summit of the Americas was meeting in Miami, Peruvian patrols confirmed previously undisclosed Ecuadorian positions in the upper Cenepa valley. Asked through military channels to leave, the Ecuadorians refused. To reach the Cordillera del Condor from Peru, it was necessary to slog without roads through miles of unforgiving jungle where even

303

helicopters could not land unless someone had first cleared the triple canopy vegetation. On foot, it took seven hours for a fit walker to reach the upper Cenepa from PV1 (*Puesto de Vigilancia* 1), Peru's closest military outpost. Moreover, Peru's military was increasingly bogged down domestically, fighting guerrillas. In 1992, President Fujimori made a state visit to Ecuador and informed President Durán Ballén that he was withdrawing observation posts near the Cenepa headwaters so as to focus Peru's resources internally, against Sendero Luminoso. Durán was an architect and builder, not a nationalist warrior. But Ecuadorian military leaders were still smarting from past debacles. Ecuador had a strategic advantage: the heights on all three sides of the unmarked Cenepa watershed were accepted Ecuadorian territory. Modern technology turned those heights into an advantage, and Ecuador now made full use of it. With advice from Israeli technicians among others, Ecuadorian military forces under highly professional leadership reinforced an existing base at Coangos, which at nearly 5000 feet could support new outposts in the Cenepa valley immediately below, where Peru had replaced manned observation posts with occasional patrols. Building new outposts in territory that would have been Peruvian had the demarcation been completed as originally planned, the Ecuadorians garrisoned them with troops armed with a variety of anti-aircraft weapons, including Soviet BM-21 multiple rocket launchers and man-portable SAMs and British Blowpipes.

In January 1995, after military-to-military contacts broke down, the Peruvians responded as in the past, counting on their air superiority and presumed Ecuadorian weakness. But this time the Ecuadorians were ready. They successfully prevented a Peruvian attempt to build a heliport in the upper Cenepa, and when Peruvian jet fighters and bombers attacked, shot some of them down, as well as several helicopters. Peru countered with their own special forces and by late February mounted an intensified assault on Tiwinza, but was unable to dislodge the Ecuadorians. After six weeks of war, the result was a tragic stalemate. Thousands of tired and hungry opposing soldiers had become hopelessly entangled in seventy square kilometers of high-altitude jungle in small units without front lines, in front, behind, above and below each other, unable to see for the dense vegetation, setting trip-wire grenades and throwing mines randomly into the jungle to defend themselves from unseen enemies. Neither could win, neither could get out without killing or being killed. In February, as the Cenepa fighting escalated, then stalled, both countries moved troops to other points in the border and started a general mobilization. Ships and submarines headed out to sea; tanks rumbled to the populated coastal border. Things threatened to get out of control.

Stu, when you interviewed him a few years ago, Jim Mack, who was at the time our DCM in Lima, told you that "Our military attachés from the embassy were prohibited from going up anywhere near the war zone by their own commander by "force protection" concerns. Instead we sent up our political counselor, not to the front line, but to Peru's forward staging area." "They were very frustrated. It was a difficult time." Stephen McFarland was that FSO, sent where our military attachés were denied. He made it to PV1, 250 kilometers from the nearest Peruvian road head but reachable by helicopter. The upper Cenepa was still many hours away, by foot.

*Q: So how did you get involved?*

EINAUDI: When fighting broke out, ARA Assistant Secretary Watson was caught up in the Mexican peso crisis. He even had a hard time getting Secretary Christopher to let him go to Rio for an emergency meeting to try to secure a cease-fire. He was finally able to go but returned after what he described as "bizarre" sleepless meetings with endless haggling over abstruse details between adversaries each of whom claimed it was the victim and one simply denying there was a problem. Watson saw the fighting as more than a conflict between two countries. A South American war would blow up the Summit Process launched in Miami the month before and encourage other disputes. He wanted the conflict "resolved once and for all," but knew doing so was going to take more time than he could possibly devote. In his oral history with ADST, he gives his reasons for turning to me, including my reputation for being unbiased, adding that he thought I was "not happy sitting in policy planning." To me, Alec stressed that I had proven at the OAS that I had the patience to deal with circuitous legal arguments and knew how to overcome suspicion and distrust.

When asked if I would take on the Peru-Ecuador conflict, I immediately remembered our failures in Nicaragua sixteen years before. First Bill Bowdler then Larry Pezzullo had been asked to deal with Somoza without clear instructions and without the backing of a united U.S. government. Both had accepted, then failed. I also remembered a family ancestor, Juan van Halen, a military adventurer whom the town fathers of Brussels summoned out of semi-retirement in 1830 to take command of their militias against the Dutch in their fight for Belgian independence. In 1980, during the 150th anniversary of Belgium's independence, I took advantage of a NATO Experts Conference to look for his traces. All I found was a worn bas relief on the base of a monument of an unnamed man at a barricade, his raised sword broken just above the hilt. But I remembered what he had asked the good burghers before accepting: "OK, but will you still be here when I need you?" [Juan van Halen, *Les quatre journées de Bruxelles*].

So, I told Alec I needed two things: first, a specific policy understanding, not just to stop the fighting but to settle the underlying dispute; and second, following the example of van Halen and as Pete Vaky had done when Vance had asked him to be Assistant Secretary, I asked for an interagency group to back me. I also told him that my first call would be to Barry McCaffrey, the Commanding General of U.S. Southern Command. Alec agreed.

*Q: Did you already know McCaffrey, or did you just feel you would need military support?*

EINAUDI: Both. I had briefed McCaffrey in Washington when he first became CINCSOUTH a year before. He was a highly decorated wounded survivor of multiple tours in Vietnam and a key architect of the Desert Storm victory against Saddam. A proud and ambitious officer from a military family, he characteristically took his role in Central and South America seriously, despite knowing that it did not involve interests then considered vital to the United States. After that briefing, in which I had told him that his primary challenge would be strengthening ties to Brazil, McCaffrey invited me to visit him in Panama and also to participate in a Milgroup Commanders conference. McCaffrey and I had an excellent relationship based on mutual respect and a desire to make things work. And I knew Peruvian and Ecuadorian military attitudes meant they would be hard nuts to crack even with the U.S. military on board.

*Q: What did you do first?*

EINAUDI: When Alec first called me, it was a Friday and I was in Mexico at a conference. My first call was to my wife, while Alec called the Director of the Policy Planning Staff, Jim Steinberg. I did not call McCaffrey until after Alec and I had talked face to face in Washington the next Monday.

Q: *What did Steinberg say?*

EINAUDI: Alec had faxed me that same Friday in Mexico that Steinberg "concurred eagerly with my request". On another occasion, Steinberg had told me he was my "boss only in theory," alluding I think to the fact that he had inherited me from Sam Lewis, and that Strobe Talbott had said I was part of the "permanent government" – whatever that meant. I had always seen myself as walking a personnel tightrope. But when he and I discussed Peru-Ecuador that Monday, Steinberg was generous. He told me to do what I needed to do. He let me keep my office, doing what I could for S/P only on the side.

Q: *What did McCaffrey say?*

EINAUDI: He was very pleased. He told me SOUTHCOM already had a liaison officer at the negotiations, that he would instruct him to provide me military advice, and that he wished me the best of luck.

On Tuesday, February 14, the fifth day after the first call, I was in Rio, having stopped first in Panama to pick up the officer who would become my military partner throughout the negotiation.

Q: *Who was he and what did he do?*

EINAUDI: Leo Rios. Colonel Leon H. Rios was Deputy Director for Plans, Policy and Strategy, USSOUTHCOM. Barry McCaffrey in effect lent him to me for the duration of the negotiation. He worked out the same flexible relation to his regular posting in

Panama that I had with mine in Washington. He proved critical in developing and maintaining military support on all of our different fronts—within the U.S. military, the Pentagon and the NSC, and with the guarantor militaries, particularly as we shall see the Brazilians. For almost three years, we were either traveling together or speaking almost daily.

Rios' first contribution originated in our first trip. We had arrived in Rio on a commercial flight, bringing with us special communications equipment and a communicator so he could stay in touch with McCaffrey. The customs line at the Rio airport was endless. It was four hours before we got through. Rios was beside himself. Never again, he swore. From then on, for the next three years, I and my State colleagues would fly commercially to Panama, where we would pick up Rios and a C-21. The C-21, the military version of the Learjet, had another advantage. As a military plane, it could land and take off at the military sections of airports. Customs delays were a thing of the past. SOUTHCOM always provided secure satellite communications equipment with a special operations officer to run it (there being no secure cell phones in those days.) Except for the Ambassador's residences in Lima and Buenos Aires, which were large enough to bring the equipment upstairs, the operator would remain locked in hotel rooms with the sensitive equipment, unable to leave, and relying on room service for all needs while we remained in country.

McCaffrey's unstinting professional and personal contributions proved critical to the peace process. The C-21, with UNITED STATES painted on its side, provided in-your-face symbolism that this was a united government-wide effort of the United States. Disembarking from it with Rios in uniform at my side meant I could not be seen as just another American diplomat of whom it could be said "yeah, he represents State but look out, the Pentagon has other views." Less externally visible aspects were just as vital. McCaffrey accepted without reserve that our goal was not just a cease fire and a separation of forces, but a resolution of the underlying causes of the conflict. And, as we shall see, he proved both a bulwark against skeptics in our own government and a mobilizer of acceptance of peace among South American military forces.

*Q: Let's go back to when you first got involved. What was happening on the ground?*

EINAUDI: Initial shock was giving way to confusion. Looking back, it is clear that the civilian governments in both Ecuador and Peru had been to a large extent blindsided by their militaries, which had been acting behind veils of secrecy and institutional opacity. Lack of internal communication within the two belligerents was compounded by the remoteness of the conflict area and surprise, particularly on the Peruvian side, at the severity and inconclusiveness of the fighting. The bizarre haggling that had so impressed Watson continued, at least partly due to the fact we guarantors did not know what was going on the ground and the Peruvians and Ecuadorian representatives were themselves operating blind, with constantly changing instructions, or both.

The day after I arrived in Brasilia, the Brazilian Deputy Minister, Sebastião do Rego Barros, who had been chairing the talks, took the lead in pulling together a proposal for a guarantor observation of a ceasefire, and accompanied that by suggesting that if it were not accepted the guarantor diplomats might disband and leave matters to the OAS or the UN. On February 17, the vice-ministers of Peru and Ecuador, Eduardo Ponce and Marcelo Fernandez de Cordoba, signed a "Declaration of Itamaraty" that announced a cease fire and committed the two countries to talks once their forces were separated. President Durán Ballén made a radio address in Quito saying that Ecuador now accepted the Rio Protocol as the basis for a definitive settlement. In Peru, however, the Presidential election was set for April 9 and the campaign was heating up. To show the flag, President Fujimori traveled to PV1, and was only dissuaded from going further by fear of coming under fire. Fujimori's main opponent in the election was Javier Pérez de Cuellar. As a former UN Secretary General, he might have been expected to encourage diplomacy and avoid jingoism. Instead, he asked, had Fujimori spilled the blood of Peruvian soldiers in vain by agreeing to a ceasefire while Ecuadorian troops were still on Peruvian soil?

In the Cenepa, meanwhile, sporadic clashes continued. Then, on February 22, Peru launched a concerted assault on the main Ecuadorian position in the upper valley, inflicting and suffering numerous casualties in what became known in Ecuador as "black Tuesday." The new fighting brought on a burst of diplomatic activity. President Cardoso of Brazil became directly involved and added a personal representative to a Guarantor military-civilian observer mission that was taking off from Brasilia to reconnoiter the fighting. Despite claims that Ecuador had again attacked Peruvian positions, it was apparent that it was Peru that had broken the cease-fire. Peruvian diplomats were desperate to counter negative reactions to Peru's offensive. In a preview of the pressures that were to come from both sides to see things their way, Ponce sent me a fax from Lima saying he had been naïve to think things would be calmer there than in Rio and Brasilia. Peru's ambassador to the United States Ricardo Luna called me privately from Washington to insist Peru could make major concessions -- so long as they were under the Rio Protocol "Anything is possible within its terms, nothing without." At the same time, Ecuadorian representatives were accusing Peru of wanting to prevent the guarantors from observing for themselves what was happening on the ground. Militarily, each side was claiming victory and claiming that it held the same key post. But they could not agree either on its precise location or its name: Ecuador spelled it Tiwintza and Peru spelled it Tiwinza.[3] As the fog of war began to lift, however, a new strategic reality stood revealed: Peru had been unable to drive Ecuadorian forces out of the Cenepa.

February 28 was the inauguration in Montevideo of Julio Sanguinetti as President of Uruguay. Both Fujimori and Durán Ballén attended. The two presidents refused to meet, but their foreign ministers met and signed a new barebones declaration that reaffirmed the February 17 declaration.

Peru and Ecuador had agreed, again, to a cease fire. But would it hold any better than the first? Would their militaries observe it? Would the fighting on the ground actually stop? There were indications that military leaders on both sides had acted with considerable autonomy, keeping plans and even decisions from civilian authorities. As for the guarantors, their diplomats had agreed to "arrange for the immediate dispatch of their observers or representatives to the area." Under what conditions would the guarantor militaries agree to go? And would the parties agree to those conditions? Would they provide security for the observers? Would they be able to? How would the warring forces be separated? Who would pay?

*Q: How did you approach getting answers to those questions?*

---

[3] I alternate the spelling, depending on the user.

EINAUDI: It was at this point that the guarantor countries each identified one person to act as the central reference point for their efforts. Brazil, the lead of the original Rio Protocol, was the undisputed chair, represented initially by Rego Barros, then Fernando Reis, who yielded almost immediately to Ivan Canabrava; Chile, by Fabio Vio, who was to be replaced by Juan Martabit; Argentina, by José Manuel Uranga, who gave way to Alfredo Chiaradia. I was the U.S. representative, the only special envoy to participate from beginning to end. My counterparts were all vice ministers. As a former ambassador to the OAS and a senior member of the Secretary's planning staff with the support of the regional bureau, I had some rank and reach, but it was far from the others' sub-cabinet positions. Still, I had key advantages: I had far and away the most time to devote, and while the others wanted to manage the dispute, I was determined to solve it.

*Q: What role did the foreign ministers play?*

EINAUDI: The foreign ministers of the three South American guarantors, Brazil's Luis Felipe Lampreia who acted as chair, Argentina's Guido di Tella, and Chile's José Miguel Insulza all remained in office throughout the period of the negotiations. Madeleine Albright replaced Warren Christopher in January 1997. The South Americans all hosted negotiating sessions in their capitals, and Secretary Albright opened a 1998 meeting of the Commission on Border Integration in Washington. All engaged from time to time on the telephone. The sensitivity of the issues involved, however, meant that the key decisions were ultimately made by the Presidents. It was Fujimori and Mahuad for the parties, and Cardoso and Clinton for the guarantors, who finally said "yes" to the peace settlement the special envoys built in their name.

*Q: So where did you all begin?*

EINAUDI: The first order of business was obviously to get the military situation under control. The Brasilia and Montevideo agreements stipulated that military observers from the guarantor countries would separate the contending forces and keep the cease fire from coming apart.

U.S. participation was committed, but not its form. The Somalia debacle memorialized in the movie *Black Hawk Down* had taken place in the fall of 1993 and was still fresh on everyone's mind. The Clinton administration's withdrawal a week later of the USS Harlan County when threatened by a Haitian mob had left a sense of humiliation and uncertainty. Two U.S. Blackhawks had been shot down by USAF F-15s in a friendly fire incident in Iraq in April 1994. Difficult commitments were on the horizon in Bosnia, Haiti and Rwanda. The White House, particularly the NSC, and within the NSC the National Security Advisor, Tony Lake, had doubts about U.S. military involvement abroad -- certainly far more than their successors after 9/11. Congress was controlled by the Republicans, some of whom were complaining that the Democrats were acting as if the U.S. was the world's fire brigade.

*Q: What was decided?*

EINAUDI: We agreed that we would join the other guarantors in providing ten men to a multinational Military Observer Mission, Ecuador-Peru, always thereafter referred to as MOMEP. The NSC reluctantly authorized U.S. military participation for 90 days. Ninety days was not enough to get anything done. I think everyone knew it. The negotiations ultimately lasted 3 ½ years. One of the fears of the NSC had been there would be a headline "American soldiers killed in the Amazon jungles" and everybody would ask what the blank is the United States doing with soldiers in the Amazon jungles? Back in Washington at the Pentagon, Army negotiators at one point were so adamant in insisting on the need for our men in MOMEP to be well armed that I said it sounded as if they wanted tactical nukes to defend against attacks from wild Indians. A second sticking point was command and control. Brazil chaired the guarantor effort, a Brazilian general had led the February reconnaissance, and Brazil immediately assigned a general officer to command MOMEP. We did not want U.S. soldiers under foreign command. This was ultimately resolved by having each national contingent under the direct control of an officer of their own nationality, with the Brazilian general named Coordinator General.

*Q: How did the other countries react?*

EINAUDI: By the time our Joint Chiefs of Staff approved reasonable Terms of Reference it was March 10. The other guarantor observers had assembled in Brasilia March 6-8 for orientation, then moved to Peru and Ecuador in Brazilian C-130s. The U.S. observers had held up in Panama waiting for JCS approval, but officers from our Milgroup in Quito scouted things out at Patuca, 65 km from the conflict zone.

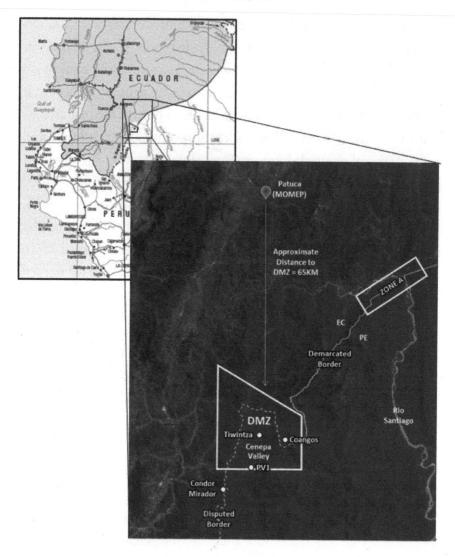

*Map of the demilitarized zone and the conflict area (Created by LR Einaudi with assistance from Colonel Leon H. Rios, personal photo)*

Patuca became the main base for MOMEP and for Joint Task Force SAFE BORDER, the U.S. logistical tail. The next day U.S. C-27s began to bring in supplies. Four UH60 Blackhawks from Panama arrived on March 13. By that time the Brazilian General and some of the South American observers had made an initial flyover of part of the area in a Peruvian helicopter.

*Q: How did our people feel about that?*

EINAUDI: Poorly. Fearing both poor maintenance and fog of war accidents, McCaffrey did not want U.S. soldiers flying in belligerent helicopters. Colonel Glenn Weidner, who took leave from his position as Milgroup commander in Honduras to lead our contingent in MOMEP, felt arriving late put him behind the eight ball. But Weidner was an outstanding officer and there was a job to be done. His men were mainly from the 7th Special Forces Group at Fort Bragg. All spoke Spanish and all had previous experience in Latin America. Like the Brazilians, they accepted Spanish as the common language of MOMEP. Each of the other guarantor contingents included officers with prior peace keeping experience, a Brazilian in Angola, one of the Argentines in Lebanon, and a Chilean in Kashmir. A few had known each other at the U.S. Army School of the Americas in Panama.

The U.S. Blackhawks were fundamental to MOMEP's success. The extraordinarily dangerous conditions—mountainous high-altitude cloud-bound jungle in roadless terrain—created extraordinarily difficult logistical problems. Helicopter support was essential, and not just ordinary helicopters, but ones that could handle heavy loads for long hauls at high altitudes. General Kenneth Bowra, who the next year became Commander of U.S. Army Special Forces (Airborne), had served in both Vietnam and Cambodia. After visiting Patuca, he told me that if Cambodia was a 10 for difficulty, the triple canopy jungle made the Cenepa a 12.

Just as MOMEP was getting underway in mid-March, one of our Blackhawks was painted by the Peruvians, meaning that the

U.S. pilot realized that his craft had been locked onto by radar, implying that someone could be readying to shoot it down. The pilot returned immediately to Patuca and would not move without McCaffrey's authorization. A dispute was brewing. Who was commanding what? The MOMEP structure and the Brazilian General, or the Americans? Weidner called McCaffrey. McCaffrey called me. I told him I was not surprised that the Peruvians would paint an American helicopter but would be very surprised if they fired. McCaffrey recognized the importance of unity in MOMEP. He relented. The Blackhawks flew.

Q: Was it that simple?

EINAUDI: Of course not. In fact, MOMEP's birth pangs on the ground were almost as difficult as the initial Washington bureaucratics. David Randolph, who was later to play a key role in Washington, was then in our embassy in Quito. He had served in the Special Forces before joining the Foreign Service, and thus, twenty years later, he was the natural choice to keep an eye on developments at Patuca. He wrote me recently: *You may recall that time you and Barry [McCaffrey] came to Quito, and Barry's one-star head of SouthCom's Special Operations Command told everyone that things were great at Patuca. I had just come back from Patuca to attend the meeting, and I said: "Well, not exactly. Actually, things are hanging by a thread. The Guarantors are really pissed by the constraints being placed on them by the US." We then went to Patuca, and the Brazilian general started the meeting by saying: "I am glad you came today, because I was just about to call Brasilia and say that this whole thing was not working and we should pull out." From my perspective, Barry had been severely micro-managing things, to the great detriment of the operation. This meeting led Barry to give Glenn [Widener] some more breathing room and keep everyone on board.*

Q: *Was McCaffrey just making sure you all knew who to salute?*

EINAUDI: No, the conditions were genuinely dangerous, and I think he felt that even one casualty would be enough to unravel NSC support for the mission. That we never suffered casualties can in large part be credited to McCaffrey as well as the professionalism of all concerned. Badly wounded twice in combat in Vietnam, McCaffrey had gone down in helicopters several times, both in combat and on maneuvers. He saw our Blackhawks as essential to safety as well as to operational capacity. Helicopter flights at altitude, with fog and drifting clouds that allowed only a few hours of visibility a day, were hazardous even with no risk of conflict. And the Cenepa was an unstable armed camp.

Operations of all kinds were greatly complicated by confused and unstable conditions on the ground. Thousands of mines had been laid, not only in the conflict zone but along much of the border. But the sketches of where the mines had been placed were questionable. At Tiwintza alone, Ecuador had scattered some 6,000 Brazilian-manufactured anti-personnel mines in what one of its officers later described as a "360 degree defensive arc." Peru had deployed thousands of Russian and Czech mines.

Q: *How were the forces ultimately separated?*

EINAUDI: The intermingling of the two countries' units made withdrawal difficult. Each had forces cutting off the other's retreat. Distrust was high. Each belligerent was accusing the other of reinfiltrating troops under cover of the ceasefire. And the politics of the dispute hung over everything. Ecuador wanted to record its advances. Peru just wanted them out. In an effort to avoid boundary implications, the Declaration of Itamaraty had specified that the geography of the conflict area had no standing beyond what was necessary to separate the forces and certainly none for the boundary.

Left to their own devices, without guarantor support and pressure, Peru and Ecuador would probably not have been able to disengage peacefully. Passing a real test of imagination and professionalism, MOMEP asked both parties to provide orders of battle and unit placements. Somewhere in my files I should have three transparencies on which MOMEP officers mapped the respective locations of the two sides. It would be easy to mistake them for magnified pictures of a bad case of a virulent bi-colored pox, the different-colored spots intermingled haphazardly. Once the locations were charted, MOMEP organized the withdrawals, one small unit at a time. A prolonged exchange of fire was documented March 27, and several cease fire violations were reported as most of the withdrawals finally took place in May. There were several casualties from mines, but there were no new deaths. When the forces were finally fully separated three months later, MOMEP had counted 5,000 men, 3,000 Ecuadorian and 2,000 Peruvian, most of them special forces, split up into some sixty different units. As provided for in the Declaration of Itamaraty, once the separation was completed, the only belligerent troops left inside what was to become the DMZ were 50 Ecuadorian troops at Coangos and 50 Peruvians at PV1 (*Puesto de Vigilancia 1*). Colonel Glenn Widener published a description of the operation, for which I believe he deserves great credit. Later, after some discussion, MOMEP also participated in the demobilization of 140,000 soldiers at other locations near the populated border.

*Q: Have we exhausted the military side of things for the moment? When we come back, I would like to turn to the diplomacy.*

EINAUDI: I agree, bearing in mind that the effectiveness of MOMEP, and the evolution of attitudes among the belligerent armed forces, proved critical to the very end. Peru and Ecuador's hardline warriors delayed the peace. And although they finally accepted it, hot heads among them almost blocked settlement at the last minute.

*Q: I gather that you saw the diplomacy developing in three phases: setting the stage, developing the solution, and finally some tension-filled months before the successful outcome.*

EINAUDI: Yes. Setting the stage for real diplomacy proved just as complicated as the military separation of forces we have just discussed.

As MOMEP was hitting the ground at Patuca, I was in Lima and Quito taking the political temperature. The Peruvians projected unyielding anger and arrogance. My long-time friend, Fernando Belaunde Terry, the cosmopolitan architect and former President of Peru, told me that Fujimori might have been "born in the hold of the ship on which his parents were traveling and on which I returned to Peru from Galveston after getting my degree in 1938 at the University of Texas at Austin." Even if Fujimori was born in Peru, Belaunde added, Fujimori had "never buried one of his own in Peruvian soil," and therefore could not be counted upon to defend Peru's territorial integrity. After my visit, *Caretas*, Peru's leading newsweekly, published a cartoon suggesting Fujimori was so weak that I would be the one to decide where the boundary would go.

*"Tell me, Mr. Fujimori, are the Ecuadorian outposts 'Etza' and 'Lieutenant Ortiz' going to remain forever inside Peruvian territory?" "Better ask Einaudi that." (Eduardo Rodriguez Díaz, Caretas Magazine, 1995. Reproduced courtesy of "Heduardo" Eduardo Rodriguez Díaz.)*

In Ecuador, attitudes were even more emotional, with defiance and pride emblazoned in the motto that had long adorned the hall of the national Congress in Quito that "Ecuador is, was, and always will be an Amazonian Country." President Durán Ballén was riding a burst of popularity. His declaration "Ni un paso atrás" – "not a step back" had been spelled out in in river boulders on a deforested riverbank at Tiwintza by Ecuadorian soldiers. Diego Cordovez, a celebrated former Ecuadorian Foreign Minister who as a UN official had negotiated the withdrawal of Soviet forces from Afghanistan, told me "The conflict will be solved, but you will be dead first." The only encouragement I got was from Oswaldo Hurtado, who told me that, despite all the nationalist hullabaloo about Ecuador as an Amazonian country, he was the first and only President of Ecuador to actually sail on the Amazon.

At the end of March, after spending three solid weeks in Ecuador, Peru, and Brazil, I cabled the Department from Brasilia that "left to their own devices, Peru and Ecuador will not make peace." Unless brought under control soon, their fighting over "three huts and a stand of corn in an impassable jungle" would unleash a nasty arms race and irrational forces that would bury regional hopes for economic development and domestic tranquility. My bottom line was that our best hope was to build on the Rio Protocol framework. In Peru, the guarantors were accepted (albeit somewhat suspiciously) as its enforcers. In Ecuador, the guarantors were suspect precisely because their authority derived from the Rio Protocol, but they still represented international law, which Ecuador saw as a shield against Peru's superior power.

*Q: Sounds complicated and unpromising.*

EINAUDI: When I was Ambassador to the OAS, I had often told the members of my Mission that we were engaged in a two-front war: with the other members of the OAS, and with our own government. The Peru-Ecuador conflict had six foreign fronts and sometimes more. We've already touched on ensuring U.S. government unity. But similar battles had to be fought in and with each of the other guarantor nations, not to mention the two belligerents, who faced all the divisive issues of addressing problems that had hung over them throughout their histories.

Let me begin with relations among the four special envoys. We each came under pressure, both at home and from the belligerents. Fortunately, the four of us developed good personal chemistry and kept in touch by phone and fax as we navigated our respective capital bureaucracies and embassies. After a while we developed a practical definition of what constituted a "guarantor meeting" or a "guarantor position." Unless all four of us were present, no meeting could be called a guarantor meeting. No statement could be considered a guarantor position unless all four of us agreed in advance. More than once, senior officials, including foreign ministers, saw this as a challenge to their authority, but this simple understanding proved very effective. There were an incredible number of angles.

*Q: Can you give an example?*

EINAUDI: Peru and Ecuador each actively sought to curry favor with the guarantors, divide them, or otherwise influence them, both officially and though the media. Ecuador had a tradition of seeking ties to Chile and Brazil to counter Peru. Chile was always worried about Peruvian (and Bolivian) revanchism for the War of the Pacific. Peru was in a period of extensive press manipulation by the regime. Argentina had diverse commercial interests and a tendency to make pronouncements. Brazil was beginning to feel its oats internationally and was jealous of its Rio Protocol leadership. The United States was far away and few people were interested in what was happening in South America. But distrust and stereotypes were universal, and the parties of war and peace had all kinds of rumors with which to play. For example, claims that the real causes of the conflict were desires to control oil and the gold in them thar hills sought to divide the guarantors and lessen their capacity to promote peace. Rumors of troop movements, war plans, and arms purchases were used regularly to prevent or interrupt negotiations or to induce statements revealing favoritism for one side or the other.

In these circumstances, trust, mutual respect, and constant communication were essential to maintain guarantor unity. But strength builds outwards. The starting point was maintaining unity at home.

Interagency coordination in Washington was essential. Peru-Ecuador matters in the USG were to run through (or at least by) me. Working out of the ARA/AND office, foreign service officer Lynn M. Sicade became engaged in the negotiation with the Pentagon of the original MOMEP Terms of Reference, then drafted reports, memoranda, and cables, also taking on the time-consuming coordinating role of the Peru-Ecuador Interagency Working Group (IWG), reminding me of the ARA-NSC IG I had run in Vaky's time. The IWG included, on a regular basis, the NSC, State, Defense, AID, ACDA, and USIA. In addition to S/P and several offices in the regional bureau (ARA), State Department functional offices that participated regularly included intelligence (INR), political-military (PM) and legal (L). Lynn Sicade was critical in keeping the State offices involved, and Leo Rios chipped in with the Pentagon, making the effort a true civil-military collaboration.

*Q: Did this civil-military cooperation extend to the guarantors as well?*

EINAUDI: Yes, and no. In May, in Brasilia, the first meeting to discuss establishment of a DMZ, tensions among and between diplomats and military officers were obvious. I felt them mainly in awkward silences, but Rios felt them as toxic. Part of the problem was that the South American civilians and military were not accustomed to working together or even really communicating. Military and civilian spheres were traditionally thought of as different *fueros*, the Spanish term for separate jurisdictions. We soon learned, however, that there was a far more poisonous factor at play. Military dictatorships of the previous decade in all three of the South American guarantor countries had included bitter clashes among some of the very persons now meeting again for the first time to discuss Ecuador and Peru. Over time, meetings of Guarantor senior civilian and military leaders proved less tense and increasingly productive. Rios felt that our facilitating a common civil-military effort within the Guarantor nations was itself significant for the stability and security of the Western Hemisphere. I felt less sure.

We did manage two successes to help consolidate the separation of forces. The first was to explicitly define a DMZ. My instructions from Washington were that this was essential to prevent mission creep for MOMEP. The territory to be included was of critical importance to both sides. Peru was adamant that it had to include all the lands they believed had been awarded to them under the Protocol plus an equal amount of Ecuadorian territory – a formula that could be read to deny Ecuador any *uti possidetis* advantage from their success in holding Tiwintza. The resolution, which met Peru's practical demands but Ecuador's only in a formal sense, was to reassert the original Itamaraty formula that the coordinates of the DMZ could not be considered in establishing the boundary. That negotiation took six weeks and did not take effect until August. The other was my initiative, to ask Peru and Ecuador to participate in MOMEP. I saw the inclusion of the antagonists in MOMEP as a confidence building measure. My reasoning was that the Peruvian and Ecuadorian militaries needed to be brought into the settlement process, and that joining MOMEP would at the very least enable their intelligence services to see for themselves what was going on. My proposal was accepted in our U.S. IWG largely as a path toward reducing the U.S. profile. The other guarantors were skeptical, but both Peru and Ecuador accepted -- on condition that the guarantors not decrease their military presence, which was helping to keep them apart. The observers on the ground had been operating under the original MOMEP terms of reference. After Peruvian and Ecuadorian officers were integrated, they helped produce an excellent MOMEP Observers Manual to further codify observation procedures.

Washington's desire to avoid mission creep had led McCaffrey to limit our observers to a square security zone immediately around the conflict area. That box was the starting point for negotiations that ultimately produced the formally defined DMZ. But there was constant trouble outside the DMZ as well. During the 1940s, concrete markers had been used to designate the border where it had been agreed. Northeast of the DMZ, a particularly prominent tree had been designated Hito 20 or Marker no. 20. The entire tree had since mysteriously disappeared, and the area between Hito 19 and Hito 21 had become a no man's land of competing outposts, among them Etza and Teniente Ortiz for Ecuador and Pachacutec and Chiqueiza for Peru. Some thirty cease-fire violations were reported there, starting in May and intensifying in August and September. Working with Peru and Ecuador's liaison officers, MOMEP succeeded in defining the area between Hitos 19 and 21 as Zone "A" and having the two sides withdraw from the zone, starting with all indirect fire, crew served, and air defense weapons. By the end of October all military personnel had left.

Fortunately for us, our participation in MOMEP was not costing us financially. The U.S. military is expensive. Peru and Ecuador each paid millions of dollars to reimburse us for our participation in MOMEP. Southern Command billed them periodically. David Randolph, then the Political Counselor in our Embassy in Ecuador, vividly remembers Ecuador's first payment. It was brought to him by hand by an Ecuadorian army officer. David could not believe his eyes: it was a check for more than a million dollars, a check of a size few of us have ever seen. A more direct form of payment was later worked out. If I remember correctly Peru and Ecuador each wound up reimbursing us more than five million dollars apiece. That was a lot of money, but as one of our military folks commented, keeping the peace that way was cheap compared to fighting, and it certainly made us feel more appreciated than sometimes happened elsewhere.

*Q: Were these military achievements appreciated in Washington?*

EINAUDI: Only to a point. JTF SAFE BORDER, our logistical tail for MOMEP, never exceeded its personnel limit of 82 and worked extremely well, providing virtually all the logistical support for MOMEP. Ecuador and Peru shared the costs, but, aside from Brazil, the other guarantors supplied little more than their ten observers. In addition, our Blackhawks were essential, and had no accidents. But their presence became an enduring political headache in Washington. Providing them implied what looked like an unending commitment. What if there was no solution? The White House and the NSC did not want "another Cyprus" where U.S. forces would be stuck indefinitely.

In the fall of 1995, taking advantage of a meeting in the Situation Room, Lake asked me to join him in his office in the Old Executive Office Building. His deputy, Nancy Soderberg, accompanied us. He had a map of the disputed area on the table. I could not believe my eyes, when he took out a ruler, and asked me to show him how to split the difference. Inwardly, I shuddered, thinking of the 1916 Sykes-Picot agreement in the Middle East. Outwardly, I explained that the academic and foreign affairs communities in both Peru and Ecuador had so exhaustively documented so many real and imagined points of dispute that no straight line solution would ever be accepted, even were the geography to allow one. Our discussion did not reassure him we would be able to withdraw from MOMEP soon.

Peru and Ecuador had committed in the Declaration of Itamaraty to "begin discussions" of remaining issues once all belligerent forces were separated and demobilized. These were referred to as "*Impases subsistentes*" (remaining impasses) because Peru refused to accept that there were problems. But the foreign ministers of Ecuador and Peru did not actually meet until January 1996, and then only in the presence of the guarantor envoys. It was in Lima, and nothing much happened. Peru's Tudela insisted there was nothing to discuss other than completing the demarcation. Ecuador's Leoro asserted the Protocol was "partially inexecutable" without giving any details. But it was the first time since 1942 that Peru and Ecuador had discussed the border officially.

Taking advantage of the meeting between Peru and Ecuador's foreign ministers, General McCaffrey took the initiative to consolidate military support for the negotiations. He invited the other guarantor military commanders to join him in Quito and Lima, then go together to inspect MOMEP on February 11, 1996.

After the event, this visit can sound very easy. I have talked about how geography and weather affected the conflict area and the separation of forces. But it was almost as hard just getting there. Built by Italy's Aermacchi under a NATO offset, SOUTHCOM's C-27s were a form of transport designed specifically to handle short dirt runways like the one at Patuca. I remember its hard precipitous bumpy landings well, but I was not along on the guarantor generals' visit. Here is Rios' description:

*When we flew into Patuca on board a C-27, the weather was precluding a good visual of the airfield for landing. The practice was to fly to the radar beacon and then dive through the ever-present rain clouds in order to gain a visual of a river that we would follow for a minute or two in order to spot the airfield at Patuca. Failing to spot the airfield, the pilot would have to make a steep climb in order to keep from smashing into the mountains that surrounded the Patuca airfield. So, as we tried to land in Patuca for this historic meeting, the four Guarantor Generals were strapped into their seats as we rapidly repeated the steep dives and climbs.*

*COL Steve Fee (the U.S. Contingent Commander at the time) and I were sitting directly across from McCaffrey and the other Guarantor Generals. After the fourth steep dive and climb, Fee puked in his cap while the Guarantor Generals all watched.*

*While their faces turned a little greener as they watched Fee puke, to their credit they didn't follow suit. Fortunately for all of us, we landed just as Fee finished in his cap. Better yet, Fee had the presence of mind to seal the contents of his cap and didn't spill a drop on the cabin floor as we took a hard landing in Patuca.*

After landing at Patuca, the generals flew by MOMEP helicopters to a spot near Hito 21 and the convergence of the Rio Santiago and the Rio Yaupi. There, they signed the "Declaration of Commitment to Peace between Ecuador and Peru by the Guarantor Nation's Armed Forces" committing them to "fully support the diplomatic initiatives toward peace" and pledging to continue MOMEP so long as there was "continuous progress" toward peace. Colonel

Rios reported to me that McCaffrey felt this was one of the greatest accomplishments of his extraordinary military career.

*11 February 1996 at the Rio Yaupi. Senior General Officers from the Guarantor Nations passing in review of an honor guard of Peruvian and Ecuadorian soldiers. In the center of the formation is the Brazilian Coordinator General. General McCaffrey is at the far right. (U.S. Army photo, 1996).*

Shortly thereafter, McCaffrey left SOUTHCOM to join President Clinton's Cabinet as Director of the Office of National Drug Control Policy (ONDCP). Early in the Clinton Administration, McCaffrey had been insulted as he arrived at the White House in full uniform, by a female staffer who greeted him saying "We don't like generals around here." Becoming Drug Czar was a bit of vindication, although he had told me he had been hoping to replace Lake as National Security Advisor.

*Q: Did it help to have an advocate at court, so to speak?*

EINAUDI: I don't really know. McCaffrey definitely set us on the right course, but our troubles with the NSC persisted. At a difficult moment in February 1996, in effort to keep everybody involved, I invited Fulton Armstrong, a CIA officer then serving on the NSC staff, to join my team for negotiations in Quito with representatives of both the guarantors and the belligerent foreign ministers. My move unfortunately backfired. Armstrong was stunned to see the close relationship that I had developed with Rios and other members of our military. He came to the conclusion that he had stumbled on a rogue operation in which the State Department and the U.S. Southern Command were cooperating to subvert the directives of the NSC. Had I not invited him, we wouldn't have had the problem. There are times when inclusion does not work. And a single person can make a lot of difference. Sicade recalls that coordination with the NSC became much smoother when Armstrong was replaced by Ted Piccone.

That summer, Deputy National Security Advisor Nancy Soderberg accompanied us to guarantor capitals together with McCaffrey's successor Wesley Clark, the very image of a modern four-star general. Progress on the diplomatic front was slow, but Brazil was considering buying helicopters to reduce the American logistical tail and calm NSC fears of U.S. overcommitment. Rios was honchoing the negotiations with Sikorsky, and Brazil would ultimately take delivery of four UH-60L aircraft the next year. This time, inclusion worked. Clark decided to follow the McCaffrey blueprint and support our efforts. Soderberg was so impressed by the attention I received that she joked that traveling with me was "like travelling with Madonna."

*Flying to Brasilia from Lima in the C-21 in August 1996. Lynn Sicade (at left margin), Nancy Soderberg, Leo Rios, Luigi Einaudi. (Photograph courtesy of LR Einaudi, personal photo.)*

In addition to the Lt. General commanding MOMEP, Brazil was providing a colonel as chief of staff and another colonel to head its ten-man contingent, plus some construction support, but neither it nor Argentina or Chile had helicopters that could operate in the Cenepa. Learning the NSC was pushing us to transition the support structure to one of the guarantors, the Brazilian army offered to assume the mission if the U.S. sold them Blackhawks. Soderberg agreed during a C-21 flight from Lima to Brasilia that the NSC would approve the sale. Colonel Rios became the point man, only to learn from Sikorsky that the only way to get UH60s in time was to divert Blackhawks already in production for the U.S. Army. Rios got it done – at the cost of some personal discomfort from his parent service. He asked for aircraft with all of the avionics necessary to operate in remote regions, with hardpoints to attach external fuel tanks for long-range operations and hoists to lift loads in dense jungle terrain. He also asked for a five-year support package, with repair parts, maintenance support and training, and then passed the information to the Brazilians who were delighted. They countered, however, that they had good offers from Euro Copter and Russia (Hind Helicopters), both of which were reportedly capable of operating at altitude. The Brazilians wanted a better price. Rios lost a month on this until the Brazilians agreed to the lowest price that Sikorsky could offer. The transition took about three months, with Rios shuttling between Panama and Brasilia for USSOUTHCOM to coordinate the plans developed by the Brazilian Joint Staff.

One of the Blackhawk helicopters Brazil bought to replace the U.S. UH60s. Note the Brazilian Army aviation patch with the flags of the four Guarantors. (Brazilian Military photograph, 1996.)

Q: While all this was going on, were you making some diplomatic progress?

EINAUDI: Keeping the military situation under control was essential for diplomacy to have a chance. Developing an exit strategy for our helicopters reduced some of the pressure for the

U.S. to leave, but the White House was still asking for evidence of substantive progress in the negotiations. And this was proving difficult. McCaffrey's initiative dramatizing guarantor military support for MOMEP but conditioning it on movement toward peace induced a flurry of diplomatic activity.

Little more than a week later, Foreign Ministers Tudela and Leoro met in Quito with the guarantor representatives. The Guarantors had told both parties it was time for both parties to define the "*impases subsistentes*" in writing and accompanied this by reminding them that MOMEP's mandate needed to be renewed. Never before had Peru admitted the existence of problems to negotiate. Never before had Ecuador defined its concerns. The encounter began February 21 with an evening meeting presided over personally by President Durán Ballén, who calmly and explicitly instructed his ever-fearful foreign minister to define Ecuador's *impases* within the framework of the Rio Protocol. Two days later, on February 23, the parties provided each guarantor an envelope containing their written list of *impases* to be negotiated. With typical obduracy, however, the envelopes were sealed with beeswax and accompanied by a signed request that asked us to witness that they be kept confidential and unopened until MOMEP reported on compliance with demobilization and troop levels in the DMZ as specified in the Itamaraty accords. At the same time, the ministers created a bilateral defense commission to negotiate transparency in military matters and formally requested an extension of MOMEP until the conclusion of the negotiations.

In Brasilia, on March 6, 1996, the ministers and the guarantors met again, MOMEP certified the military conditions had been met, and the envelopes were opened. The United States immediately sought to capitalize on this mote of progress. Secretary Christopher included the other three Guarantors in a five-nation trip to the region in March, and President Clinton met with President Fujimori in May and Durán Ballén in June.

But the second half of 1996 and much of 1997 produced mostly frustrations. Neither government was willing to make substantive concessions. The parties were stubbornly unwilling to move beyond formalities and sought to cross every "t" and dot every "i". And it became obvious that both were rebuilding their forces. Ecuador bought Kfir fighter bombers from Israel, and Peru countered with Sukhoi's and MiG-29s from Belarus. Military activities would flare up. Patrols outside the DMZ would exchange a few shots. Forces would be repositioned. Never much hard intelligence, but lots of rumors. In all four guarantor capitals the tensions and delays were generally seen as proof of stalemated negotiations that were going nowhere. The guarantors were desperate to crack the frozen immobility of the two parties.

In August 1996, Abdalá Bucaram succeeded Durán Ballén as president of Ecuador. Bucaram, a coastal populist, was not a good fit with the austere folks from the Quito highlands, but he was expansively positive with the White House delegation to his inaugural that he wanted to make peace with Peru. The NSC was pushing me to turn Bucaram's words into real progress. I discussed the situation with the other Guarantors, and proposed that I take advantage of the invitation and my relative freedom from other responsibilities to go to Quito for an extended effort to identify possible avenues for progress. Lynn Sicade remembers you could hear a pin drop after I described my intentions. The other three were not happy and implored me to remember that "everything we do we have to do together." They had some disquiet at my undertaking a form of shuttle diplomacy. They worried that the U.S. bilateral Ambassadors to Peru and Ecuador were complicating the issues. They suggested Bucaram was playing the guarantors and trying to divide us. I assured them I would not say anything without them, and would meet with them before doing anything, reminding them that I had a record of traveling to guarantor capitals to consult them first. Finally, Ivan Canabrava, the Brazilian chair, spoke up with a sort of pleading tone, saying in essence, "Well, if you really have to go, Godspeed. But if you fail, we're blaming you."

I went to Quito and stayed for ten days to listen and try to pry out proposals the Ecuadorians could live with. After my extended stay in Quito, a Peruvian paper revealed that I was plotting with Ecuador because General Moncayo and I had gone to high school together. Fake news is not new!

My stay in Quito proved useful in many ways, all of them helpful to the settlement. I am a careful listener, and that builds trust. Leaders of the Shuar indigenous people took me to task for referring to the conflict territories as "empty" or "unpopulated," which they said revealed my white man's urban-centered mentality. They argued that the Shuar, Peru's Aguarunas and other Amazon peoples populated enormous areas they only visited occasionally. Indeed, they had long used a cave in the upper Cenepa called Cueva de los Tayos, abandoning it only after military activities had increased in recent years. So much for UCLA geographer George McCutcheon McBride's romantic image in his 1942 report to Sumner Welles that the Cordillera del Condor was located "where no human foot had trod." These discussions led directly to the provision in the final settlement that indigenous peoples would have unrestricted freedom of access to the ecological reserves created by the peace agreement. More importantly, during our extended conversations

Ecuadorian military and diplomatic leaders told me that one reason for their failure to make proposals in the negotiations is that they feared automatic rejection by Peru for the sole reason that it was they who were making them. They armed me with several ideas that I succeeded in having the guarantors introduce later into the negotiations as our own.

As the negotiations dragged, we learned to use time positively. One method was to keep the ball in the air, knowing that then it was sure to come down again. For example, after a mind numbingly negative session in which no agreement seemed possible on anything, we consciously decided to allow no meeting, no matter how unproductive, to end without a specific date to meet again to resume talks. Moreover, while skeptics saw the creation of Commissions and technical committees as a waste of time, all this, and even the mere passage of time, was having an impact on both public opinion and the parties of peace and war in each country. The parties of war were regrouping, rearming and planning for renewed conflict, but the parties of peace were also organizing and taking advantage of public opinion that was getting away from the fever-pitch initially induced by the Cenepa combats. Time well used was also exhausting the naysayers in the negotiations, who were finding their complaints methodically investigated and set aside by the very Commissions and technical committees some thought were simply a waste of time.

*Q: I'm sure our people were on the impatient side.*

EINAUDI: Yes. But we were working on that also. To keep pressure on the belligerents, I endeavored to obtain shows of U.S. political support for an active negotiation. While mobilizing interagency support, we also succeeded in having the Congress

"applaud [our] earnest work . . . as guarantor of the Rio Protocol."
When agreement was reached on the demilitarized zone, President
Clinton wrote to Fujimori congratulating him and stressing the
agreement's importance to continuation of the Observer Mission. I
thought Fujimori could use it against the war party in his military.
Similarly, when negotiations were stalling in 1997, my former
colleagues Michele Manatt and Roger Noriega helped generate
letters to the presidents of Peru and Ecuador from House and
Senate foreign affairs leaders of both parties, Ben Gilman, Lee
Hamilton and Jesse Helms.

In December 1996 Peruvian foreign minister Tudela was among
the hostages taken by the MRTA (Tupac Amaru Revolutionary
Movement, a terrorist group akin to better known *Sendero
Luminoso*) in the Japanese Embassy in Lima; he was not released
until April, 126 days later, by a commando raid that killed all 14
hostage takers at the loss of one hostage and two commandos. In
the meantime, in February 1997, Ecuador's President Bucaram was
impeached. Popularly known as "Crazy Abdalá," he was judged
unprecedentedly corrupt and impeached by Congress as unfit
for office. But nothing I ever knew personally that he did was as
crazy as his sister, who on a campaign stage had suddenly bared a
breast and squeezed it out toward the crowd saying "Vote for us,
no oligarch is ever going to suck on this tit." The chaos in Quito
and the hostage crisis in Lima underscored another overarching
reality: settlements require having governments in each country
stable enough so that each party can trust the other to be capable
of delivering when peace is made.

*Q: Fujimori got a lot of credit in some quarters for the ruthless ending
of the hostage crisis, but he was also much criticized. How did you
see him?*

EINAUDI: I had dealt with Fujimori after reaction to his 1992 *autogolpe* shutting Peru's Congress led to the negotiation in which the regional community pushed for the calling of new elections for a new congress later that year. He and I had learned to approach each other with wary respect. He was a micromanager and a stickler for detail, a loner who often slept in his office. His political rise had been meteoric, but he was an outsider – politically, ethnically and personally. He belonged to no organized political party. He was a "chino" as Orientals are known in Peru regardless of national origin. His wife had left him, leaving their daughter to act as first lady. He admired the United States but distrusted Americans. During the observation of the new elections for Congress that Fujimori convened under duress in 1992, I asked the Japanese Ambassador to Peru to support me on a certain point and was rebuffed, with the comment, "Don't come to me. Fujimori speaks better English than he does Japanese." Lynn Sicade could not get over the fact that when we called on him, a large block of melted residue from Hiroshima was on prominent display in his anteroom. I was more struck by Fujimori's statement that when he visited the front, "I needed to look at the uniforms to tell the Peruvian dead apart from the Ecuadorian dead." But I knew that, even after his 1995 reelection, the authoritarianism of his regime hid great weakness. Fujimori was too lonely and too much of an outsider in Peru to lead the peace by himself.

Meanwhile our U.S. team was being tempered by common effort. Being on the C-21 engendered a sense of a team in quick order. Some of our best ideas began or developed on the plane. Lynn remembers watching Leo and I work together and thinking that we proved good civil-military relations were possible. One day, cruising along at something like 40,000 feet, suddenly Sicade and Rios approached me one on each side. Sicade said "Now we have you." I look at Rios, he said "Apache." I looked back at Lynn. She said "Puyallup." I was stunned by their references to their Native American heritages, which in fact I had never even realized. I had always thought of them as just "Americans" like me, with no hyphenation. Which we all were and remained. Afterwards, Lynn joked about it as "our plot to surround the U.S. Ambassador." I was still learning about my own country.

I was also learning the importance of strengthening in each belligerent a party of peace to counter the party of war. This is critical, but very difficult for outsiders. And doubly difficult as a member of the guarantors, who were supposed to be strictly neutral. In Quito Brazilian Ambassador Osmar Chohfi was a constant source of support. In Ecuador, Heinz Moeller Freire, a president of Congress who had received the most votes ever in his election to Congress, and Julio Prado Vallejo, an Ambassador and human rights lawyer who had as a young diplomat been the one to receive the U.S. aerial survey that had provided the basis for Ecuador's claim of *inejecutabilidad*, were encouraging.

I never had any doubt that public opinion would swing our way. Once, while the C-21 was refueling on our way to Santiago, I was standing outside the military section of the terminal in Quito when I was approached by a middle-aged woman in traditional Indian garb. I had never seen her before. She curtsied and said "Thank you for making peace and saving lives. I baked this for you." She handed me a small package and was gone before I could even react. It was a tiny panettone, a fruity Italian Christmas cake that, when I ate it, had the absolutely correct inimitable flavor. The morale boost for me was as astounding as the cultural chaos of the experience.

Changes in the parties' negotiating teams helped. Peru's Foreign Minister Francisco Tudela was drained by his hostage experience and gave way to Eduardo Ferrero, whose brother Carlos, as President of the Peruvian Congress, made him very politically correct. But the Peruvian negotiators were proving more creative, including Ambassadors to the U.S., Ricardo Luna, and to Brazil, Hugo de Zela. Critically, the brilliant international lawyer Fernando de Trazegnies joined the Peruvian negotiating delegation. In Ecuador, Foreign Minister Galo Leoro was a successful public international lawyer, and contributed procedurally at first, but the conflict made him "afraid of his shadow." He entrusted the negotiations to a former Foreign Minister and Ambassador to the US, the brilliant pro-American lawyer, Edgar Terán, who was head of Ecuador's negotiating Commission. In the spring of 1997, as decisions were needed, Ecuador's new President, Fabián Alarcón, who had been President of Congress, quietly moved to support the peace process. He replaced Leoro with the distinguished Ambassador José Ayala Lasso. Ayala had been serving as the first UN High Commissioner for Human Rights but resigned to become Ecuador's foreign minister. Ayala brought audacity and commitment, even campaigning in Ecuador on behalf of the settlement. Leading Ecuadorian generals were also evolving in their views, particularly their commander of theater operations, General Paco Moncayo, who was later to be elected mayor of Quito.

I got to know and respect Moncayo and some of his colleagues— the defense minister, General José Gallardo, General Calle, and others. They had collectively planned the war. But it was Moncayo who told me the Ecuadorian command had finally concluded that "to continue the war would have been to bankrupt the country and force us to rule by bayonets." Afterwards, Moncayo also told me that the peace had destroyed military morale: "You have taken away their reason for being." His son, a lieutenant on the front, resigned his Commission, asking his father "You sent us to war for this?"

I was never able to develop similar relationships with Generals Hermoza Rios, Lopez Trigoso and the other Peruvian military leaders. They were smarting from their failures. Fujimori did not trust them. And weakening everything was the Montesinos factor. The ambitious and corrupt Vladimiro Montesinos was the head of the aptly named SIN, Peru's national intelligence service. A cashiered former officer, he was a key supporter of Fujimori. Montesinos' maneuvers sapped institutional strength and ultimately left the military sidelined (later, Montesinos' bribes were to destroy Fujimori as well, but that is a different story).

In 1997, as we were trying to exhaust all avenues by which the stalemated negotiators could try to escape reaching agreement, we even brought U.S. space technology to bear. Rios knew that the National Imagery and Mapping Agency (NIMA, the forerunner of the current National Geospatial Intelligence Agency) controlled radar satellites that could provide accurate three-dimensional views of otherwise obscured terrain. With endorsements from me and General Clark, Rios called NIMA to explain the problem. National assets were redirected to take radar-satellite imagery of the area in dispute. For the first time, leaders from Peru and Ecuador were able to see the conflict area in detail. To this day, "influencing world events by creating animated renditions of imagery and geospatial data that allowed users to visualize inaccessible terrain and resolving international boundary disputes" is listed as a major NIMA accomplishment. The unstated reference is to the Ecuador-Peru border.

April and again September 1997 brought disappointing formalistic presentations of *Impases* in Brasilia, in which both sides presented maximalist claims. I retired from the State Department for personal reasons in July 1997. Jeff Davidow had replaced Alec Watson as Assistant Secretary. He insisted I stay on as special envoy. To make it possible for me retire but remain in charge of the Peru-Ecuador effort, Davidow created a new full-time position as Special Coordinator for Ecuador/Peru Border Operations and appointed senior FSO David Randolph to act as my primary back-up. Lynn Sicade, who was also moving on to new responsibilities, prepared a planning document that stressed the objectives of demarcating the border with the help of NIMA satellite technology, supporting demining and development initiatives for the border, and keeping the Guarantors together. In September, Randolph and I met with both Presidents Fujimori and Alarcón on the margins of the UN General Assembly in New York to impress our continuing interest in a settlement. Even so, a Peruvian diplomat commented despondently, "The least Ecuador can accept is more than the most Peru can give."

*Q: I take it this was not a moment of great optimism?*

EINAUDI: Quite right, in the sense that at the time neither Peru or Ecuador had the political will to go forward. But I emphasize "at the time." I had no doubt that the elements we were developing would come together when the circumstances were ripe. Still, we had a curious debate about "ripeness". At a SAIS seminar, Professor William Zartman said I was overlooking that the conflict was not "ripe" for settlement. I got on my high horse and said that being of Italian background I loved pears and knew all about judging ripeness. I told the story of my grandfather asking at a state dinner when he was president whether there was anyone at the table who might share a pear with him so that it would not be wasted if he only ate half. In Italian politics, that pear became the symbol of lost parsimony after he left office. In the Peru-Ecuador negotiations, I said, the pear risked becoming a symbol of opportunity lost to the academic abstraction of "ripeness." Whether the pear was ripe or unripe became something of an in joke among the negotiating teams. The Peruvian diplomat José Boza gave Lynn Sicade a beautiful ceramic pear when he left his Washington posting.

*Q: What finally led to the breakthrough, the final step toward developing the elements of a successful settlement?*

EINAUDI: In the fall of 1997, after an October meeting in Buenos Aires that was full of possibilities but went nowhere, the guarantors decided to change the framework of debate. They asked the parties to consider new issues that could be agreed upon and thus help both sides to claim victories. Meeting in Brasilia, Brazil's Foreign Minister Lampreia formally proposed talks on navigation, integration, and security as well as the border. The parties agreed, and the new phase was recorded on November 26, 1997 in a "Declaration of Brasilia." Four commissions were named, with members chosen with the concurrence and participation of the parties. The half a dozen boundary impasses that had been identified were referred to one commission, chaired by Nelson Jobim, then Chief Justice of the Brazilian supreme court, and later to become the first civilian minister of defense. I proposed NIMA's John Gates as the U.S. expert. He was rejected because the Peruvians and Ecuadorians feared the influence of his Chilean wife, but fortunately the University of Tennessee's Clarence W. Minkel, an eminent U.S. geographer and the successor to Preston James, agreed to represent us.

Another commission was created to deal with the Amazon. Article VI of the Rio Protocol provided for a treaty to enable Ecuador to enjoy free and untaxed navigation on the Amazon and its tributaries. No such treaty had ever been negotiated. I remembered the 1903 Panama treaty that had granted the U.S. rights to the Canal Zone "in perpetuity as if sovereign". I suggested Ecuador could be given access to the Amazon "in perpetuity as if sovereign," arguing this would reflect modern usage rather than traditional concepts of sovereignty. Peru and Ecuador accepted to draft a treaty giving Ecuador control of ports on the Amazon, with free passage "as if sovereign" for 99 years, renewable. A separate commission was established to work on border development, including integration of electricity grids, oil pipelines, and transport. Another was assigned national security and confidence building measures. These Commissions were made up of Ecuadorians and Peruvians chosen as leaders in the fields under consideration.

Progress was immediate. On January 19, 1998, meeting this time in Rio de Janeiro at the old Itamaraty palace where the Rio Protocol had originally been signed, Ecuador and Peru agreed to seek a comprehensive settlement by May 30. Positions on the border remained far apart. We did not know it then, but Ecuadorian forces secretly began to build a new base downslope from Condor Mirador, to south and outside of the DMZ and not readily detectable.

On May 8, 1998, the advisory findings by independent guarantor technical and juridical experts were communicated to the parties privately. On the boundary, they backed Ecuador's positions on some minor points, but on the critical Cenepa conflict area, they came down squarely in support of Peru's position. Edgar Terán was personally devastated; he had become Ecuador's chief interface with the guarantors and was immediately scapegoated by the territorial maximalists.

On May 19, the Peruvian diplomat Jorge Valdez told me Ecuador had built a new base one kilometer inside Peru and that it had been expanded into a garrison of 300. He said that Peru had not only discovered it, but placed military units on two sides. President Fujimori had told President Cardoso, he said, that the two countries' troops faced each other "50 to 70 meters apart." This sudden threat had emerged with no warning from U.S. intelligence.

And the deal killer was still there: The Commission chaired by Brazil's Chief Justice had ruled that Tiwintza was clearly inside Peruvian territory. But the Ecuadorians at Tiwintza had not "run like rabbits" as their predecessors had been accused of doing. They had stood and fought and died. And they had had buried some of their dead there. Venezuela's President Rafael Caldera had once raised his fist to my eye height, saying, "See this arm?" He shook it. "As long as there is blood in this arm, I will never accept [X]." The nationality was different, and the issue was different, but no one needed to tell me how the Ecuadorian military would react to a finding that NI UN PASO ATRÁS, and those who had died to put and keep it there, was in Peru. Tiwintza, with its buried Ecuadorian dead, was a deal killer.

*Q: How many dead are we talking about?*

EINAUDI: Not that many. Ecuador probably buried at Tiwintza less than a dozen of the one hundred or so killed in the fighting on both sides. But blood is memory whose screams are far thicker than the waters of the Amazon for which Ecuador's soldiers fought and died.

The negotiations had advanced so far that a win-win solution was almost at hand. Yet the potential settlement, so far advanced, now suddenly coexisted with a real threat of renewed war. On May 21, as the parties and the guarantors prepared to meet again in Buenos Aires, Alfredo Chiaradia, my Argentine counterpart, feared the week could as readily lead to war as to peace. He did not want it happening on his turf.

It was in Buenos Aires that necessity begat invention. We had long talked of the possibility of transforming the conflict area into a binational park or ecological preserve. The area of the fighting, it had turned out, was almost entirely in Peruvian territory. The territorial contributions for a park could be equalized by having each country devote the same amount of land. The boundary would be demarcated through it but in effect erased by having a single binational administration and allowing free transit to those indigenous peoples who might want to resume the visits interrupted by the conflict. In Buenos Aires, I was suddenly struck that Tiwintza, the epicenter of fighting, where Ecuador had buried its dead, was tiny. Putting a matchbox on the table to symbolize how small it was, I proposed that we find a special status for one square km that would include Ecuador's graves. It was the Peruvian negotiator, Fernando de Trazegnies, who immediately identified the specific modality: The square kilometer could remain sovereign Peruvian territory, but could be the property of Ecuador under Peruvian law, subject only to two qualifications: Ecuador could not sell its property, and Peru could not expropriate it. Peru would have its sovereignty. Ecuador would have dignity for its dead. A sanctuary so defined could offer a win-win solution to both belligerents. It would be, Trazegnies commented, an effective "management of symbols." But it was still just a proposal.

On May 29, the Chilean guarantor, Juan Martabit, articulated the still negative atmosphere this way: "Ecuador does not have the strength to lose, and Peru does not have the grandeur (*grandeza*) to win." Word circulated that in both Peru and Ecuador key military leaders and some politicians thought a permanent stalemate was preferable to the concessions needed to breach settlement. Many Peruvians felt their country's relative size guaranteed victory should fighting begin again.

This is the moment the stars of presidential politics aligned with those of the peacemakers. On May 31, Jamil Mahuad was elected President of Ecuador. Mahuad was mayor of Quito, but had been born in Loja, a city in southern Ecuador that had been occupied by Peru in 1941. His grandfather had fought against Peru. This background impelled him toward peace. And there was another factor as well, his Lebanese family origins. One of his important backers, Ivonne A-Baki, from Guayaquil, also had Lebanese origins. Trained as an artist, A-Baki was wealthy and ambitious. She was later to become Ecuador's ambassador to the United States, then run for President as a successful minister and entrepreneur. But her biggest contribution came when she was Ecuador's honorary Consul in Boston. While there, she met Roger Fisher, a professor at Harvard Law School who specialized in negotiations. Together, they anointed Mahuad as the man who would make peace. She told me, "We cannot allow the same thing to happen here [in Ecuador] that happened to Beirut." She brought in James Carville to advise Mahuad's winning presidential campaign.

In July, after his victory, but before he took office, A-Baki brought Mahuad to Washington to go over the status of the conflict. As mayor and candidate, Mahuad had not been directly involved in the negotiations. And while the military situation seemed stalemated, a host of economic problems (the highest debt/GDP ratio in Latin America, falling oil prices, high inflation, and losses caused by the El Niño current) were building to a crisis point. In hushed voices, A-Baki and Mahuad told me they had also just learned from friendly officers that their own military had introduced fresh forces below Condor Mirador. I told them the Peruvians knew and had countered with forces of their own. Mahuad asked what would happen if, acting as both President and the new boy on the block, he was to "patear el tablero" (kick over the playing board) and start the negotiations all over again. I told him Ecuador could only lose. It was too late. Everywhere Mahuad turned in Washington, from the IMF to the Inter-American Development Bank, he was told he had to make peace to salvage Ecuador's credibility.

It was at this point that Fernando Henrique Cardoso, President of Brazil and in effect the lead Guarantor, stepped in personally to ensure that Mahuad and Fujimori got the support they needed to counter their respective parties of war. Tensions were too high for Fujimori to attend Mahuad's inauguration on August 10. But Cardoso personally encouraged both presidents and designed a flurry of meetings to overcome opposition to a settlement. He arranged for Fujimori and Mahuad to meet quietly while they were both in Asunción for the inauguration of the new President of Paraguay on August 15. Randolph and Jack Leonard (then DAS for South America) flew to Asunción. Randolph writes "as best I recall, the Guarantors at this meeting decided to have their bosses (the presidents) deliver a stern message to Fujimori and Mahuad to the effect: "Get your militaries and any other troublemakers under control and put a stop to any shenanigans. We have gone too far to have things fall apart this close to the end."

Discipline among the Peruvian and Ecuadorean troops facing other at point blank range at Condor Mirador held. Not a shot was fired. By late August, MOMEP certified that both countries had pulled back their forces.

On September 4, Mahuad and Fujimori met in Panama before the opening of a Rio Group Summit. Over breakfast before he was to meet Fujimori later that morning, Mahuad used me as a sounding board for two hours and forty minutes for what he intended to say to President Fujimori. Our session was far from easy. At one point I felt constrained to tell Mahuad that "Fujimori will kill you if you put it that way." After breakfast, with only fifteen minutes to go before the Presidents were to start their meeting, I reached Peru's Ferrero to ask him to warn Fujimori that Mahuad was still focused on territory, but also asked him to urge Fujimori to hear Mahuad out.

The presidents met over lunch for four hours, alone at all times. Their aides were reduced to speculating how things were going by how the presidents looked (generally ok) during their bathroom breaks. When they finally came out, Fujimori told the press "There is no white smoke, but the atmosphere is positive." Mahuad said there was much at stake, that the foreign ministries would finalize areas of agreement, and that the two would meet again "as soon as possible." At breakfast with me the next morning, Mahuad opened by saying "I'm still alive." Then, turning serious, he said Fujimori had behaved as I had predicted, firmly rejecting any land swap. But, he said, he, Mahuad, had been right in believing Fujimori would understand the political imperative that each president would have to cover the other's rear to get to a lasting agreement.

On September 25, President Clinton wrote separately to both Fujimori and Mahuad urging them, as leaders of vision and principle, to take advantage of their upcoming visit to President Cardoso to announce a definitive agreement to put to rest the possibility of fighting between fellow citizens of the Americas.

On October 8, as he left for Brasilia to visit President Cardoso, Fujimori replaced Foreign Minister Ferrero with Trazegnies. Arriving in Brasilia, Fujimori and Mahuad signed a joint letter to Cardoso informing him that they were agreed on specific treaties on trade, navigation, and frontier integration, as well as confidence and security measures, but that they had been "unable to find a mutually acceptable formula to complete the common land frontier." In fact, they had both bought in principle into the package we had developed. But as Martabit had worried, neither felt in a position to admit it publicly. Their solution was to turn to the Guarantor Presidents as *Dei ex machina*. An accord we had reached in Santiago in 1996 stipulated that the Guarantor countries would "propose the procedures best suited to definitively resolve those points of disagreement that the parties will have been unable to resolve themselves." In their letter to Cardoso, Fujimori and Mahuad asked him to obtain a proposal from the guarantor presidents that would enable the definitive solution of the remaining differences. We envoys had assured them that our presidents would do so *if* they asked us formally to do so *and* if the agreement was ratified in advance, sight unseen, by the two congresses.

*Q: Is that how it happened?*

EINAUDI: Yes. Except that first we had to resolve a fresh problem created by the NSC in my own government. On previous occasions, when I had wanted an appointment for one of the two presidents to meet with President Clinton, the initial reaction had always been: "They're never going to settle, why expose the president to failure?" This time, the first reaction was, "they've decided to settle, why waste the president's time?" Please understand, I am not being critical. The world looks entirely different from the White House than it does from the State Department. In a functioning government, a solution can usually be found. But this time there was another wrinkle: Fujimori was desperately afraid of leaks and did not want to provide the details of what had been decided. Not unreasonably, Fujimori feared that a prematurely leaked decision would be interpreted as coming from them rather than from the guarantors. Both he and Mahuad would be accused of treason. Equally reasonably, since the details were to be contained a few days later as a decision of the Guarantor Presidents in a letter Clinton would have to sign, Jim Dobbins, the NSC Latin America Director, and National Security Advisor Sandy Berger said flatly "The President of the U.S. cannot not know."

The issue was left to the prebrief in the Oval Office. I prepared Fujimori. If Clinton decided he wanted to be told, we agreed Fujimori would tell him, but I would try to keep the others away while he and Clinton moved as far away as possible (the Oval Office is a big room). The meeting took place October 9, 1998. The impeachment trial in the Senate of William Jefferson Clinton had begun the day before. Even more than the details of this decisive visit, what I remember most is Clinton's appearance. During the pre-brief, Clinton moved over to the fireplace and leaned on the mantel as if for support. The dark circles under his eyes were impressive; his whole face expressed a deep sadness, as though this brilliant politician felt he had destroyed his presidency by his own hand. But, when the issue was presented to him, Bill

Clinton showed his political smarts, deciding he did not need to know the details in advance: "It's his country, after all," he said to me.

At the press event after the meeting, Mahuad and Fujimori said Clinton had promised a response to their appeal and that they were both optimistic.

On October 16, the Congresses of Ecuador and Peru both voted to accept the future guarantor finding, sight unseen. Before the vote, a Peruvian opposition leader in Congress, my friend Lourdes Flores Nano, called me to ask in confidence if Peru would lose territory in the decision. I said no, without giving her details, knowing that although one square kilometer at Tiwinza was to be owned by Ecuador, it would remain sovereign Peruvian territory and under Peruvian law. She and her bloc voted to accept. The guarantor's pending finding was accepted by margins about 3 to 1 in both countries. When she later ran for the Presidency, critics dubbed her "Miss Tiwinza," and some suggested her vote may have cost her the Presidency, although other factors, including anti-indigenous comments by her aging father, certainly hurt her far more.

The final touches were put together October 17-18 during side meetings at the Ibero-American Summit in Oporto, Portugal. The guarantor Presidents, minus only Bill Clinton, met with Fujimori and Mahuad, their foreign ministers, and the four special envoys for one last review of the text of the finding and the settlement package. On October 21, Cardoso wrote Clinton that "Ambassador Einaudi has, I am sure, brought to your attention" that a conclusion was at hand and invited Clinton to act as co-host for the signing ceremony Monday, October 26.

*At the signing ceremony. From the left, Hugo Banzer, Thomas McLarty, King Juan Carlos, Dario Castrillón Hoyos, Jamil Mahuad, Luigi Einaudi, Carlos Menem, Fernando Henrique Cardoso, Alberto Fujimori, Eduardo Frei, Juan Martabit, Alfredo Chiaradia, Ivan Canabrava. This photo was sent to me by Canabrava with a note that it recorded "almost four years of joint effort that led to unique professional achievement and great personal enrichment." (Brazilian Foreign Ministry photo, gift of Ivan Canabrava, 1998.)*

On October 23, the guarantor finding was made public in a long letter addressed separately to Mahuad and Fujimori. It began painstakingly laying out the legal antecedents and their conditions, then expressed their "point of view, which the parties have agreed to accept as binding, in the following points that conclude the fixing of the common land boundary and complete the comprehensive and definitive settlement." There followed nine points and a map. The coordinates for boundary markers to be put in place made clear that, in accordance with the Rio Protocol, Peru was sovereign over the Cenepa watershed. The finding continued that Peru must "grant as private property to the government of Ecuador an area of one square kilometer, at the center of which will be the point Ecuador identified to MOMEP as being Tiwinza." "This transfer," the letter continued, "will not affect sovereignty" and "will not be subject to expropriation by the government of Peru. The government of Ecuador, as owner, will enjoy all rights conferred under the laws of Peru for private property, except the right to transfer the property. . . . The government of Ecuador will have no police or military forces on its property nor undertake therein any such activities except for memorial services previously coordinated with the government of Peru." The letter specified that the square kilometer would be inside "a protected ecological zone" which "members of native communities of the region will be able to transit freely." Finally, the presidents wrote, they had informed His Holiness Pope John Paul II, "who has given his approval and moral support." Two days later, the Inter-American Development Bank (IDB) announced a $500 million loan for social and economic development along the border.

On October 26, 1998, the diplomatic corps in Brasilia gathered with invited luminaries to celebrate the signing of the "Acta Presidencial de Brasilia." Presidents Mahuad and Fujimori signed accompanied by their foreign ministers. The witnesses were the Presidents of Brazil, Argentina, and Chile, with Mack McLarty representing the President of the United States. The King and Queen of Spain, the President of Bolivia, a Cardinal representing the Pope, and the four guarantor special envoys were on the dais. The President of Colombia, Andres Pastrana and Secretary General of the OAS Cesar Gaviria also attended.

Six months later, in mid-May 1999, Ecuador and Peru erected the final marker completing the border. John Gates of NIMA assisted. Their mission complete after four years and two months on the ground, MOMEP's last elements withdrew.

*Q: Did you have a problem of keeping other elements of our government from crowing?*

EINAUDI: Except for moments of real crisis that can be counted on the fingers of one hand, Latin America isn't considered terribly important in the United States. So, who is going to crow about things that aren't terribly important? I did more than any other single individual to create the peace between Peru and Ecuador. Those directly involved recognized that. In February 1999, Presidents Fujimori and Mahuad rented the ballroom at the Mayflower Hotel to decorate me in front of several hundred guests with Peru's Order of the Sun and Ecuador's Order of Merit. Secretary Albright gave me the Frasure Memorial Award "for extraordinary diplomatic skill and vision in brokering a ceasefire and masterminding the historic process to bring a definitive end to the centuries-old Ecuador-Peru border dispute." On my recommendation, the Department gave awards to both Sicade and Rios.

*With President Clinton celebrating the peace between Ecuador and Peru. February 5, 1999. (Sharon Farmer, official White House photograph, 1999.)*

The general reaction was different. There was none.

After the settlement, I ran into Tony Lake who had been National Security Advisor when the process had begun. We were both teaching at Georgetown University. Instead of congratulating me or crowing as you said about the fact that the U.S. really had done something here, he immediately said that he would never forgive me for keeping the U.S. military on the border longer than the 90 days that he had first authorized. He felt outmaneuvered. No crowing there.

Leo Rios had a worse experience. Brazil decorated him for his support of MOMEP, and particularly for his brokering of their purchase of the UH-60 Blackhawks. When I had briefed McCaffrey in 1994 when he first became CINCSOUTH, I had told him that Brazil was becoming increasingly important and that he would do well to focus on overcoming Brazilian military skepticism about the U.S. And now here was Brazil decorating an American officer, one of his officers. But McCaffrey was long gone. Rios himself had been reassigned to our border with Mexico. Rios was denied duty time to receive the medal. He had to take annual leave to go -- on his own time and his own dime -- to be decorated by the President of Brazil.

I was later interviewed by a leading Brazilian scholar who was interested in assessing Brazilian foreign policy. Appendix Six reproduces our discussion. South American diplomats and many of my foreign service colleagues understood the momentous significance of our achievement, but Americans in general did not recognize the strategic significance of what we had done. They did not know and did not care. Many of the CIA's sources in the belligerent militaries had told them a settlement was impossible, and they were not always on top of the situation – there were no suspected Communists involved. Our military folks who knew about it were happy because it was a unique case of having a military mission abroad that was successful, paid for by others, without leading to U.S. casualties. But even there, the absence of casualties deprived the case of notoriety and the closing of ranks that comes with heroic pain. I owe my office at the National Defense University to that success, but, overall, nobody did any crowing because in terms of American public perceptions the solution didn't matter because they never knew the problem existed. This should not have surprised me. Fame is fleeting. Pio

Baroja's novel on my forebear *Juan van Halen, El oficial aventurero,* ends with a grinning horse skull on the beach in Cadiz and the comment *Sic transit gloria mundi.*

*Q: How do you judge the experience of being a "Special Envoy"? I've often thought that special envoys are something of a bureaucratic disruption, outside the normal system.*

EINAUDI: You're quite right. A special envoy by definition fouls up the normal chain of command. This negotiation involved five embassies. Ambassador Mel Levitsky in Brasilia was the pillar of our initial effort while Watson and I sorted out ourselves and the Washington bureaucracy. He was supportive afterwards, even teaching Peru-Ecuador as a case study at Syracuse and Michigan. His political counselor, Ted Wilkinson, went on the original guarantor observer reconnaissance at the end of February 1995, and then in 1997 became part of a guarantor support committee in Brasilia. Our ambassadors in Peru and Ecuador were central to the process, but sometimes less than helpful. In Peru, Alvin Adams and I worked well together as we had previously when he was Ambassador to Haiti, but his successor, Dennis Jett, minimized the conflict as a "silly border dispute" and concentrated on criticizing the Peruvians with what they considered paternalistic arrogance, particularly over human rights and their purchase of MIGs and Sukhois from Belarus. In Ecuador, Pete Romero defended his host country but still drew fire from the Ecuadorian press for referring to Tiwintza, accurately but not very empathetically, as a "lugarcito" [little place]. Later, in his oral history, Romero ignored MOMEP and the guarantors and attributed the peace largely to himself and Roger Fisher. In Washington, however, I could not have asked for more from Assistant Secretary Watson, his deputies Ed Casey and Mike Skol, or from his successor Jeff Davidow and his deputy Jack Leonard. At the NSC, Nancy Soderberg and Jim Dobbins were ultimately helpful, as was Mack McLarty at the White House. But it was the support and respect accorded me by General McCaffrey and his successors that sealed the deal. And the symbolism of that C-21.

*With presidents Fujimori and Mahuad in February 1999 at the US Institute of Peace, 1999. (Rick Reinhard, 1999, reproduced with permission of Rick Reinhard.)*

*Q: What lessons did you take from the negotiating experience?*

EINAUDI: Above all, patience. Patience to participate in interminable negotiating sessions and stubborn, unyielding wrangling by the parties. Patience to deal with our own government and its people. Patience to learn the history of the conflict. Patience to listen to the complaints and fears of all sides. Patience to assess interests and if necessary, help redefine them. Patience to identify local and regional interests involved. Patience to mobilize support for a settlement, internationally as well as domestically. With Peru and Ecuador, given their Catholic cultures and the origins of conflict during Spanish Colonial rule, patience to keep the Vatican and the Spanish government informed throughout.

*Q: OK, but I remember hearing that you developed specific "rules of the road," so to speak, for the negotiations.*

EINAUDI: Yes, but let me emphasize that these are my formulations, developed out of practical experience, and almost as a matter of survival as we went along. I say "my formulations" because I am articulating them, but these were not just my rules. We four guarantor envoys succeeded in driving the process only because we were all accepted these five basic considerations:

First of all, *Maintain Unity*, within the U.S. government and outside with other governments. We have talked a lot about our own internal problems. Let me stress now that all governments directly involved in the conflict and all their allies and rivals also need to be accounted for. The guarantor experience gave me an operating definition of multilateralism. Whatever course of action was decided was ultimately the product of our interaction, of the four special envoys meeting together and deciding, on the basis of everybody's inputs, everybody's knowledge. In some cases, others had better intelligence than I did. No one came out of a meeting with the same position with which they had started. Decisions were hammered out collegially. But that meant that everyone was also committed to the outcome. But unity did not stop with diplomats sticking together. It meant making sure their governments had the political support to meet their commitments. At the end, we made sure we also had the endorsement of the

King of Spain and the Pope. This is far from what is often sold these days as multilateralism, where either nothing happens, or we decide on our own what we want to do and then try to coerce others into following.

Second, *ensure military support for diplomacy and diplomatic support for the military.* Never assume automatic cooperation or similar perspectives or interests even when joint operations are underway. Military opposition can prevent a solution. McCaffrey was critical to U.S. unity in support of the mission; and by convening the leaders of the Brazilian, Argentine and Chilean armies in early 1996 he also helped unify the guarantor militaries in support for peace. Peruvian and Ecuadorian military leaders were slow in coming around, but the Cenepa standoff, their inclusion in MOMEP, and their own limitations and sense of duty ultimately led them to accept the negotiated peace, even to claim it as a victory for their side.

Third, *always remember that those who must live with the result must buy in.* If not, whatever is negotiated will not last. That meant the Parties must lead or be put in the lead. Even if there is a total impasse, never let a negotiating session end without publicly agreeing to a date for a new session. Very importantly, also, never surrender the autonomy of the outside negotiators, because even if they do not have arbitral authority, they have moral and political authority. Maintaining their authority was what enabled the guarantors, on request of the parties, to shift responsibility to themselves for the final decision the parties could not make publicly themselves. But no matter how much the parties may need to be nudged, would-be peacemakers must remember that it will be the parties who will ultimately determine whether a settlement holds in the future.

A fourth rule, especially important for the powerful United States, is _Use the law_. Domestic and international laws and explicit operating agreements are the foundation for common action, predictability, and legitimacy. The military have a practical operational term for it: interoperability – ensuring that cooperating forces have common rules and equipment to work together. Diplomatically, interoperability is set by multilateral bodies and treaties. Encourage support from the UN, regional organizations, other multilateral bodies and treaty organizations. The Guarantors did all that and more. We lived by the Rio Protocol, the ensuing declarations, and the Terms of Reference for MOMEP. And then we created a special commission of geographers and jurists to rule on the territorial issues which was chaired by the Chief Justice of the Brazilian Supreme Court. And when the parties could not bring themselves to publicly accept even that, we arranged to have our presidents take responsibility, and arranged for the presidents of their other neighbors and the Pope to cheer them on.

Lastly, but not least, _Keep sights high_. If you don't harness optimism and even the power of illusion, the unyielding difficulties, delays, interruptions, the freezing mud or the tropical heat will bog you down if you do not harness optimism and the power of illusion. Shift focus from points of contention where one party must "lose" to areas that have a "win-win" potential. Ecuador's sovereign territorial claims proved largely invalid, but the negotiating process itself provided dignity, respect for its dead, commercial access to the Amazon, and border development. Peace became possible because it brought a dignified resolution of the immediate dispute and put it in a broader context with a mix of both quantifiable and unquantifiable benefits, including the removal of a historical millstone that was mortgaging the future for both countries.

These five points are of course abstractions from more complicated realities. For example, unrelated discontinuities had to be overcome (for example, in Peru, the Foreign Minister was taken hostage by terrorists for months and in Ecuador there was a coup), and the role of individual presidents proved essential (Mahuad. Fujimori. Cardoso. Clinton).

*Q: Rather than go back to those aspects, let me ask if you believe the Peru-Ecuador experience is relevant to the fighting that has just broken out (February 2022) between Russia and Ukraine?*

EINAUDI: After the 1941 war, the Ecuadoran delegation appealed to the Brazilian foreign minister that the proposed settlement violated international law. He is said to have responded "Ecuador, with its lack of military resistance, is not a problem for international law."

When Russia invaded Ukraine, my first thought went back to that moment. And my first thought was, unless it resists effectively, Ukraine, like Ecuador in 1941, will not be a problem, either, any more than it was in Russia's invasion of Crimea in 2014.

Ukrainian survival depends on its resistance weakening Russia enough for Russia to accept that Ukraine will survive. Once that happens, a solution will then have to be developed that will enable each party to claim some degree of success. As with Peru and Ecuador, territorial claims will need to be balanced by economic and security arrangements. Like today's sanctions, some of these arrangements will need to be multilateral. The cultural and humanitarian disaster will be as challenging as that of security. The whole will require the Americans to learn more diplomacy, the Europeans more force, and the Chinese and other fence-sitters to engage more positively.

Finally, looking forward, a more stable global future will depend on whether real resources are put into regional and global institutions capable of solving the riddle of sovereignty in a globalized world.

*Q: What do you mean by the riddle of sovereignty?*

EINAUDI: Let us leave the riddle of sovereignty to our later discussion of globalism (cf pages 472 ff.).

*Q: Looking back, how do you see the peace settlement and its legacy?*

EINAUDI: Let me answer with the statement I made at a meeting of the Peru and Ecuador Consultative Group, convened in New Orleans on March 23, 2000 by the Inter-American Development Bank.

*Thank you, President Iglesias. It is a real honor to speak to this distinguished audience, especially since I am retired and no longer speaking in an official capacity.*

*My objective is to share with you the perspective gained as the Special Envoy of the United States in the Guarantor effort, together with Argentina, Brazil and Chile, under the chairmanship of Brazil. I do so as the only guarantor envoy who covered the entire period, from the start of the armed conflict in January 1995 to the signing of the peace in October 1998.*

*From the very start until about two months before the signing of the peace agreements, the entire effort took place in an aura of impossibility. The conflict had always been there. The two republics were born in its shadow. This noxious history has been evident even in the excellent statements made just now by the ministers of foreign affairs [Fernando de Trazegnies and José Ayala] of the two countries, who, let it be said, each played a critical role in the actual negotiation of the accord. Their presence today is proof of continuity, conviction and leadership beyond what one might expect in what many assume to be unstable conditions.*

*So we know the conflict had always been latent, that the republics were born with it, and that therefore it would always be there. Our first challenge was to separate the armies in conflict. We were told we would never be able to do it without casualties because there were five thousand special forces soldiers from both sides inextricably entwined in the impenetrable jungles of the upper Cenepa. Nonetheless, thanks to the skill of the military observers from the four guarantor countries, all forces were separated in the course of three months without a single new victim.*

*Next it was said that we would never reach agreement on procedures because that discussion was just an excuse to avoid negotiating the real issues. When we reached agreement on procedures and began substantive negotiations, it was said we would never be able to decide anything, first, because it would be impossible to reconcile the demands of international law—by which we were bound—with political viability in the two countries, without which no solution could work.*

*Then it was said that, in any case, these countries were too violent and unstable: nothing would ever work. And, in fact, we ran into serious problems when the Minister of Foreign Affairs of Peru became one of the hostages in the residence of the Japanese ambassador in Lima, and again, when the President of Ecuador was removed by his Congress.*

*Finally, it was said that we could play all the diplomatic games we wanted, but that the military would never accept a settlement, that they wanted revenge, that they wanted to have an excuse to buy arms, that they needed the conflict to obtain support for their institutional survival. The conflict might be managed, but it would never be resolved.*

*Well, we are here today because we were all part of the solution. In saying "all", I do not wish to detract from the merits of Peru and of Ecuador who, obviously, are the ones who built the solution, nor do I wish to detract from the solution itself, which provided for an appropriate land boundary and, free and contiguous access to the Amazon in perpetuity for Ecuador, while also providing for dignity, all of which made the solution possible.*

*The implementation of the solution is also something for which we are all responsible. And that is why we are meeting here today. I remember that in one of the many moments in which everything seemed impossible, I came under great pressure. In today's United States, it is not easy to maintain troops abroad. The President's National Security Advisor told me he was disappointed, because he had only authorized military observers for ninety days. He asked me what were we doing there three hundred and sixty days later. So we had a meeting in the Situation Room in which I was asked "What is your plan?" At that point, things were going reasonably well. We were showing patience as well as resolve, the two parties were committed to the negotiations, and the building blocks of a future agreement were being put in place one on top of another. Even so, seen from the outside, everything seemed impossible. So I answered "Well, since you ask, and if you promise not to tell anyone, here is my plan: I am going to hire a bunch of publicity agents and have them carry big signs through the streets of Lima and Quito, banging bells and singing out 'the Millennium is coming! the Millennium is coming!' The plan is simple: there will be a settlement because no one in either Ecuador or Peru wants to enter the Twenty-first Century weighed down by the conflicts of the Nineteenth Century."*

*And if you look at the final agreement, it is, as someone said earlier in this hall, a bet on modernity, a bet on progress, a bet on the idea that international cooperation can work. If you examine the elements of the solution, you find that it deals with matters like trade, integration, navigation, environmental protections, national security, and confidence building measures, including respect for the rights of indigenous peoples. What you find is precisely that: a bet on the future and on modernity.*

*So, where are we today? It is sixteen months since the peace was signed.*

*Has political instability or popular anger created difficulties? No. In fact, polls show the peace is more popular in both countries today than it was when it was signed.*

*Have the countries failed in implementation? No. Demarcation of the land frontier is complete. Two ports serving Ecuador, one of them in the Amazon itself beyond Iquitos toward Brazil, have been identified and are being developed.*

*Is there any risk of renewed conflict? No. Quite the contrary. The armed forces themselves managed the demarcation. And the discipline and restraint both have shown in arms acquisitions is a new element that is transforming the strategic balance in South America from one of tension to one of cooperation.*

*Has development failed? No. At least not as concerns Peru and Ecuador. Before the peace, their provinces near the frontier had been held back and even punished for the simple fact of being in the way of a possible attack from the neighboring country. Roads could not be built because they might be used by an invading army. Now, as those of you who have visited have seen for yourselves, people on the frontier are hard at work building a new and more common future.*

*No, the real question, the real risk lies with us. The real risk is that, somehow, we in the international community will allow the settlement to be orphaned, bereft of the international support it had at birth and which it still merits.*

*Let me conclude with what is for me an emotional note. I have spent 45 years working to improve U.S. relations with Latin America. In these years, I have, like you, seen some extraordinary things happen. We have seen the end of military dictatorships in Latin America. We have seen the end of colonialism in the Caribbean. Even so, we remain filled with doubts. We ask ourselves, is the progress we have seen reversible? Will the details work?*

*I think Peru and Ecuador are demonstrating that the details can work. But the fact is, we cannot be absent. We must create an **engranaje** (a strong meshing of gears) of mutual support, of integration, cooperation and sensitivity to each other's interests, that will ensure that peace will last and that we will harvest, together, the benefits of the Twenty-first Century.*

*Q: You talked about risk, and ended with the fear that the settlement might be "orphaned." Was it?*

EINAUDI: Inside the region, of course, there was support as well as appreciation. The Inter-American Development Bank (IDB) followed up its initial $500 million loan by establishing a Consultative Group that raised significant sums in a series of fund-raising meetings like the one in New Orleans at which I made the statement above. Ciro de Falco, who had by then moved from the US Treasury to become Executive Vice President of the IDB, wrote me that *"While the investment [for Peru and Ecuador] initially focused on development, it eventually morphed mainly into a program to combat illegal drug production. Both the Clinton and*

*W Bush administrations got deeply involved in drug eradication. In 1999, we also got Plan Colombia, an anti-drug and anti-guerrilla program. . . back to business as usual."*

In effect, de Falco concluded, what happened was a good example of how domestic politics can drive foreign policy down the wrong path, and in the case of drugs, an ineffective path. By ignoring the demand side, regional drug policies failed to stop the flows to the United States but enabled the illegal cartels to make so much money that they had ample means to corrupt law enforcement and local politicians. In Central America and even the Caribbean some national governments became powerless to stop the cartels' negative influence. But that is another tale.

*Q: Returning to the Peru-Ecuador peace, was there any immediate opposition in the two countries themselves?*

EINAUDI: Nationalists on both sides were disappointed. In Peru, there was a month of unrest and even a few deaths. But the troubles were limited almost entirely to Iquitos and Loreto province, where the granting to Ecuador of port facilities on the Amazon was taken as just another example of the provinces being ignored and discriminated against by the central government in Lima. Since the settlement, the peace has not only held but solidified, perhaps particularly in the border populations on both sides.

Mahuad and Fujimori, the two presidents who made peace, were each forced out of office in 2000 for other reasons. Mahuad was overthrown by opposition to his economic policies, particularly the immediate costs of dollarization; he wound up in prolonged unmerited exile in the United States. Fujimori fled to Japan after revelations of extensive corruption directed by his man Vladimiro

Montesinos; his subsequent odyssey included detention in both Chile and Peru. These events, coupled with controversies over human rights and his reelection overreach in 2000, permanently tarnished Fujimori's achievements, which included economic stabilization and defeat of the Sendero Luminoso insurgents as well as peace with Ecuador. In Peru, the political sociologist Julio Cotler wrote quite unfairly that Fujimori had always depended on others, at home on Montesinos, on Ecuador on Cardoso and Einaudi.

*Q: You have said this was the last conventional war in Latin America. Why?*

EINAUDI: Ending the conflict had a major impact on South American geopolitics. Since the days of the Alliance for Progress, U.S. policies had opposed arms races in poor countries, seen as diversion of resources for development. Peace between Ecuador and Peru ended aerial arms races, which had started with F-5, A37, or Canberra military jets, and moved on to increasingly expensive Mirage, Kfir, Sukhoi and MiG aircraft. Peace meant they didn't all need to buy jet fighters to keep up against each other. This did not just affect Ecuador and Peru. The Brazilian air force had been looking for modern jet fighters for years. After Peru and Ecuador settled, they wound up not buying anything for another generation.

Unfortunately, disputes in the name of sovereignty will always be vitamins for bad politicians. And there are still many unresolved disputes, including a whole ocean of unsettled maritime boundaries. Fortunately, despite the decline of international law and international organizations, recent trends have been in the direction of nonviolence if not necessarily legal resolution.

# OAS Assistant Secretary General

*Q: After you retired from the State Department, you began to work for the OAS proper, I believe. What was that new role? How did it develop?*

EINAUDI: I was elected Assistant Secretary General of the Organization of American States in June 2000. The term was five years, the last of which I served as Acting Secretary General, replacing former Costa Rican President, Miguel Angel Rodriguez, who resigned as Secretary General a month after he was elected to go home to face corruption charges.

My election was the direct result of the Peru Ecuador settlement, which had given me some prominence among what my uncle Roberto Einaudi used to call the region's "very litigious countries." I had retired from State but was keeping my hand in at the Inter-American Dialogue in Washington. In December 1999, OAS Secretary General César Gaviria invited me to become his special representative to tamp down a dispute between Nicaragua and Honduras that threatened violence in those already exhausted countries. I was able to prevent the immediate crisis from escalating.

Trinidad and Tobago's Christopher Thomas was completing his term as Assistant Secretary General (ASG). Bolivia's Ambassador to the United States, Marlene Fernandez, began to lobby to have me replace him. That possibility had been broached by Argentina and Guatemala back when I was with S/P. It had been scotched by Hattie Babbitt, my successor as U.S. representative to the OAS and my then boss, Policy Planning Director Jim Steinberg. I have a note to myself recording that on January 19, 1995, Steinberg called me into his office literally minutes after his return from Geneva with the Secretary. He told me that "there is a consensus at senior levels of the United States Government" that a candidacy on my part to the OAS was a problem and would not be in the U.S. interest.

*Q: Why did they do that? I would have thought having you there would be in our interest.*

EINAUDI: Steinberg did not elaborate. He did not question that others were coming to me, but simply told me I should "call them off." So I informed everyone that I had received my instructions and was not and would not be a candidate. The possibility of a U.S. citizen in the OAS leadership had come up in 1994 when Senator Chris Dodd (D-Conn.), who had served in the Peace Corps in the Dominican Republic, thought he might like to be OAS Secretary General. I understand the Clinton White House quickly put an end to that, telling Dodd he was needed far more in the Senate. No American had ever been elected for a leadership post at the OAS, and some thought we would just get a black eye.

By the time Bolivia started pushing again for my candidacy in 1999, I was retired and presumably able to decide for myself whether I wanted to run. Marlene Fernandez enlisted the support of the Peruvian and Ecuadorian foreign ministers. The Ambassadors to the United States of the three countries visited me together to say their governments wanted me to run. I was flattered, but my answer was simple. "I may no longer be on active service, but I am still a U.S. citizen and I am not going to do anything unless I am nominated by the United States." I told them that if they wanted me, they had to get the State Department to nominate me. I remembered what had happened to me previously, and I also wanted to avoid the Orfila effect. Alejandro Orfila had become OAS Secretary General in 1975 without the support of Argentina. He had not been a success. The lesson was clear: As an international public servant, it is unwise to be at cross purposes with your own government.

I knew some in the regional bureau for Latin America were not overjoyed at the thought of my candidacy. It turned out the White House was also reluctant. They had just said no to someone else, Ronald Scheman, a Democratic loyalist who had been angling for their support for a run at the ASG position. The "no" to Scheman had been on the grounds that no American could ever be elected, and that having an American in the leadership would reduce the value of OAS support for U.S. policies. Scheman objected to that reasoning and telephoned Bolivia's President Hugo Banzer, whom he also knew, to get his support. I was told Banzer replied "Of course Einaudi is my candidate." Scheman's call may have redounded to my benefit.

Undersecretary for Political Affairs Tom Pickering ultimately proved decisive. He had been ambassador to El Salvador and to the UN and understood the skills and issues involved. Pickering told me: "This is your business. This is what you are good at and it makes a great deal of sense." To dilute fears that my candidacy might be challenged as "Made in the USA," he worked out that I would be formally nominated in a joint diplomatic note signed by the OAS ambassadors of Bolivia, Ecuador and Peru as well as the U.S. Permanent Representative, Luis Lauredo, a Florida Democrat. I was still a private citizen.

I was up against Lawrence Chewning, a distinguished Panamanian ambassador who ten years earlier had resigned to protest Noriega's electoral abuses. Chewning had the support of Mexico and had been actively campaigning throughout the hemisphere. But my web of friends was large and active and Secretary of State Madeleine Albright personally endorsed me at a CARICOM meeting that had a large block of votes. A hint of what was to come was provided by a journalist who printed that he had asked the Brazilian foreign ministry for a comment and was told they thought Einaudi was the only candidate. The final vote, in a secret ballot at the OAS General Assembly in Windsor, Canada, was 27-7. I carried every region. North America, 2 to 1 because Canada, which traditionally gives a lot of weight to multilateralism, supported me. South America and the Caribbean backed me overwhelmingly. I even carried Central America, Panama's own subregion. The only surprise was Chile, which voted against me fearing I might favor Bolivia's efforts to regain the outlet to the sea it had lost to Chile after the 1879 War of the Pacific.

*Q: Did you make any campaign promises?*

EINAUDI: Yes, two. The Assistant Secretary Generalship had traditionally been held by a small country, so I sought to lessen the break in precedent by saying I would not seek reelection. My second promise, responding to accusations of U.S. domination, was that I would not hire any U.S. citizens to my immediate staff.

*Q: Were you able to keep those promises?*

Yes. I was enormously fortunate in the critical choice of Chief of Staff. Out of a number of suitable candidates, Sandra Honoré stood out. She was then serving as Deputy Chief of Mission of the Republic of Trinidad and Tobago in Washington. Fluent in all four official languages of the OAS plus Creole, Sandra served with total distinction the full five years of my term, and when I became Acting Secretary General in 2004-5, she accompanied me seamlessly and indefatigably. When I sought her government's approval, their ambassador told me "You are taking my right hand." He paused, "And my left hand as well." Sandra proved to be all of that and more for me and the OAS. Afterwards, Sandra served as Trinidad and Tobago's Ambassador to Costa Rica, with concurrent accreditation to Guatemala and Panama, and as Director of its CARICOM and Caribbean Affairs Division. In May, 2013, Sandra was appointed by the U.N. Secretary General as his Special Representative and Head of the United Nations Stabilization Mission in Haiti (MINUSTAH), and served in Port-au-Prince until the end of that Mission in October, 2017.

The rest of my staff was also outstanding. I asked Chris Hernandez Roy, a dual citizen of Canada and Spain who had been my OAS aide on Nicaragua-Honduras, to join my office. Cristina Tomassoni of Argentina ran the day-to-day work of the Permanent Council. Paul Spencer of Antigua and Barbuda acted as the link to the National Offices. Denneth Modeste of Grenada had previously been Grenada's White House Ambassador and was later to play key roles in Haiti, including as director of the OAS office in Port-au-Prince. Dalcy Cabrera of Bolivia floated. Elba Molina, of Chile, whom I had known when she worked for the Peruvian Hugo de Zela, Secretary General Baena's Chief of Staff, became my secretary, a role in which she rivaled the best in the Department of State. Other key collaborators in the Secretariat included Argentina's Santiago Murray and Sergio Caramagna, who played key roles on elections and in Nicaragua and later Colombia respectively; Uruguayans Jean Michel Arrighi, the head of the legal department and Stella Villagrán, the reference librarian, and the Mexican Yisrael "Arturo" Garzon, who ran the Conferences Department. Two U.S. citizens were also very much in the mix, Linda Poole and legal advisor Bill Berenson, but they were at the OAS when I arrived and were not on my immediate staff. Ana Colomar O'Brien, a U.S. citizen of Cuban origins, was Chief of Protocol. Several other US citizens in the OAS Secretariat were idealists from the days of the Alliance for Progress.

*Some of my key advisors in my OAS office as Assistant Secretary General. From the left, Paul Spencer from Antigua and Barbuda, Chief of Staff Sandra Honoré from Trinidad and Tobago; me; Linda Poole from the United States, and Christopher Hernandez-Roy from Canada and Spain. (Organization of American States (OAS), 2000, reproduced with permission of the General Secretariat of the Organization of American States.)*

*Q: Did Bolivia ever attempt to collect on its support?*

EINAUDI: The occasion never arose. Ambassador Fernandez joined Ecuador's Ambassador A-Baki and Peru's Chargé d'Affairs to give a dinner in my honor. President Banzer had intended to come but underwent chemotherapy two days before the dinner and died of lung cancer a few months later. Fernandez had had a long career as a CNN reporter, with infinite drive and savvy. For the dinner, Fernandez obtained a letter from Henry Kissinger praising "Luigi's life of public service," and in which he somewhat prophetically added that mine had been a "sometimes a lonely" voice in calling for U.S. attention to Latin America. This time, again, Bolivia's efforts to stimulate support for an end to its landlocked status failed.

*Q: What were your prime responsibilities or issues as ASG?*

EINAUDI: Article 115 of the OAS Charter reads "The Assistant Secretary General shall be the Secretary of the Permanent Council. He shall serve as advisory officer to the Secretary General and shall act as his delegate in all matters the Secretary General may entrust to him." In other words, the ASG is to do what the SG wants him to do. Secretary General César Gaviria, a former president of Colombia and a very bright man, also liked to run everything by himself. He felt no need to consult me, and sometimes gave me the impression he would have liked me to have no functions. The only problem with that, as he himself put it to me, is that I was elected too. And I had independent credentials. One was as a successful international mediator, earned as a result of the Peru Ecuador settlement. The fact that Gaviria had brought me in even before my election as ASG to help defuse a Nicaragua-Honduras dispute suggested he was willing to work with me, at least in that area. And border problems were an important concern. As ASG, I followed up on Nicaragua-Honduras, settled the El Salvador-Honduras border, and calmed tensions between Belize and Guatemala before coming a cropper attempting to negotiate the largely domestic dispute in Haiti between President Aristide and his opponents. Conflict resolution was my niche.

*Q: Ok, let's start with conflict resolution. How did the Peace Fund come into being?*

EINAUDI: The Peace Fund, in Spanish *Fondo de Paz*, was approved at the same General Assembly in Canada at which I was elected ASG. It was my initiative. My experience with Peru and Ecuador had made me fear that peace settlements are vulnerable to being orphaned, because once peace is made, everybody loses interest. And resources are often critical, both to arrive at a settlement and to ensure follow-on. My proposal to create a Peace Fund at the OAS was resisted by some on the grounds that calling it a "peace" fund would imply that Latin America was at war and needed pacification. Others thought it would be an empty gesture because no one would contribute any money to it in any case. Enthusiastic support from Honduras, both at the Assembly and later in the development of implementing rules by the Permanent Council, helped greatly.

*Q: What can you tell us about the genesis of OAS involvement in Honduras-El Salvador matters?*

In the 1969 so-called Soccer War between Honduras and El Salvador, the OAS had managed the end of hostilities, with U.S. military observers and helicopters under the aegis of the OAS helping the separation of forces. Everything had quieted down, but over time certain areas along their common but undefined border, referred to as "*bolsones*," or "pockets," had become no-man's lands and safe-havens for guerillas. On a visit to El Salvador in early 1980 as ARA Director of Policy Planning, I realized that there had never been a peace treaty between El Salvador and Honduras. How could one fight lawlessness in the *bolsones* if no one knew whose law to apply? I told Assistant Secretary Bill Bowdler that José Luis Bustamante y Rivero, a judge on the International Court of Justice, would be an ideal mediator. Bustamante was a former elected president of Peru. I had met him in the '60's and admired his practical knowledge of border problems between Peru and Chile, particularly the issues affecting Tacna (where he was from) and Arica. Bowdler suggested Bustamante to El Salvador and Honduras. Working with the OAS, they invited him and he accepted. The "General Peace Treaty Between the Republics of El Salvador and Honduras" was signed in Lima in late 1980 with Bustamante as the mediator. It was a comprehensive document covering trade, human rights and other matters as well as frontiers. A few points on the border were not agreed and referred to the World Court for later decision.

A quick parenthesis: I believe the parties to a dispute, the people that have to live with the results, are always best placed to reach agreements that will last. If a dispute is referred to distant august bodies like the World Court, the decisions that the justices may make in their brilliance and fairness will also be made at great distance and usually without personal knowledge of the impact on the people involved. Such decisions could turn out to be less useful than ones the human beings involved could have reached, had they been sensible and reached them themselves. And that is what happened here, because when the World Court finally issued a judgment in 1992, Honduras and El Salvador found that they could not implement it. The issue was referred to the UN Security

Council, which in the structures of world power is the supposed enforcer on behalf of the World Court. Nothing happened. The border remained open.

In the spring of 2003, the Honduran and Salvadoran Foreign Ministers came to see me in my lovely wood-paneled office at OAS headquarters at Constitution and Seventeenth Street. The initiative was probably that of the Salvadoran foreign minister, Maria Eugenia Brizuela de Avila. The ministers said they wanted to close the border and asked if I could help. They said they both trusted me personally. After all, they were coming to me, the ASG; anybody who knows the OAS knows that the ASG is not the Secretary General. They explained that they were ready to apply Article 25 of the 1980 peace treaty which said that in case of disagreements they could not resolve themselves, they could turn to a third party to *dirimir* it. *Dirimir* is a Spanish term meaning to "untangle" or "resolve" not to decide or settle. In other words, this was not to be presented as a political issue, but as something to deal with technically. They knew what I had done with Ecuador and Peru, and they both trusted what I had done with each of them before. I had worked very hard with El Salvador throughout their years of pain, and I had also worked very closely with Honduras between 1999 and 2001 in their dispute with Nicaragua. Both sides trusted me to consider their interests.

Q: *Interesting that they came together to meet you.*

EINAUDI: Well, that was essential. The OAS cannot do anything in conflicts unless both sides want it.

Q: *Was the request precipitated by a crisis? How did they reach a mutual agreement to come?*

EINAUDI: There was no particular crisis. But it was ten years since the World Court decision, which had allocated roughly twice as much of the disputed territory to Honduras, and El Salvador had run out of appeals. These were smart people who understood unsettled borders are trouble. And they were looking for a solution that could be defended as technical adjustments to implement a long-standing Court order.

Appearances were important. They wanted to come to an international body that would give this broad legitimacy. At the same time, they also came to me as an American, because they also believed in U.S. power and technology. They did not want the settlement to be labeled "made in USA," but still wanted it to work.

My solution was to turn to the Pan American Institute of Geography and History, a specialized organ of the OAS located in Mexico City. I told the PAIGH to ask the U.S. delegation there to provide the OAS a U.S. expert I could trust. At the same time, I sought out John Gates, who had supervised the final demarcation of the Peru-Ecuador border. Gates worked for the U.S. Army Mapping Agency, by then called NIMA, the National Imaging and Mapping Agency. Gates is a very good cartographer, an American married to a Chilean, which gave him the advantage of knowing how to operate in a Latin environment. I could count on him to do things well.

Q: *When the foreign ministers came to you —is there anything written out?*

EINAUDI: No. I just told them that I would see if I could do it. ASGs do not go about making commitments to member states without checking with the Secretary General. And I had not been in touch with Gates in a while. So the ministers and I had a nice positive conversation, at the end of which I said "Yes, yes, yes, but — let me get back to you."

Q: *So did the Institute hire Gates or did they subcontract him?*

EINAUDI: They didn't need to. Once I found Gates again (I seem to remember he was in Cambodia), I asked the State Department to have him take on the assignment, and they probably asked the NSC to go to NIMA to arrange it. If I hadn't been able to get Gates, I don't know what I would have done. I might have said, "I can't do it." But once I found Gates, all PAIGH had to do was issue him credentials, and all I had to do was to find somebody who could give him political advice. I gave that task to Chris Hernandez on my staff, who accompanied Gates on his initial visits. I needed to not expose Gates to political madness, and that always comes when sovereignty is involved. In this business you have to be a spider and you have to weave webs constantly to bring people together and keep them together. That was my strength.

The instructions I gave Gates were that he was to take the decision of the ICJ and develop technical explanations on how to implement it. How? By applying cartographic principles in consultation with the two parties *in ways that would harm the fewest people.* In other words, in ways that would benefit the most people. I put it that way because El Salvador is a heavily populated country, and Honduras is an under-populated country. The issue was to draw an honest line without suddenly turning a bunch of Salvadorans into Hondurans – or vice versa, neither of which would have been useful. In effect, John Gates was redrawing the World Court's lines as the Salvadorans and Hondurans would have drawn them themselves in the first place without going to court. That this whole rigmarole was necessary was due to the fact that questions of sovereignty are incredibly emotional. Think of the U.S. and the John Birch Society or the Tea Party people; they're afraid the UN is going to come in and tell them what to do. They're even afraid the OAS is going to change U.S. gun laws.

When it comes to sovereignty, form is everything. That seems like an exaggeration, but it really is not. If you can't get the form right, you can get everything else right and it will still go wrong. The key to form in this case was that both governments agreed the work would be presented as technical, and not political. Once you get the form right, in this case with an international organization, not a particular government, responsible for the work, then it is possible to have Americans doing the work because then the technical capabilities of the Americans are presumably being applied in accordance with the general interests of all concerned. This was 2003 when the only people who had GPSs were American government people. Nowadays, everyone has GPSs in their phones, but these were different times. Another element of form was that it wasn't a high mucky muck like the Secretary General or ASG traveling to the disputed areas and turning things into a political circus. Getting the form right means giving the countries a way to get a result they can sell domestically, that won't be undermined by politics and sovereignty concerns.

*Q: Did you have to do anything else to do to keep the mission technical?*

EINAUDI: Monitor the mission, which lasted from May 2003 until August 2004. Chris advised me privately so I could keep John Gates' coat dry politically; there were no big titles, no big names, no political pronouncements, nothing of that sort. Just dry technical findings and boring press releases.

The idea was to keep the mission, and of course its recommendations, quietly technical: one border, one mission, one lonely guy with his GPS, armed only with common sense and the professional engineering ability to write things up properly. Gates developed recommendations point by point — there were about forty it turned out — and then it was up to me to review them and make sure they would work and were in language appropriate to submit to the Special El Salvador-Honduras Border Demarcation Commission, which assumed responsibility for the implementation.

*Q: Were issues raised during that time that could have gotten Gates' work politicized?*

EINAUDI: Yes, but I won't go into the details. Time has passed, but these issues of sovereignty can still raise emotions. I met privately with one or another of the ministers to keep them informed of what was happening and what our recommendation was going to be so that there wouldn't be any surprises. Life is personal. The ministers were taking risks themselves, and they're the ones that had to know. They came to me and I would go to them, but it was out of sight and it's going to stay out of sight, because, as Henry Kissinger used to say about Bismarck and the founding of Bosnia-Herzegovina "Only two persons knew, the King and I. The King is dead and I have forgotten."

*Q: So the meetings with the ministers took place based on specific needs at the time; there was no sort of official process where "we will meet every two weeks or every few months,' as you had done with Peru-Ecuador? It was according to the need for information?*

EINAUDI: Absolutely. If you fear improvisation and think it is too amateurish or too difficult to defend, you create rules. But life is fluid, situations are fluid, and rigid rules often don't work. The

State Department does not provide much training or education to its officers. It basically believes in on-the-job training, or as one FSO put it to me, learning to operate off the seat of your pants. Trusting our people will be smart enough to make the right decision when they have to make it. That sounds extreme, but diplomacy often involves situations that don't respond to predetermined rules. Every situation is different and has to be handled differently.

However, there are a couple of lessons that emerge here. One of them is the importance of trust, another is the importance of finding the right face or presentation, for the solution. Rather than rules, these lessons should be taken as checkpoints. They may or may not fit in all cases. As I say, disputes that involve sovereignty are particularly sensitive, because sovereignty is presented to people as life essence, so you want to be careful with it.

*Q: Was the Peace Fund used to further the work?*

EINAUDI: Of course. To do anything you need money. In general, lack of funding is one of the tragedies of the OAS. If you are bankrupt and don't have money, people aren't going to come to ask you to do anything. If people assume that the people you have as leaders can't do the job, or have become lighting-rods for criticism, you aren't going to come to them to ask for help. In this case, the Peace Fund was able to cover the staff support and travel required.

*Q: Were the governments comfortable with the outcome?*

EINAUDI: Yes. In April 2006, after I had left the OAS and was out of any kind of government position, the government of Honduras still paid for me to come down to be its guest at the ceremony at which the two presidents blessed the final pilon that closed their land border. That speaks for itself.

*Q; Was the Honduras – Nicaragua conflict similar?*

EINAUDI: Not at all. In some ways it was the opposite. El Salvador and Honduras came to me at an end game, when fighting was remote, legal recourse had been had, and what was needed was a practical, almost private solution. That I was a U.S. citizen was important as a security blanket but kept in the background. In the case of Nicaragua and Honduras, it was early times in the dispute, and I was thrust on them at a moment of great tension in a highly public effort to keep them from fighting. In that case, my being a citizen of the regional superpower was probably a main reason the Secretary General asked me to be his special representative. I was retired, but the retirement was so recent it seemed like a technicality.

Tensions had broken out in early December 1999 between the two countries as the result of the ratification of a Maritime Delimitation Treaty Honduras had signed with Colombia. In it, Honduras ceded to Colombia islands claimed also by Nicaragua. Nicaragua felt blindsided and victimized. Fishing rights were involved. Politicians began to enflame public opinion in both countries. Nicaragua imposed a 35% retaliatory tariff against Honduras, undercutting the progress toward a regional customs union (that tariff was not lifted until 2002 during the negotiation with the U.S. and the rest of Central America on the Central America Free Trade Agreement, CAFTA). Communities along the land border began to seethe. Both sides appealed to the OAS for help.

On December 7, the OAS Permanent Council welcomed their commitment to solve their conflict by peaceful means, invited them to refrain from exacerbating the situation, and asked the Secretary General to appoint a special representative "with the greatest possible urgency" to facilitate dialogue and "formulate recommendations aimed at easing tension and preventing acts that could affect peace in the Hemisphere."

On December 8, Nicaragua sued Honduras in the World Court. On December 10, the Secretary General named me his Special Representative. After consulting with the State Department, I accepted and arrived in Managua on December 15. Two days later, I was in Tegucigalpa.

In each country I met with government officials, President Arnoldo Alemán in Nicaragua and President Carlos Alberto Flores in Honduras, their cabinets, and civilian and military leaders. President Alemán received me at his *finca* outside Managua. President Flores gave me the red-carpet treatment in Tegucigalpa. (Both receptions were personally jolting for me. In Nicaragua, the freshly paved roads to the President's farm reminded me that my grandfather had refused while president to allow the dirt road to his country home to be paved. In Honduras, official ostentation contrasted sharply with my grandfather's parsimony.)

My instructions were generic, and I was to be impartial, so my line of argument was the same in both countries. I had come to listen and work. Their positions deserved to be heard. Their rights could best be defined and defended in the law. The new century had to be approached with dignity and discipline, not violence. In today's world, border wars don't stay on the frontiers as in the past, but spread fast to endanger national life and development.

It was essential to prevent unintended clashes while waiting for a decision from the International Court on the substance.

In relaying this message, I brazenly attempted to impersonate the entire international community and sought maximum publicity. I asked the OAS director in each country to convene the entire diplomatic corps, including the Papal Nuncios (representatives of the Vatican), the Ambassadors of the United States, Colombia and Mexico, and UN representatives. I made a point of seeking the support of the Catholic Church by meeting separately with bishops Obando y Bravo and Maradiaga. The Miami-based *Diario las Américas*, founded by my friend the Nicaraguan anti-Somoza exile Francisco Aguirre, was all too happy to publicize my efforts. The local press followed suit.

Between Christmas and New Year, I met in Miami with the foreign ministers, Roberto Flores Bermúdez of Honduras and Eduardo Montealegre of Nicaragua. On December 30, after several fits and starts, they agreed publicly to establish a military exclusion zone in the Caribbean Sea and to immediately freeze military personnel and border posts along and near the land border at the levels that existed on September 1, 1999. Perhaps even better news came New Year's Day, 2000. The risk of fighting ended because the Honduran church under Archbishop Rodriguez Maradiaga (who now as Cardinal is a member of Pope Francis' special commission) and the Nicaraguan church under Bishop Obando organized, at my suggestion, a march to the border to oppose renewed armed conflict.

*Q: How did you coordinate with the State Department on all this?*

EINAUDI: By phone and in person, in Washington and in the field. On January 3, I met with my former State Department colleagues in the regional bureau for a full debrief. The Office of Central American Affairs and the U.S. Mission to the OAS then undertook to have our embassies, the Agency for International Development, and the Inter-American Development Bank reinforce the message. We emphasized the economic costs that failure to keep the peace would have for both countries. My notes stress the need to move expeditiously because the issue was volatile, a juicy target for politicians to exploit.

Applying the Peru-Ecuador lesson of keeping the ball in the air, the ministers and I met again in Miami in mid-January, then again on February 6 and 7 in San Salvador at the headquarters of the Central American Integration System (SICA).

*Foreign Ministers Roberto Flores Bermudez of Honduras and Eduardo Montealegre of Nicaragua flank Einaudi after signing the Memorandum of Understanding. (Organization of American States (OAS), 2000,*

*reproduced with permission of the General Secretariat of the Organization of American States.)*

On March 7, 2000, the two foreign ministers signed a Memorandum of Understanding at OAS headquarters in Washington that set forth detailed provisions for combined patrols in Caribbean waters and limitations on military activity on and near the land border.

Tensions calmed down for several months. That June, I was elected ASG. By February of 2001, however, a surge of claims and counter claims arose, with each side accusing the other of violating the confidence-building measures agreed to the year before. Talks in March in Washington at the OAS with the two vice foreign ministers led to the development of a Technical Verification Agreement to develop data on the agreed security measures. Chris Hernandez played a major role in its drafting, and he and I traveled in April to discuss implementation. We started in Managua, then drove to Tegucigalpa rather than flying. The drive took about five hours, and we made a show of it, riding with Nicaragua's vice minister to the border, where we were met by the vice minister of Honduras who took us the rest of the way to Tegucigalpa. When we met at the border, I encouraged the two vice ministers to wave to the reporters to show that everything was going well. Put on the spot, they performed for the press. And if they were less than enthusiastic, they were clearly not fighting.

*At the border between Nicaragua and Honduras at Las Manos, Honduras, opposite El Paraiso, Nicaragua. From left to right, Guillermo Molina, Director, OAS Office in Honduras, Tomas Arita Del Valle, Vice Minister of Honduras; Bertha Marina Arguello Roman, Vice Minister of Nicaragua; OAS ASG Luigi R. Einaudi. In the background, Christopher Hernandez-Roy, OAS Secretariat, and Sergio Caramagna (face concealed), Director, OAS Office in Nicaragua. April 25, 2001. (Organization of American States (OAS), 2001, reproduced with permission of the General Secretariat of the Organization of American States.)*

The OAS Verification Mission visited border posts in July, August and October. Nicaragua and Honduras each participated with representatives from the foreign and defense ministries. Hernandez Roy and Cristina Tomassoni from my staff were accompanied by four technical advisors, two for land inspections, and two for the Caribbean. These advisors were field grade officers from the Brazilian and Argentine armies and navies. Their presence was most unusual, since the OAS Charter conveys no coercive authority and its organs had not sanctioned military participation in any operations since the 1960s. To provide credible reports on the forces on Honduras-Nicaragua border and to provide an example of civil-military comity, I insisted that we needed military people. To overcome deep seated OAS resistance to anything military, the Brazilian and Argentine officers were not called "officers." They were always referred to as "technicians." To avoid creating a precedent for military involvement, Mexico had agreed in the Permanent Council to including military officers so long as words "military" and "officer" were never used. Military professionals were key to our success, but they were just "technicians."

*Q: I want to be conscious of your time, but I do want to get Belize-Guatemala—*

EINAUDI: Also an interesting case. Sovereignty, again. But in its most extreme form, Guatemala challenges the very existence of Belize. The dispute was a direct residue of colonialism. Guatemala had long claimed that an 1859 treaty with the U.K. was null and void. In fact, Guatemala's constitution specified that its territory included the lands occupied by British Honduras. When Belize became independent in 1981, the United Kingdom kept British forces there to guarantee its defense. Guatemala recognized Belize as an independent country, but reasserted to the United Nations Guatemala's claim to Belize's territory.

*Q: How did the OAS get involved?*

EINAUDI: Several bilateral efforts to reach agreement proved inconclusive, and in the meantime Guatemalan slash and burn farmers and loggers increasingly penetrated forest preserves claimed by Belize. In the spring of 2000, the two countries turned to the OAS to develop a framework for confidence building measures and a mediation process. After I was elected that summer, the SG asked me to handle the negotiations on a day-to-day basis.

In November 2000, the parties agreed to an "adjacency zone" extending one kilometer on either side of a de facto line first marked in 1860. They also agreed in principle to remove illegal settlements and discourage incursions. Most importantly, they agreed to a mediation process to resolve underling issues. Each side named an outside "facilitator." Guatemala chose the American lawyer Paul Reichler, Belize chose Sir Shridath Ramphal of Guyana. In September 2002, after a painstaking process, both foreign ministers signed on to a report that covered development and maritime as well as the land boundary. The proposals were to be put to simultaneous public referendum in both countries. As part of its preparations, the government of Belize invited me to come down to explain the report. I did. But then congressional conservatives in Guatemala forced the foreign minister to resign. Plans for a plebiscite were shelved.

*Q: Were you surprised?*

EINAUDI: Disappointed, after all the effort we had put in and particularly because of the opportunity lost. But not really surprised. We had always known that the *Comisión de Belice* in Guatemala's Foreign Ministry was very hard line. And during my visit to Belize, I was struck by the ferocity of the local opposition slogan to yield "not one square centimetre, not one blade of grass." The situation was simply not "ripe" for solution.

*Q: What happened next?*

EINAUDI: Let me cite the preamble of what followed:

*Delegations from Belize and Guatemala, headed by H.E. Assad Shoman, Minister of Foreign Affairs of Belize, and by H.E. Edgar A. Gutiérrez, Minister of Foreign Affairs of Guatemala, met at OAS Headquarters in Washington D.C. on February 7, 2003, with Assistant Secretary General, in charge of the General Secretariat, Ambassador Luigi R. Einaudi to continue their discussions aimed at concluding an Agreement to Establish a Transition Process and Confidence Building Measures Between Belize and Guatemala, within the framework of a just, equitable and permanent solution to the territorial differendum between the two countries.*

Everyone understood that too much had been gained to let things evaporate, even though a negotiated solution now seemed unlikely. The result was a double innovation. The OAS was to build a small office in the "Adjacency Zone" between Belize and Guatemala to serve as an international presence to help keep things more or less peaceful. It was to be staffed and managed by the OAS and supported by a "Group of Friends" convened by the OAS. The Adjacency Zone Office opened July 1, 2003, a simple four-room building that stood alone at a strategic location with unimpeded access between the customs houses in the Melchor de Mencos - Benque Viejo area. The Group of Friends met for the first time that October, with the U.K. and Spain, the former colonial powers, taking an active interest and supporting our operations by contributing to the Peace Fund.

*Q: Did this work out as intended?*

EINAUDI: Yes. Since its establishment the Office has investigated hundreds of incidents, but not a single shooting confrontation has taken place between security forces. I visited the office in its first year, and invited representatives of both sides to meet with me there. I was reassured when the local Guatemalan Army commanders told me they felt the OAS presence reduced uncertainties associated with policing an open border on land the Guatemalan Constitution asserted belonged to Guatemala.

You may remember in the El Salvador-Honduras case I mentioned El Salvador as being more heavily populated than Honduras. There were far more Guatemalans than Belizeans in their border area. In long stretches of forest without supervision, stone markers had disappeared or changed position magically as Guatemalan agricultural and rare wood mining activities penetrated more deeply into what Belizeans considered theirs. The definition of an adjacency zone with outside supervision stabilizes the situation but does not resolve the underlying issue.

The presentation of the final agreement will be critical. The situations are different, but in this sense the Belize-Guatemala case is similar to Honduras-El Salvador and for that matter, to Peru-Ecuador. By the time the ministers of Honduras and El Salvador had come to see me, their dispute was far removed from armed conflict, and could be solved quietly, as a technical issue, carefully avoiding awakening new political decisions or power politics. In Peru-Ecuador, the parties knew by the end what had to be done but needed an outside force, the Guarantors, to tell them to do it.

In Belize-Guatemala, resolving the issue—which still isn't solved—will require deciding who has the authority to do so. It has to be solved by the two of them, but it can't be solved by the two of them alone. It can't be solved by Belize agreeing with Guatemala, because then Belize is selling out by yielding a blade of grass, and it can't be solved by Guatemala agreeing with Belize because then Guatemala is selling out to a tiny country that doesn't even exist.

The two had gone formally to the OAS hoping that the OAS could help them come up with a solution. It turned out that the OAS did not have the standing, in either Belize or Guatemala, to be the court of last resort. And therefore, with the OAS Adjacency Office providing a transient buffer on the ground, the countries turned in 2008 to the ICJ, the highest court in this poor world of ours, so they will then be able to say that "yes, we have no choice but to agree with this."

The lesson common to all of these conflicts is that you have to think about how you will sell the solution to public opinion. How are you going to get people to not only reach an agreement but also really accept it and make it last.

*Q: But when the Court does decide Guatemala-Belize, it's going to end up being the same situation with Honduras-El Salvador; that it will be partly impractical. Again, the reality will be that there will be more decisions to be made, don't you think?*

EINAUDI: Almost certainly you're right. In the El Salvador-Honduras dispute, El Salvador existed, Honduras existed, and no one questioned that. The issue was just where to put the line between them, so that you could draw it and forget about it, which is what in effect happened.

I am hesitating in the case of Belize-Guatemala because I'm trying to wrap my aging mind around the existential problem. For Belize, "Not one blade of grass" prevented applying technology or some other means to adjust the boundary line just enough to buy off Guatemala. But for Guatemala you had and still have the existential question, "does Belize even exist?" and that radicalizes the situation still further. Whenever the World Court decision comes down and makes clear that Belize exists, will the Court's authority be enough? And how difficult will the small collateral issues be? Are they going to be very difficult or are they going to be fairly simple? I don't know. But I think you're almost certainly right that they will probably not be made to everyone's satisfaction by the Court decision. After spending millions and millions of dollars to go to the Court in the first place, the parties will still have issues to settle.

*Q: Did dealing with these disputes affect your sense of the peace-making lessons you learned from dealing with Peru and Ecuador?*

The specifics of interstate conflicts are never the same. Even if they seem to be, they are made different by different sovereignties.

Everybody thinks their problem is unique. When somebody comes to you for help and you say, "Well, we solved the Peru – Ecuador problem doing this," they'll say, "Of course, BUT I AM NICARAGUA! I have NOTHING to do with Peru-Ecuador, don't try to put me in that box, you have to deal with MY problem." The conviction of uniqueness affects not just the parties, the victims, if you will, but also the would-be peacemaker, who might well react exactly the wrong way "Of course I know what is best! Why are you questioning me?" The more productive response is "I understand each solution has to be different. Tell me what your problem is." Then you go to the other party and the other party says "Well, I'm different." And you say, "Yes, you are different, good! Tell me about how you're different."

The absolutely most important prerequisite for reaching agreement between parties in conflict is to understand what each party wants. They are going to be different, all of these countries, any two people, are different. They are not all the same. What they want, will be different. Then you look at what they want, and you see where it overlaps, and where it doesn't. There may be something on which there's never going to be agreement, ever. I mean, I want X, and you want X too... So then you have to look and say well, there are these other areas around X that they both want differently, and then you can look for ways to agree. And you can build up those areas, so that the area of disagreement becomes smaller relative to the whole. And that's another reason for the Peace Fund. You don't want the agreement to be an orphan. If, for example, this is a simple example, they are fighting because they each want the same machine, and they can't each have the same machine. You could say, well, what do you want to use it for? Isn't that machine getting kind of old? If we work together, maybe you can each have a new machine that basically does the same job, or, better yet, a better job, or even build a machine you can share. And then we can forget about this one. But it may be that in spite of our greatest inventiveness or intelligence, that new machine or that system is going to cost something! And you've got to invest in it. And that is why it is good to have a Peace Fund to follow up, If you reach agreement, and then leave it orphan, the odds are it will be another of those pretend agreements that last only until you are out the door.

Sovereignty is at once the foundation and the bane of the modern world. The modern state system is based on it. The OAS started with Franklin Roosevelt's acceptance of the principle of non-intervention. But today's world demands cooperation with others. Which means we need to redefine sovereignty to include cooperation.

Quarta Reunião
Anual do Fórum Interamericano
sobre Partidos Políticos

Brasília-DF, Brasil
9 a 11 de novembro de 2004

*My Chief of Staff, Ambassador Sandra Honoré of Trinidad and Tobago, advises me on how to relate opposing viewpoints. (Organization of American States (OAS), 2004, reproduced with permission of the General Secretariat of the Organization of American States.)*

*Q: That may be a touch above our pay grades! But let's take another big issue key to our times. What can you tell me about the evolution of the OAS with regard to support for democracy? You had been instrumental in starting the legal framework in this regard ten years earlier.*

EINAUDI: Yes. In 1990, the General Assembly Resolution 1080 authorized action against "sudden or irregular interruption" of democratic processes. The September 1991 coup against President Aristide in Haiti was the first test of 1080. Carlos Andrés Pérez remained active, even appointing me to be his representative in Caracas talks with the Haitian Congress and its president Duly Brutus to restore Aristide with René Theodore as Prime

Minister. But that formula failed. 1080 was also invoked to other "interruptions," in Peru and Guatemala, among others. In 1993, the OAS Charter was amended to allow the suspension of a member state whose democratically constituted government had been overthrown by force. In 1994, heads of state and government met at a summit in Miami and agreed to negotiate a Free Trade Area for the Americas. Electoral observation and concern for human rights, often driven by NGOs, became the core of the OAS's public image.

*Q: I take it this was the lead up to the Inter-American Democratic Charter?*

EINAUDI: Yes. In the fall of 2000, efforts began to codify the emerging regional jurisprudence on democracy. Secretary General César Gaviria and Colombia's OAS Ambassador Humberto de la Calle, who chaired a special Permanent Council Working Group for the purpose, managed the drafting. The negotiators had to overcome nationalist and non-interventionist concerns. The final text dropped the automaticity established by Resolution 1080 and emphasized that elections were the sole responsibility of member states, but the Charter's Article 3 defined for the first time the "essential elements of representative democracy," among them respect for human rights, the rule of law, the separation of powers, and freedom of assembly and the press. On paper, it was a major conceptual step forward. It had the great merit of identifying many of the principles in greatest dispute, but their development was subsequently ignored, partly for ideological reasons, partly for renewed distrust of the United States, and importantly because no one was willing to assign resources to multilateral cooperation.

The Inter-American Democratic Charter was signed in Lima, Peru, on September 11, 2001. That morning I was among the horrified delegates in the hotel lobby as we actually saw on live television the second plane hit the second twin tower. Colin Powell earned the respect of all present by waiting a few hours to participate with his fellow foreign ministers in the signing ceremony instead of leaving immediately. The atmosphere was one of instant solidarity with the United States. Many of those present had ties to New York. Some had relatives there. The daughter of the vice minister of foreign affairs of Brazil was actually employed in one of the towers. Powell had an Air Force Plane for his return. I and others had to wait a week in Lima for airports in the U.S. to reopen. I was reduced to hearing from my wife Carol, who, from the safety of her downtown office, watched the sidewalks fill up with people. The government and the subways had closed, and they were walking home. When the streets of Washington, D.C., emptied, she drove home.

*Q: Did the fact that the Charter was signed on 9/11 have repercussions on its implementation?*

EINAUDI: I believe 9/11 fundamentally shifted the focus of U.S. foreign policy. The war on terrorism simply erased the Bush Administration's early focus on Mexico and Latin America in general. Everybody started worrying about terrorism in the United States. Brazil even supported the invocation of the Rio Treaty in support of the United States against the terrorist attack at the Twin Towers. At the OAS, we negotiated and concluded an anti-terrorism convention in record time. But in the U.S. no one noticed. We were so obsessed with Al-Qaeda that we couldn't pay attention to our own hemisphere. With neither sustained attention nor resources, the operationalization of democratic principles suddenly became essentially hortatory. I discussed with Enrique Iglesias, President of the Inter-American Development Bank, the possibility of coordinating OAS political stances with the lending practices of the bank. But neither of us found much support from our member states. Economic conditionality is difficult enough without adding political conditions except in genuinely extreme cases.

In March 2005, at the preparatory meeting in Buenos Aires for the Summit of the Americas, I made an effort to counter fears of interventionism and promote common understandings that could help put some meat on the Democratic Charter's bones. Speaking as the Acting Secretary General, I proposed the creation of a multilateral evaluation mechanism on democracy. I suggested it could be modeled on the successful Multilateral Evaluation Mechanism (MEM) on illegal drugs developed by CICAD (The Inter-American Drug Abuse Control Commission). CICAD and its MEM had replaced the often empty but always troubling threat of Congressional sanctions and aid cut-offs against countries judged not to be cooperating sufficiently with the United States against illegal drugs with a mechanism that created a framework for evaluating and supporting drug control efforts. My objective was to develop a similar mechanism to enable governments to reach agreement on specific, practical, actionable ways to apply the Democratic Charter's principles by supporting democratic institutions. I argued that antidemocratic practices anywhere weakened all countries and that not finding ways to combat them meant the OAS would lose effectiveness, credibility and funding. A stitch in time could have a preemptive effect. It could strengthen local institutions, making them more difficult to challenge, and provide channels for practical outside support instead of after the fact denunciatory rhetoric.

My proposal was actively opposed by Venezuela. In 1989, Hugo Chávez had attempted to overthrow Carlos Andrés Pérez. Elected President himself in 1999, he mounted an assault on representative democracy, arguing that popular interests required "direct democracy." It is one of history's ironies that both the promoter of resolution 1080 in defense of representative democracy and its leading antagonist were Venezuelans. Chávez' populist and authoritarian concept of democracy helped divide the hemisphere and weaken the democratic solidarity we and Pérez had worked so hard to develop. As social redistributive rhetoric began to polarize politics and Hugo Chávez applied Venezuela's oil revenues to subsidize popular support abroad as well as at home, governments found excuses to look the other way. No one wanted to turn international relations and the OAS into platforms for their domestic opponents.

The U.S., meanwhile, was focused on Osama bin Laden. Our OAS delegation was living in its own world and had earlier complained to me that I had provided an opening for dictators by saying that the promotion of democracy should allow for national idiosyncrasies. By that fall, when the Kirchners acted as if they were hostile to the Summit they were themselves hosting, my term of office had ended. The Mar del Plata Summit abandoned efforts to advance democratic cooperation as well as the proposal for a Free Trade Area of the Americas. It became known as the Errata del Plata.

*Q: That must have been frustrating.*

EINAUDI: Yes. But times have changed. The irony is that by the time the Inter-American Democratic Charter was adopted, solidarity in support of democracy was already breaking down.

Back in 1991, the adoption of 1080 was the direct result of the end of the Pinochet period and a desire to avoid a repeat of the U.S. military action in Panama in 1989. Chile was the host of the OAS General Assembly and wanted to prove its renewed democratic vocation. Military dictatorships had been failing throughout the hemisphere. U.S. intervention in Panama had been something of a surprise. After 9/11, with the U.S. engaged far from the Americas, a repeat seemed increasingly unlikely. Moreover, nobody had done anything with the third resolutory paragraph of resolution 1080, which had sought to balance negative approaches like sanctions, exclusions and breaking of relations with incentives to strengthen democratic systems based on international solidarity and cooperation. This could cover a lot of things, from collaboration on elections, human rights and judicial reform to public administration and anticorruption activities. It could also be considered and was so understood by some of the poorer countries, as a possible mandate for increased economic assistance and institutional support. In my experience most sanctions rarely produce results unless they are part of a broader policy package that provides rewards or at least reasonable escape valves.

On democracy, this broader package of positive measures was never developed. The opportunity to support the thrust for democracy was lost. Quite the opposite happened. OAS quotas – the member dues that funded the Organization's regular budget -- shrank even as more mandates were added. In addition, the definition of democracy itself came under fire, and it came under fire because of Latin America's deep and pervasive social injustice. The old saying from pre-revolutionary Cuba's cane fields was "What good does it do me to go to school and become literate, if I will simply remain a cane cutter and I will not be able to escape that back-breaking misery?" Or the litany of the 1940's Guatemala landowners, to make sure that rural workers were kept illiterate because an education might give them ideas. When societies open up to mass media and education, all kinds of ideas start bubbling up until suddenly you have a discussion not just about elections or even freedom of speech, but also about social inclusion, worker's rights, the economy and an infinite array of other matters. Regional cooperation is becoming more difficult even as the need for it grows and its potential expands.

*Q: Can you give me an example?*

EINAUDI: Consider the negotiations on the Declaration of the Rights of Indigenous Peoples, which came under my purview as ASG. In today's world, everyone has rights. And problems arise when they are not observed. But who are indigenous peoples? And who are to observe their rights? Many indigenous peoples believe their nation has boundaries different from those of today's sovereign states. The Yaqui Indians, for example, consider themselves a nation that covers Mexico's Sonora and parts of the American Southwest. Or the Shuar, whose territory reaches into Ecuador, Peru, and Brazil. These people are minorities in our modern nation states. But what happens when they might be a majority, like the Maya in Guatemala and Belize, and who are also present in Honduras, El Salvador and Mexico? The Aymara in Bolivia, Peru and Chile? Or the Quechua, whose reach extends from Peru into all of Peru's neighbors and north to Colombia? Indian rights is an issue that is prime for regional cooperation but also extremely complicated.

*Q: I can see that would be a puzzlement. I want to pick up on your comments about Venezuela and Chávez. Were you at the OAS during the anti-Chávez coup attempt?*

EINAUDI: I was Assistant Secretary General of the OAS in April 2002 when Chávez was briefly ousted, yes.

*Q: Here was Chávez, duly elected as President of Venezuela. But it looked like we in the U.S. government were jumping in, Condoleezza Rice and all, sort of giving support to the coup people because we happened to agree with them. This is a very dubious period.*

EINAUDI: Well, those were very complicated relationships to sort out. There were specific actors, for example, the IRI, the International Republican Institute, which had made its choices and was actively working in Haiti against Aristide and in Venezuela against Chávez. I think there was also a lack of realism and of caution on the part of official U.S. policy when the coup against Chávez was attempted and at first appeared to succeed.

Being at the OAS, I did not have access to what U.S. intelligence might have been. But the move against Chávez seemed ill fated from the start. The Brazilian ambassador told me right away that the reports that he was getting from his people in Venezuela was that there was a tremendous spontaneous popular mobilization of support for Chávez while he was being held by the coup plotters. If the Brazilians saw that, we should have seen it too. There should be a big difference between being conservative and believing something you hear just because you would like it to be true.

I felt from the start that Chávez and his people were actively hostile to the United States and that they were sought to undermine the existing international order. At the OAS, they enjoyed the rights of any legitimate government. I felt they needed to be not only opposed, but worked against, but not in big dispendious garrulous public ways. To be effective, it is important to know how to throw your weight around. One of our Foreign Service colleagues who spent time in Venezuela under Chávez commented, "just because a hog wants to wrestle you in the mud, you don't necessarily have to get in there and wrestle with him." The United States needs to be careful how it uses its power in this part of the world. Secondly, Chávez was responding to a series of problems in Venezuela that were genuine and had preceded him. In an earlier stage of this interview, I talked about my friendship and respect for Carlos Andrés Pérez. Under Chávez, Carlos Andrés was driven into exile. When he died, Chávez wouldn't even let his remains be returned to Caracas for burial. I consider that absolutely despicable.

Since then, the situation in Venezuela has been very difficult, and armed repression has become key. The Venezuelan-Cuban relationship is not a normal diplomatic alliance, but one that allows for Cuban involvement in intimate internal security matters, military intelligence and control, and Cuban-style bloc surveillance (called Bolivarian circles in Venezuela). Most foreign press coverage deals with either government imposition or opposition protesters, and, depending on who is doing the reporting, whether the actions are peaceful or not. What is not being discussed is the semi-official armed bands created under Chávez that are neither police nor military, but that do the thug work that enables the official uniformed services to remain relatively clean because others are doing the actual physical repression. When that happens, a country is really doing very badly. I think the judgment on Chávez has to be that he destroyed his country. A less impassioned and less hostile appreciation might be to say that Venezuela had been corrupted long before Chávez by the easy returns and socially divisive effects of the black gold of oil. Either way, Venezuela is in very bad shape, and the war of attrition between Maduro and Venezuela's now largely exiled elite is having tragic effects for its people.

After the failed attempted coup of 2002, the OAS attempted to foster dialogue in Venezuela, establishing a *Mesa de Negociación y Acuerdos* to try to bridge political differences between the Chávez government and an opposition umbrella group, the *Coordinadora democrática*. As a Colombian as well as OAS Secretary General, Gaviria felt he had to lead that himself. As president of Colombia, Gaviria had successfully steered the development of a new Constitution. In Venezuela, the attempted dialogue turned out to be a massive and fruitless headache that ultimately led to a recall referendum won by Chávez in the presence of inhibited OAS observers. I was fortunate not to be involved.

*Q: What were you doing at that point other than boundary disputes?*

EINAUDI: Whatever the Secretary General didn't want to do, or that he found inconvenient or embarrassing. Sometimes that turned out very well for me. The President of Brazil is traditionally inaugurated on New Year's Day. That is a very inconvenient time for outsiders to go to an inauguration. Gaviria said, "You go and represent the OAS at the Lula inauguration."

January 1, 2003 was a great experience. Carol accompanied me. We spent New Year's Eve in Rio de Janeiro, on Copacabana beach. Lost in a totally egalitarian crowd of two to three million people, we watched fascinated as tens of thousands of floats bearing flowers and candles were sent out to sea in the night waters by white clad celebrants. At our side, Enrique Iglesias, a former Foreign Minister of Uruguay then serving as President of the Inter-American

Development Bank, kept muttering, unbelieving "Look at this crowd. There are more people here than live in my entire country." The next morning, we flew to Brasilia. Lula's inauguration was fascinating. The ceremony was held at the Presidential Palace, displacing the Foreign Ministry's Palace of Itamaraty, where previous Presidential inaugurations had been held. But the main events were the parades and mass outdoor gatherings, including one starring Fidel Castro. Itamaraty was reduced to an event hosting foreign delegations. I had the impression that the Brazilian Foreign Service was losing its monopoly as Brazil's face to the world. Itamaraty's skilled diplomats, known to their critics as the "barbudos" or bearded ones, were being reeled in by their own national realities.

*Q: Did you also have the impression that a pink tide was sweeping Latin America?*

EINAUDI: No. The region's countries are too different to be lumped that way. I had met Lula several years before and though I knew there was a radical streak to some of his associates, I thought of him then – and still do now – as basically a union leader rooted in bread-and-butter issues more than ideology. In any case, for me, the real pink tide inauguration had been the summer before, in Bolivia. The President being inaugurated there was Gonzalo Sanchez de Losada, a cosmopolitan former president, whom I had first met when he was Minister of Planning nearly twenty years before. But the show was totally stolen by the visiting Hugo Chávez, with Evo Morales a close second. Chávez was greeted everywhere by flower-bearing schoolchildren and crowds bearing "ALBA" signs that had obviously been paid for with petrodollars. ALBA stood for *Alianza Bolivariana Americana,* the leftist bloc Chávez was creating. Not by accident, the acronym also means "Dawn".

I had met Chávez in Washington after he had been first elected. Now he had survived the abortive coup against him. As we watched the swearing-in ceremony in Bolivia, Chávez insistently invited me to come to Venezuela to see for myself his revolution's Bolivarian glories. Meanwhile, on the floor of Congress, Morales and other deputies from his MAS (*Movimiento al Socialismo* – Movement to Socialism) party were preening in traditional Indian garb as if the 1952 Revolution and land reform had never happened.

I represented the OAS at two other inaugurations the Secretary General wanted to avoid, that of Alberto Fujimori for his third term in Peru which began badly in 2000 and ended disastrously a few months later, and the inauguration in 2001 of Jean-Bertrand Aristide for his second term as the questioned president of Haiti.

*Q: Were you sent as a slight?*

EINAUDI: To whom? Well, yes, perhaps to both me and to them. The number two is never the number one. A Chilean diplomat once said he felt that when I was there the OAS had the luxury of having two Secretary Generals. But that statement papered over a less comfortable reality.

From Secretary General Gaviria's standpoint, the issue was the same in both Peru and Haiti: a controversial election that meant that anyone who attended the inauguration would be accused of legitimizing it. I had dealt quite a bit with both Fujimori and Aristide over many years. Both were lonely authoritarians who would recoil into a tense inward-focused silence when a subject not to their liking was broached with them without their permission. With Aristide, the taboos were voodoo or illegal drug dealing. With Fujimori, it was an American telling him what to do, even if it was something he was personally inclined to do in any case.

Fujimori should never have run for reelection in 2000. I had not seen him since he decorated me in January 1999. That fall, his niece took my class at Georgetown. After class one day, she asked what I thought about his running for reelection. I told her a third term was too much and that, if he were to ask me, I would advise him not to run.

In April, running with Tudela for Vice President, Fujimori won a plurality, but not enough to avoid a runoff. On May 28 he faced Alejandro Toledo, who ran with Carlos Ferrero, the brother of the Foreign Minister Fujimori had dismissed just before settling with Ecuador. Eduardo Stein, a former Vice President of Guatemala, headed an OAS electoral observation mission that reported major irregularities. In the wake of the election, and at the instigation of Canada's Foreign Minister Lloyd Axworthy, the OAS sent first a mission and then established a Mesa de Diálogo between government and opposition. Other than representing the OAS at Fujimori's inauguration on the 28th of July, I was just a spectator in the extraordinary sequence of events that followed.

Fujimori had long been operationally dependent on Vladimiro Montesinos, a cashiered military officer who was the most ambitious individual I have ever known. In September, the corruption that Montesinos managed as head of SIN, the national intelligence service, was revealed in videotapes in which he was personally paying bribes. By November, Fujimori fled to Japan, attempted to resign and was impeached. The OAS Mesa played a major stabilizing role during the crisis, particularly after the flight of Fujimori. A caretaker government conducted new elections, which Alejandro Toledo won. When Toledo was inaugurated on July 28, 2001, Gaviria represented the OAS. By then, I was fully engaged in Haiti.

*Q: Tell me about Haiti.*

EINAUDI: Haiti absorbed an enormous amount of my time and energy. Haiti was an unstable society with weak institutions, a controversial messianic leader in Jean-Bertrand Aristide, an entrenched elite, and very complicated domestic and international circumstances. This was very different from the interstate conflicts with which I had previously dealt. A foreigner cannot have the legitimacy in internal affairs that he might have in an interstate dispute. In a domestic dispute, you can't appeal the same way to international law.

So that was very difficult, and it was made more difficult by extreme polarization within American politics over Haiti and particularly over President Aristide. I had been on the policy planning staff when President Clinton and the Democratic administration sent troops to restore Aristide to power in 1994. The Congressional Black Caucus supported Aristide, but many Republicans were very dubious, and some of them were passionately anti-Aristide. Then, when I was ASG, I found myself dealing again with Haiti. I must have traveled 30 times to Haiti in my five years at the OAS. In the second Bush administration, conservative political appointees and Republican anti-Aristide congressional staffers ultimately undermined my efforts and those of the OAS to avoid violence and increase democratic space in Haiti. We wound up in 2004 with more violence and another interruption to Haiti's institutional continuity.

*President Jean-Bertrand Aristide of Haiti and I at the OAS. Between us is Ambassador Bernardo Pericas of Brazil. (Organization of American States (OAS), 1991, reproduced with permission of the General Secretariat of the Organization of American States.)*

*Q: What is your own personal evaluation of Aristide? I gather some liked him, but many thought he was bad news. Some said he was on drugs.*

EINAUDI: Let me start with a premise: it is not for me to judge foreign leaders.

*Q: But you do.*

EINAUDI: Of course, but in private. I started my answer about Aristide that way because many Americans worked actively for and against him on grounds polarized by American politics and often a virtually racist rush to judgment, disregarding that Haiti is a foreign country, a sovereign country.

Having said that, I would say this. I got to know Aristide fairly well. He and I occasionally spoke in Italian, which he had learned from Italian Salesians in Israel. He was a strange and difficult person out of a very humble background who rapidly developed many powerful enemies. And he is a very complicated character with a lot of Haitian overlays. For example, he was ordained as a Roman Catholic priest but I found him interested in the occult and in voodoo. A much-cited CIA report I have never seen reportedly identified Aristide as a drug addict, apparently largely on the basis of what was reputed to be the content of his medical cabinet when he was overthrown by General Cedras. Elsa Boccheciampe was the Venezuelan ambassador to Haiti. With our Ambassador Al Adams, she saved Aristide's life during the 1991 coup, then flew him to Caracas in a Venezuelan air force plane and took care of him while he was in exile there. She assured me that Aristide was clean, that he did not use drugs. She was a sound person and she was convinced that reports otherwise were nothing more than character assassination, propaganda invented to discredit Aristide. All I can say is that I met many many times with Jean-Bertrand Aristide, in Venezuela, Atlanta and Washington as well as Haiti. I never had occasion to sense any drug use by him.

But if you are asking whether Aristide was a good organizer, I would say he was lousy. He was President of the Republic a second time from 2000 to 2004, holding all the authority and levers of control that being President gives you even in a weak country like

Haiti. He was outmaneuvered, outorganized and thrown out of power by a handful of businessmen who, it is true, had money and were very skilled. But still. So, yes, I would say he was lousy from the standpoint of management and administration. I think some of his political judgments were also questionable.

But, again, my job is to understand rather than to judge. Aristide began life as a preacher, not a politician. He lived in a hard society that you and I do not know. Personally humiliated by his military captors during the first coup, he made a vow never to be caught in that kind of situation again. His experience instilled in him a hatred of the military, but it also made him see violence as a social given. And his hatred of the military fed into something that in the Clinton administration had U.S. support -- the abolishment of the Haitian army.

The Haitian Army was dissolved in 1995, after Aristide was returned to office by U.S. military intervention. The Army was disbanded, but the weapons were not collected from the soldiers, many of whom were disgruntled, and most of whom squirreled their guns away for future use. After the elimination of the national army, Haiti developed many private armies. In 2002, I calculated there were perhaps 40 or more major armed units and gangs. Some were security forces for companies and wealthy individuals, others were criminal gangs (some of them narcotraffickers), still others acted as armed enforcers for political groupings. Some were all of the above. This fragmentation of organized violence and lack of central authority ultimately brought down both Haiti and Aristide.

I never took the position that some did, that since Aristide was popular his flaws should be overlooked. In our whole relationship I consistently pressed him to follow the law and to allow democratic space. My focus was on defending the rule of law, not Aristide. After a December 2001 attack by unknowns on the Presidential Palace, gangs associated with Aristide followers burned the homes and offices of opposition leaders. I organized an International Commission of Inquiry that was scrupulously neutral but still wound up asking the government to pay for some of the damages. In short, I always maintained a certain amount of tension with Aristide – while I also accepting that he was Haitian and I was not. So that is a very long and very complicated answer describing an extraordinarily complex situation.

*Q: Let us go back to the beginning. What was the situation in Haiti when you became involved this time?*

EINAUDI: The negotiations went through several phases: an initial period of several months in which everyone was sounding out everyone else, followed by a year that almost produced a solution but during which spasms of violence changed calculations, and finally two years of efforts to build a political center that aborted when regime weakness enabled supporters of regime change to bring about still another violent denouement.

*Q: Can you summarize?*

EINAUDI: I would be glad to do so. There are boxes and boxes of detailed files on Haiti at the OAS' Columbus Memorial Library should anyone want more.

Here are some highlights.

When Aristide was returned by the United States to office in the fall of 1994, he had lost more than half of his term, a full three years. However, to maintain constitutional form, Presidential elections went ahead as originally scheduled in December 1995. René Préval, an Aristide ally, was elected overwhelmingly for a five-year term beginning February 7, 1996. Parliamentary and local elections in 1997 and again in May 2000 were controversial. In the latter, OAS observers concluded that 8 of 17 senators who were declared elected by the CEP (*Conseil Electoral Provisoire*), the formally independent Electoral Council, should have gone to a run off.

In August 2000, a few weeks after I was elected, the Secretary General and I went to Haiti with a mandate from the OAS General Assembly to offer our good offices to resolve an electoral dispute, so as to pave the way for the presidential election scheduled for November. After that initial visit, I returned twice in September and then for more than a week in late October. The last visit produced the first face-to-face meeting between Aristide's Fanmi Lavalas party and the main opposition coalition, the *Convergence Démocratique*, which included the *Organisation du Peuple en Lutte* (OPL), led by Gérard Pierre Charles, which was a breakaway from Aristide's Fanmi Lavalas. The OPL was probably the most important of the Convergence parties, which covered the ideological spectrum, including evangelicals. Throughout the years, Convergence representatives were fairly stable. In addition to Pierre Charles, they included Victor Benoit, Serge Gilles and Ariel Henry. Micha Gaillard and Evans Paul also joined the talks many times. That first meeting in the fall of 2000 produced a great deal of acrimonious debate and no agreement. However, my staff and I compiled the main points made by the two sides into a document we entitled "Elements of Reflection concerning the components of a National Agreement." I suspended the dialogue on October 20, but left the document behind, indicating the OAS was open to receiving comments.

Before leaving, I learned that the head of the CEP, Haiti's electoral council, had made a diatribe in Creole calling for the election of Aristide. I don't remember where I got the transcript, perhaps the Foreign Broadcast Information Service. But its authenticity was unquestioned. I called on President René Préval and told him this was a violation of the neutrality required to administer fair elections. The President heard me out, then said, "Here, sit in my chair and tell me what you would do in my shoes." We traded places. Sitting on the presidential throne, I said, "I learned from my Grandfather, when he was President of Italy in hard times, that the number one rule, particularly when uncertainty reigns, is to set a good example. I know I am not setting a good example if I allow the Head of the National Electoral Council to campaign for one of the candidates. I must change him, or the election will not be fair." We traded places again, and Préval said "I'm sorry, but he is the only person I have who knows how to run an election."

*Q: That must have been a bit of a downer —*

EINAUDI: That certainly crystallized the government's intransigence at that point. Aristide had felt cheated of three years of his presidency by the 1991 coup. He believed he was legitimate, basically that he should be able to do what he wanted.

On November 26, Aristide received more than 90% of the vote while running against six minor candidates. The Convergence groupings boycotted. The only international observers were a small team from CARICOM. The OAS, faced with the government's intransigence, did not attend and issued a statement that the election "avoids an interruption in the timetable for presidential succession established by the Constitution of Haiti, but does not alter the need to ensure the broad political representation and citizen participation critical to the development of Haitian democracy." Even before the election, the UN Secretary General had recommended that, in light of the political turmoil and instability, the UN International Civilian Support Mission in Haiti (MICAH) be terminated at the end of its mandate on February 6, 2001.

*Q: That certainly marked where the international community stood.*

EINAUDI: Yes, but nothing about Haiti is ever cast in stone. The ten weeks between Aristide's election and the inauguration were filled with maneuvers on all sides. At the end of December, after a visit from U.S. officials, President-elect Aristide declared in a letter to outgoing President Clinton that he intended to implement eight commitments, the fifth of which was to establish "a semi-permanent OAS commission to facilitate dialogue among Haitian political, civic and business leaders and through international monitoring of the protection of human rights." As a result, during January, the Secretary General and I were literally flooded with letters and visits from the outgoing and incoming Haitian authorities and civil society. On January 31, a five-member delegation from the Convergence Démocratique visited me. They explained that, given the illegality of Aristide's election, they wanted a transitional government to hold new elections.

*Q: So what happened?*

EINAUDI: On February 7, 2001, Aristide was inaugurated the second time, and for the second time his term was to be interrupted. The Secretary General asked me to attend, and gave me instructions to keep lines of communication open with all parties and assess whether the OAS could have a positive role. In four frenetic days, I met not only with the other visiting foreigners (including UN, EU and CARICOM representatives and former Venezuelan President Carlos Andrés Pérez), but especially with a broad swath of Haitians, from Aristide, who introduced me to his yet to be designated foreign minister, to business and civil society leaders, the Convergence and others in the political opposition, and the local diplomatic corps. All were supportive of an OAS effort. Luigi Bonazzi, the Papal Nuncio, Serge Miot, the Archbishop of Port au Prince, and Hubert Constant, the President of the Episcopal Conference, were particularly encouraging.

On April 17, President George W. Bush visited the OAS. In the meeting in the Secretary General's office before he spoke to the Permanent Council, Bush asked about Haiti. Gaviria told me to summarize the state of affairs. I did so, recalling that his father had always been very interested in Haiti. The new President of the United States did not engage. Instead, he looked at me and said, with a smile, "Well I am glad it is your problem, not mine. Better you than me." In his address to the Council, he was positive about the OAS, saying "Along borders where tensions run high, the OAS helps build confidence and avoids crises. And, in lands where freedom's hold is fragile, the OAS is there to strengthen it."

*President George W. Bush at the OAS Permanent Council, April 17, 2001. The Chair of the Council, Colombian Ambassador Humberto de la Calle and I preside to his left. (Organization of American States (OAS), 2001, reproduced with permission of the General Secretariat of the Organization of American States.)*

The following week, Aristide participated, though under a cloud, in the Summit of the Americas in Quebec. The Summit Chair, Canadian Prime Minister Jean Chrétien, closed the meeting asking the Secretary General to lead what became a joint OAS-CARICOM mission to Haiti. Led by Gaviria and former Prime Minister Dame Eugenia Charles of Dominica, the mission concluded that "mutual lack of trust" meant face-to-face negotiations would be unlikely to overcome the "problems arising from the May 21, 2000 election." External facilitation would be required. Aristide kept the ball in the air by writing a letter to the OAS General Assembly containing five points—including the resignation of seven May 21 senators and the normalization of Haiti's relations with the international financial institutions—to "foster an end to this situation." Clearly the government hoped that some flexibility on its part could end what Aristide would later call the "embargo" holding up Haiti's badly needed IDB (Inter-American Development Bank) and World Bank loans. Conversely, the opposition feared repression and realized their demand for a transitional government was not meeting much support from an international community more interested in course correction than the unknowns of regime change.

OAS General Assembly resolution 1831 of June 5, 2001 instructed the Secretary General to monitor Aristide's commitments and increase efforts to resolve the political crisis. Negotiations got underway immediately, with either the Secretary General or more usually me in the chair. We were aided by several constituents of civil society and by the Group of Friends, led by the ambassadors to Haiti of France, Canada and the United States and chaired at the time by the Argentine. A civil society institution that played an important role over time was the *Fondation Nouvelle Haiti* (FNH – New Haiti Foundation), founded by wealthy businessman Andy Apaid. Unlike some others of the Haitian elite, who slept in Haiti but went to Miami for shopping and medical treatment, Apaid was fully committed to Haiti.

The *Convergence Démocratique* was represented by the group I have already described. The government was usually represented by the prime minister, foreign minister, and Aristide's chief of staff or some combination thereof. Fritz Longchamp, Leslie Voltaire, Duly Brutus, Jean Casimir, and Jean Claude Desgranges all played important roles at one point or another. On rare occasions, Aristide himself would participate. Once, while Gérard Pierre Charles was maneuvering his polio damaged legs to get to his place at the negotiating table, Aristide whispered to me "It is important to be nice to cripples. You never know when you will meet them in the afterlife."

After great effort, the government and the opposition reached important agreements in July 2001. The one with the greatest long-range implications was to create a new CEP, or electoral tribunal, with nine members to be nominated by the Executive, the Judiciary, political parties from both government and opposition, the Catholic and Protestant churches, the Chamber of Commerce and Industry, and human rights organizations. When the agreement was concluded, all present broke out in spontaneous and apparently heartfelt applause. Other agreed measures included pledges to avoid violence and to run new elections in 2002 for the eight disputed senate seats. But the negotiators adjourned without being able to agree on new elections for local authorities.

Agreement on the CEP was to prove the closest we ever came to success. The maximal balance of the new electoral body, with representation of parties, government, religious bodies and civil society, was to remain an almost utopian ideal. But neither it nor any of the other points agreed were ever implemented. Within days, at the end of July, armed men attacked the police academy in Pétionville and three police stations, killing five and wounding fourteen as they melted away without encountering resistance. Then, in the early hours of December 17, 2001, about 20 armed men attacked the national palace. Five guards were killed, offices including that of the president, were ransacked, and there was a lot of shooting as the attackers fled, chased by a police helicopter. In response, mobs set fire to the offices of three parties belonging to the Convergence Démocratique, the homes of key opposition leaders, and a research center run by Suzy Castor, the wife of Gérard Pierre Charles, leader of the OPL party of the Convergence

Démocratique. The next day, books from its library turned up for sale on the streets of Port au Prince.

In the old days, under the Duvaliers, the regular army and police, supported by unofficial gangs known as the Tonton Macoutes and Chimères, organized controlled (and sometimes uncontrolled) violence. After the U.S. intervention led to the dissolution in 1995 of the Haitian Army, fragmentation of authority and gang warfare became king. These informal, unofficial, often local gangs were generally lumped together as *Organisations Populaires*. The Haitian National Police was undersized and corrupt. With no army and no reliable police, and fearing his opponents wanted to drive him out the way they had in 1991, Aristide fell back on traditional gang methods. The *Organisations Populaires* loyal to him and to *La Fanmi Lavalas*, and also known as the *Chimères* ("Ghosts"), served to neutralize the armed gangs of his opponents. Haiti was too disarticulated a society to polarize, but it was beginning to be dominated by armed camps.

Each fresh outburst of violence damaged the negotiations. Apparently mindless rage directed against unpopular targets was referred to locally as *déchoucage* or "uprooting." I imagined them as the equivalent of the usually fruitless *jacqueries*, the French peasant uprisings of the late Middle Ages. But the July and December outbursts of 2001, whose masterminds were never identified, were different. They did not bring down the government, but the violence emboldened the opposition. Each new outburst proved Aristide could not maintain order. Why compromise with a regime that might not last? The opposition could drag out the negotiations and deny legitimacy to the government while they worked for regime change. The weakness of the government meant the OAS was no longer viewed as needed for protection.

Formally, and on the surface, everything went on more or less as before. In March, Aristide named a new Prime Minister, the intelligent and dignified Yvon Neptune. Aristide also named his rival from the 1990 elections, the conservative former World Bank official Marc Bazin, as Minister without portfolio to facilitate the negotiations. For our part, we at the OAS appointed an Independent Commission of Inquiry. I chose my friend, the former Honduran foreign minister, Roberto Flores Bermudez, to head it along with jurists from Mexico and the Caribbean. The Mexican was a distinguished professor of international law, Alonso Gómez Robledo. CARICOM was represented by OECS Supreme Court Justice Dr. Nicholas Liverpool, who later became President of the Commonwealth of Dominica. Berta Santoscoy, a Mexican citizen, took leave from the Inter-American Commission on Human Rights to serve as their Executive Secretary. The report of their May 2002 visit is a revealing and troubling document still worth reading today. It described what happened in detail, including the many failures of the police. It recommended, among other things, that the *Organisations Populaires* be disarmed and reparations paid to the victims of the December rampage. The head of the OAS Legal Department, the Uruguayan Jean Michel Arrighi, traveled not very happily to Haiti afterwards to help assess the reparations.

*Q: Was the OAS in effect working against Aristide by seeking reparations for his opponents? Particularly since the December attack had been against Aristide in the first place?*

EINAUDI: I would have objected to that implication at the time. By getting reparations, I was attempting to keep the opposition in the game, to expand the space for democratic politics, and to facilitate the normalization of Haiti's relations with the international financial institutions. But by the time reparations were actually paid to the opposition leaders and organizations whose properties had suffered in the retaliation for the attack, conditions had changed, and paying reparations was by then only one of the demands of the international community before releasing funds for Haiti from the international financial institutions.

As this example suggests, this whole phase of the negotiations turned into an abyss of moving goal posts, mutual reneging on commitments by all concerned, the whole much complicated by the very Haitian tactic of *marronnage*. The *Marrons*, or maroons, were slaves who escaped to the interiors of the colonies of the New World. I have not found a dictionary that goes much beyond the imagery of the fugitive slave of the past, and none that goes beyond a confused link to illegality. In cultural reality today, however, *marronnage* refers to all the antics of deception invented by the weak to put off the powerful, and to avoid doing what is wanted, even if the cost is looking foolish or lazy. For example, we had agreed on the composition of the electoral council. But what staff will it have? Where will it be housed? What will be its relations to the police? To the press? To the local authorities? Its budget?

*CARICOM meets with Haitian opposition and NGOs in the Bahamas, January 2004. Seated are Fred Mitchell, Patrick Manning, Perry Christie, P.J. Patterson and Knowlson Gift. Standing in the rear are Haitian delegates, among them Victor Benoit, Ariel Henri, Luc Mesadieu and Micha Gaillard. I am at the far left, representing the OAS with Canada's Paul Durand. CARICOM leaders met with President Aristide and Famille Lavalas in Kingston, Jamaica, a week later. (Organization of American States (OAS), 2004, reproduced with permission of the General Secretariat of the Organization of American States.)*

All this was taking place against a background of economic decline and extraordinary institutional frailty. Amazingly, the international community has contributed, sometimes intentionally, to the weakness of Haiti's governmental institutions. President George W. Bush successfully expanded U.S. global efforts against AIDS. These world-wide efforts, conducted mainly on a government-to-government basis, had remarkable results in Africa and elsewhere. But in Haiti, the assistance went to NGOs, ubiquitous private non-governmental organizations, on grounds that the Ministry of Health was corrupt. According to the President of the Pan American Health Organization, my friend Sir George Alleyne, who also served as the United Nations Secretary General's Special Envoy for HIV/AIDS in the Caribbean, the ministry would have been perfectly capable of administering AIDS prevention and training programs. But suspicion of Aristide prevailed. By the time of the 2010 earthquake, Haiti had a different government, but U.S. hesitancy about working with the Haitian government remained. A former senior Haitian official sadly told my wife and me that the United States found it easier to send aid in the form of bottled water from Miami than to help Haitians bottle it in Haiti. U.S. assistance was critical, but it was being provided in ways that were undermining the already weak state Haiti needed to function.

As 2002 turned into 2003, I increasingly attempted to develop new formulas to break the mounting impasses. In March 2003, Julian Hunte, who as Foreign Minister of St. Lucia was President of the UN General Assembly, joined me in heading a joint OAS-CARICOM delegation to Haiti. We brought with us the President's Special Envoy to Latin America Ambassador Otto Reich, hoping that his Cuban American and Republican credentials would add to our authority. That August, at my suggestion, the Secretary General named retired U.S. Ambassador Terence Todman as an additional facilitator of dialogue in Haiti. Denneth Modeste staffed him.

Every time we made some progress in the negotiation between Aristide and his political opposition, the members of the opposition who opposed any kind of negotiation used their ties to the U.S. Congress and to conservatives and to IRI, the International Republican Institute, to obstruct. They would get on the phone to Republican congressmen and staffers and the White House and they would say: "It looks as though the OAS is again doing something stupid in support of Aristide, they don't really represent U.S. policy, do they? You must do something about this."

Aristide had friends in Washington also, chief among them Randall Robinson, Ron Dellums, Maxine Waters, and other members of the Black Caucus, as well as a few others, including Bill Delahunt, and Chris Dodd in the Senate. But they had had their moment in 1994 with Bill Clinton, and now was the Republicans' moment, led by Congressmen Benjamin Gilman and Porter Goss and Senators Jesse Helms and Mike DeWine. The organizing lynchpins of the anti-Aristide movement were not the principals. They were Congressional staffers, foremost among them Caleb McCarry, whose passionate opposition to Aristide was matched only by his hatred of Castro's Cuba, and a Haitian-American at IRI named Stanley Lucas, who was active in the Dominican Republic and Haiti as well as Washington and later ran unsuccessfully for Congress in Florida.

Every time I was flying home to Washington, I knew that before I even landed calls were being made to Washington to undo whatever had just been agreed. Dean Curran, the U.S. Ambassador to Haiti, was worried that a member of the International Republican Institute was in touch with persons in Haiti and the Dominican Republic who were preparing an armed campaign against Aristide. Curran was a career diplomat and something of a scholar. His concerns rang a bell with me. At an IRI fund raising Gala in Florida in 2001, I had suddenly found myself surrounded by several Haitian businessmen. They told me they were contributing heavily to IRI to organize against Aristide and were sharply critical of Apaid for negotiating with Aristide. The contributions from these Haitians made it possible for IRI to undertake programs not subject to the controls that existed for U.S. taxpayer funds.

Ambassador Curran feared that IRI, particularly Stanley Lucas, was helping to organize regime change. Curran referred to Lucas and his cohorts as the "Washington *Chimères*" (ghost gangs).

*Q: How were the Latin American members of the OAS responding to all of this?*

EINAUDI: Mainly with indifference. Haiti is not a Latin American country. In geographic terms it is a Caribbean country, a member of CARICOM but in practice a secondary member of CARICOM, since it's not English speaking. For the last century, it has been heavily dependent on the United States. The French and the Canadians have an interest, as do Cuba and Venezuela, but the rest of Latin America has never shown much interest. In the period we've been discussing, Brazil, Mexico, Chile perhaps most, have had an interest in Haiti but still their interests were secondary and their influence was secondary. So, the real issue was the political problem inside Haiti and how it related to the political problem inside the United States.

*Secretary of State Powell confers on Haiti with Einaudi and St. Lucia Foreign Minister Julian Hunte at the OAS General Assembly in Barbados in 2002. (Organization of American States (OAS), 2002, reproduced with permission of the General Secretariat of the Organization of American States.)*

*Q: All right. Back to Haiti. What happened next?*

EINAUDI: In 2003, the *Organisation Populaire* known as the Cannibal Army, previously favorable to Aristide, turned against him. There were rumors of former Haitian military training in the Dominican Republic. The line between legal opposition and armed opposition was blurring. Andy Apaid's wife, Elisabeth, took over day to day management of their businesses so that her husband could dedicate himself to the Group of 184, an Anti-Aristide umbrella group that began to challenge the *Organisations Populaires* for control of the streets in Port au Prince. In Haiti, arguments surfaced that Ambassador Curran was not representing the Bush Administration properly, and that the OAS and I were out of step with U.S. policy. Armed anarchy was growing. Palms were being greased, more and more easily as uncertainties grew. The supporters of regime change were growing more and more emboldened.

In August-September 2003, with anarchy at the door, Apaid and Aristide each told me they could agree to a foreign police force to help stabilize the security situation. Apaid was a businessman and a Haitian patriot, and while he was strongly against Aristide, he had a businessman's appreciation of predictability and "law and order." Aristide was more ethereal, but he could sense his ability to control things slipping away. We settled on a hypothetical number of police, on the order of 600. I told them that the OAS was allergic to anything that looked like the military, that unlike the UN's Chapter VII, the OAS Charter provides no coercive authority. But I knew we had found a way to involve Argentine and Brazilian officers in Nicaragua-Honduras, and I thought that perhaps Haiti being Haiti, and the United States being the United States, we might be able to finesse the issue in some way. Canada might also be helpful.

So I consulted with friends in the U.S. military and at the Justice Department and FBI to see what a force and training requirements might look like and what a package might cost. If I remember correctly, I got an estimate on the order of $100 million. I then raised the issue with Assistant Secretary Noriega. After a few days, the answer came back. It was not possible. The cost was just too high. That was certainly true, under normal circumstances, but I suspect that Noriega, a conservative who had served in Senator Helms' office, also felt he would be accused of helping to prop up Aristide. I insisted. The next election was only two years away. It would be a small investment compared to the cost of boots on the ground, which the President did not want, and would help ensure institutional continuity. He said "I'll check," then called back. "They said no."

Thinking back, this was a classic case of our government, indeed our society, being unable to respond to a crisis when it was still manageable, before it blew out of control. We were unable to act when action was required. We could not come up with funding we knew would be necessary and a fraction of what it would cost if we waited until a full-scale military operation became necessary.

In desperation, I hit on a stratagem. The negotiations had always, almost religiously, taken place at politically neutral Haitian sites. The Hotel El Rancho, the Hotel Montana, the Nunciatura, etc. What if we met at the U.S. Ambassador's residence? Not even Stanley Lucas could then argue that what was agreed in the U.S. Ambassador's residence did not represent U.S. policy. The new U.S. Ambassador was James Foley, an FSO I had known when he was Eagleburger's aide, fifteen years before. I proposed it to him and he agreed. We settled on a date: October 5, a Sunday. Holding the talks in his residence would be a clear sign the U.S. supported negotiations, not regime change. We moved to invite. Then on Friday, less than forty-eight hours before the meeting, we got word that Foley had canceled the meeting.

Watching my language, I sent an unclassified e-mail that night to Foley describing the immediate results of what he had done. At the State Department, I copied Director of Caribbean Affairs Mary Ellen Gilroy, Assistant Secretary Roger Noriega and U.S. Ambassador to the OAS John Maisto. At the OAS, I sent copies to David Lee, Denneth Modeste, Sandra Honoré and Paul Spencer.

*Subject: Next steps, please read before you see Aristide*
*Jim:*

*None of us appreciated your unconsulted decision, giving us no role and putting the SG and myself in the position of appearing without effect. The OAS has now probably again become too obvious an appendage to play much of a useful role as proclaimed in publicly articulated U.S. policy. As you will see below, we are trying to preserve some space by adopting some of your arguments.*

*But the pressure on you personally will be much greater and it will now take a virtuoso performance on your part to win; we will of course do our part, and part of that is telling you what we think, what we are saying, and what is said to us.*

*[Bishop Hubert] Constant and the Nuncio had formally accepted. Constant after a visit to Fort Liberte by Modeste, the nuncio with a very nice note to me, noting that he was convinced the Catholic bishops were not alone in expressing the unacceptability of the politics of permanent confrontation and that he hoped that those voices would be heard Sunday. David and Denneth are calling all invitees to postpone, but I answered the nuncio myself. I told him you had concluded some sectors of the opposition were not prepared to support positions that would prove feasible in the short term. The Secretary General therefore had authorized a postponement of two to three weeks but not longer, the time during which we can evaluate and prepare positions better suited to ensuring success.*

*President Aristide called me at about 6pm PaP time. I told him that Ambassador Foley had decided to postpone the lunch to have more time to prepare and that I did not fully agree with the postponement because of the risks involved, but that the SG and I agreed that the U.S. is vital to any success. JBA responded "tout à fait. Tout à fait."*

*I said he should keep his mind open as to where you stood and why until after hearing you out tomorrow, and that I believed you were not setting up for an indefinite postponement.*

*I then told him that I feared some in the opposition would use the time not to seek compromises but to attempt to accelerate efforts to provoke situations they could claim prove that Haiti is ungovernable and a dictatorship and to promote military action by the US. They will fail in the latter purpose, I said, and perhaps the American Administration might in the process discover who among the opposition are democrats and who are playing a double game. But, I told Aristide, that would depend to a large extent on the success of the Haitian National Police in avoiding the provocations and reactions that the anti-democrats could use to make their case. Aristide said he agreed.*

*Aristide and I parted on apparently good terms, with him saying that he understood your concern for prior agreements so as not to step into the void (a great fear of his as well).*

*David and Denneth will make every effort tonight in their individual conversations to postpone to stress the need for better preparation, prior agreements, and the importance of getting the right people to attend. Our thought is that by complicating the reasons for the delay, we not only reduce the pressure on you but keep ourselves from just looking as your tools.*

*Bonne chance.*

I felt blind-sided and betrayed. A few days later, Assistant Secretary Noriega brought his entire front office to visit me at the OAS and told them in front of me that I should always be consulted in the future. But it was too late. Noriega and his colleagues almost certainly did not realize it, but the die was cast.

There never was a rescheduled meeting under OAS auspices. Without security support, without viable political negotiations and with an incompetent Haitian government, order collapsed over the next several months. Once it collapsed, of course the same American authorities who could not spend money for a little bit of security support before the collapse, suddenly had to face putting boots on the ground, with all the extravagant expenses military action requires.

On December 3, students at the State University in Port au Prince were assembling to march out to demonstrate against the government when members of the *Organisations Populaires* supporting Aristide broke into the campus and started to beat them. Before disappearing, as usual without resistance from the police, the attackers broke both legs of the rector and wounded some 20 other persons. OAS offices were broken into. The event was met with outrage by some, and indifference by others, with both emotions reflecting an advancing state of near anarchy.

In the midst of it all, January 1, 2004 was the 200th anniversary of the Independence of the first Black Republic of modern times. Foreign attendance at the celebration was sparse. The only head of state present was Thabo Mbeki of South Africa. Prime Minister Christie of The Bahamas represented CARICOM, Maxine Waters, the Black Caucus. I was there for the OAS. The King of Benin, the traditional ruler of the Edo people of Nigeria, whence many had been brought as slaves to Sainte Domingue, was in full ceremonial garb. Thousands of Haitians danced before the platform, their sinuous beauty marred by occasional distant bursts of gunfire and the thought that Aristide was probably running out of funds to pay them.

Over the next weeks, chaos spread. The Cannibal Army was active in the North. Former soldiers were returning from the neighboring Dominican Republic. CARICOM, then the U.S., directly, first with Noriega and finally Colin Powell, were caught up in a spate of desperate negotiations following the script I had developed over the previous three years for an institutionally coherent compromise. But it was too late. The opposition was again openly demanding that Aristide step down. Aristide was offering concessions but holding on. Efforts to hold the center were doomed. Here is how the McNeil-Lehrer Newshour described it with me on February 25, 2004: [4]

MARGARET WARNER: As violence continued in Haiti today, international diplomats were still struggling to broker a deal between President Jean-Bertrand Aristide and opposition groups demanding his ouster. A delegation came to the capital, Port-au-Prince, last Saturday to present a U.S.-drafted proposal in which Aristide would remain as president, but share power with his rivals. Secretary of State Colin Powell had said the U.S. would not endorse forcible regime change. *Clip of Powell saying: "We cannot buy into a proposition that says the elected president must be forced out of office by thugs and those who do not respect law."* Aristide promptly accepted the proposed deal Sunday, but yesterday the political and civic opposition leaders said "no." *Clip of opposition leaders saying "And there will be a worsening of the violence as long as Mr. Aristide is in power..."* The violence, which has killed 70 people, began with an armed rebel uprising three weeks ago. The rebels, who say they're not connected to the civic opposition, now

---

[4] "The NewsHour with Jim Lehrer," 2004-02-25, NewsHour Productions, American Archive of Public Broadcasting (GBH and the Library of Congress), Boston, MA and Washington, DC, accessed January 2, 2022, http://americanarchive.org/catalog/cpb-aacip-507-930ns0mj15.

control the northern half of Haiti and are threatening to seize the capital. Yesterday, Aristide appealed for foreign assistance to his outmanned Haitian police force. Otherwise, he warned, thousands will die or flee to U.S. shores. *Clip of Aristide "The world sees this kind of tragedy, it is a genocide, it is a crime against humanity."* On Capitol Hill today, the congressional black caucus urged the president to act quickly to end the violence without waiting for a negotiated settlement. *Clip of U.S. Rep. Charles Rangel: We don't want the blood, any more blood, Haitian blood on American hands, on the international community's hands. And no matter what the French or anyone thinks of Aristide, we cannot have his life taken away on our watch."*

MARGARET WARNER: Now for the latest on diplomatic efforts to solve the Haiti crisis, we turn to Luigi Einaudi. He's Assistant Secretary General of the Organization of American States, he's also the OAS point person on Haiti. He's met frequently with President Aristide and with many of the political opposition leaders.

Let's start with what Congressman Rangel just said at the end of the tape. Is President Aristide in danger of losing his life here? Is the situation that dire?

EINAUDI: Quite possibly. Basically, the situation is as bad as it is because President Aristide was humiliated and nearly killed in a military coup in September of 1991. He has vowed never to let that happen again. And it's one of the reasons for his attempt to control power in ways that a lot of people find objectionable. Conversely, there are people who moved against him then who are sorry they left him alive.

WARNER: So, take us back to this weekend, this latest effort to negotiate a settlement. Secretary Powell got personally involved.

He even interceded with the opposition trying to get them to agree. It failed. Give us your political analysis of why it didn't work.

EINAUDI: I think the only people who wanted it really to work are us foreigners. It's hard to be Haitian. If you're Haitian, you're poor, you live in a very difficult environment. You are forced to be suspicious. You're aware of your slave heritage. But it is also hard to be a friend of Haitians because they suspect the motives of the outsiders and I think basically for two years we've had a hidden war that has been escalating into the present.

The opposition did not want to do anything that might legitimate Aristide. Aristide did not want to do anything that would really undermine his power. And the outside community, to some extent, was a bit late in reacting to all of this, although we have made… the OAS has made a major effort . . .

WARNER: Let me ask you this. The way it has been portrayed here, Aristide was willing to share power and the opposition wasn't. Is that the case? Or is the opposition right to be suspicious of Aristide and whether he really means it?

EINAUDI: Yes. Yes, they are right to be suspicious. And, Yes, it is also true he was willing to offer. The problem is that on the basis of past history, distrust reigns supreme. I have often told Haitians they distrust people and they come back at me saying it's not that we distrust, it's that we know that everybody's planning how to get out of whatever commitment has been made.

WARNER: Now, what is the connection between the civic or political opposition? First, let me ask you a quick question about them. Is that a unified group or are they also split?

EINAUDI: The one unifying factor for much of the opposition is anti-Aristide. And they themselves are divided. There are some very optimistic long-term elements here. Used to be that Haitian politics was left to the hands of the professional politicians and the military. Now the military's largely out and disbanded, although, as we've seen, some of them are coming back. Now we've also had the growth of civic movements and the like. The problem is that they have all united in a way that creates a further polarization and division for the time being.

WARNER: Now what's the connection, they insist there isn't one of course, between the political opposition in the city and these armed rebels out in the countryside. But is there a connection?

EINAUDI: Well, if you spend all of your time talking and the government is not particularly responsive, after a while, you feel that you need some bite and you don't necessarily object that others mobilize and give you some bite. The difficulty in Haiti now is that I think things have really gone to a further pass than anybody expected.

The government never expected its police to crumple the way it has. The opposition, until recently, was hoping to provoke an armed intervention from the United States or somebody else to change things. They didn't think they could take things into their own hands. One of the reasons they turned down the peace plan over the weekend was that they now think they don't need the outside. They think they can win.

WARNER: You mean because the rebels are providing the pressure?

EINAUDI: Yes.

WARNER: Now President Aristide, as we just saw, warned yesterday, if somebody doesn't intervene and shore up his police force, thousands will be killed and many will try to flee to the U.S. as refugees. Do you think that's true?

EINAUDI: Yes, I do think that's true.

WARNER: On both counts?

EINAUDI: Yes, I think the flights have already begun. The deaths are gradually growing. I think the expectation and the fear right now in Port-au-Prince itself, the capital, is that there could be loosed some terrible revenge taking. There's a sad lesson from what's happened in the North. There's a report from the United Nations that they have been unable to open a humanitarian corridor for fuel and food and medicine. That's one thing that the entire international community is in total unity about. But we just saw the clip of some of their workers leaving now, and the U.N. is saying, they can't do it, because there are too many fiefdoms with barricades and demands. That to me is a description of growing anarchy.

WARNER: Now, do you also have a split in the international community? The way at least the wires reported, the French put out a statement that seemed to be calling for a force right away and we heard President Bush say: happy to support a force but only after there is a compromise. Is there a lack of unity also among the foreign diplomats and foreign countries that would like to solve this?

EINAUDI: I think there has been a lack of unity. Whether that lack of unity will continue under the pressure of these events is not clear. We saw Secretary Powell say very clearly, and he has repeated it a number of times recently, and when we met with him ten days ago, that we have to recognize that President Aristide is an elected president.

There are others who are less interested in that principle, and are willing to say, look, this man must go. On the other hand, I think the U.S., reeling still from the experience of 1994 when we did, under President Clinton, put Aristide back in power after a coup, but didn't really ultimately feel that we had achieved a major result, so the U.S. is not clear that it wants to go in and defend a regime that's under attack.

WARNER: And a regime whose record it's not exactly proud of or can't really stand behind.

EINAUDI: That's right. Although frankly I think the political reasoning is that we don't want to get involved in a conflict where we will be losing more casualties. And that is true of everybody. I think the French would like to do things, but are constrained. They're far away. They're the former colonial power. The Caribbean countries are small.

WARNER: Let me ask you about something the French said today at the end of their statement: Aristide bears ultimate responsibility for the current situation, they said. It is his decision but a new page must be opened in Haiti's history. Do you read that as the French pressing Aristide to leave, to step down before his two years are up?

EINAUDI: The whole French statement is parallel to the position of the opposition and it's a very intelligently and well-crafted position.

WARNER: And from what you know of President Aristide, would he ever do that?

EINAUDI: I think we are in this trouble in part because he vowed that he'd never be thrown out.

WARNER: All right, Mr. Ambassador, thank you so much.

Not even four days later, in the early hours of February 29, 2004, Aristide left Haiti on a plane chartered by the United States. That very evening the United States had boots on the ground in Haiti again.

The journalist Walt Bogdanich quoted me years later as saying "Haiti is a tragedy, and it is a tragedy of partisanship and hate and hostility. These were divides among Haitians and there are also divides among Americans, because Haiti came to symbolize within the United States a point of friction between Democrats and Republicans that did not facilitate bipartisanship or stable policy or communication." ["Democracy Undone: Mixed U.S. Signals Helped Tilt Haiti Toward Chaos," *The New York Times*, January 29, 2006.] That is correct as far as it goes. But the real tragedy was that U.S. behavior -- partisan domestic divisions, unwillingness to back words with resources, and policy reversals in 2003-2004, combined with Haiti's own equally great difficulties and Aristide's incompetence—produced a political collapse that was as hard on Haiti as the disastrous earthquake that was to follow six years later, in 2010. In the words of Trinidad and Tobago's Reginal Dumas, "Fevered ideology overcame common sense." Also overcome, unfortunately as much in the Commonwealth Caribbean as in the United States, was knowledge of Haiti and empathy for its people.

*Q: Did you have anything to do with that, what happened next?*

EINAUDI: When Aristide fled, Denneth Modeste, the OAS representative in Haiti, helped maintain a thread of constitutional order by convincing Prime Minister Yvon Neptune to stay on even after the Chief Justice of the Supreme Court assumed the presidency. However, once the UN force came in and the anti-Aristide forces took over, Neptune was shamefully arrested by the new authorities on charges of having participated in murders by Lavalas gangs in the climactic February events before Aristide fled. He undertook a hunger strike. I visited him in jail in 2005 accompanied by members of the Permanent Council. Juan Gabriel Valdés, the head of the UN Mission did what he could, harboring Neptune when he turned himself in to the UN after escaping in a mass jail break, then voluntarily returning to jail, where he was treated even worse than before.

I was able to seize one last opportunity to stimulate the democratic space and fairness I had been working to help develop in Haiti before everything fell apart. In November 2004 I reached an agreement with UN Undersecretary Prendergast that gave the OAS the lead in the registration process for fresh elections. In January, I became the first OAS Secretary General, Acting or not, to speak before the UN Security Council. To my astonishment, I had discovered that the United States and the international community had in the past spent millions of dollars for elections in which voters had been issued pieces of paper valid only for that particular election. A one-time scrap of paper provides no institutional development or foundation for the future. At the same time, Haitians had no ID cards, meaning that ordinary Haitians had no legal status with which to defend their property, their rights or their lives. Without IDs, Haitians without means or power literally did not exist. I told the U.N. Security Council that it is "very difficult for local authorities to do things well in a globalized world without international support, and it is very difficult for the international community to achieve things if it is not capable of enlisting the support of the local authorities." To my knowledge, I am still the only OAS Secretary General to address the U.N. Security Council

In mid-2005, in virtually my last act as Acting Secretary General of the Organization of American States, I successfully engineered the introduction of Haiti's first permanent identity card instead of issuing those old one-time paper voting slips. Checking around, I had learned that proper identity cards had been introduced in Mexico for the 2000 Presidential election, a step which probably had helped end the monopoly the PRI had held on power since the Mexican Revolution. I asked OAS staff to get in touch with the Mexican electoral authorities and get a bid from the company that had manufactured the Mexican IDs to develop a system for Haiti. This time the United States government supported me, along with Canada, Norway, and Switzerland, to provide the necessary funds.

*A sample of the original ID cards I successfully introduced through the OAS for the 2006 elections. (République d'Haiti, Carte d'Identification Nationale; Organization of American States (OAS), 2006, reproduced with permission of the General Secretariat of the Organization of American States.)*

The *Carte d'Identification Nationale* (CIN) is laminated plastic. Valid for 10 years, the card has a photograph and fingerprints of the bearer and meets security standards to avoid counterfeiting. Reasonable elections were held in 2006. René Préval was elected President of Haiti for the second time, to become, also for the second time, Haiti's only president ever to hand over power to an elected successor. Haiti's institutions, and even elections, have since been subjected to grave stresses, but the ID card system begun in 2005 has become one of the few constants in Haiti's turmoil, evolving to become the key to many official transactions. I am very proud of my role in developing that bit of functional sanity.

*Q: Do you have any final words of wisdom on Haiti?*

EINAUDI: My wife Carol and I traveled to Haiti November 30-December 5, 2013, to deliver the Ivy Humanitarian Prize for 2013 to a nun teaching school in Cité Soleil, Port au Prince's worst slum. It was my wife's first time in Haiti and my first since 2005. We stayed with Ambassador Sandra Honoré, my former OAS Chief of Staff, who had just arrived as the Special Representative of the UN Secretary General to head the UN Stabilization Mission in Haiti (MINUSTAH).

The 2010 earthquake had made Haiti seem doubly cursed, as it struck just as economic progress under Préval had begun to take hold. On Sunday, the new Nuncio, Msgr. Bernardino Auza, took us to the grave of Joseph Serge Miot, Archbishop of Port-au-Prince, who was among the earthquake's many dead. A brilliant man from a humble provincial background, Archbishop Miot had worked with us to resolve problems arising from the 2000 legislative elections. He and I had become friends. The earthquake did not make political distinctions. In destroying the Justice Ministry, it killed both dedicated public servants and opposition leader Micha Gaillard, who had also participated in our negotiations. Killed that day also was my friend Gerardo Chevalier, a Salvadoran Christian Democrat working in Haiti for the National Democratic Institute. Seventy persons died in the collapse of the Montana Hotel's living quarters. The owners, the Cardozo sisters, one of whom survived 100 hours in the rubble before she was rescued, were scammed by their insurance carrier.

I visited Aristide on that 2013 trip. After seven years in South Africa, he was back in his old house. As ambiguous as ever, he claimed to be out of politics but had kept his position as head of his party. Jean Claude Duvalier was also back in Haiti. He had been in exile 25 years in France; Jean-Bertrand Aristide was in exile 10 years, 3 in Venezuela and the United States, then 7 in South Africa. Their returns were long delayed by fears that they would prove destabilizing. Duvalier and Aristide remained polarizing figures, but President Martelly met with them both, as well as with his predecessors Prosper Avril, René Préval and former Prime Minister Yvon Neptune. My wife and I also met with both Préval and Neptune. I interpreted the fact that all are able to live in Haiti without being hounded is a sign of progress. Haitians' strong sense of being "Haitian in Haiti" is evolving to include more tolerance. One of my oldest definitions of development is having room to live and work even if you oppose the current government.

Another sign of progress came at a dinner for about twenty persons Ambassador Honoré gave for us. It was attended by many who had participated in all sides of the negotiations and evoked many positive memories. Andy Apaid came late but made up for it by waving his ID card, reminding everyone I had been its originator.

Under Brazil's leadership, MINUSTAH units proved professional and technically proficient. But MINUSTAH cannot guarantee stability for the long term. Not being Haitian, MINUSTAH will always appear a foreign occupation force. To the extent that MINUSTAH's mere presence instills confidence, Haitians could be less motivated to modernize their own government to increase its legitimacy. A former minister told us "The important thing is to try to make sure demonstrations do not get out of hand. If they are left alone, Haitians will fight." The Commonwealth Caribbean's democratic traditions may ultimately help repay the inspiration Haiti's independence gave them, but they have very limited resources and all its countries together lack the population of Haiti. CARICOM cannot replace MINUSTAH. If the cycle of instability is to be broken, a Haitian alternative is needed.

*Q: At the end of the day, did MINUSTAH become what the OAS police force would have been if the negotiation and Aristide's government hadn't fallen apart?*

EINAUDI: I've never been asked that before. It is a very interesting question. The first obvious point is that an OAS police force would not have brought cholera to Haiti. The basic point, however, is legal and political. A potential police force under OAS auspices would have been to prevent a violent change in government (remember, however, that the idea of a police force died aborning before what concessions Apaid and the Convergence might have wrested from Aristide could even be discussed). MINUSTAH was a peacekeeping force necessary after a violent change in government had already taken place. Had the OAS police force been successful as conceived, it would have lasted only until 2006, when Aristide was to leave and a new elected President take office. MINUSTAH stayed until 2017. How important that is may depend on one's politics and the importance one assigns to the gradual strengthening of democratic institutions in Haiti, which still have far to go.

The best answer, of course, is that Haiti needs its own professional security institutions to channel political conflict into peaceful activities, neutralize criminal gangs and narcotraffickers, help respond to natural disasters, and "show the flag" domestically and internationally. Haiti's history of partisan manipulation of armed force by those in power—whether through Leopards, Tonton Macoutes, Chimères, or partisan military or police forces—makes this impossible unless an improved national security capacity is linked to the checks and balances that only a legitimate democratic government can provide. As Max Weber pointed out a century ago, the use of force contributes to stability only if it "constitutes obedience to a norm, rather than an arbitrary decision, a favor, or a privilege." Where legal authority is lacking, gangs rule.

Haiti's government is handicapped by external assistance and the ways it is delivered as well as by Haiti's own history of internal conflict. The Haitian government needs to reconstruct, democratize and develop; the international community should provide more of its support directly to Haitian state institutions rather than to foreign-linked NGOs. As in some other countries of the greater Caribbean Basin, including Central America, greater progress and stability depend on the development of consensual ways to strengthen security on a basis of democratic legitimacy. Certainly, in Haiti and its neighbors, neither the government nor the international community can succeed without the other.

*Q: How did your experience with Haiti affect the lessons on conflict resolution that you developed out of your experience with Peru-Ecuador?*

EINAUDI: I was too busy, too tired and too upset to give that question much thought at the time. One obvious lesson from Haiti is that domestic disputes are different from international disputes. In disputes between countries, the ultimate deciders are the states involved. That is a key consequence of sovereignty as traditionally defined. States decide, meaning the government in office at the time decides. When a dispute is domestic, and particularly when the dispute is over the very legitimacy of the government, who is to decide? The would-be resolver is without a key reference point. Haiti did confirm other lessons, including the critical importance of multilateral engagement. The failure to maintain unified and effective external support for negotiations contributed directly to the 2004 rupture of Haiti's legal order.

In pondering the many conflicts recounted in this oral history, readers could find many generalizable lessons or sub-lessons in addition to those I have identified. For example, "use of law" could be spelled out to include the role of institutional development, of experts, of technology, of international commissions. Haiti's experience raises a question about another lesson I drew from Peru-Ecuador: how do you maintain military support for peace in a country where the military has been abolished? Or, what material resources will be required? For how long? Institution building requires time and patience.

Perhaps the most important lesson is that there are no hard and fast rules that apply universally, only awareness that possible lessons may need to be adjusted and relearned every time. Like politics itself, dispute settlement is an art, not a science.

*Q: Did you find the second Bush administration a difficult one from the perspective of being in the OAS?*

EINAUDI: The U.S. ambassadors to the OAS under George W. Bush were first Roger Noriega, a political appointee, then John Maisto, a career officer. Both had worked for me earlier in their careers. The U.S. Mission supported me on a lot of things. However, they were not, as we have seen, in a position to defend the Haiti negotiations against a group of committed anti-Aristide Republicans, both in Congress and in the Administration. Most of all, they were limited by the Department's inbred focus on bilateral relations at the expense of multilateral ones.

The Department's focus on bilateralism goes beyond any particular administration. We have yet to learn that many contemporary problems require multilateral approaches and frameworks. This does not mean everything or even most things, should be decided multilaterally, let alone carried out that way. But bilateral actions are always rendered more effective, and sometimes even made possible, if they take place in the context of common effort in support of universal ideals codified in international law. The asymmetry of power between the United States and all of its neighbors makes multilateralism a critical element for success. And U.S. behavior is critical for the OAS, whether it be support, opposition, or, as is more often the case, indifference. As Senator Jesse Helms once asked, what use is it for the United States to belong to an organization we do not use?

*Q: You were Acting Secretary General when Ecuador's instability surfaced again in 2004, were you not? Did the OAS do anything under the Democratic Charter?*

EINAUDI: Good question. I had a lot of contacts and friends in Ecuador and I knew that there was tension between the government, the Congress and the Supreme Court. Ecuador is Brazil's neighbor, and Brazil at that point was very much feeling its oats, its ability to project soft power. In November 2004, I was in Brasilia on another matter as Acting Secretary General, so I asked for an appointment with Foreign Minister Celso Amorim to discuss Ecuador. He made me wait for two hours and then said: "Stay out of it, don't worry about it, we will take care of it."

*Q: What happened next?*

EINAUDI: Brazil did not "take care of it." In April, President Lucio Gutierrez was removed by the Congress, Brazil offered him asylum, and I found myself leading a delegation of Ambassadors to see what measures were available to support some form of democratic continuity.

*Q: This didn't arouse much of a fuss, though, did it? It looks like it wasn't a problem or it wasn't considered a real problem. When Lucio Gutierrez started to act like a dictator or a little bit undemocratically it wasn't really a problem.*

EINAUDI: The OAS is an organization of States represented through their executive branches. The problem in Ecuador started as tensions between the Executive and the Supreme Court and the Congress. Unless the government of Ecuador itself raised the issue, it would probably not have been discussed publicly. When I went to Brasilia and spoke to Amorim, I was acting on my own, not because I was being asked to do so by a member state. When you act independently, you are weak; you are not acting on behalf of a government or of a group of governments. And even when you move with support, as I did after the coup, visiting Ecuador with the Chair of the Permanent Council and a delegation of Ambassadors, the results can be limited. A gifted Ecuadorian caricaturist had fun at my expense, depicting me as a would-be Don Quixote on a wooden rocking horse attempting to clean up problems beyond his reach.

*Q: Did the U.S. bring the issue to the OAS?*

EINAUDI: No. I don't remember what the U.S. delegation did, if anything. The U.S. ambassador to the OAS was John Maisto and you can find what he had to say in the minutes of the Permanent Council, where you can find the records of all the debates. His deputy, Tim Dunn, accompanied me on the mission to Ecuador.

*Q: Do you think the leadership style of the Secretary General can make a difference when it comes to the protection of democracy?*

EINAUDI: Resolutions by the Permanent Council, the General Assembly, or in unusual cases by a special meeting of foreign ministers are required to set policy. Article 110 of the OAS Charter sharply limits the executive authority of the Secretary General. But the occupant can still make quite a difference. And times and situations change. João Baena Soares' low-key style and traditional non-interventionism made it easier to adopt Resolution 1080 because the member states felt he would not exaggerate his authorities. Today, Secretary General Luis Almagro has made Venezuela a personal crusade. On February 14, 2019, I attended a meeting convened at OAS headquarters in Washington to talk over the internet to Venezuela's opposition leader Juan Guaidó. While waiting for a connection that ultimately failed to materialize, Almagro said "We need humanitarian aid, but most of all we need regime change." He repeated the same idea a moment later, saying "La principal ayuda humanitaria es sacar a Maduro." ["The best humanitarian assistance is to oust Maduro."] This kind of personal activism is at odds with Article 110, is opposed by key member states and makes it harder to generate broad support for effective OAS action. But Almagro's refusal to be silent may also be one of the few reasons that the OAS is still being discussed in this time of decline of multilateralism and polarized politics. The 2005 coup in Ecuador came when I was Acting Secretary General. On the big issues, at that time, we were necessarily treading water.

*Q: So, it was a hard time for the organization in that period, also, right? You had a campaign for Secretary General going on between Mexico and Chile, and I've read that the OAS had some financial problems. The organization had other problems to face than the crisis in Ecuador.*

EINAUDI: Well, that's certainly true. It's also true that the OAS has long had financial problems. But I think outsiders, including my successors, had difficulty understanding how bad the money problems had become until they actually took office.

*Q: We'll go into that, but first, let's go to the other extreme for a moment. Did you enjoy the ceremonial functions of the office?*

EINAUDI: Very much. I even enjoyed signing circulars. I had a rubber signature stamp. But as an indication of respect for the recipient, I preferred to sign in person each of the thirty-odd copies of documents to member states.

Ceremonies celebrating Pan American Day or honoring the statue of Isabella la Católica were often not quite up to what they were meant to symbolize. On the other hand, presidential visits could be quite stimulating. Argentina's President Menem used to call the OAS the "megaphone of the Americas" and certainly the foreign press paid the most attention to the OAS when Presidents spoke there. The U.S. press was more cynical. The Brazilians used to say it did not matter unless they read about it in the New York Times, which meant that the OAS and generally Latin America did not matter much.

*I enjoy a common moment with Henry Kissinger and Enrique Iglesias at a charitable function in the Hall of the Americas at OAS headquarters, 17th and Constitution, Washington, D.C. (Organization of American States (OAS), reproduced with permission of the General Secretariat of the Organization of American States.)*

The ceremonies I remember with the most pleasure were the visit to the OAS of Italy's President Carlo Azeglio Ciampi and the signing of CAFTA, the Central America-US Free Trade Agreement (later to include the Dominican Republic as well). On both occasions, the Secretary General was traveling, leaving me in charge of the Secretariat. So I presided. Ciampi was a distinguished economist and a leading builder of the Euro. Italian migrants have contributed much to the New World. With Spain and France, Italy is one of just three countries to accredit a full-time ambassador as observer to the OAS. Italy just then occupied the presidency of the European Union, with which I had organized consultations, hoping to activate greater cooperation. Most importantly for me, Ciampi was also a man who had followed in the footsteps of my grandfather as both Governor of the Central Bank and as President. His visit, on November 13, 2003, gave me the chance to be a bit shameless. I welcomed him to the Permanent Council, saying "Your presence in this House of the Americas has special personal significance for me and for my wife Carol, since it affords me the opportunity as the grandson of the first full-term President (1948-1955) of the Republic that arose from the tumult of the Second World War, to receive you, Sir, the tenth President of the same Italian Republic (1999-2006)." I was happy.

Presiding over the signing of the free trade agreement between the United States and Central America, CAFTA, was just as personally satisfying and certainly more significant professionally. It was May 28, 2004. In my remarks I noted the extraordinary contrast between the "1970s and 1980s [when] Central America was one of the last battlegrounds of the Cold War" and CAFTA's promise of the rule of law, openness, and relations that took into account the interests of all nations, small as well as large. Some of the Central American ministers there and I had known each other during the wars. Up on stage, we literally had tears in our eyes. Hope is often much needed in our lives, and the CAFTA ceremony symbolized the hope that the future would be better than the past.

My wife and I represented the OAS at the celebration of Panama's 100 years of independence in 2003. In 1977, I had attended the signing of the Carter-Torrijos Treaties at the OAS in Washington. Now, Mireya Moscoso, widow of Panama's 3-time president Arnulfo Arias, was herself President. She was squired for the ceremonies by Sean Connery, and a good time was had by all. For us it was also a bitter-sweet moment, as we made a private visit to the Miraflores locks, where Carol manually shut the locks, turning for the last time the wheel of their original mechanism. Built by the General Electric Company at the Lynn, Massachusetts, plant where her father and grandfather had worked, it was being replaced by new engines built in China that operated on a push-button. Symbolically and personally, it felt like the passing of an era.

*Q: Talking of symbols, the OAS is often associated with electoral observation. Did you have anything to do with that?*

EINAUDI: Yes. Electoral observations are important conveyors of international support as well as scrutiny. They also depend heavily on voluntary contributions. I remember desperately scrounging for funds for an election observation in a small Caribbean country none of the wealthy countries wanted to help pay for.

In April 2003, I headed an Electoral Observation Mission (EOM) to Paraguay. It was not likely to be a particularly competitive election, Colorado party dominance still being strong. But things were opening up, and the new national electoral authority was planning to use Brazil's new portable electronic voting machines.

Santiago Murray, the best electoral technician the OAS ever had, organized an observation that included informatics specialists from Bolivia, Chile, Colombia, Ecuador, Nicaragua and Peru. This multilateral presence contributed confidence and a sense of progress, and the whole effort was a substantial success.

In May 2004 in the Dominican Republic, President Hipólito Mejía ran for reelection against former President Leonel Fernández. This was likely to be a close one. Murray headed an EOM that began its work in February, three months before the election. I attended for the election itself. Everything turned out well. But had our observation not been both thorough and proficient, old habits might have prevailed.

*Q: What do you mean by "old habits might have prevailed"?*

EINAUDI: Without going into details, let's just say that irregularities are more likely to occur in the dark of night. Murray's modeling enabled us to preempt any overnight funny business by issuing a communiqué on the fairness of the process and the results, just four hours after the urns had closed.

*Q: Alright, what about the election of the new Secretary General?*

EINAUDI: Miguel Angel Rodriguez was elected to succeed César Gaviria. A former president of Costa Rica replaced a former president of Colombia. On September 15, 2004, Rodriguez, the first Central American to be elected Secretary General, was inaugurated in a showy ceremony attended by several sitting presidents.

Within days Rodriguez was accused in Costa Rica of having accepted a bribe from Alcatel, the French telecommunications company. It was a terrible shock for the organization. It was just as big a shock for me. I had spent four years without a break. I was worn out. I was expecting that Rodriguez would reduce the pressures Gaviria's increasing absenteeism had put on me. At first, Rodriguez suggested that I should play the front man, letting him stay in the background while he defended himself. I had to tell him that would not work. After barely three weeks in office, Rodriguez resigned to go home to face the music. In 1984, when Alejandro Orfila had resigned under similar pressure, new elections were held immediately. This time, the Permanent Council decided I should serve as Acting Secretary General until May, when a proper election could be organized. However, it did not see fit to name anyone Acting ASG. I found myself with extra work without extra help. As my role expanded, so did that of Sandra Honoré, my Chief of Staff. She wound up doing the work of Gaviria and Rodriguez's entire gaggle of advisors, with a bravura performance that helped save the General Secretariat.

In his brief time there, Rodriguez had begun to understand the problems the OAS faced. After reviewing the Organization's finances, he described heads of the different offices of the Secretariat as "beggars with tin cups fighting for a place on the sidewalk to scrounge for money."

*Q: What did he mean by that?*

EINAUDI: The OAS budget has two sources: The regular fund, made up of mandatory membership quotas, and the voluntary funds, made up of grants member and observer states make to the Organization for specific programs. The regular fund had been frozen, without even cost of living increases, since the early 1990s. Yet the regular fund is what keeps together the entire structure of the Inter-American system, from the General Secretariat in Washington to the country offices in the member states, and the numerous entities that make up the "Inter-American System" loosely coordinated by the OAS. The Pan American Health Organization (PAHO) was founded in 1902, the Inter-American Juridical Committee, headquartered in Brazil, in 1906. In 1928, came the Inter-American Children's Institute in Uruguay, the Pan American Institute of Geography and History (PAIGH), headquartered in Mexico, and the Inter-American Commission of Women (CIM), the first international body dedicated to the advancement of women. The Inter-American Defense Board (IADB) and the Inter-American Institute for Cooperation in Agriculture (IICA), based in Costa Rica and with a unique focus on tropical agriculture, came in 1942. 1959 saw the formation of the Inter-American Commission on Human Rights (IACHR). The Inter-American Drug Abuse Control Commission (CICAD) was founded in 1986. The Inter-American Indian Institute (1940) and the Inter-American Development Bank (IDB, 1959) were the only parts of the "system" that did not in some way depend on the cash-strapped OAS. Since the 1990s, ministers for domestic affairs – education, justice, labor, trade, science and technology, security -- have also met fairly regularly under OAS auspices. Sixty-eight states from outside the hemisphere and the European Union are permanent observers.

In referring to "beggars with tin cups," Rodriguez was referring to the competition for voluntary contributions as the regular funds dried up. Countries with money to spend on their projects of primary interest to them, primarily the United States, Canada and Spain, were shaping the Organization's programs by using voluntary contributions to push activities they favored, while depleting staff and allowing the rest of the "system" to become skeletal.

Notwithstanding lack of funding from the member states, this hemispheric system and the OAS Secretariat that supports it, has some notable achievements. The CIM led in the development and adoption in 1994 of the Inter-American Convention on the Prevention, Punishment, and Eradication of Violence against Women, better known as the Convention of Belém do Pará), the first legally binding international treaty that criminalizes violence against women. OAS staff, among them an American, Linda Poole, played a major role in developing the convention and establishing a follow-up mechanism in 2004. CICAD, whose founding Executive Secretary, Irving Tragen, was also an American citizen and former FSO, played a key role in moving antidrug efforts from a U.S. focus on sanctions toward the development of common standards for cooperation.

*Q: Did you try to do something about lack of funding when you became Acting Secretary General?*

EINAUDI: I tried two things: to simplify the structure and to raise consciousness of the problem. Neither had much effect. The OAS is the hub of a multifunctional web of regional institutions, ministerial meetings and summits, but it is run by foreign ministries that find it easier to agree on mandates, that is, things to do, than to come up with the funding to do them, which often depends on other agencies of government. My favorite example is support for democracy. In 1991, Resolution 1080 called for "incentives to preserve and strengthen democratic systems, based on international solidarity and cooperation." Since it was given this mandate, resources available to the OAS regular fund have been cut in real terms by more than 25%. The Organization was trapped between a stagnant budget and growing mandates with increasing market-driven costs.

The worst of it was that outsiders assumed the OAS had the resources it needed. When I was Acting Secretary General, we founded a lecture series entitled the "Cátedra de las Américas" at which distinguished leaders were to address problems of common interest. The program was made possible only because a special grant by Peru provided funding unavailable through the Regular Fund. I asked Jimmy Carter, who made much use of the OAS both during and after his Presidency, to give the inaugural lecture. He was literally amazed by what I told him when we met before he spoke. He could hardly believe his ears when I explained our financial woes.

*Former President Carter and I in my OAS office as Acting Secretary General, January 25, 2005. Why are we smiling? I had just told him that OAS work in support of democracy was crippled by lack of resources and*

*that the Inter-American System was becoming skeletal. (Organization of American States (OAS), 2005, reproduced with permission of the General Secretariat of the Organization of American States.)*

*Q: I gather that Rodriguez had already begun to put in effect a General Assembly request for a restructuring plan before he had to resign.*

EINAUDI: Yes. With a few exceptions, I continued what Rodriguez had begun, eliminating Assistant Secretary positions and downgrading others to save funds and simplify reporting. My report also sought to "clarify that while it is inevitable that different offices must engage in a degree of fundraising, it is also essential that we have a degree of coordination and coherence" (Rodriguez would have called that assigning places on the sidewalk where units could stand to wave their tin cups). The savings were just enough to stay within the ceiling of $76.275 million established by the General Assembly. They also cut so close to the bone that my successor as Secretary General, who had downplayed my appeals for resources, called me in on my last day in office to ask how come "everyone else," meaning the office directors, had some flexible funds except him, and complained that his staff posts were all filled with people he could not send away.

My most important structural change was to eliminate Rodriguez' new Department of Human Rights. This had interposed a new layer between the Inter-American Commission on Human Rights (IACHR) and the Secretary General. The IACHR is an important exception to the general rule of direct governmental control of international organizations. Unlike the United Nations Human Rights Commission, which is made up of government representatives, IACHR members are elected by governments but serve in their own right rather than as representatives of their countries. The Commission helped keep liberal democratic values alive during the quarter century of authoritarian governments that dominated Latin America from the 1960s to the 1980s. A number of states, led by Chávez' Venezuela, were increasingly critical of the Commission's independence. Rodriguez's new department was meant to look like an upgrade, but in practice would have made it easier for governments to resist the Commission's findings.

*Q: How did your defense of the human rights commission go over?*

EINAUDI: Quietly. By spring 2005, attention had shifted to the race for a new Secretary General, which was shaping up as a donnybrook between the Foreign Ministers of Chile and Mexico. Early on, when Honduras put out feelers suggesting I should be persuaded to give up my "no reelection" pledge and enter the race, Venezuela immediately sent them a private aide-memoire attacking me. Neither Honduras nor Venezuela had consulted me, and nothing became public. I was exhausted and in no mood to run. A candidacy of mine was in any event a non-starter. I did not have the rank. And Roger Noriega had decided the U.S. would support El Salvador's former President Francisco Flores.

*Q: Flores was not a brilliant choice!*

EINAUDI: Hardly. Flores campaigned widely, but was utterly unable to generate support and withdrew. In the end, the race between José Miguel Insulza of Chile and Luis Ernesto Derbez of Mexico was literally too close to call. The secret ballot of member states came out a tie. Five votes were required, spread over two days, before Insulza won.

*Q: Did you have an easy transition out?*

EINAUDI: Very. On June 5, I delivered the opening address of the General Assembly in Fort Lauderdale, with Jeb Bush and Condoleezza Rice in attendance. Over lunch Jeb Bush and I had a marvelous chat about my thoughts on the OAS and his on education. That night, at John Maisto's urging, Condoleezza Rice gave a farewell dinner in my honor at which she gave a toast telling me to "hang your uniform by the door" so I could be ready to be called back to serve again.

Back in Washington, on July 11, 2005, the Permanent Council gave me a rousing farewell at which Insulza declared that "As a politician and negotiator [Einaudi] went into all the crises body and soul," bringing "a rare generosity to how he handled everyone."

Appendix Seven discusses the continuing decline of the OAS and of multilateral institutions in general, victims of nationalist interpretations of sovereignty.

*Much material on the OAS, including my statements as Acting Secretary General, can be found at its web site, OAS - Organization of American States: Democracy for peace, security, and development. The catalogue of my library and many articles, papers, and speeches are available at OAS :: Columbus Memorial Library : Ambassador Luigi R. Einaudi.*

# Afterwords

*Q: In this final session, I would like to ask you about how you view your career and diplomacy more generally.*

EINAUDI: I welcome that.

*Q: Let's start with nuts and bolts. What is the story of your personnel status in the Department?*

EINAUDI: I came into the Department in 1974 as a Foreign Service Reserve officer under the old Foreign Service Act. A few days before Christmas 1978, I was put in the street by Harry Barnes, who was implementing the new Foreign Service Act. Fortunately for me, the Chair of the House Foreign Affairs Committee was Dante Fascell (whose last name was originally Fascelli, ending in a good Italian "i" like mine, and whom I had first met when Kissinger brought him along to Tlatelolco in 1974). Fascell had his aide Mike Finley call Barnes. Barnes and Vaky found a way out by enrolling me as a charter member of the new Senior Executive Service (SES). Then, five years later, in 1984, the Secretary of State and the National Security Advisor, George Shultz and Robert McFarlane, both wrote separately to convince the Director of the

Office of Personnel Management, Don Devine, to make me a career member of the SES.

*Q: That means that you wound up a senior civil service officer in a building dominated by the foreign service. This was particularly true in the geographic bureaus like ARA, where the number of SES positions was (and still is) extremely limited. Your own university and RAND experience also meant that you always had a deeper knowledge and wider network of Latin American contacts than your colleagues. Was that difficult?*

EINAUDI: I sometimes felt like an outsider – partly because I was initially grafted in with Kissinger, but most of all because I was not an FSO. The FSO culture I came to know was suspicious of outsiders. Even FSOs who had started as FSIOs with USIA, were considered almost as unbaptized as if they had been part of the old Consular Service. USIA's focus was on cultivating foreign audiences rather than reporting. Frances Coughlin was my model. She went from the Women Airforce Service Pilots, the WASPS of World War II, to USIA via Claremont, Stanford and an instructorship in the Brazilian Air Force. In Santiago and Lima in the 1970s she still flew and drove like a demon. And she knew everyone in the world of ideas. Her parties for me were like being at home. In contrast, a political counselor in our Embassy in Buenos Aires turned down my offer to introduce him to a major public intellectual because "I can read what he has to say in the newspaper." Fortunately, Coughlin was not alone. Their outward orientation and capacity for working with foreigners enabled USIA officers like Mary Ellen Gilroy, Cresencio Arcos, Steven Dachi, Bob and Pat Chatten, Ed Purcell, Linda Jewell and Sally Cowal to build foreign relationships as much and sometimes more than some regular FSOs.

*Q: Ouch! As an active-duty economic officer and senior FSO, I want to assure you we have worked hard to overcome deficiencies. Continuing with the theme of having FSOs broaden their contacts and understanding of other cultures, did you make suggestions for improving the situation?*

EINAUDI: What I am saying is less that FSOs are deficient, and more that they do not have the support they need for their many roles, roles that go far beyond reporting, in the field as well as in Washington's national policy machinery.

A comparison to the Defense Department is illustrative. Defense has an educational system of its own (on which the State Department builds to economize, e.g. shutting down the Senior Seminar and sending officers to the National War College). The military promotion system makes training one of the requirements for promotion. Granting that it is important to distinguish between education and training, but there is a lot to be said for linking knowledge to promotion. When Arnold Kanter, whom I had known at RAND, became Undersecretary for Management, he told me one of his first tasks was to choose the head of State's Foreign Building Office (FBO). He was startled at the difference between candidates from the Foreign Service and from the military. Those with a military background all had graduate degrees in management and related fields. The FSO candidates had none. In 2010, an FSO in the Secretary's office told me new FSO's were being shipped off to Afghanistan with no training at all.

The State Department cannot function without more resources. With a recruitment system that brings in already educated officers, we may not need a "West Point" for diplomats, but we certainly and at the very least need opportunities for mid-career reflection and consolidation of skills. Perhaps something analogous to a Command and General Staff College. As things now stand, lack of resources makes this impossible and leads to the disaster of gapping between assignments – which inevitably means having no personnel float that allows time for training or education. Education stretches the mind. We may also need a new Foreign Service Act. And a National Diplomatic University where other agencies can study diplomacy, the way we now study national security at the National Defense University. The Foreign Service deserves it. Our national interests require it.

*Q: We talked earlier about Kissinger's 1974 GLOP, Global Outlook Program. What do you think is needed to have a global outlook?*

EINAUDI: First, what is for me an emotional point. Having a global outlook does not mean putting America down. Of course, we must always put America first. To keep America safe, you need to understand the world in which we live.

Since I was first on the Policy Planning staff I have argued against "foreign aid" as the label to cover activities most of which we actually need to make America first and keep it there. Is it really "foreign" aid to engender institutions and norms that will advance U.S. interests? I told Art Hartman that if the aid was needed to make others capable of supporting our interests, calling it "foreign aid" was a misnomer. The label "Foreign aid," I argued, leads to public misunderstanding, images of giveaways to foreigners when in fact most assistance funds go to U.S. agencies, personnel, contractors, and NGO's.

In a similar vein, international law in practice has been less a surrender of U.S. sovereignty than it is an effort to get others to accept the rules we live by. Karl Marx was correct for once when he wrote that the law reflects the superstructure of an existing order. That the Reagan administration could mine Nicaragua's harbors was as self-defeating as the Senate's recent record of refusing to ratify international treaties – even when they simply copy the provisions of U.S. law and make them apply to other countries.

Our lack of global sensitivity takes many forms. At RAND I was unable at a certain point to find funds to continue my Peru research. I told a Peruvian friend that I was switching to global issues. He objected, saying "But we are part of the globe, too." Foreigners are not just underdeveloped or dirty would-be Americans. They have their own histories and cultures. And interests they will try to defend.

Here is another example. A global foreign multinational I know tried for years to find a senior American to fill a leadership position. It failed repeatedly because the Americans they hired were, in their view, "incapable of thinking globally." The Americans they found could not take into account that not everyone is as powerful as the U.S. but still needs a modicum of respect for those things they can do, or that others have ways of doing things that have validity, or simply that when you look at a situation you need to look around, see who else is affected, then find a way to involve them – or if that is impossible, identify correctly what you need to do to keep them from harming your interests.

I have long advocated the importance of *listening* in order to understand where others are coming from and treating them with respect. The Mexican Benito Juárez put it succinctly: "El respeto al derecho ajeno es la paz." Peace is respecting the rights of others.

In a world in which our actions increasingly impact others (and vice versa), it is important to remember something my grandfather wrote in the wake of World War I: "We must abolish the dogma of perfect sovereignty. The truth, reality, is the interdependence of free peoples, not their absolute independence ... A state isolated and sovereign that can survive on its own is a fiction, it cannot be reality. Reality is that states can be equal and independent among themselves only when they realize that their life and development will be impossible if they are not ready to help each other."[5] In my own mind, I call this "the riddle of sovereignty": how to retain your integrity and independence while also working with others.

My former Treasury and IDB colleague Ciro de Falco suggests this approach may come more naturally to persons brought up outside the United States, particularly in smaller countries, or ones in close contact with many neighbors, different languages and cultures. For example, the inhabitants of a divided Italy had to adjust to so many centuries of occupying powers before unification, that they had to learn flexibility just to survive. This, he suggests, may teach humility, the ability to see the other side's position, and help develop social skills like admitting mistakes, looking for allies, and giving credit to others. Coming to a somewhat similar conclusion from a different starting point, Cornell professor Matthew Evangelista commented that my concern for democracy among countries as well as within them "is not a value that a country that considers itself both exceptional and indispensable should be expected to favor." That is an important and telling insight about one of the consequences of American hubris. Even so, I am not sure nationality or culture is always overriding. I have met many persons from small countries who had little patience for others. And it was a fellow American who taught me early on that every

---

[5] Luigi Einaudi "Il dogma della sovranità e l'idea della Società delle nazioni," *Corriere della Sera*, 28 Dicembre 1918.

audience I spoke to would include at least one person who was smarter than me.

Pete Vaky and I had a secretary in common, Jeanne Rogers, a gal with a sharp tongue from Normalville in the Pennsylvania coal country. She dismissed one of our interminable discussions by announcing: "Pete Vaky conceptualizes in public." Here is a note about "conceptual premises" that Pete sent me in 2007, when we were both retired but still conceptualizing:

*For much of our history -- whether we were being the Good Neighbor, opposing Communism, running the Alliance for Progress or more recently fighting terrorism – we in the United States have tended to assume we knew how to do the operational things better than anyone else. That approach doesn't work anymore. More than ever before, we need to understand and respect the space and dignity of those with whom we need to cooperate. But the reflex in Washington and in public opinion at large is still often patronizing and teacher to pupil.*

*Our very success and power will be a handicap until we understand (and really believe) the fundamental reality that this new world requires an honest give and take. Competence must be learned, trust must be earned, both sides must be reliable, and all must benefit to be able to work together effectively. Long-term cooperation can only be based on activities that serve the interests of others as well as ourselves.*

*Q: You obviously thought a lot of Vaky, and I know many others did too. What did you think, in general, of the people with whom you worked?*

EINAUDI: I could not have done or enjoyed my work without the people I worked with. With only a couple of exceptions, I dealt with every Assistant Secretary of State for the hemisphere, starting with Robert F. Woodward in 1961. I worked directly with Secretaries of State from Kissinger to Powell. And I had a series of excellent secretaries with a small s. Jeannie Rae Rogers came with me from S/P to PPC. When she moved on through the Mustang program to apply her wit to investigating fraud, her position in PPC was taken by Florence "God willing and the creek don't rise" Allen, and a second secretary, the self-effacing always reliable Delancey Turner. And I have already mentioned the skilled Bernadette McCarron at USOAS (and Chile's Elba Molina when I was at the OAS).

The tone, however, was set neither by the bosses or the helpers. It was set by the Foreign Service. In addition to Vaky, I have recorded how Bowdler, Shlaudeman and Lewis shaped my career, not to mention Eagleburger and Pickering. The names of others are sprinkled throughout these pages. A great many more are not but could easily have been or even should have been mentioned. The Foreign Service is a trying and exacting profession. Those outsiders who see only the pleasures of travel and (sometimes) of life abroad often fail to appreciate that foreign service life can be very lonely. Unfortunately, the commonplace that the State Department is less than the sum of its parts is accurate. There is probably more talent in the Foreign Service than in any other executive agency, but we do not put FSOs into a system that supports them with training and makes them proud of their professional advancement. By not doing so, we not only fail to recognize their achievements, but we also demoralize them and we put them at the mercy of outside specialists, political interlopers, and the vagaries of domestic opinion. Above all, we damage national interests, which depend on dealing effectively with the rest of the world.

*Q: What are the major changes since you came to Washington?*

EINAUDI: Let me take that in stages.

First, the U.S. government has come under siege. I came to Washington after twelve years in California. Carol had become a driving force locally, founding the No Oil movement in Pacific Palisades, and Fair Housing in broader Los Angeles. We were rooted there. We knew our neighbors and what they thought. After we moved to Washington, "inside the beltway," I increasingly found myself looking uneasily over my shoulder, wondering what the rest of the country thought. Vietnam had already stimulated popular dismay with official policies, but the divide between the country and the government has continued to grow steadily since then. There is a tendency in American politics to campaign against the government, to campaign against Washington. Government is essential to how our society runs and its servants need to have a modicum of respect; all of us look for respect. To be constantly battered down, to always hear Washington is corrupt, Washington is wasteful, Washington is all these bad things, after a while that creates a self-fulfilling prophecy; young people are not going to be interested in working in government. Good people already in are going to leave when they feel they won't be treated well. As a government bureaucrat, I felt Barack Obama was the first Presidential candidate in my time who did not campaign against me.

Second, the world is transformed, its instability brought to the fore by the end of the Cold War and the rise of the internet. When I came to the Department, e-mails did not exist and airgrams were still the source of thoughtful analysis. Today's instant communication has had quite an impact. The spread of information and the multiplication of options has led to the decline of the state and the rise of opposition to government.

That, in turn, has stimulated government secrecy and conscious miscommunication and misdirection. As an Italian friend put it, the answer to fake news is not official news.

Third, the government's people have also changed greatly. McGeorge Bundy and many others in the Kennedy Administration came from what was still a functioning Eastern establishment. Administration leaders went in and out, they were professors in universities, consultants in business, they worked in the government in two-year or four-year increments -- it didn't matter, they just jumped in and out. They knew each other; they could make the government work or not work, and they pretty much knew what was going on and why. It could lead to counterproductive elite-think, as in the Bay of Pigs plans. But it also facilitated operational effectiveness.

The foreign affairs community now is drawn from people all over. Those from Virginia or New Hampshire are near outliers of the old Eastern Establishment centered on Massachusetts, Connecticut and New York. But more and more come from UCLA, Chicago and Michigan, from the West and the Mid-West. The country has democratized, and the government has swelled; the situation is very different from the inbred old boys club that characterized the United States until long after World War II, even into the 1970s. The addition of fresh people, ideas and viewpoints is very positive, but it has also contributed to a breakdown of knowledge of how government functions. Much information is classified today that does not really deserve to be classified. As a result, even the interested public has fewer opportunities to learn what is going on. Changes in administration bring in a lot of people who don't know anything about governing. The need for intermediation between career officials and political appointees has grown but has not been met.

Finally, there has been a change in society at large that concerns me greatly. Immigration has become an emotional problem. There are no accepted and enforceable rules. The greatness of the United States is closely tied to the fact that we have been the country that has best realized a utopia consisting of a rule of law that accepts the rights of *all* individuals. The U.S. has been the energizer of the world's democratic revolution, realizing to an unprecedented extent equality of opportunity regardless of gender, race, class, religion or nationality. My generation was part of the civil rights movement that helped affirm the rights of American blacks as citizens who are free, as the black historian Roger Wilkins once put it, to "exert relentless energy to hold up [their] end." For years migration across our southern land borders has brought us countless men and women who daily exert relentless energies to better themselves in ways impossible in their countries of origin. We are individually and economically the better for it, but the sheer mass is bringing growing controversy.

To say that our civilization is at threat misses the point. *They* are now part of *us*. Lashing out and repeating the mass expulsions of Mexicans in the 1930s will uselessly compound the pain. We already send repatriation flights daily to Mexico and countries in Central America and the Caribbean -- with effects that are strategically ineffective, locally destabilizing, and regionally dispiriting. Refugees from the civil war in El Salvador in the 1980s met resistance in South Central Los Angeles from the previously established Mexican American "18th Street" gangs. We in turn deported veterans of the resulting gang wars – some of them with new-found criminal skills – back to El Salvador and Guatemala in the early 1990s, where they founded the *salvatruchas* in El Salvador even as gangs grew in many parts of the United States.

What is needed is a return to the spirit of equality before the law that made America great. My friend, the University of California's Caesar Sereseres, once commented wistfully that Native Americans had a lot of experience with what happens if you lose control of immigration. We need immigrants. But we do not need shadow communities that live in the dark, at the margin of the law. That is not the American way. To regain control in a way that is worthy of our civilization, we need to develop immigration laws that will shape an open system, with dignity and responsibility for all. The controls should define the qualifications and rights of guest-workers, distinguish between migrants and refugees, specify requirements for citizenship, and identify national security and health concerns. And they should be multilaterally accepted and hence enforceable also by sending countries. And then those laws should be applied fairly but rigorously. As the old Roman saying goes, *Dura lex sed lex*. The law is hard but it is the law.

A major consequence of all these changes is that the level of mud in the trenches in which public servants in foreign affairs must wallow has risen. It is vital to keep our head high and our eyes on our goals. Again, I turn to Pete Vaky. After leaving the Foreign Service, he held his head high at Georgetown, at Carnegie, and at the Inter-American Dialogue, and promoted multilateralism. Not the false multilateralism of coalitions of those willing to simply follow, or the equally false multilateralism of using the like-minded without regard for the rights of others, but, as Vaky and I believed, one of cooperation based on generalized principles of conduct that go beyond the transactional or the bilateral, multilateralism based on respect for international law.

The times have not been particularly good to our vision. Back in the days when Pete and I were both in the State Department, Jeanne Rogers, the same sharp-tongued secretary I mentioned a moment ago, ran into us out in the street, absorbed in one of our usual discussions, and exclaimed "you two look like Dr. Doom and Mr. Gloom." Pete and I both laughed. To this day I do not know who was Doom and who Gloom.

*Q: What would you say has changed in U.S.-Latin American relations?*

EINAUDI: This oral history has focused necessarily on the past. But perhaps the most important point to make is that, while conditions in the United States, in Latin America, and in the Caribbean have all changed, a lot has NOT changed in our relations. The asymmetry in power remains. The mutual ignorance and stereotyping remain. Inter-American relations labor under the triple burden of ideas about migration, imperialism, and the black legend of the Spanish conquest. Our neighbors for the most part still think we are more important to them than we are, and we still think they are less important to us than they are. Even the extraordinary increase in the numbers of *latino* U.S. citizens and residents has not changed that. We remain, as the journalist Alan Riding once said of Mexico, "distant neighbors." If anything, in fact, we are increasingly distant, as what Arthur Whitaker called the "Western Hemisphere ideal" fades, and publications like the OAS' *Americas* magazine go out of existence.

HENRY A. KISSINGER

October 24, 2001

Dear Madame Ambassador:

Thank you for the opportunity to add my own sentiments to the other honors coming Ambassador Einaudi's way this evening.

Luigi was serving his country when I arrived at the State Department in 1973. He remained at State, serving our interests in the Americas, for long years after I left. Now, more than a quarter century later, he is the senior American at the pinnacle of the inter-American system. Luigi's has been a life of public service.

But that service is not only impressive quantitatively; the quality of his contribution to the conduct of diplomacy in this Hemisphere has been outstanding, indeed historic.

I am a witness. At the Department, he provided wisdom, common sense and clear-headed counsel to legions of senior officials over the years. He has been a consistent and leading voice, sometimes a lonely one, in insisting that Latin America should have a high priority on the foreign policy agenda of the United States. The new strength of the Hemisphere's democratic ethic owes much to his tireless work as U.S. Ambassador to the OAS. And who knows better than the people of Peru and Ecuador that there is peace in the Andes in no small measure due to him. Now, the evidence of his strong, vigorous hand is everywhere evident in the work of the Organization of American States.

The United States owes much to Ambassador Einaudi -- as does the Hemisphere. He merits our enduring thanks.

Warm regards,

Henry A. Kissinger

Her Excellency
Marlene Fernandez del Granado
Ambassador of the Republic of Bolivia
3014 Massachusetts Avenue, N.W.
Washington, DC 20008

TWENTY-SIXTH FLOOR · 350 PARK AVENUE · NEW YORK, NEW YORK 10022 · (212) 759-7919
FACSIMILE (212) 759-0042

*Kissinger described me as a "lonely voice" in advocating for a higher priority for Latin America in U.S. foreign policy. Appendix Eight sets forth my views on the Americas in the world, as I expressed them to the Washington Institute of Foreign Affairs in 2020. (Photograph by LR Einaudi, reproduced with permission of Henry A. Kissinger.)*

*Q: You spent a lot of your career on interagency coordination. How has that evolved?*

EINAUDI: Governing requires coherence and the NSC is essential to that. Coordination is necessary for an infinite number of reasons. One is to defeat stove piping, which we discussed earlier. Another quite innocent reason for coordination is that people with different specialties interact extraordinarily little. Peter Hakim once observed that Washington is in many ways a government-centered small town, but that economists and political folks still manage to live in their own separate worlds, without overlap. But other reasons are profoundly structural. The U.S. government is a many-headed monster and each monster works to protect its own turf. This may be particularly dangerous with regard to the CIA because their claim to secrecy means they can even justify to themselves lying to the president. That means you need an NSC that can keep the agencies honest and is able to intermediate between them to get proper policy assessments. Not just an NSC that will choose its preferred source of information and then slap its own staff memo on top of the interagency recommendation to the President and head policy down the road of disconnect from reality. If you are in the State Department, which is all too often left to implement whatever are the results of this process, the implicit lesson is that you need to try to get control of a proper interagency system.

Vaky believed the NSC worked best under Brent Scowcroft. The so-called "Scowcroft model" focused on coordination rather than control. I first met Scowcroft when he was a Lieutenant Colonel covering the Peru Desk in the Defense Department. He was utterly unpretentious, knew how to listen, and was extraordinarily efficient. He believed the NSC was at its best when it ensured that the recommendations that reached the president were fully staffed and scrubbed of special interests. Bob Pastor, who became the Latin American person at the NSC when Jimmy Carter took office, epitomized the opposite approach. Pastor believed that the purpose of the NSC was to advance the president's agenda. He was like Menges under Reagan, though from a totally different ideological angle. Menges was an angry conservative, Pastor a conventional liberal. Both wanted to use the NSC to advance their causes, to pressure and hound and kick the bureaucracy into doing what they thought it should do to advance their ideological causes. The Vaky view was that we in the United States have given ourselves an extraordinarily diverse government in which many different agencies have a hand in the foreign policy pie, and with a lot of institutional self-interests. The job of the NSC is to protect the president and serve the country by forcing government agencies to set forth honest and workable options.

I do not see this view of the NSC as a partisan political matter. Vaky was celebrated as a liberal in the NGO community for criticizing U.S. complicity in the use of torture in Guatemala. I think it is inappropriate to consider someone a liberal just because he or she finds torture offensive. All of us should find torture offensive. Pete was willing to stand up to the CIA when it was lying – even if the CIA argued it was doing so for the common good.

In 2008, I was invited by the Center for Strategic and International Studies (CSIS) in Washington to talk about the Smart Power Commission's report that had concluded with a call for *"a strategic reassessment of how the U.S. government is organized, coordinated, and budgeted . . . including the appointment of senior personnel who could reach across agencies to better align strategy and resources."*

I asked "What happens if we in the U.S. solve all of our own internal interagency and civil-military problems only to then find we and other countries still lack the trust and know-how to work together?"

It takes expertise to reconcile national interests that differ. A multilateral Academy of Public Administration, with students nominated by the member states to study a broad curriculum, would over time produce a network of professionals who know how to work together to contain issues that might otherwise degenerate into quagmires of missed opportunities or even escalate into conflict. The Inter-American System, now starved and skeletal, has a long tradition of professional studies in two specialized areas, the Inter-American Defense College and the Inter-American Juridical Committee's summer Seminar for member state diplomats and lawyers. But it has no "Academy of Public Administration." The Multilateral Evaluation Mechanism developed by the OAS to assess and coordinate national drug programs showed multilateralism can work. But though U.S. support for the MEM has been essential (along with that of Mexico and other countries), cuts were made to accommodate other foreign assistance needs. This is a bad mistake. International professional training and coordination should not be considered foreign aid – they are necessary to build the capacity required to make programs sustainable regionally and internationally. It is all well and good to have great initiatives, but what happens if you don't have people who can make them work? Every U.S. department and agency should have a core of public servants who spend part of their careers working in the UN, the OAS, or other international organizations. Stealing a page from Goldwater-Nichols, such a tour might even be a requirement for promotion to the Senior Executive Service and the Senior Foreign Service![6]

Institutional ties maintained by a network of professionals who know how to work together can provide both early warning and containment of issues that might otherwise escalate into problems—in effect, a valuable insurance policy for progress and peace.

*Q: Secretary Shultz called this "tending the garden," right?*

EINAUDI: Absolutely. But this is of necessity a long-term approach. It takes time to educate and train people, time to build trust. It is not enough to know where you want to go. You also need to know how to get there. You need skill. And you need friends. Nothing will last unless the interests of all concerned are advanced. In international politics there is no MapQuest where you can punch up directions. There is just a lot of hard and unpredictable work with others. Maybe we should call this approach a "Diplomatic surge" or a "Smart Power Surge."

During the Obama Presidency, the NSC continued to grow in numbers. The model continuing to emerge was the attempt to not just decide but implement sensitive initiatives using the NSC rather than the agencies. I heard the opening to Cuba was negotiated by the NSC, excluding the State Department until the point at which the technical firepower was needed to develop the agreements and legal/regulatory modifications required to actually implement the decision. When they are excluded, the agencies naturally recoil into

---

[6] Making multilateral experience a requirement for promotion appears in Appendix Five, "Multilateralism Matters," remarks I made when receiving a defense education award in 2016.

themselves, each doing less, and each doing only its thing. After the Trump administration had been in office several months, I asked a very senior official how interagency coordination had changed. His answer was that Principals meetings were taking place more regularly, but they had no guidance to discuss. Without political leadership interested in making the government work, agencies were beginning to shrink and drift.

*Q: In addition to politics, did racial and ethnic stereotypes complicate your work?*

EINAUDI: Of course. Stereotypes take many forms, are impossible to avoid, and can strike at the most unexpected times and ways. Some people identify nationality by race. Some people like the comfort of a world where everyone looks like them. Others would prefer to live in a world that is totally mixed up, as in parts of today's United States.

When my wife and I lived in Peru in 1964-5, our daughters were two little blondies. The Indian population would look at them and would come close and ask permission to touch their hair and just look at them; skin and hair color is an automatic badge of identity. The Peruvian melting pot is particularly complicated because Indians were conquered by Whites then joined on the coast by Asians and Blacks. One day I was talking to a Peruvian Army officer who was so upset that I had to ask why. He answered, "Well, one of my men just came to me all unhappy and said his girlfriend had broken up with him." "How come?" my friend asked. "Well, we were lying there, and she put her forearm up against my forearm and said 'See, mine is lighter and yours is darker. I can't stay with you.'" In the Caribbean this was referred to as a woman wanting to put some milk in her coffee.

The philosopher José Vasconcelos set the creation of a "Cosmic Race" as a goal of the Mexican Revolution. In *La raza cósmica*, published in 1925, he wrote to the effect that "Here are the raw materials: the Indian, the Spaniard, the Black. Brothers, the revolution is the forge. Build." A good friend of mine, the Italian diplomat Paolo Janni, who lived long in the United States, entitled his book explaining President Obama *"L'uomo venuto da ogni dove"* – "The Man from Everywhere." In essence, Janni was saying that the cosmic man had arrived. Birtherism showed both how right and how wrong that insight was.

*Q: I liked your story about the importance at times of bringing in diverse viewpoints, particularly in the context of the Peru-Ecuador border.*

EINAUDI: Thank you. Listening to the indigenous inhabitants of the disputed areas contributed to the peace. Cultural conflicts and race have influenced things in the Americas at least since the European discovery. And it was not just the conquest of the native populations. The Spanish crown used to grant (and sometimes sell) certificates of *limpieza de sangre* (cleanliness of blood) to those who needed to prove they were neither Muslim nor Jewish. I was certainly not thinking of all that while milling around in the holding area before the Peru-Ecuador peace was signed. Without warning, a former President of the Venezuelan Chamber of Deputies grabbed me and brought me over to Queen Sofía and introduced me saying "This North American knows more about us than we do." Without a word, the Queen took me by the arm, and guided me to King Juan Carlos I, saying, still without a word to me, "Sire, this gentleman has something to tell you." After a pause while I (metaphorically) picked my jaw up from the floor, I said, "Sire, I merely wished to record that your presence here completes this occasion, since the dispute we are settling today began under Spanish rule." And then I paused, as the devil within me took control, and I myself became a stereotyper, adding "But do you realize that it took *un chino y un turco* (literally a Chinaman and a Turk, which is how a Japanese and an Arab are referred to in South America) to solve it?" The King's reaction was controlled, but a listening Brazilian diplomat was horrified and told me I had ruined our chance to be decorated for our work (a prediction that turned out to be inaccurate, at least for me, as the King later awarded me the *Orden de Isabella la Católica*, established originally to recognize valiant defenders of the Spanish crown against the Moors).

Perceptions of race lead to assumptions about culture. In the early seventies, I had lunch alone at the White House with then Lt. Col. Colin Powell. Powell was a White House Fellow and clearly on the way up. We had been introduced by Bernie Loeffke, then a Colonel and the coordinator of the program. As we parted, I asked Powell how come he was so free of many of the inhibitions I had encountered in other Black officers. He answered "My parents were from Jamaica. American slavery did not weigh as heavily on me."

In 1977, Colombia refused agrément to the nomination of José Cabranes, Puerto Rico's representative in Washington, to be the U.S. Ambassador. I interceded on José's behalf with Colombian Ambassador (and future President) Virgilio Barco, but to no avail. Barco told me his government was convinced no Hispanic would have clout in the U.S. government or influence at the White House. Cabranes moved on to a distinguished career on the U.S. Court of Appeals, Second Circuit, even being rumored at one point for the Supreme Court. But Colombia was hit with the law of unintended consequences. The Carter administration replaced Cabranes with Phillip V. Sanchez, and this time Colombia yielded. Sanchez did not last a year, proving to be what Colombia had feared in Cabranes.

Visiting Bogota, Kissinger included Assistant Secretary Bill Rogers and me at a lunch with the Colombian Foreign Minister hosted by Pete Vaky, who at that point was our Ambassador to Colombia. Both Vaky and I participated actively in a lively discussion. Rogers was largely quiet. As we got up, Kissinger turned to the Colombian Minister and said "with a Greek and an Italian around me, you see why I have to keep an Anglo as front man." Kissinger's comment reflected his insecurities and his sometimes nasty sense of the jugular more than any disrespect for Rogers, whom he valued highly.

Roger Noriega had Kansas roots with Mexican antecedents, with family members who fought for the United States in WWII. In 2004, he was the political choice over FSO Anne Patterson to replace Otto Reich as Assistant Secretary for Western Hemisphere Affairs. After his interview with Colin Powell, he told me that he had gotten the impression Powell thought he was "a Cuban." I agreed to stand in with Roger at his swearing in.

When Bill Colby first arrived in Rome, he was under cover as a State Department officer. Colby later told me our Ambassador, Ellsworth Bunker, was so afraid his presence would draw attention to the CIA's activities with the Italian left, that he forbade Colby to leave the embassy except to go home. Finally, Colby wangled permission to go to a political gathering, promising he would do nothing to attract attention. The first Italian he met clapped him jovially on the shoulder, and said loudly "You're an American?"

Colby, fearing the worst, nodded wordlessly. His interlocutor continued remorselessly, "Then you must know my cousin. He lives in America." Colby, still trying to recover his aplomb, answered "Where?" "Outside Buenos Aires," came the response.

As "Americans," U.S. citizens are not the only inhabitants of "the Americas." In the Spanish-speaking countries of the hemisphere, we are referred to as "*norteamericanos*" –or, to differentiate us from Mexicans and Canadians, who also live in North America, as "*estadounidenses*," As Americans from the United States, however, most of us simply think of ourselves as "Americans." And unlike Europeans, who live in a world of languages, the only language many Americans (*estadounidenses*) hear growing up is English. The power and dynamism of the United States make speaking English an enormous global privilege. The fact that English is the language of more than half of the world's web sites is a great asset for us, but it is important to remember that half of the users of even the sites in English are not native English speakers. And then there are all the rest, for whom English remains completely alien.

Looking at us and contrasting our wars of independence and values with those of South Americans, Mariano Grondona, an Argentine friend since my first trip in 1955, commented "Latin Americans fear anarchy. You fear dictatorship." There is some truth to that insight, just as there is to other stereotypes that bedevil hemispheric relations, from our black legend of the Spanish Conquest to their fears of imperialism, the legacies of colonialism and slavery, the allures of the frontier and the persistence of racism. Stereotypes gorge on mutual ignorance and lack of contact.

*Q: How well do most Latin American countries and embassies understand the U.S. and Washington?*

EINAUDI: With a few momentary exceptions, poorly. The best example for me was always the difference between Canada and Mexico. Our two immediate neighbors in North America obviously have similar stakes in their relations with us. Most of the time Canada was all over the place, penetrating our government almost seamlessly, always aware they might need to duck quickly when something unexpected came their way. Mexico certainly knew all about U.S. power but was much less engaged. From my California days I remember how a Mexican effort to encourage the development of a Mexican version of "the Israeli lobby" was sharply rejected by local *chicanos* who wanted nothing to do with a government they associated with the conditions that led them to emigrate. Mexico did provide consular services for its citizens, but when it came to the U.S. government, I always suspected that at least on some things it relied more on intelligence channels rather than the State Department.

*Q: This may have changed some in the years since. I was the director of the Office of Mexican Affairs in 2014-2015 and I can tell you for certain that the Mexican foreign minister texted our Assistant Secretary daily. And, Mexican officials were working directly with Cabinet officials in the Departments of Homeland Security, Commerce, and many others.*

EINAUDI: I am delighted and reassured to hear that. In my time, Mexico and many other Latin American and Caribbean countries focused their embassies more on their emigrant communities than on the sprawling and often impenetrable U.S. government. On the other hand, foreign contacts and "arrangements" with DOD and the CIA were largely unknown to us in State. When Caesar Sereseres looked at the embassies for me in 1986-7, when he was in PPC, he discovered they were almost exclusively focused on the White House. They assumed we were the same as their own countries, with power concentrated in the presidency. Sereseres also reported that most of the smaller Latin American embassies lacked the modern technology to communicate to the U.S. government and even their own capitals. The Latin embassies, he felt, were also "segregated" internally -- the Ambassador, the military, cultural/ information people did not talk to each other and were often reduced to using paid lobbyists to do their policy work. One of my Central American friends, who had done graduate work in the United States, then later returned as his country's ambassador, was always amazed that his foreign ministry made no special effort to follow U.S. politics and policy. As with all rules, however, there are exceptions. It was a foreigner, Val McComie, the Ambassador of Barbados, who first introduced me to U.S. Congressman Charlie Rangel, thus expanding my ties to my own country.

*Q: You described a few important foreign policy areas like Central America and Haiti, that got unduly partisan. Did you find it hard to convince politicians and political appointees that you were impartial?*

EINAUDI: I was a registered Democrat, but, as I have said before, I never ran for office, and always accepted that I had to work with those who did and won. And I think that, with few exceptions, most politicians saw me more as an expert, a professional, as a member of the deep state or "permanent government," rather than as a partisan.

The big problem for me was always partisan politics. And, in particular, partisan opposition to whatever party occupied the White House. Central America blew up with Carter in office, so the Republicans blamed that on the Democrats' destabilizing human rights policies, to which the Democrats replied once Reagan came in that the Republicans favored oligarchs and dictators. The Contra program was both the beneficiary and then the victim of this polarization. Started as a means to resist the Sandinistas, it was later sacrificed as duplicitous Republican militarism. The Bipartisan Commission on Central America was created to offset what the Democratic opposition was calling the Republicans militarization of policy. The very same intense partisan divide carried over later to Haiti after Clinton used our military to put Aristide back in power. Republican hatred of Aristide contributed greatly to preventing the creation of a middle ground in Haiti in the decade from 1994 to 2004. It was fueled operationally by the tit for tat of U.S. domestic politics and driven ideologically by the same staffers shaped by the partisan battles over Central America in the 1980s. This partisanship was exploited to their advantage by local elites in both Central America and Haiti. Right-wing groups influenced Reagan administration policies on Central America, but the Guatemalan government got aid from the Democrats by opposing the Contras. The Haitian right enlisted Republicans to block compromise with Aristide. Sereseres used to say the big Yankee dog was being wagged by its tail.

It should go without saying that foreign policy must ultimately reflect domestic interests. But it is important to realize that this has costs abroad. The distortions imposed on U.S. policy toward Latin America by the Cold War are generally known. Immigration and even exile are now discussed as if they were purely domestic matters. Global trade policies adopted for reasons of abstract efficiency were undermined by their domestic consequences. The inability of the United States to establish domestic controls over its own drug demand, money laundering, or illegal arms transfers has had devastating consequences for our immediate neighbors. The success of the Haitian right in weakening Aristide and influencing

U.S. policy was clearly based partly on the successful exploitation of American racism. My problems with the NSC on MOMEP would have been even harder to manage had Peru-Ecuador been a higher profile issue domestically in the United States. The challenge for statesmanship is to convert as many interactions as possible into win-win propositions.

*Q: But sometimes there are too many conflicts to develop win-win outcomes . . .*

EINAUDI: Of course. But the right approach can sometimes work miracles. Even on the highly polarized issue of Central America, some reconciling of different viewpoints could be found. The key was to focus on points of potential overlap and seek ways to expand them. For example, common opposition to "Communism" could lead to support for "Democracy," and "Democracy" could provide cover for policies acceptable to both conservatives seeking "Freedom" and to liberals seeking "Social Progress." Developing win-win formulations and syntheses of this kind is not easy. My 1980 talk on Central America in Appendix One was an attempt to do that. The results proved mixed, because the swing in personnel and politics between Carter and Reagan was just too great, and a viable center did not exist on the ground in Central America. Later, when I was the U.S. Ambassador to the OAS, I would say that I looked forward to the day when a democratic Cuba could return to the OAS – a simple formula that enabled me to point toward a goal stated in a way that bridged the enormous chasm between those who hated Castro and those who opposed the expulsion of Cuba. Ambiguities like that are about as far as an unelected public servant can go without betraying his obligation to represent all his people.

Bridging formulas can help build coalitions to develop new policies. To take advantage of the openings they provide requires cooperation between insiders and outsiders – that is, between operating people in the governmental bureaucracy like the State Department, and the political people in the White House, the Congress and pressure groups. In foreign policy, that is not the rule.

*Q: I was just thinking in the foreign affairs context, you were doing a job an incredibly long time and dealing with essentially the same issues. Did you get any feel for our political people both in the White House and in Congress as a group were they more aware later on, less aware, were they learning, were they effective? I mean the people who were outside of essentially the system. How were they dealing with this? Did you see a change in them?*

EINAUDI: That is a marvelous question, and it is one on which I have been on both sides. I came from outside the system. I came to the State Department at the age of thirty-eight in what was then a "plum list" job, a job reserved for appointees at the discretion of the president. For the first ten years in the State Department, through both Republican and Democrat administrations, I defined my role as one of interpreter, not in the sense of language, nor between Americans and foreigners, but as interpreter between the American political class and the career public service. That is to say between the political people who came in with changes of administrations and filled many of the top rungs and the career people who carry out policy under them. I had experience in both roles, and I felt that I often had to mediate, interpreting each to the other. And I think that is a function that is very much needed.

I have always been an optimist. I have always believed that people can learn. I felt that when an administration first came into office, those first four years amounted to a cold bath in the realities of government, and therefore that it could not help but do better the second four years. I have been very disappointed in that expectation. Things have not worked that way. I think it is in part because Presidents bring their A-team when they first come in, then in their second term they are left with their B-team because the best ones have moved on and the new people come in with fewer ambitions and illusions.

As to how much political folks know when they first hit Washington, I think there has been a decline. This is an old man speaking and I don't want to sound like an old man, but I will for a moment. I used to have a great many friends on the Hill in both the House and the Senate. Their core was made up of moderates. My personal political preferences were Democratic, but I rose through Republican administrations. I knew, liked, and worked with people of both parties and of all colors. On the democratic side Chris Dodd, Senator from Connecticut, served in the Peace Corps then became key on the Foreign Relations Committee. He was very important to me. I wound up having a lot of respect for Ted Kennedy which I had not had when I was younger. There was a group, perhaps they can be called Rockefeller Republicans, the Jacob Javitses or more recently Richard Lugar, and others willing to look for common ground. Those people are all out of office. One day Senator Mathias, Mac Mathias of Maryland, and I had been at a meeting together. I don't remember what it was. He had a car; I did not. He asked me where I lived and said, "I will drop you home." As he drove, we talked about the ineffectiveness of Congress. He says, "You know it is not going to change until we get rid of the yahoos." I said, "What do you mean?" He said, "All these new people who don't know anything." "What party do they belong to?" I asked. He said, "They are the majority in both parties." Then Mathias became the first to tell me that a majority of the representatives in the Congress of the United States do not have a passport.

On the House side, Charles Rangel once told me proudly that he had been renominated for Congress by all three parties in his district: Democratic, Republican and Liberal. Ben Gilman was a Republican, but I traveled with him twice, both times with Democrats, with Michael Barnes to Venezuela, and with Rangel, John Lewis and other members of the Black Caucus to Haiti. The big issue in the House, I thought, was the disconnect between the foreign and the domestic. John Conyers looked at me sadly, "I always voted for free trade, but now . . . look at Detroit." I recall one public-spirited congressman from a Midwestern state telling me that he was home once when there were floods, and he was hauling sandbags, helping to build a levee. One of his constituents, working next to him, recognized him, turned and said, "Tell me Congressman, if we were foreigners would we have gotten aid faster?"

We are dealing with a very difficult and contradictory world. Our country is more intertwined than ever with others by globalization, yet we seem also more primitively nationalist than ever. Somehow our politics do not catch up to world realities. I am not implying that the U.S. should have a more interventionist foreign policy. In my view, the U.S. most of the time ought to do less but learn to do it better and to cooperate more effectively with others. Those are things we are not particularly good at.

Generally speaking, I also think our leaders deserve more respect than they get in normal discourse. That includes foreign leaders. My notes record by name more than one hundred presidents and heads of government with whom I had direct personal contact in the course of my career. As I look back, a handful obviously left something to be desired. But something else stands out: the national leaders I dealt with were for the most part able individuals. Are we to hope for a better future because generally competent people rise? Or are we in a pickle despite the efforts of our best and brightest?

I am concerned now that the disruptions of globalization can also undermine our sense of the onward progress of civilization. My consciousness as an American-educated person is that we somehow embody the march of history toward freedom, away from dictatorship, racism, feudalism and colonialism toward a more civilized world of greater democracy and opportunity and economic well-being. By extension toward a better and more universal world order. You don't need to be a world federalist to believe this. But I fear we have lost the sense that this is the general march of civilization. At the same time, the U.S. is in decline as a model. In some ways it was easier during the Cold War. The current world is hard and difficult to understand. Kissinger once commented that the cold war favored those with political/strategic skills; those elites were not prepared for the economic issues that emerged after the Cold War ended. The speed of change is disorienting, the information age has multiplied available knowledge while simultaneously destroying common reference points. We are all delegitimized.

I am proud of the contributions my State Department colleagues and I made in our times. I worry about what my friend Ed Casey calls the "eternal contempt of Congress towards the Foreign Service." And I worry that our successors will have to refight our battles with domestic politics and other cultures all over again.

*Q: How do you view the "gap" between how Washington makes decisions affecting Latin America and how the academic community portrays Washington decision making?*

EINAUDI: Teodoro Petkoff, a former guerrilla later to become a moderate minister in Venezuela, visited a number of Latin American studies centers at U.S. universities in the 1980s. At the end of his trip, he told me "U.S. libraries, data bases and students have incredible amounts of information about Latin America. Fortunately for us, they do not know what to do with it." He was implying that despite our many assets, our lack of understanding allowed Latin Americans greater freedom of maneuver. But he was also saying that much academic understanding of our relations was lacking.

The long list of U.S. misadventures in the hemisphere has contributed to almost instinctive alienation from U.S. policy, in both the academic world and the general public. I will never forget the reaction of Kalman Silvert, at the time the undisputed dean of U.S. political scientists dealing with Latin America, at a meeting in the fall of 1961 whose purpose was to help policy makers regroup after the fiasco at the Bay of Pigs. After listening to an initial presentation by the government sponsors, Silvert organized a walkout of the academic participants, exclaiming "Do they want us to choose a new beach?" As I noted earlier, events in Chile and Central America brought out similar hostile public reactions and misgivings.

This is not to say that there is not sometimes a great deal to criticize about U.S. policy. But the application of rational yardsticks to human affairs is often misleading. In the absence of knowledge of particular situations, reason leads almost perforce to radical conclusions. To reason correctly, you need to know the facts, take them seriously, and interpret them in their context. Accepting conventional abstractions is an occupational hazard for anyone who tries to look beyond their nose.

*Q: Does that hold for you? Were there differences in your knowledge and analyses between your time at RAND and your time at State?*

EINAUDI: It certainly does hold for me. Bill Stedman was the Director of Andean Affairs when I first joined the Department. What I had written on Peru included a classified study of our assistance policies. Bill quietly pointed out that the facts did not always support my conclusions. I am a great admirer of Stedman, who has been running the Ford Latin American group at DACOR which is a marvelous way for old hands to stay in touch. [FLAG went out of existence in 2017 and Bill Stedman passed away at 95 on March 25, 2018.]

There is a constant tension between having an analysis emerge from data and imposing an analysis on data. This tension increases the less data is available. When you know everything, you don't need to think. But the fact is, you can never know everything. In 1953, responding to my pride at graduating from Exeter with honors, grandfather Einaudi wrote me *The joy you feel when you do something well must always be accompanied by a tacit mental reservation. What I know, what I have learned, is nothing compared to what I do not know. This mental reservation must accompany you to the end of your life. This does not mean that in life you will not have to decide, or that in doubt you must behave like Buridan's ass, frozen at the moment of choice. Unfortunately, the choice is never clean: between good and evil. . ... The essential thing is to realize that you DON'T know. If you think you know, you will almost certainly take the wrong path; as the things to learn are infinite, and knowing but few of them, it would be a miracle if those few things you know were both morally good and logically true, so that the risk of error is great . . ... What you need to do is to learn how to tell the more true from the less true; you need to learn how to reason.*

Experience has taught me to be ever more careful of generalizations, ever more aware that good government is an art, not a science. Never think conspiracy when incompetence or human error will explain (Were the doctors who examined President Kennedy after he was shot trying to hide the course of the bullet? Or were they simply in such shock they did not have the heart to turn his head over to complete all aspects of the autopsy?). Similarly, I have always thought Graham Allison's much ballyhooed analysis of bureaucratic models of decision-making mostly meant that his exposure to government during the Kennedy Administration was too brief. Of course, getting things done in government is complex! Of course, different bureaucracies have different interests. But those who learn the subtleties of politics and bureaucracies can transcend them. What cannot be transcended are ignorance, cultural blinders, and arrogance.

*Q: You are beginning to sound hostile to academic work and theorizing in general.*

EINAUDI: I don't mean to. And there is an important counterbalance to what I just said. The theoreticians may be in need of more facts and to deal better with those they have, but the practitioners are just as much in need of better theories to order their work in the trenches. That was why I invited Huntington to speak to S/P and why I advocate a mid-career educational break for Foreign Service officers. Academic work in search of theories regularly distorts reality by simplifying it. Government work is sometimes done mechanically, without necessary reflection. Some analysts try to make decision-making seem rational; others claim it is irrational. A better answer would be it depends. And it depends not just on the situation, but also on the ability and training of the decision-maker. Good government is hard work, and it deserves far more respect than it gets.

*Q: Would you say that about diplomacy? That it is not well understood or given its due?*

EINAUDI: Absolutely. Diplomacy is hard. Its key starting points are simple: to listen, to know, and to share so as to find grounds for cooperation. But diplomacy is not easy to practice. And part of the reason is that it depends on force as well as reason.

To reach and structure lasting agreements, the first rule is to listen. A diplomat cannot be constantly on transmit, lecturing others. He or she must listen, be empathetic, and understand the essential interests of all sides. Listening is not enough. It is important to understand. When a moderate Caribbean Foreign Minister out of the British tradition told Colin Powell that something revealed "Man's inhumanity to man," Otto Reich whispered to Powell that this proved the Foreign Minister was a Marxist. "Man's inhumanity to man" is certainly a high impact phrase, but it comes from a poem by Robert Burns, not from a diatribe by Karl Marx. Otto Reich was a U.S. citizen born in Cuba after his father's path from Nazi Germany to the United States had been interrupted by marriage to his Cuban mother. Fidel Castro was part of Otto's world, not Scotsman Robert Burns. The result of not understanding is, at best, frustration and ineffectiveness.

A second rule is that all parties, including the weakest, must benefit from any agreement, if that agreement is to last. Lasting results do not require equal benefits – it being in the nature of things that the strong will usually prosper most -- but even the weak must get at least a crumb. Conversely, even the weak must contribute. The failures of the OAS and of U.S. migration policies are not just U.S. failures. They are failures of all the member states and of sending as well as receiving countries. All must benefit, but all must also contribute.

The need for creativity is another dimension of diplomacy that is generally undervalued by nonpractitioners. Even in an age of instant communication, instructions have sharp limits. Situations change, opportunities arise, and a diplomat has to be quick to adjust. When I talked to an audience of students or prospective diplomats, I would often tell them to "Look at the person sitting next to you. What do you think they would do?" I would then say that the way to act effectively when in doubt, or when uninstructed, is to have confidence in how your fellow citizens would think and act. You are, after all, representing them. The old hand will also know he has to guard his own back. If he expects to have to act at variance with instructions, remember UNODIR (UNless Otherwise DIRected). Wait to the last minute, then let Washington know that, unless otherwise directed, you will do something tomorrow you know will raise hackles. Not in order to abandon American interests, but the opposite, to move them forward in situations not understood or anticipated in Washington.

The need for creativity in diplomacy, the fact that formulaic straightjacketing will often not work, leaps out at you if you look at the sweep of history just in our lifetimes. We were born during the depression, with instability, poverty and the consolidation of fascism in Western Europe -- but also FDR's New Deal reconciling industrial civilization and democracy; then came World War II with fear death, destruction and social mobilization on unprecedented global range and scale -- followed by post-war reconstruction and a new, largely U.S.-designed international order that was accompanied also by the Cold War, which drew resources to security and produced conformism and intellectual bankruptcy; more recently, globalization has stimulated broad growth but also dislocation and terrorism, the assertion of the marginalized but also growing anarchy and decline of international law and institutions. All this accompanied by a generalized and growing disdain for history, even in the academic world. All that in less than a lifetime. No time for fixed formulas.

Finally, diplomacy cannot be just talk or just sophisticated understanding. It needs something behind it. Whether it is fear, money, brute force or simply shared ideals, diplomats need something to work with. Sometimes it is "all of the above" and more. Usually it is a mix. But certainly the politically popular juxtaposition of solutions as being either military or diplomatic is misleading. As a diplomat, I would like to say that the military must always be part of a solution but can never be all of it. The military's basic training and operating rule is to follow orders; a good diplomat shows his worth in a UNODIR moment when he must advance our interests when his instructions cannot tell him what to do.

Q: *What do you think was your most important accomplishment in your lifetime?*

EINAUDI: The Peru-Ecuador peace saved lives. Resolution 1080 kept freedom alive as an objective for the Americas. Surviving with honor while working on Central America in the 1980s was a miracle.

Q: *And your biggest disappointments?*

EINAUDI: Our collective failures in Haiti. Watching the OAS shrivel. Sensing that we are not keeping up with what we need to understand about the world beyond our borders.

Q: *Have you offered advice to people in the Department since you left?*

EINAUDI: Not much. In the military, once you lose troop command, you lose influence. The State Department is a bit like that. Tom Shannon once asked me about Haiti in behalf of Secretary Kerry, but I was too far removed from events to tell him anything he did not already know. At the start of the Obama administration, I did volunteer to Arturo Valenzuela when he became Assistant Secretary that he should try to avoid the Todman-Pastor-Derian rivalries that bedeviled Carter's policies by seeking to work with Restrepo, Otero and others. I also suggested he get the weightiest possible U.S. Ambassador to the OAS and instruct his regional bureau's country offices to involve our OAS Mission in advancing policy.

Q: *Q: Clearly that last point did not work. Have you tried to influence particular policies?*

EINAUDI: Just once. I remembered seeing a report from the mid-1990s that Mexican authorities had, with the help of the Justice Department's Bureau of Alcohol, Tobacco, Firearms and Explosives (commonly known simply as ATF), traced the origins of a large cache of weapons captured from drug gangs. Many of us, myself included, had believed most would turn out to be leftovers from El Salvador and the Central American wars. In fact, almost ninety per cent came directly from or through the U.S., many simply transshipped through California or Texas from China.

Aware that countries to their south were also being victimized by similar illegal weapons transfers, Mexico consulted, first with South America, and then with CARICOM and developed a multilateral treaty to "eradicate illicit transnational trafficking in firearms." Mexico then brought the draft in the OAS and sought the support of the United States. The key ambassadors leading the negotiations were both women, Carmen Moreno for Mexico, and Hattie Babbitt for the United States. Hattie added an advisor from the National Rifle Association (NRA) to the US delegation. The delegates finally agreed on an *Inter-American Convention against the Illicit Manufacturing of and Trafficking in Firearms, Ammunition, Explosives, and Other Related Materials*, known as CIFTA from its acronym in Spanish. The text encouraged increased regional cooperation but left each country free to enforce its own laws. It also stated explicitly that it was "not intended to discourage or diminish lawful leisure or recreational activities such as travel or tourism for sport shooting, hunting and other forms of lawful ownership and use." The result seemed a win-win for all sides. President Clinton signed for the United States during a visit to Mexico in 1997. Ten years later, it had been signed by 33 countries and ratified by 29 but had languished in our Senate.

So in early 2009 I drafted a letter to the Senate Foreign Relations Committee urging ratification. It makes clear that the treaty's purpose was to "create a framework to combat illegal trafficking in the kinds of weapons used by drug gangs and criminal enterprises in Mexico" without affecting existing U.S. gun laws and explicitly recognizing U.S. citizens' rights. I got on the phone and obtained the signatures of all Assistant Secretaries of State for the Western Hemisphere since 1976, all Ambassadors to the OAS since 1989, all Chairmen of the Inter-American Defense Board since 1989, and two thirds of SOUTHCOM Commanders since 1983. The letter is reproduced at Appendix 9. We were 27 signatories in all, including 11 generals and 13 ambassadors. Our talking points emphasized we were not asking for more U.S. gun laws or new U.S. gun laws. Hattie Babbitt, my successor as OAS Ambassador, testified that her own Texas hunting childhood would in no way be affected. We were merely asking for a legal endorsement of hemispheric cooperation against *illegal* weapons flows, many of which came through the U.S. but originated in China.

*Q: Remarkable. How did it turn out?*

EINAUDI: At the Summit of the Americas in Trinidad and Tobago in April 2009, President Obama pledged to seek ratification of CIFTA. A thirtieth country did ratify after the Summit, but it was not the U.S., which is still missing.

One of my biggest frustrations is that the United States, a key contributor to the emergence of modern international law and organization, has since the end of the twentieth century become an absentee on modern treaty law. Our lawyers have been reduced to saying lamely that we support "customary" practices. But not ratifying CIFTA is not just a "customary" matter: it makes it seem that we are simply not interested in cooperating with our neighbors against illegal arms transfers.

Q: *Well, what else have you been up to since you retired?*

EINAUDI: During my years at the State Department, I had very little in the way of vacations or downtimes. And I did almost nothing in Italy, where my father had founded the Fondazione Luigi Einaudi, a research institute in Turin that houses my grandfather's unique economic library. Homepage EN - Fondazione Luigi Einaudi (fondazioneeinaudi.it) The Fondazione needed my support after my father's death in 1994. My resignation from the State Department came after receiving an opinion from the Legal Advisor's office that it would be a conflict of interest for me to go to the EU in Brussels to ask for money for an Italian institution while still being an American diplomat with ambassadorial rank. I think the person who told me that thought that I would just say fine, I will stop.

Instead, I said, fine, I can't stop, so I will have to leave. At Jeff Davidow's request, I stayed on as the Special Envoy for Peru Ecuador, but retired in July 1997 to an office at the Inter-American Dialogue and devoted much of my time to the Fondazione in Turin. It turned out that Italians are just as resistant as anybody else to outside meddling. They were happy to have me around, but weren't particularly happy to support my initiatives, which they thought were flawed by American optimism.

In contrast, when Bolivia, Peru and Ecuador asked me to run for OAS Assistant Secretary General, I felt I would be doing something that people wanted me to do. I completed my term at the OAS in 2005, and Carol retired from her law firm in 2006. Since then, we have split our time between Italy and the United

States, more in Washington than anywhere else. In Italy, we have been living in my grandfather's old house, writing and working on things that have to do with both Einaudi and Michels (including the introduction to a study on Michels I used to compare my two grandfathers!) and occasionally lecturing academically in Turin and Rome. In 2016, the local administration in Dogliani, our small home town, gave me the "Schi-na Cinà" (piedmontese dialect for "bent back") award for those who work as hard out in the big world as in peasant agriculture. Three trips to Poland helped my wife Carol uncover much about the family of her mother, who arrived as a babe in arms in 1907. Turns out Carol was not named for Carol Lombard after all, but after her great grandfather Karol Wankowsky, a mayor and administrator in Wielkopolska whose progeny have been active on all sides of Polish politics from the 1863 uprisings against Russia to modern Solidarność. Here in the States, our four children are all well and productive, and nine of our ten grandchildren are Lake Wobegon kids. The tenth is also beautiful but his severe autism blocks normal expression.

In the United States, I have spoken in various settings, including at Cornell's Center for International Studies, founded by and later named for my father Mario Einaudi. I also taught as an adjunct professor at Georgetown, where I was exposed to the immediate and indiscriminate impact of the internet. It gave my students unprecedented cross-cultural access, but in limited time frames and it fostered laziness ("You put the reading on reserve at the library? We don't go to the library; the assigned readings must be available to us on line"). At the National Defense University, I had an office from 2007 to 2018 and received the 2016 William J. Perry Award. In 2011, I published a paper on *Brazil and the United States: The Need for Strategic Engagement*, INSS-NDU Strategic Forum No. 266. It was inspired by Hans Binnendijk, an old hand at both State and Defense, who said "No one knows that" when I told him that Brazil saw itself as part of the world rather than as part of Latin America.

In 2016, I began to transfer my library and many of my papers to the Columbus Memorial Library at the OAS, which also has put my speeches and some other materials on line at http://www.oas. org/en/columbus/amb_einaudi.asp

*Q: Thank you so much for the work you have put into this oral history. I know this account will be valuable to many now and in the future.*

EINAUDI: I am very grateful to you. I was putting together notes for a possible memoir. You have preempted that, and you have had me cover things that I would not have done by myself.

*End of interview*

# APPENDIX ONE

Informal Remarks on Central America and the Caribbean
by
Luigi R. Einaudi
Director of Policy Planning and Coordination
Bureau of Inter-American Affairs
at a Conference Sponsored by
American Enterprise Institute - Konrad Adenauer Stiftung
Washington, D.C.
May 22, 1980

I am delighted to have this opportunity to share some thoughts with this distinguished company.

The countries of the Caribbean Basin are changing rapidly. The region as we have known it is passing and so is the structure of relationships between its countries and the West. The challenge before us is not to resist change but to participate in it in new and constructive ways.

In Central America, a once stagnant order is disintegrating before our eyes. New groups are emerging; old ones are changing. Traditional alliances among landowners, generals, and bishops lie shattered. The landed gentry's economic monopoly has been broken by modern businessmen. The Armed Forces are developing broader and more modern perspectives as institutions. The Church has ceased to bless the status quo, and sometimes actively supports change.

The complex nature of these transformations is reflected in the very different situations of individual Central American nations. Nicaragua is struggling for economic recovery and searching for ways to implement a national consensus against dictatorship; in El Salvador, a civil-military coalition is carrying out unprecedented reforms against violent opposition from right and left extremes; in Guatemala, a conservative government must decide how to develop that country's unique potential without falling prey to tensions similar to those that have created turmoil in its neighbors; in Honduras, a delicate transition toward full constitutional rule is taking place under the pressure of regional uncertainties; in Costa Rica, a functioning democracy is adjusting to new political and economic stresses.

In the island states of the Caribbean, the signs of change are less dramatic but equally undeniable. In a single generation, colonialism has given way to independence for a dozen countries. Since the early seventies, the region has experienced severe economic problems: rising energy costs, falling prices for commodity exports, declining investment and loss of skilled manpower through emigration. Young people are leaving rural areas with high aspirations only to become frustrated dwellers of urban slums. Last year's quantum leap in oil prices is having a devastating impact on most of the small island economies. External pressures are thus aggravating internal problems, such as the tension between social benefits and economic productivity that is straining democratic institutions in Jamaica. There is no guarantee that the coups in Grenada and Suriname are not portents of more generalized instability to come.

The differences between Central America and the Caribbean are significant. The English-speaking Caribbean has inherited a potentially important source of strength in parliamentary democracy. In contrast, Central American democracy has too often served as a mask for authoritarianism, and popular aspirations have too often not been expressed effectively through normal constitutional channels. In the Caribbean, cultural and even ideological differences are sharper than in Central America, and fragmented sovereignties have undermined early efforts at federation. In both regions, nevertheless, there are nuclei for better cooperation -- the CARICOM and the Central American Common Market.

Despite differences among individual countries and sub-regions, the Caribbean Basin is a geopolitical unity. Events in one part of the region inevitably affect the others. Western interests, particularly security interests, in the region are largely undifferentiated. Events in one country affect others -- not in a simple domino effect, but importantly nonetheless.

Were we dealing with a series of unrelated crises, we could assume the relaxed attitude of monitoring the painful but necessary birth pangs of a new and possibly more just order. Certainly, the dispersal of power now taking place introduces new hope for democracy. The erosion of central authority, however, facilitates the growth of extremist factions. Taken together, these developments make plain governing difficult, and increase uncertainty about what the future will bring.

One of the major uncertainties concerns Cuba's role. Cuba is larger than any other Caribbean or Central American country. The region is of unique importance to Cuba, and Cuba's enormous dependence on the Soviet Union creates a dangerous link to global East-West problems.

Cuba is clearly not the cause of the region's turmoil.
Just as clearly, however, Cuba could become a major beneficiary. Cuba's longstanding ties with indigenous revolutionaries, and the concrete assistance it provides
them, could make a critical difference. Mounting domestic
failures could provoke Cuba into even more dangerous
adventurism.

It is important to remember in such circumstances
that Central America's future will ultimately be decided
by Central Americans. Few of them want to repeat Cuba's
experience. Most want to build modern and open societies
that take into consideration their own history, traditions,
and special economic circumstances.

Helping them to do so, and formulating an adequate
response to these developments, is a complex policy problem
for the West. Our choices are not as simple as those
of Cuba. The Cubans have little choice but to support
the violent left. We cannot support the violent right,
although they may consider themselves -- or be considered
by others -- our natural allies. The weakness of legitimacy
based on traditional authority, and our own values --
support for human rights and for development with equity
-- combine to preclude this alternative. We must, rather,
work patiently and steadily with those individuals, groups,
and institutions capable of building a more pluralistic
and democratic future.

In contrast to the Caribbean, moderate and democratic
groups in Central America are often fragmented and demoralized.
Too often, they accent their weaknesses by squabbling
with each other and working at cross-purposes. But they
do exist -- among businessmen and military officers,
among labor and peasant organizations, and among political
parties with views ranging from populism to christian
and social democracy.

These many different local groups all deserve our
understanding and support. For although changes -- and
a certain amount of instability -- are in fact inevitable,
we can make a major difference in how the forces of change
ultimately work themselves out. As Dr. Hans Morgenthau
once wrote: "The real issue facing American foreign
policy ... is not how to preserve stability in the face
of revolution, but how to create stability out of revolution."

U.S. policy is currently based on two guiding principles:

First, because traditional patterns are in many
respects both unjust and unstable, we recognize that
change is both natural and inevitable. We believe that

peace and democracy depend, in Central America in particular, on broadly-based and fundamental socio-economic
and political reforms that will increase national well-
being and strengthen the rights of the individual.

Second, while we hold these views, we will not attempt
to impose them. We will not use military force in situations where only domestic groups are in contention.
We harbor no illusion that we can define the nature of
change or substitute ourselves for local leadership;
but, as in El Salvador today, we can and will support
local reform initiatives.

This approach reflects both local realities and
American interests. For that reason, and despite certain
suggestions to the contrary, I believe U.S. policy is
unlikely to change significantly in the future. Indeed,
we anticipate that our European and Latin American friends
will join us in this cooperative approach. If we --
and they -- do not participate in shaping the future,
we would be reduced to accepting and adjusting passively
to whatever comes. And it would not be pleasant. The
alternatives are intolerable: violence followed by dictatorships
-- first of the right, then of the left.

In sum, the multiple crises of the Caribbean Basin
present the West with a very complex and, I submit, important challenge. We must:

   --  encourage moderate and democratic forces through-
       out the area on the basis of constructive relation-
       ships free of dogmas and sectarianisms;

   --  facilitate the development of economies where
       the fruits of modern entrepreneurship and labor
       are rewarded;

   --  find ways to rejuvenate processes of regional
       cooperation and economic integration;

   --  deal effectively with Cuban aggressiveness;
       and

   --  maintain, and if necessary, increase development
       assistance, to levels commensurate with the
       area's pressing needs.

These objectives are all immeasurably strengthened
by meetings such as this, where Central Americans and
Caribbeans, Americans and Europeans -- men of the West
all -- come together to discuss how urgency and serenity
can be combined . . . in action.

Thank you very much.

# APPENDIX TWO

FIRST DRAFT        $1994$        26 July 0800   FIRST DRAFT

### Sources of Conflict after the Cold War:
Neither Original Sins nor Passing Fancies

Less than five years after the fall of the Berlin Wall, the peacekeeping and the humanitarian capacities of the world community are being overwhelmed. Bosnia festers in the Old World and Haiti in the New, while Rwanda's nightmare reaches beyond Africa to challenge our practise of humanity and our concept of organized society.

This draft analysis considers three factors present to some degree in all of today's major troublespots. They are:

--the dispersal of power among nations,

--the weakening of central governments within nations, and

--technology's erosion of traditional frontiers and structures.

Each of these trends has positive aspects; indeed each can be said to be a "downside" of positive consequences of the end of the Cold War: the dispersal of power is partly a result of the end of bipolar rigidities; challenges to central authorities are not unrelated to reduced militarization and repression; and the spread of technology is tied directly to global economic growth and greater social openness.

Importantly, however, these are all trends which began **before** the Cold War ended. Indeed, while Leninist legitimacy and command economics were among their early victims, these trends are affecting all societies, including our own. Their impact seems likely to be felt for some time into the future.

The pervasiveness, origin and nature of these trends puts them "beyond politics," at least in the sense that their impact is without regard to partisan politics and cannot be blamed on particular decisions by particular leaders or parties.

To channel these new forces as constructively as possible, this draft argues, will require an approach based on enlarging democracy among nations as well as within nations. Policies of open regionalism can be used to foster greater integration. Greater burdensharing will be essential for international institutions to improve their effectiveness.

As the world's leading military and economic power, the United States should seek to ensure that future historians record today's crises as the birthpangs of a better world rather than the deaththroes of the hopes generated by the triumph of freedom in both World War II and the Cold War.

## I.  Three Key Trends

**Dispersal of State Power**.  One of the most obvious changes is the transformation from a world aligned along the bipolar lines of antagonistic superpower-led blocs to one where none of the world's major powers sees any of the others as an immediate military threat.  We still have our disputes with Russia and with China -- and, for that matter, on certain issues with Western Europe and Japan -- but not one of us considers any of the others an adversary.  Many of our overall foreign policy objectives, from the security of key regions to nonproliferation to economic prosperity, can be greatly facilitated by cooperation among the major powers.

The downside of this basically positive trend is that, with the likelihood of armed conflict among the major powers reduced, many states will be less likely to compromise their objectives in order to find shelter under the American military or nuclear umbrella.  This applies to more than just security or political objectives:  with the end of the Cold War, some of the frictions originating in economic competition need no longer be submerged under a common security blanket.

Many of today's hot spots -- Bosnia, Rwanda, Somalia, Haiti -- originate in the refusal of smaller states to act according to the interests of the major powers.  The very number of crises now evolving with minimal effective outside intervention reduces perceptions of the influence of the major powers, including the United States.

**Weakened Central Governments**.  A second trend is undermining both the traditional foundations of the international system and the authority of individual governments.

The state-system was built around the idea of sovereign equality and non-interference by foreign powers into a nation's internal affairs.  In the late 18th century, with the American and French Revolutions and the rise of democracy, the sovereign state began to evolve into the modern nation-state, characterized by the growing reliance on the consent of the governed -- the principle of self-determination.  Together, sovereignty and self-determination became the basic organizing principles governing legitimate order within and among states. For the most part, when conflicts arose, the principle of territorial integrity took precedence; self-determination was accepted as valid only within pre-existing borders.

At the end of World War I, President Woodrow Wilson proposed to elevate the place of self-determination. Yet because granting self-determination to groups within existing states could imperil the international order, the Covenant of the League of Nations did not mention self-determination.

The end of World War II saw a new impetus in favor of self-determination, in part spurred on by decolonization. The UN Charter explicitly recognized the right of self-determination and referred, if ambiguously, to self-determination of "peoples." But the Charter, like the Covenant, put self-determination second to the traditional principles of the state system.

The Cold War had made self-determination a dead letter for countries and peoples under the Soviet Empire. But the collapse of the Berlin Wall revealed the artificiality of the Stalin's internal "administrative" boundaries -- and more. Ancient ethnic hatreds are re-inflamed not by Soviet fifth columns, but by local demagogues -- who, as President Clinton put it in his speech to the French National Assembly, are "transforming the healthy pride of nations, tribes, religious and ethnic groups into cancerous prejudice."

Nor is this simply a problem of the ethnically mixed republics of the former Soviet Union, or of Yugoslavia, or Northern Ireland, or Rwanda alone. The characteristic conflicts of today's world are **within established boundaries** rather than **among states**, and are typically generated by centrifugal forces claiming rights against traditional centrally organized authority.

**Technology.** Weapons and weapons technology proliferation, terrorism, population growth and demographic change, drug trafficking and international crime, and global environmental degradation are no longer issues merely of quality of life, but for some societies of stability itself.

At least 20 nations have acquired or are attempting to acquire various forms of weapons of mass destruction. A small number of states, including North Korea and Iran, have active nuclear programs. About a dozen nations have missile and biological weapons programs. Because of less demanding technical requirements, even more states have chemical weapons programs. Moreover, radical states and terrorist groups could purchase or steal some of the thousands of nuclear weapons that remain deployed in several former Soviet republics or hire former Soviet scientists. The combination of weapons of mass destruction and ballistic missiles is particularly dangerous because of the difficulty of defending against missile attacks.

In the past, threats of the type posed by weapons of mass destruction came from major industrial powers. Today, weapons of mass destruction give smaller states, and theoretically even terrorist groups, the potential to inflict enormous damage everywhere. In the near future, states with unconventional weapons could launch devastating attacks on U.S. armed forces abroad and on regional friends and allies.

Technology-generated or linked processes can vitiate economic progress, destabilize fragile new democracies and cause debilitating systemic crises. For example:

o    The rapid rise in the world's population, caused directly by our capacity to save life, strains educational and social infrastructures and in extreme cases can contribute to humanitarian crises. Growing fuel and food consumption strains the carrying capacity of many nations, and contributes to periodic famines and endemic dietary insufficiencies, poor health and low productivity.

o    Recent mass migrations pose demands on governments and international relief organizations. There were an estimated 19 million refugees worldwide before Rwanda. Haitians and Chinese on overcrowded boats and ships have illegally sought entry for employment in this country. Refugees in Southeast Asia, Burundi, Somalia and elsewhere in Africa reflect and add to instability in those regions. Several million Eastern European peoples have left the Balkans and the Caucasus for West Europe.

o    Cocaine and heroin destroy the lives of users and innocent victims, with huge attendant economic and social costs. Narcotics production and trafficking corrupt societies and distort economies throughout the world, multiplying the dangers of international terrorism and crime.

o    The apparent ideological clarity of the cold war, with its defining criteria of communist, anti-communist and even anti-anti-communist, has given way to a fragmentation of localisms. At a time when computers, faxes, fiber optic cables and satellites all speed the flow of information across frontiers, the information itself is increasingly lacking unifying characteristics that impart meaning. Both doctors and terrorists can now share their technical secrets more quickly. Both pro-democracy activists and promoters of ethnic cleansing can more broadly spread their views.


## II.  Nostalgia is inappropriate

Our frustration with today's conflicted world should not lead us to rewrite history. Cold War stability came at the price of an overhanging nuclear nightmare and deprivations suffered by those living under Communism.  Moreover, even the Cold War witnessed massive bloodletting, famine and refugee flows:  Cambodia's million dead rival Rwanda; Central American casualties and refugees surpassed Bosnia; China quietly slaughtered untold numbers; Mozambique alone produced 1.3 million refugees.  Ethiopia, Angola, South Africa, Liberia, Sudan, Afghanistan, Iran-Iraq, Lebanon, not to mention Vietnam, all took their toll.

The period some now fondly recall as stable or orderly reveals our eurocentrism: success was averting war in Europe and among the great powers, often at the cost of proxy wars fought elsewhere.  Indeed, Bosnia horrifies today partly because it risks fracturing NATO and the Western alliance, the underpinnings of the long peace.

Violence is not new, but our ability to tolerate, justify and manipulate it has changed.  Proxy wars were justified in ways that found public support; slaughters in China, Cambodia, Ethiopia, Iran were dismissed as evidence of communist misrule or otherwise deficient systems fulfilling their doomed destinies beyond our control or concern.

Today's global issues involve a dynamic very different from that of containing communism.  Facing a military threat, order, hierarchy, centralized governments, strong militaries, secrecy, and strong economies and stable power elites acquired an importance that could be set aside only in extreme circumstances.  Promoting democracy involves new assumptions, players and prescriptions: decentralization, transparency, public accountability, civilian authority, reallocation of resources and shifting elites; in sum, the exhilaration and chaos of democracy.  The change may not be readily grasped or welcomed by all concerned -- but it is the essential message of the American revolution.

### III.  Longer Range Risks

Current U.S. relations with the larger powers -- Russia, Germany, China, Japan -- are essentially free of conflict (albeit not uniformly free of strain).  All of these powers currently desire cooperative relations with us and an active U.S. presence and role in their region.  The question is whether this condition will persist or whether difficulty in managing the post-Cold War transition, future changes within one of the powers, or changes in America's role abroad will, over time, introduce new sources of tension among the larger powers.

In Europe, the three key powers since 1914 have been
Germany, Russia and America, each of which has been up or down
at one time or another. Relations among them have varied from
alliance to enmity, with each having been on both sides with
each of the other two. Since WW II the U.S. has drawn Germany
into a tight alliance within NATO, supported the European
Community as an instrument to channel German economic and
political power and, under Presidents Bush and Clinton,
regarded Germany as our core Western ally, in name as well as
in fact. Our efforts since 1989 to draw the USSR (now Russia)
into the kind of binding ties we developed after WW II with
Germany have not yet had the time to bear fruit.

Sustaining these goals will depend on the perception that
America will continue to play the role of stabilizer. Should
this perception change -- should, for example, resource
considerations cause a drawdown well below the President's
100,000 U.S. troop level commitment, we could not dismiss the
possibility of more assertive Russian or German policies, or of
Russo-German competition in Eastern Europe should further
economic deterioration there again open a vaccuum. More
generally, a reduction of U.S. forces to what would be
perceived to be symbolic levels would have a wide range of
negative repercussions in economic and political as well as
security terms.

Contemporary Asia is marked by a profound economic
modernization (of great importance to the U.S.), potentially
secular political change in Japan and what may come to be seen
by the year 2000 as dynastic change in China. All this occurs
in the midst of the Korean nuclear crisis which may in turn be
the harbinger of a united and nuclear armed Korea. The opening
of free markets in India (with a middle class now approaching
100 million and a nuclear capability), the explosion of growth
in the ASEAN states and the re-emergence of Indochinese in the
world economy add to this mosaic of increasing international
weight.

For America the bottom line in Asia remains averting
hostile relations with China and Japan simultaneously. We want
to ensure that cooperation between them, or between China and
Russia is not at our expense. The same applies for a united
Korea, which could be inclined to swing between China and Japan
should the U.S. security guaranty be put in question. A
particular flashpoint could be Taiwan -- or even Hong Kong
should tough new Chinese leaders choose to play the transition
hard rather than by the treaty. The implications for our
overall economic and security interests in East Asia, as well
as domestic politics here, could be considerable.

This paper has not considered parts of the world (eg, the Mideast) which could intitiate developments that might skew the outcome or could become the object of competition between the U.S. and some of the sub-great powers. Nor does it do more than allude to the benefits of cooperation, above all in the economic realm or through new political institutions. However, there is an important relationship between economic and political developments: political tensions can undermine the vast potential for economic cooperation as readily as developing economic ties can mitigate political differences. Much will depend on our setting priorities and proceding with a broad strategic sense of U.S. goals in the world of the 1990s.

## IV. Policies for an Uncertain Future

Historians may well look back at our times as the opening chapter in a radically altered international system, where instantaneous communications and the globalization of trade and culture build both new possibilities for cooperation and new sources of conflict. Alternatively, the aspirations that many feel today for a new global order may prove as misplaced as the 1920's belief that war had been abolished.

There are many reasons to give ourselves a tentative pat on the back. So far we have avoided turning inward despite enormous popular pressures. Economically, we have maintained the post-WWII multilateral architecture for economic relations, and even strengthened it at key points (NAFTA, GATT), instead of retreating as so often in the past into economic as well as poltical isolationism.

With this architecture in place, we have a chance of incorporating the newly emerging great powers, China and Russia, as well as Eastern Europe and the former Soviet Union, into a common international system in which, over time, they may have a stake in the status quo. Despite the strains and reversals, as they struggle for economic reform and democratic pluralism, historians will see that we have set in place and kept in place the right architectural framework.

To consolidate this more optimistic outcome requires that we now also learn to channel the new forces as constructively as possible. Three possibilities can be identified, all linked to central themes of greater international integration and more effective institutions.

**To respond to the dispersal of power, enlarge democracy among nations.** Democratize the global system by broadening membership of the United Nations Security Council. Use policies of open regionalism to foster greater integration for small as well as large countries in globally compatible ways. Exploit regionalism as a building block for world order, drawing on the unique U.S. role as the only multi-regional player. Insist on greater burdensharing to strengthen international institutions and lay a foundation for mutually engaged cooperation.

**To respond to the weakening of central governments, nurture evolution within nation state structures, seeking to make them as open and democratic as possible.** Whether it is ethnic, religious, racial, political, economic or gender-based, violence (war) is diplomacy (compromise/change in the power structure) by other means. Time might be better spent on exploring and adapting/updating conflicted societies' own power allocating/conflict adjudicating systems than introducing our own.

**To respond to the destabilizing impacts of technology, engage ngo's and governments in common efforts to respond to global issues.** Accept that transnational or subnational institutions may serve popular needs and contribute to the creation of a more stable and peaceful world. Provide positive incentives to governments that make decisions compatible with our key objectives. (For example, decisions to forego nuclear weapons deserve active U.S. encouragement as in the agreement between Brazil and Argentina and South Africa's decision to abandon its nuclear program.)

If the world is to fulfill mankind's more hopeful future, the United States has a critical part to play, not only because we have unique military, economic and political assets, but equally important because collective action requires leadership.

In the world today, only the United States has the global interests to galvanize action which benefits not only the United States, but all states, but which each, acting out of its own narrow self-interest, is unlikely to undertake. It is not a question of the US playing global cop on the one hand, or ceding sovereignty and responsibility to international institutions on the other. Rather, international institutions and mechanisms can provide the fulcrum for leveraging our efforts, the consensus building structures and the burden-sharing mechanisms that are necessary for effective collective responses. Our leadership is essential to kick these mechanisms into gear. We will act alone when we must, but our leadership is most effective when we bring others with us.

DRAFTED FOR D
by S/P Staff

524

# APPENDIX THREE

SEPARATA

COMITÉ JURÍDICO INTERAMERICANO

**CURSO DE
DERECHO INTERNACIONAL**

**XXVIII
2001**

LUIGI EINAUDI

THE POLITICS OF THE UNITED STATES POLICY TOWARD
HUMAN RIGHTS

SECRETARÍA GENERAL

# THE POLITICS OF UNITED STATES POLICY TOWARD HUMAN RIGHTS

## LUIGI EINAUDI [*]

---

[*]    Assistant Secretary General of the Organization of American States.    Secretario General Adjunto de la Organización de Estados Americanos.

Muy buenos días y muchísimas gracias, Dr. Lagos. Reconozco la presencia de los distinguidos miembros del Comité Jurídico Interamericano en su Presidente y de mi gran amigo João Clemente Baena Soares.

When we get to discussion, I will be glad to take questions in whatever language each of you feels most comfortable. But I thought that I would speak in English now because I am going to speak about things I lived in English. I am not going to speak as the Assistant Secretary General of the OAS. Nor am I going to speak as somebody trained in the law. Indeed, my training even tended to question whether international law exists. At Harvard, Professor Stanley Hoffman, who taught international relations, denied that international law existed. He would have sided with Ambassador Baena yesterday in saying that power has a tendency to destroy law.

I found Baena's talk yesterday extremely stimulating. I agree with him absolutely that it is important to preserve utopia in one's thinking. I would even say that, for me, the struggle to do so has kept me intellectually alive. It is very hard, because as Baena said, utopia refers to the future. And it is hard because existence constantly contradicts utopia. Anyone who works in a government, as many of you do or will, will continually have to undertake or accept actions that contradict utopia. And that is why utopia is so important, because sometimes the only place you can keep it alive is within your own being. It is, of course, also important to keep it alive with the people with whom you work. If you cannot do that, then you really cannot inspire teamwork and movement, and jointness, because cooperation requires a common goal toward which to work.

When at the beginning I recognized some of the powerful people here today, I did not recognize them all. I did not recognize you, the participants. But I learned a long time ago that in any class, particularly any group that lasts for a while, it is the members of that group that count, not the professors. You will learn from each other and with each other in the years ahead, in ways that will be far more important than anything that we the professors can say or can try to teach you. I know one of you reasonably well, I had the pleasure of working for some years with Marcelo Biato, of Brazil. I have run into a few of you in other places and I hope I will do so again in the future. And I hope very much that you will all continue to stay in touch with each other and with the utopia of the OAS.

I liked two other things that Ambassador Baena said. One was the very specific point he made about translation and about how the word *liability* does not have, to his knowledge, an effective translation in Spanish or Portuguese, because it tends to be translated as *responsibility*. All of us with even the most minimal power to make distinctions understand that *liability* is a much more specific and narrow concept than *responsibility*, even if sometimes it is translated that way. While I am not a lawyer, my wife combines the law with prior scientific training and is a specialist in intellectual property. She observes that on commercial matters international law has progressed much further than in some of the more political fields in which I work. And I was interested that Baena yesterday commented that one of the problems that we face is the fragmentation of the sources of law. He too recognized the importance that international corporations have on the forging of law. The importance of this course and the importance of your future work are increased by the fact that, without doubt, we are dealing with a period in which we are seeing a progressive development of law. Those of us who deal with politics and diplomacy cannot afford to be left behind.

I do have one disagreement with Ambassador Baena: he spoke to you of the conflict between power and the law. I would prefer, particularly given what I have just said about my belief in the progressive development of the law, to think of conflict as being between power and utopia, or between power and the ideal, rather than between power and the law. Certainly, out of conflict gradually can begin to emerge elements of consensus of law, grounded sometimes, as Baena said, in international opinion.

My main subject today is the politics of United States policy on human rights. I am speaking on the understanding that this is a totally academic setting. I do not expect any of you, even if you have journalistic ties, to turn back into journalists and start quoting any of it. What I will say is very personal. But I am doing it because I thought that it would tell you something about the United States. When I was elected Assistant Secretary General of the OAS, I took great pride in telling my fellow United States citizens that I no longer worked just for them, that I only worked 1/34th of my time for them, and 1/34th of my time for every single other member State of the OAS. Even so, the United States carries enormous weight in the hemisphere. And one of the things I have learned is that many outsiders have difficulty understanding the internal tensions that often arise within the United State government.

My starting point is that there is no such thing as "the Americans". There are many Americans, many views, many different groups, and many different processes at work on any given issue. So today I will draw on my memory about how the human rights policies of the United States developed from the standpoint of somebody who worked inside the government throughout the past quarter of a century. Changes of government and of political party in the United States as elsewhere have always led to changes of political leaders. And unfortunately also sometimes to purges of senior career officials. For a variety of reasons, I was lucky - in politics luck is often more important than skill - I was lucky enough to be able to survive all of these changes from 1973 until my voluntary retirement in 1998. Only once was I asked to turn in my resignation. I did so and six months later they came to me embarrassed and told me that they had lost it, and that, please, I shouldn't write a new one. This proved to be the strangest way of saying "we've decided to keep you".

528

As Dr. Lagos said, I spent eight years on the policy planning staff of the Secretary of State, first with Henry Kissinger and then, at the end of my time in the Department, with Warren Christopher. The first was a Republican, the second a Democrat. In between I spent, in addition to my period as Ambassador to the OAS, twelve years as the Director of Policy Planning for Latin America.

I came to Washington In December of 1973. My wife and I drove across the country from Los Angeles with two of our four children. It was a few months after Kissinger had moved from the White House to the State Department as Secretary of State. It was a very difficult time, because in Nixon we had a wounded President in the White House and in Vietnam we had a bloody and hard to explain war. The self-confidence of the United States as a nation was eroding. In California, I had worked in Santa Monica at The RAND Corporation, which had been one of the creators of the computer world. On the other side of Los Angeles, in Anaheim, one of the early applications of computerization, Disneyland, was just beginning to carry animation to previously unimaginable heights. Yet at the same time that our civilization was producing Disneyland, it was killing its young in the fields of Vietnam. The basic psychological contradiction created the sense that we were becoming dehumanized by technology. Not too many people spoke about it quite that directly, but that was an important concern in the world into which I moved when I went to Washington. A government under siege from a people that did not understand why it was behaving the way it was behaving.

When I say a government under siege, I recall a small taste of the times. When Kissinger became Secretary of State, many around him felt that somehow it was up to them to save the Republic. We had a weakened Presidency and such internal confusion that the country somehow needed to find stability and direction. Into that United State equation the 1973 *coup* in Chile and its bloody sequel produced an extraordinary marriage of events affecting the center of political consciousness in both Latin America and the United States. Contrary to much of the talk of the time, what happened in September of 1973 in Chile came as a complete surprise to most of Washington. The United State government had had some involvements, some very unfortunate and repugnant involvements, in Chilean internal politics in 1970, attempting to block the accession to power of Salvador Allende. But they had failed, and by the time 1973 came along, Chile was not a big problem for Washington anymore. Of course when evidence of repression emerged for all to see, the Pinochet coup suddenly fitted exactly into what I just described to you as the Vietnam-Disneyland syndrome. Somehow United States politics and United States policies had become dehumanized. They had become computerized and the human being had been left out.

The public reaction came, as it often does in the United States, through Congress. Until Nixon left office, the Kissinger team had managed to be somewhat above the immediate partisan battle. But under Ford suddenly Kissinger became known as the President for Foreign Affairs, and it hurt both of them. It was one of the reasons why Jimmy Carter won; there was a sense in the country that it was time to make a clean break.

For those of us in government, these were very difficult years. We were constantly fighting a rearguard battle against rising pressures in Congress against our various policies. The rebellion of Congress against the Executive branch is not easily understood in Latin America, where Congresses generally do not have the power that they do in the United States. In the mid-seventies under Ford and by the time Carter came to power, Congressional committees had hired so much staff that it sometimes seemed they had as many staff members as the Executive did. The State Department would go and they would find themselves confronted by Congressional staff working for the Foreign Relations Committees in the House and Senate who knew as much about foreign policy problems and foreign conditions as did the experts from the Executive Branch. Frequently the competition led to distrust. This breakdown of trust is very important not just on human rights, it has been important across the board. I used to tell my American colleagues who had chosen diplomacy as their life work, that they had chosen the most difficult of professions. They would be ground down between American nationalism and the foreign nationalisms with which they would come into contact. Because every time they would attempt to defend foreign realities in the American reality, they would not be believed, they would lose their credibility. By the late 1970s, there were probably about 100 reports which the Executive Branch was required to present to the Congress to explain and justify its policies. And the underlying premise behind all these reports was "you people in government are not to be trusted, you people in government are liars, you people in government are traitors to the national interest". The Hickenlooper amendment assumed that the State Department would not defend the rights of American corporations when they were expropriated abroad, and therefore mandated cutting off economic assistance unless satisfactory compensation was paid. The Pelly amendment did the same on fishing disputes. More recently, the same dynamic of distrust in the Congress toward the United State Executive Branch, produced the law requiring certification of countries for cooperation in anti-narcotics activity. In each of these examples and many more, the common if implicit assumption was that the Executive had to be kept honest through pressure from Congress.

In 1976, as President Ford was ending his term, the Congress adopted the first reporting requirements on human rights. The Department of State was to prepare reports on human rights conditions in all countries receiving United States assistance. The United States labels most normal international intercourse among States to which the United States makes a financial contribution as "foreign aid". This is true even when the activity is clearly assisting the United States as much as the foreign recipient. I have been arguing against this practice for 30 years without success. Many types of cooperation are required for reasonable relations among States, and if you do not have them, or if you suspend them, you create distrust, disappointment, even havoc. However, under the normal definition of aid, everybody received aid, and therefore everybody was subject to a human rights report. I had the dubious honor of actually losing my Christmas and New Year's holidays of 1976-77 to supervise and in some cases personally write the entire first series of reports on Latin American countries. I did this because I believed in utopia. I believed in human rights defined as the rights of individuals and private citizens. At the same time, I believed in the State system, in sovereignty, in attacking problems in their different national settings. That first set of human rights reports, sent to Congress in early 1977 by Jimmy Carter, had actually been written under Gerald Ford by career people, and reflected a conscious attempt to report on human rights conditions in the context of the State in question -- its jurisprudence, its sovereignty, its development.

Many of you will remember the shock waves that followed after the Carter Administration assumed office and placed human rights at the center of United States policy. Carter implemented what previous administrations had talked about, but without much political will, that is, human rights, a new treaty for the Panama Canal, etc. The immediate shock of the Carter presidency was the cut-off of all aid to Argentina, Brazil, Uruguay. Then-Vice President Mondale criticized Brazil's nuclear program and threatened retaliation. These acts resulted directly from the change of government. They were not consulted within the permanent bureaucracy. In fact, one of the first reforms at the State Department was the creation of a new Bureau dedicated to Human Rights Affairs, which came to be known as HA. To head it was appointed a very bright and very single-minded lady named Pat Derian. Under Derian, HA suddenly became the center for United State policy towards Latin America, virtually displacing the Bureau of Inter-American Affairs, known as ARA in those days. In recent years we have seen a similar development in the rise of counter-narcotics as a central concern, with the accompanying tension between the Inter-American Bureau and the Bureau of Anti-Narcotics Affairs.

In their first flush of victory, the Carter people saw themselves as re-humanizing American policy, they were going to end all of this Kissinger right wing military fascist business and they were going to do things right. In an act that is still unique to this day, no other American administration since has ever dared do it - the Carter Administration sent the American Convention on Human Rights to the Senate for ratification. The Carter people were doing something fundamental to regional relations. They were saying that the United States would bind itself to the rules of regional international law on human rights. The Senate refused to ratify. No other American administration has proposed ratification since then. But during the Carter Administration, when the United States realized that there were a number of countries that had not yet acted on the convention, particularly in the English speaking Caribbean, Andrew Young, at the time the United State Ambassador to the United Nations, was even dispatched to seek Caribbean ratification.

The emergence of revolution and counterrevolution in Central America provoked sharp polarizations over human rights. On one occasion the military regime in El Salvador headed by General Romero asked for assistance on human rights. The HA reaction was straightforward. "These people are a bunch of criminals", and you do not advise criminals. The view left little room for compromise. Over time, it created a substantial backlash. Kissinger was one of the first to denounce this approach to human rights. He said simply that this was the unleashing of a principle that would have unforeseen consequences and create instability. A great many American conservatives agreed. At the Republican Presidential Convention, one of the most famous speeches in American political history was made by Jeanne Kirkpatrick on the theme of "Blame America First." Her contention was that the Carter people behaved as if human rights violations were always the fault of the United States and its activities abroad.

The mounting conservative criticisms of the new United States approach to human rights worried me. Serving as something of an intermediary between the political level and the bureaucracy, I found myself spending more time serving as an interpreter within the American government, unable to meet the even greater need for interpretation between the American government and foreign governments. I saw the Reagan counterreaction coming. A bureaucrat normally has to stay within channels, and not appear publicly. I was given a chance to give a speech by one of the international political party organizations supported by the Konrad Adenauer Stiftung. In that speech I argued that the traditional order in Central America was breaking down because it had proved too rigid to withstand economic growth and the accompanying demands for political participation. The issue was not whether to change or not to change, but how to change. Without change, the result would be chaos, explosion, anarchy. Change was inevitable. Let us accept, I argued, that human rights are not an aberration in the minds of crazy left-wing idealists, but fundamental social rule of general utility, no more radical than the predictability in law that corporations demand and that most conservative thinkers accept as being the basis of progress.

The first people to attack me were the Sandinistas. One of the Nine explained that I had revealed that the United States would never be a revolutionary power. Well, that did not surprise me very much, but certainly I fared little better with the Conservatives. By the time Reagan won election, American conservatives felt that it was time to really completely clean house and reverse course. I was not present at the meeting, but I was told that at the highest levels of the White House, the instruction was given to the State Department to "reverse" policy in Central America. You will remember Kirkpatrick had articulated the intellectual justification: her distinction between totalitarian and dictatorial regimes. Totalitarian regimes were seen as permanent and therefore evil to be fought at all costs. Dictatorships were seen as transitory and therefore acceptable in certain circumstances.

This period was an extraordinarily difficult one. In the Carter years, it was difficult to keep alive the idea of the State as distinct from the people, the idea that the right need not always be condemned or that as I said to my detriment at the time to a New York Times correspondent, even right wingers have rights. In the Reagan years, it was just as difficult to keep a balance in the other direction, to argue for example that the left had its rights. Arguments became so heated that gradually the internal planning mechanism within the foreign affairs community, the NSC inter-agency system, was affected. Meetings became less frequent and coherent, because people would fight. The regular Inter-Agency Group, which had functioned well under Nixon, was under Reagan often replaced by the RIG, the Restricted Inter-Agency Group, where only three or four officials would meet to decide policy.

But policy is not something that can be set on specific cases alone. Policy, if it is to work, has to follow principles and be communicable as rules to those affected by it. Again, the importance of utopia. There has to be some guideline, some direction. Given the intensity of the battle between left and right, in Washington and in the field, it is remarkable that human rights concerns survived to become a permanent component of United States policy. A number of individuals made critical contributions.

One of the most important was Jimmy Carter's first Assistant Secretary for Inter-American Affairs, Terence A. Todman. Todman was a career diplomat from the U.S. Virgin Islands who served with distinction as US Ambassador on three continents through more than two decades. Todman carried in his very being the righteous knowledge that as a black man in America, his whole life had been a battle for dignity and human rights. As head of ARA, he came under constant pressure from Pat Derian in HA, who was frequently supported by Bob Pastor at the NSC. Caught up between their liberal political correctness and his own sense of gradualism, Todman did not last one year. But he decided to resign in flames, and it was really very interesting. He and I fought like cats and dogs. My job was to be the writer. He, of course, was the boss. He was saying everything that was wrong with the Carter Administration's approach to human rights. "They shall not condemn an entire nation for the behaviour of one of its officials" he would thunder. I kept saying "Look, you may be gone but I will survive and I want to make this policy last and you therefore have to formulate a sensible set of objections and provide alternatives that will work". "No, I do not want to say this!" We fought through a dozen drafts and finally laughed and ended it. We had come up with a list of negative rules. We had fought so much we both forgot to count how many rules there were. It turned out there were ten. Todman's 10 no's: they shall not do this. Todman's Ten Commandments. The speech immediately became a "*cause célèbre*" and forced Todman's replacement and transfer to Spain as Ambassador. But it left a legacy of necessary restraint on the liberal approach to human rights.

An equivalent restraint on the conservative approach was provided by a subsequent Assistant Secretary, this one under Ronald Reagan. Thomas Ostrom Enders was, like Todman, a career diplomat. We used to call him "too tall Tom" because of his size. Enders was as intelligent as he was tall. Enders took orders from no one. In El Salvador where Soviet bloc support was flowing to rebel forces, there was a war to fight. When you fight a war it is easy to forget about rules. First you fight then after you have won you clean up. That was known in Washington as the Argentine solution and some argued internally that we should simply ignore democracy building in El Salvador. That is where Enders fought his battle. He said "No, we are going to continue to support elections in El Salvador", "no, we are not going to reverse the agrarian reform." Conservatives had strongly criticized the Carter Administration for "betrayal of alliances." The Republican utopia was "You shall be loyal, you shall be consistent, you shall not abandon your friends". So we argued with the White House that having begun to forge new democratic alliances, we should be loyal and consistent. We succeeded and were able to continue to work to build a political center that could reach beyond the violence.

Henry Kissinger, who had earlier led the criticism of the human rights policy, ultimately became an instrument for saving it. By the mid-1980s, the war in Central America had become increasingly partisan and bitter. The Administration did what often is done under such circumstances, it created a bi-partisan commission to define a more acceptable course for policy on Central America. Kissinger was named chairman. Many practical issues had to be fought over: economic versus amount of military aid, use of U.S. forces, negotiations, government organization, practical day-to-day governance matters. In the end, the Kissinger report also addressed a matter of principle, asserting that the days when dictatorships could be guarantors of stability in Latin America are gone and that democracy is the only viable path to stability. Thus was the Enders contribution confirmed. The fighting continued, and with it some activities that were not conducive to progress on human rights, but the foundations of policy were set.

When George H.W. Bush came to office the operating tensions were still there. Their resolution was due as much to United States domestic concerns as to events in Central America. If it could be said that the Reagan administration destroyed the Soviet empire by making it spend more than it could afford, it could also be argued that U.S. policy in Central America was affected by U.S. taxpayers who no longer believed that it was worth raising money for Central America in the name of anti-communism. Moreover, the internal struggles in Central America were beginning to affect the United States. In the barrios of Los Angeles, Nicaraguans and other Central Americans were mobilizing to fight on both sides. Distrust was beginning to poison domestic politics beyond Central America.

It is to the eternal credits of George Bush Sr. that he was smart enough to choose Jim Baker as the Secretary of State and Jim Baker was smart enough to go look for a Democrat, (a real one, with good Democratic Party credentials, not a fake Democrat) in Bernard Aronson to be the Assistant Secretary for Latin America. Baker and Aronson injected a multilateral and democratic commitment into the strategy that was ultimately the basis of the end of the strife. Human rights were no longer a divisive issue. Support for human rights had become as acceptable on the right as it was on the left.

The United States, however, still lacked a coherent policy with regard to the inter-American system of human rights. When I became Ambassador to the

OAS, one of my priorities was to make the United States part of the general system of legal obligation that is the core of the Inter-American System. In 1992, I succeeded in negotiating the "Acuerdo Sede", the Headquarters Agreement for the OAS, so that the OAS was actually legally recognized as existing and with privileges in Washington, D.C. When the Senate ratified the Agreement in 1994, It was the first time since the 1950s that the United States had ratified a Headquarters Agreement for an international organization.

But I failed on the American Convention on Human Rights. Provisions concerning the death penalty, the inception of life, and federalism, among others, created an impassable barrier. But so did an unwillingness to engage seriously. A State Department lawyer once said to me "the American Convention was meant to apply to South American Indians, not to American Eskimos". I find that an extraordinary expression, and one of the crudest forms I have ever heard of American exceptionalism. To understand the United States, it is important to keep in mind that the feeling that the United States is unique, incomparable, and thus not subject to the same rules as others can emerge at the most unexpected moments .

When Clinton came to office, I thought that perhaps we would be able to push for Senate ratification of the Convention. I even put it in my farewell to the OAS Permanent Council, because I had by then had positive contacts about it with the Clinton transition team and with my successor, Ambassador Babbitt. Nothing happened.

American exceptionalism is a very important concern. As a United State citizen in dealing with my own country, I see it as my most difficult problem. The engagement of the United States on human rights and democracy in the hemisphere suffers from exceptionalism and the refusal to ratify the American Convention. By not accepting multilateral jurisdiction on human rights matters, the United States weakens its own example, and that is most unfortunate for the country most others take as their example on human rights and democracy.

# APPENDIX FOUR

*On Public Service*
Exeter Assembly Remarks
Luigi R. Einaudi '53
May 9, 2006

Principal Tingley, thank you. Students, faculty, friends. My wife Carol and I are very happy to be here. This Academy was a key force in my life.

I came to Exeter as a Lower Middler and graduated in 1953 after three formative years. Thirty-six years later, as a newly confirmed Ambassador, I met the President who had nominated me at a White House reception. As we shook hands, the first thing I said to him was "I am delighted, Sir, to finally meet the enemy." George Herbert Walker Bush, the father of our current President, was taken aback (I am not sure that any President of the United States had been greeted quite that way in a perfectly friendly setting). So I explained: "You went to Andover. I am an Exeter man. You are the enemy." He laughed. I laughed. And we agreed to work together for the common good.

And that is what I want to talk with you about today: Public service for the common good. I was deeply honored when Bill

Dakin, the President of our Class of 1953, and the members of our Visitors Program Committee, asked me to come before you to suggest that public service has real merits and rewards, even in a world that is less than the Utopia we would wish it to be.

As I am speaking at Exeter, I can invoke NON SIBI as a Utopia all of us in this Academy can understand. [Our Academy motto] NON SIBI does not mean selfless in the sense of denial of self; rather, it means working beyond your self with others, in society and in the world, for the common good. That is what I would call a genuine Utopia, a goal that is not always attainable, but a goal so constantly present and so powerful that it can serve as an organizing beacon for our lives.

I was chosen to visit with you because I had a successful diplomatic career. I do not know what you know or think about diplomats. So let me start with a straw man. It is often said that diplomats are persons who are paid to lie for their country. Let me tell you that that statement exemplifies one of the most corrosive aspects of public life: cynicism. The truth about serious diplomats is rather the opposite: a good diplomat is a person who knows how to advance his or her country's interests without lying. Every lie is a failure. A liar loses credibility and respect. And without respect and credibility he or she will not be able to do the job. So my first point is:

**Fight Cynicism**: Cynicism is a recipe for failure and inaction. Exeter is such a unique haven that when you leave it will be hard not to be cynical about something, even if it is only the claim that whatever college you next attend is "the best." The problem is that cynicism is the enemy of progress, both personally and for the community at large. I came to Washington as a public servant during Watergate. I was proud to have been asked by Henry Kissinger to serve on his Policy Planning Staff. I was proud to have become a bureaucrat. Bureaucracy emerged with the birth of the nation state and the specialization of functions in organized society. Good government is impossible without a good bureaucracy. Yet every President elected since Richard Nixon has run for office against the "bureaucrats in Washington." To put it bluntly, politicians have discovered they can get votes by equating civil servants with wasteful dundering idiots. Don't expect to get a lot of recognition, even if you are working for Utopia.

So here is my second point:

**Accept Reality, but uphold Utopia:** Sometimes life is trench warfare in freezing mud. Sometimes it is simply boring. Too often cynicism seems a prudent response forced upon us by promises not kept, the incompetence of others, our own failings, or similar harsh realities. Keep your head up. Develop your inner compass. It does help to think beyond yourself; it is not easy to survive without a Utopia for which to strive.

My third point is

**Learn to listen and never underestimate others**. Never forget that in every audience, in every situation, there will be some who will be ahead of you, just as there will be some who will need your help. Respect all of them and respect their interests. Benito Juárez said *La paz es el respeto al derecho ajeno.* Peace is respect for the rights of others. My favorite extrapolation of that concept is: *Democracy among nations is as important as democracy within nations.* Small countries have the same rights under the law as big ones. These caveats are particularly important for the United States, the world's only superpower. Fearing our displeasure, and assuming that our power and resources mean we know what is going on, foreign leaders often keep silent. Beware of silence and do not assume it implies agreement. Agreements that do not advance the interests of all concerned will not be well implemented, and will not last.

My next point is

**Rules matter.** Your mind is an inherently revolutionary instrument, but imagine your computer without default settings! Descartes wrote that when you are thinking about a particular problem, you must accept the conventional wisdom on all other matters. Only then can you keep your mind clear to concentrate. In societal matters, whether domestic or foreign, the rules are codified in the law. Only under the law can you work, produce, save and invest effectively. If you want to change the rules, you must learn to make rules, to influence government or to participate in public service. The United States is too developed and too big for guerrilla warfare.

Let me open a topical parenthesis. One of the biggest reasons immigration has become such an emotional problem in the United States today is that there are no enforceable rules. The greatness of the United States is closely tied to the fact that the US has been the country that has best realized a Utopia consisting of a rule of law that accepts the rights of ALL individuals. The US has been energizer of the world's exploding democratic revolution, realizing to an unprecedented extent equality of opportunity regardless of gender, race, class, religion or nationality.

My generation – the class of '53 and a few privileged others -- were part of the great explosion and healing of the US civil rights movement that helped affirm the rights of American blacks.

Henceforth they were CIVI (as our teacher would have boomed in Latin class at Exeter), citizens entitled (as the black historian Roger Wilkins once put it) to "exert relentless energy to hold up [their] end."

For some years now the sheer mass of uncontrolled migration from across our southern land borders has brought us countless men and women who daily exert relentless energies to better themselves in ways impossible in their countries of origin. We are individually and economically the better for it, but the sheer mass is bringing growing controversy.

To say that our civilization is at threat misses the point. THEY are now part of US. Lashing out and repeating the mass expulsions of Mexicans in the 1930s will uselessly compound the pain. In any case, Mexico and countries in Central America and the Caribbean already receive repatriation flights daily -- with effects that are strategically ineffective, locally destabilizing and regionally dispiriting.

What is needed is a return to the spirit of equality before the law that made America great. We need immigrants. But we do not need shadow communities that live in the dark, at the margin of the law. To regain control in a way that is worthy of our civilization, we need a law that will shape an open system, with dignity and responsibility for all. We need internationally enforced controls defining guest-worker rights, requirements for citizenship, and national security.

My fifth point is that

**Theories that do not fit the facts cannot explain them**. The days of the *Encyclopédie Française,* when knowledge was so limited serious people could attempt to publish all that was known in a single set of volumes, are over. Now less than ever can education be just a matter of rote learning. Today education is a process of stretching the mind so you can learn to think, find facts and fit them together to find meaning. The trouble starts when we are lazy and accept shortcuts to help us give meaning to a complicated world. When I was growing up, the shortcut was "communism." Today it is "terrorism." Tomorrow it may be "global warming." We must resist allowing symbols like these to become a substitute for thought. And in the long run, they lose their value even as political rallying cries.

**Learn to write.** A leader must know how to communicate. Speaking matters. But writing is the discipline that brings clarity and influence to speaking. I remember when I was a student at Exeter being repelled at the thought that then President Eisenhower read nothing longer than one page. Twenty years later, I had become a specialist at putting what mattered for decisions into a one page decision memorandum. I think it was at Exeter that I learned that Napoleon was reputed to have said that *Armies travel on their Stomachs*. Well, if armies travel on their stomachs, then I would say *Bureaucracies travel on paper*. And papers carry words. Most people do not know how to write. If you write well, you will stand out.

**You will have to decide.** If you become a leader or a senior official to whom people look to for guidance, and with a duty to provide it, all the precedents, instructions and field manuals in the world will never cover every situation you will encounter. Yet you will have to decide how to act. And you will never have precisely the information you will need to cover all aspects of your decision. Many times you will know so little it will be like trying to find a light in the dark in a strange room. Sometimes, rarely, you will have too much information. A great study once demonstrated that the US government had information about the impending Japanese attack on Pearl Harbor, but could not pick it out of what the analyst called "static." So, most of the time you will starve for information, and the rest of the time you will have to pick through the static. But always you will have to decide. Fifty-four years ago, in English class at Exeter, I learned that without free will Buridan's Ass would have starved, unable to choose between the two buckets of oats set before him in perfect symmetry. Look at each other. Look at the persons sitting next to you. You are each other's base. Staying in touch with your friends, parents, siblings, the family you will create, your neighbors, that is what will enable you to know what to decide. It will even enable you to fight for your utopia and be a good bureaucrat at the same time. In the State Department, Ambassadors had a formula for it: The UNODIR cable. UNless Otherwise DIRected, I will do/say the following.

Finally, to conclude:

Act *sub specie aeternitatis,* act in the light of eternity. Think of how what you do or say will look like to you and others ten or fifteen years from now (not quite eternity, but long enough). Think of tomorrow, not just today. Yours will be a career, not a job. Think of others, not just yourself. Act with dignity and respect, and never forget your Utopia.

# APPENDIX FIVE

*MULTILATERALISM MATTERS*
Luigi R. Einaudi

This essay, published initially in *Recollections and Reflections*, A book of Essays for the 60ᵗʰ Reunion of the Harvard College Class of 1957 and reprinted here with permission, is based on my remarks accepting the *2016 William J. Perry Award for Excellence in Security and Defense Education* at a ceremony held at Fort McNair, Washington, D.C. on January 12, 2017. Sponsored by the Center for Hemispheric Defense Studies, the award ceremony symbolized State-Defense cooperation by including Ambassador Thomas A. Shannon, Undersecretary of State for Political Affairs, and was attended by some 200 persons, including some 40 U.S. and foreign ambassadors and flag officers.

\* \* \*

I am proud to accept this award. I met Bill Perry when he was Secretary of Defense, and have just finished reading what he calls *his "selective memoir."*[7] With a forward by my old boss George Shultz, Perry writes how honored he was to have this Center named

---

[7] William J. Perry, *My Journey at the Nuclear Brink* (Stanford, CA, Stanford University Press, 2015).

for him, and makes a passionate plea to *eliminate nuclear weapons before they eliminate us.*[8] It is a good read, and I recommend it.

My values have been shaped by a belief in Western civilization. That bold phrase *Civis romanus sum* (I am a Roman citizen) is its cornerstone. I was born in the United States and am a citizen of the United States alone. But I believe the rights and obligations of citizenship that began in Rome are at the heart of mankind's progress.

## Diplomacy *Today and Tomorrow – The OAS Example*

I would like to share some thoughts about where we are now and what may lie ahead.

The last twenty years or so have been hard on the ***international order***. So much so that *disorder* increasingly seems a better description.

> The current *Foreign Affairs* asks whether the situation should simply be seen as *"Out of Order."*[9] Governing has become harder and more complicated. Citizen demands for a better life have grown, but disparities in power and cultural differences have not been erased; in some cases, they have sharpened.
>
> World War II ended with winners and losers; the Cold War had blocs and anti-blocs; in contrast, with what has been called the *"end of ideology,"*

---

[8] Perry's website, www.wjperryproject.org, is co-sponsored by the Nuclear Threat Initiative.

[9] *Foreign Affairs*, Volume 96, Number 1, January/February 2017.

shared reference points and perspectives are fewer than ever.

These conditions hamper international understanding and disrupt long-held concepts. My professional career has focused on United States relations with countries in the Western Hemisphere. In my service on the Policy Planning Staff for Secretaries of State from two different parties, I always tried to see our neighbors in the Americas a global context.

In that spirit, I will use the **Organization of American States**, the world's oldest regional organization, to *exemplify the difficulties of today's international scene.*

The OAS is a multilateral organization of the sovereign states of the Western Hemisphere. This simple definition combines *three concepts.*

- *Multilateralism*, based on "generalized principles of conduct" – the creation of predictable universal rules rather than a temporary coalition of a few countries on a specific problem.
- *Sovereignty*, the sovereign equality of states, the organizing principle of the international system since the 1648 Peace of Westphalia.
- *Geography*, as in the proposition that "the peoples of this Hemisphere stand in a special relationship to one another which sets them apart from the rest of the world."

Today, these three concepts are all operationally challenged.

**Multilateralism** is associated with inefficiency more than order. International law has been weakened by repeated failures to ratify treaties or abide by their obligations. A cynic might argue that *multilateralism is now just an idealistic illusion in an increasingly Hobbesian world.*

***Sovereignty*** has long meant that individual states are inviolate from outside intervention and free to decide whether or not to participate in any particular activity. The problem is that our times *require* cooperation. Cyberspace, illegal drugs, weapons from small arms to drones and nukes, migration, terrorism, disease, climate and most economic activity cannot be dealt with by any one state acting alone. Does this mean *sovereignty is obsolete?*

Finally, in the age of the jet and the internet, ***does geography still matter?*** Twenty years ago, a senior administration official told me flatly that geography was no longer relevant to foreign policy.

My colleagues at the Perry Center and the National Defense University are among those who know better. *War is intimately related to sovereignty, geography and even multilateralism.*

The *League of Nations* was created to end war but had no military authority.

The *United Nations Charter* authorized the use of force in Chapter VII.

The *OAS Charter* purposely conveyed no coercive authority.

These formulas are all incomplete. *Neither force nor diplomacy can work alone.* What is needed, of course, is to *integrate* the various elements of power.

> You can't say *"We'll deal with this militarily, or just economically, or just diplomatically."*

> You can't say *"We'll deal with this multilaterally, that bilaterally, and this unilaterally."*

Major problems require the application in some form of *all elements of power, civil and military, hard and soft, multilateral, bilateral and unilateral.*

### Integrating Power

Trying to integrate power by making the inter-agency system work is how I survived in Washington.[10] My mentors at the State Department all served on the National Security Council.[11] One of them conditioned his acceptance of becoming Assistant Secretary on also chairing the NSC Inter-Departmental Group, then promptly appointed me its Executive Secretary. Years later, in 1995, when I was asked to represent the United States in the effort to end fighting between Ecuador and Peru, I did the same thing so as to have the authority to team with U.S. Southern Command.[12]

In a dispute that went back to colonial times, five thousand Special Forces soldiers from the two countries had become entangled in mountainous jungle terrain. To prevent escalation, Brazil,

---

[10] Although I served in the State Department under 6 presidents, 9 secretaries of state and 12 assistant secretaries, I was never a career officer, thus always vulnerable to being replaced at the will of whoever had command authority.

[11] Viron Peter Vaky, William G. Bowdler, and Samuel W. Lewis.

[12] Then headed by General Barry McCaffrey, who proved an invaluable ally.

Argentina, Chile and the United States – all guarantors of an earlier treaty -- contributed soldiers to a military observation mission, known as *MOMEP*, to separate forces and give diplomacy a chance.

My counterparts from the *guarantor countries*, all of us senior diplomats, and I would share intelligence, listen to each other's views and meet until we hammered out a course our governments could all support. We approached things from different perspectives and different interests. But the give and take was mutual. Often our *guarantor meetings* led to a course different from anything any one of us had started with.

> One example was our decision to invite Peru and Ecuador to send soldiers to join the observation mission, a potentially risky move, but one designed to build confidence between the antagonists and demonstrate our position as honest brokers.

> Another was our decision to ask our four guarantor presidents to consult and reach a joint decision on issues the two parties felt they could not resolve themselves.

Whenever innovations like these took place, interagency coordination was key to keeping Washington (and of course the other capitals) in sync as well. Sometimes I felt as though I was dealing with two wars, one abroad, and the other here at home.

> The NSC had initially authorized the military deployment for a maximum of 90 days, fearing that

any U.S. military casualties in the Amazon would lead to a political backlash at home.[13]

Others feared MOMEP would drag our forces into a Cyprus-like eternal deadlock. *Each 90-day extension had to be approved* – and each approval was won only because State and Defense kept on the same page.

The *peace agreements* ultimately *settled the land boundaries* at the origins of the conflict, but extended also to *river navigation, trade, parks, burial of casualties, human rights, and economic development.* It took almost four years, but we succeeded where few believed we could.

The peace between Ecuador and Peru has now lasted almost a generation.[14] It resolved the last active territorial conflict on the South American mainland and removed the arms race contagion in the region. *Conventional war among states in the Americas today is almost unthinkable.*

## Security

In this lower threat environment, collective security obligations have given way to a concept championed initially by the countries of the

---

[13] Not incidentally, the loss of U.S. soldiers and a Blackhawk in Somalia had taken place just a year before.

[14] Readers wishing more on this conflict, known also as the Cenepa War, may enjoy a lecture I gave at Cornell University in 2015: http://www.cornell.edu/video/ambassador-luigi-einaudi-peru-ecuador-war-impact/?utm_source=cornellcast_weekly_update&utm_medium=email&utm_campaign=5860

Commonwealth Caribbean[15] that security should be understood as *"multidimensional."* This approach expanded security concerns from traditional defense matters like weapons acquisitions and confidence building measures to trafficking in persons, drug abuse and the special security concerns of small island states.

Yet even with this more consensual approach, security and defense matters remain problematic. Uncertainty about military and police roles creates confusion. Asymmetries in power breed illusions and distrust. Tensions among neighbors still flare up. The end of the Cold War reduced but did not eliminate concerns about the activities of countries outside the hemisphere. The variety and complexity of contemporary security issues makes clear that no one policy fits all. Every country has tended to set its own course. Nothing is automatic.

## Principles of Diplomatic Strategy

So what should we do in the midst of this uncertainty? [16]

---

[15] CARICOM – the Caribbean Community -- brings together 15 states in the Caribbean Basin, geographically our near neighborhood quite as much as Canada and Mexico. CARICOM members are Antigua and Barbuda, Bahamas, Barbados, Belize, Dominica, Haiti, Jamaica, Grenada, Guyana, Montserrat, St. Lucia, Suriname, St. Kitts and Nevis, St. Vincent and the Grenadines, and Trinidad and Tobago. A majority are members of the British Commonwealth.

[16] I had a childhood lesson on dealing with disorder. In December 1944, when I was a boy, my grandfather returned to Italy from Swiss exile on an American Flying Fortress to help run post-war reconstruction, then became the first President under the new Republic that replaced the monarchy. Italy had come out of the war in economic free fall and intermittent civil war. There were few precedents or rules. My grandfather taught me that those in authority are always required to behave in ways that will show the way to a better order, and that this becomes critical in the midst of disorder. He called this *setting a good example,* and he thought it increased both moral authority and chances for survival.

### First, multilateral consultations should be part of any strategy.

Multilateralism was the core of the international order the United States led in creating after World War II. The United States today is more focused inward and faces competition from many quarters. The multilateral order has eroded, and U.S. participation has been reduced. Yet even when agreement is elusive, broad consultation can reduce confusion and set the stage for future cooperation.

> The excellent lead article in the *Foreign Affairs* issue cited earlier calls for a system of "Sovereign obligation" to deal with the world's growing common problems. I was amused, however, that the author suggests the United States consult only half a dozen "other major powers."[17] I was delighted to read that the powerful have obligations as well as rights. But in my experience, *democracy is as important among countries as within them*. If smaller countries do not receive respect, they are unlikely to be part of the solution. Democracy is as important among countries as within them.

Our Founding Fathers set a good example in our *Declaration of Independence*: *"a decent respect to the opinions of mankind"* requires that all be heard. Idealism quite aside, success is harder if you don't consult.

### Second, respect the law and support local institutions.

In the Peru-Ecuador conflict, the Rio Protocol authorized the guarantors only to "assist" the parties, not to decide. Peru and

---

[17] Richard Haass, "World Order 2.0, The case for Sovereign Obligation," *Foreign Affairs*, Volume 96, Number 1, January/February 2017, p. 9.

Ecuador had to agree; and a Terms of Reference had to be negotiated for the military observers. Once the rules were agreed, however, everything could be dealt with.

> Early on MOMEP helicopters maneuvering to find ways to separate the hostile intertwined forces found that they had been locked in upon by radar that could have targeted them for being shot down. Later, both parties at different moments secretly built up fresh forces near the conflict area. Both activities were in contravention of explicit agreements and when discovered were reversed.

Using the law gradually enabled the parties of peace within Peru and Ecuador to seize the initiative. A key dispute was resolved by a panel headed by the Chief Justice of Brazil's Supreme Court. That Chief Justice, Nelson Jobim, later became Brazil's Minister of Defense. Jobim received the Perry Award in 2011.

But just as the peace between Ecuador and Peru was proving the value of the law, the *United States Senate stopped ratifying key international treaties.*

> We have not ratified the global *Law of the Sea*, even after it was re-written to help meet U.S. objections.

> We have also not ratified *conventions* that advance U.S. regional interests in *human rights* or in fighting drugs by *controlling illegal firearms.*[18]

---

[18] The Inter-American Convention Against the Illicit Manufacturing of and Trafficking in Firearms, Ammunition, Explosives, and Other Related Materials, known as *CIFTA* after its Spanish acronym, is of particular significance. CIFTA is aimed at illegal transactions not at weapons. The NRA provided an advisor to the

Laws are obviously not self-enforcing, but they do provide agreed goals legitimating international cooperation. Sandra Day O'Connor summarized the consequences of U.S. absenteeism:

> "*The decision **not** to sign on to legal frameworks the rest of the world supports is central to the **decline in American influence in the world**.*"[19]

In 1991, OAS Resolution 1080 established common grounds for *action against interruptions of the democratic process*. But it also called for proposals and *incentives to support democracy*, a call that was never followed up with resources or specifics.

The current tragedy in Venezuela is due to failures in implementation by the member states, starting with Venezuela, rather than to a failure of multilateralism.

> The Inter-American Charter stipulates in Article 3 that the *"essential elements of representative democracy include, inter alia, respect for human rights and fundamental freedoms, access to and the exercise of*

---

US delegation negotiating the treaty on the basis of existing US laws, and explicitly recognizing US citizen rights.

The 1997 treaty was signed by President Clinton on a visit to Mexico, responding to an upsurge of weapons manufactured in China and transiting the US illegally to Mexican drug cartels.

In 2009, with the treaty still unratified, I organized a letter to the Senate Foreign Relations Committee seeking ratification of CIFTA that was signed by all Assistant Secretaries of State for the Western Hemisphere since 1976, all U.S. Ambassadors to the OAS since 1989, all Chairmen of the Inter-American Defense Board since 1989, and two thirds of US Southern Command Commanders since 1983.

At the Summit of the Americas in 2009 President Obama pledged to seek ratification. Thirty-one of thirty-four OAS member states have done so. The United States remains an absentee.

[19] Smart Power Commission Report, 2008.

*power in accordance with the rule of law, the holding of periodic, free, and fair elections based on secret balloting and universal suffrage as an expression of the sovereignty of the people, the pluralistic system of political parties and organizations, and the separation of powers and independence of the branches of government."[20]*

Despite the clarity of the language, specifics are still subject to interpretation and challenge. What is striking is that no serious independent multilateral effort has been made to reconcile differing interpretations or to seek ways to reward good performance.

Much the same principle should apply to other hot-button issues like *migration* and *trade*. Sovereign nations have the right to decide who and what enters and leaves their territory. A wall that channels people and goods to an entry/exit point at which clear rules are enforced is fine, but if the wall is breached or circumvented, or if there are no rules, even a beautiful wall becomes a Maginot line, impressive but ineffectual.

*The world needs laws and relationship-building, not walls or nation-building.* Lectures and barriers are less effective than relations built on respect and shared rules. Nothing will last unless all concerned feel at least some of their interests are being advanced.

Which brings me to my third and last point:

---

[20] Texts of regional agreements and treaties are available at http://www.oas.org.

### *Prepare professionals to cooperate across cultures.*

Even if interagency differences were all miraculously resolved here in the United States, we would still need to work efficiently with other countries.

*To reconcile different national interests requires knowledge.* Institutional ties maintained by a network of professionals who know how to work together can help contain issues that might otherwise escalate into conflict—in effect, a valuable insurance policy for progress and peace.

> Bill Perry understood this. As Secretary of Defense in the years after the fall of the Berlin wall, he supported the establishment of the *Marshall Center* in Germany to help military and civilian officials from both NATO and the Warsaw Pact learn to work together. And because he understood that geography matters, he then supported the creation of similar centers for other parts of the world.

The *Center for Hemispheric Defense Studies* or CHDS, now known simply as the Perry Center, has an *international faculty and students*, ties to countries and institutions large and small, and an annual fall program that examines U.S. security and defense structures and policy.

For years, the graduates of the *Inter-American Course in International Law* in Rio de Janeiro and of the *Inter-American Defense College* here at Fort McNair have had enviable records.

Between them, the OAS and the Perry Center are forging relationships and cadres of public servants who can help turn a difficult world to mutual advantage. They provide a unique foundation for a safe neighborhood.[21]

***And this brings me to a personnel recommendation.***

In this increasingly disorderly world, we in the United States might do well *to link cultural sensitivity and knowledge of how to make things work to eligibility for promotion.* In 1986, the Goldwater-Nichols Act established that to be eligible for promotion to General or Flag Officer, a military officer had to have both senior education and a completed a Joint Duty Tour. Stealing a page from Goldwater-Nichols, might *a tour in the UN, the OAS, the IMF, or some other international organization become a requirement for promotion to the Senior Executive Service and the Senior Foreign Service?*

## Summing Up

Times have changed, but some old truths still apply. *Geography* and *neighborhood* still matter. *Sovereignty* still matters. Yet in today's world, we can no longer retreat like Voltaire to cultivate our own garden. To take care of ourselves, we must also deal with the outside world, our neighbors perhaps most of all.

In international politics and security, there is no MapQuest to click for directions. There is just a lot of time consuming and necessarily inclusive hard work. It will not be easy.

The logo at the bottom of the Perry Center's crest -- ***Mens et Fides Mutua* (Mutual understanding and trust)** has guided the Center during twenty years of progress.

---

[21] John A. Cope (Colonel, USA, Ret), the founding Director of the Perry Center, and a colleague of mine at both State and NDU, nominated me for this award; his career has embodied the best in public service.

*It must continue.*

The intimate relationship between law, multilateralism and cooperation was symbolized in this **1992 Headquarters Agreement** signing giving the Organization of American States *(OAS)* legal status for the first time since its founding in 1948. Ambassador Luigi R. Einaudi *(left)*, Permanent Representative from the US to the OAS and Ambassador João Baena Soares of Brazil, Secretary General of the OAS, are shown signing the agreement at OAS headquarters[22] in Washington D.C. The Headquarters Agreement set forth the legal status of the OAS properties and employees in the US. *Photograph courtesy of the Columbus Memorial Library.*

---

[22] The OAS main building was built in 1908 for the OAS's predecessor institutions, the *International Union of American Republics* (1890) later changed to the *Pan American Union*. The OAS Charter was signed in 1948 at the *9th Inter-American Conference*, Bogota, Colombia.

# APPENDIX SIX

Pax Brasiliana? A Study of Brazil's Role in Constitutional and Political Crises in Latin America (1990-2015)

Pax Brasiliana? Um Estudo da Atuação Brasileira em Crises Constitucionais e Políticas na América Latina (1990-2015)

¿Pax Brasiliana? Un Estudio de la Actuación Brasileña en Crisis Constitucionales y Políticas en América Latina (1990-2015)

## Luigi R. Einaudi

### Interview, 2018

Luigi R. Einaudi was US ambassador to the OAS (1989-1993), US special envoy to the Peru-Ecuador peace talks (1995-1998) and secretary general of the OAS (2004-2005).

Luigi R. Einaudi foi o embaixador dos EUA na OEA (1989-1993), enviado especial dos EUA nas negociações de paz entre Peru e Equador (1995-1998) e secretário geral da OAS (2004-2005).

Luigi R. Einaudi fue el embajador de EEUU en la OEA (1989-1993), enviado especial de EEUU en las negociaciones de paz entre Perú y Ecuador (1995-1998) y secretario general de OAS (2004-2005).

To cite this interview:

## Luigi R. Einaudi

Luigi Roberto Einaudi was born in Cambridge, Massachusetts, in 1936. He received a Bachelor of Arts degree from Harvard (1957), was drafted into the United States Army, serving from 1957 to 1959, and later returned to Harvard for a Ph.D. (1966). He worked at the RAND Corporation in Santa Monica, California, where he led the institution's social science research on Latin America from 1963 to 1974.

He then joined the State Department, having served twice on the secretary of State's policy planning staff (1974-1977 and 1993-1997). Einaudi was also director of policy planning for the Bureau of Inter-American Affairs (1977-1989) and US ambassador to the Organization of American States (1989-1993).

From 1995 to 1998, Luigi Einaudi was the US Special Envoy in the peace talks that led to a comprehensive settlement of the long-lasting territorial and boundary conflict between Ecuador and Peru. He was widely considered a key mediator in the negotiation process.

In June, 2000, Dr. Einaudi was elected to a five-year term as assistant secretary general of the OAS. He proceeded to serve as acting secretary general upon the resignation of Secretary General Miguel Angel Rodríguez, from October 2004, to May 2005. During his time at the OAS, Einaudi was strongly involved in attempts to find solutions to the crisis in Haiti.

He moved on to be a distinguished visiting fellow at the Institute for National Strategic Studies at the National Defense University in Washington D.C. and a member of the Comitato Scientifico of the Fondazione Luigi Einaudi, in Turin, Italy.

Technical information

Interview type: thematic interview
Interviewer: Oliver Stuenkel
Research and script: Caio Simoneti, Oliver Stuenkel
Transcription: Ariane Costa
Editors: Caio Simoneti, Oliver Stuenkel
Location: Washington, D.C.
Date of interview: April 12, 2018
Date of final edition: December 6, 2018
Language: English
Duration: 01:43:40
Pages: 19

This interview was conducted as part of the project "Pax Brasiliana? A Study of Brazil's Role in Constitutional and Political Crises in Latin America (1990-2015)," developed by Oliver Stuenkel and funded by FAPESP and CNPq. This project aims to provide, through analysis and oral history interviews with main actors, a deeper understanding of several political and institutional crises occurred in Latin America since 1990, as well as the Brazilian connection and agency regarding each of them.

Keywords: Latin America, Peru, Ecuador, Brazil, United States, Argentina, Chile, Haiti, Jean-Bertrand Aristide, Alberto Fujimori, US-Latin America relations, political crisis, Cenepa War, Organization of American States, Inter-American Democratic Charter, Rio Group, Fernando Henrique Cardoso.

**Interview: April 12, 2018**

O.S. – Ambassador Einaudi, thank you so much for taking the time for this interview. I think that, in Brazil we sometimes tend to overestimate Brazil's influence was in certain historical events in Latin America. That's why, last year, we decided to focus on moments of diplomatic, constitutional and political crisis, because crises – the way we understand it – sometimes are moments when particular dynamics and power relations, become obvious. So it allows us to tell History based on the personal impressions and memories of those who engaged in it. Since then, we have selected a series of policymakers who could tell us their stories, which allows us to add important perspectives. Now, in your case, you have written a lot, you have given many talks, and I have listened to or read all of them, so I will ask questions that are based on what you have said, so you don't have to repeat yourself.

L.E. – You know, my State Department Oral History interview is still not finished because the person they sent to interview me, who was its founder and a very interesting gentleman, had never been to Latin America. So he was unable to ask me many relevant questions.

O.S. – That's fascinating. I think that says a lot, right? It reminds me of an oral history interview we conducted with [Brazilian diplomat and former secretary general of the Organization of American States] Baena Soares[1], and he said: "You know... this guy [Einaudi] understood us."

L.E. – Yes. The quote that is most interesting from this exact point point of view is that, many years after we were both out of the Government, I had an occasion to sit down and talk a little about the past with Bernard Aronson[2] – who was the assistant secretary of State under James Baker.[3] Aronson was a Democrat who was named to help us to get out of the Central America mess, and with whom I worked very closely on many things. He didn't like me very much, I think in part because people in Latin America liked me – he once said to me when he returned from a trip to the region, "I bring you greetings from 'boom boom' and 'boom' but I will never do that again."

O.S. – [Laughter].

L.E. – In any case, in another conversation, long after we were both out of government, he said: "You know, when I was talking to you, I never knew whether I was talking to one of us or one of them" [laughter].

O.S. – That is very interesting. This reminds me of a story that, back in the day, the Brazilian government feared that the Brazilian diplomats who went to France enjoyed Paris so much that they started to represent the interests of Paris rather than Brazil, so the Foreign Ministry supposedly shortened the period of time they spent in Paris. But in the case of the United States, I think, there is such a lack of people who understand Latin America, and these comments, seem to underestimate the strategic value of having somebody who is seen as an interlocutor.

---

[1] João Clemente Baena Soares was a Brazilian diplomat who served as secretary general to the OAS from 1984 to 1994. In 2014, professors Oliver Stuenkel and Marcos Tourinho conducted an oral history interview with Ambassador Baena Soares, which can be accessed through this link: http://www.fgv.br/cpdoc/acervo/historia-oral/entrevista-tematica/joao-clemente-baena-soares-ii

[2] Bernard Aronson was the United States assistant secretary of State for Inter-American Affairs from 1989 to 1993.

[3] James Baker served as US secretary of State from 1989 to 1992 under President George H. W. Bush. He was also White House chief of staff from 1981 to 1985 and from 1992 to 1993.

L.E. – That's right.

O.S. – But it also says a lot about priorities: perhaps mainstream Washington doesn't necessarily regard Latin America or somebody who understands Latin America as something that is so crucial to the overall foreign policy.

L.E. – But they understood that I did [understand Latin America] and therefore I had a lot of unofficial power for a very long time, because people understood that I understood. And most of the time the smart ones understood that they didn't understand. *That* enabled me to survive in spite of the fact that I was never a career diplomat, that I didn't come from the Foreign Service. I always had to survive the politics – that was very difficult during those years.

O.S. – Right. Ambassador, I would like to ask you about three episodes: the first is your time as ambassador to the OAS from 1989 to 1993; then, your role in the Peru-Ecuador peace talks in 1995 – you have given a tremendous amount of highly valuable information: I used, for example, your talk at Cornell in 2015[4] in my class. And the third episode is your time as assistant secretary and secretary general of the OAS from 2000 to 2005, and I'd like to talk about particular perceptions concerning how do you think dynamics have changed over those three periods. So, my first question is: how do you remember the time when you come to the OAS, in 1989? Which dynamics shaped the Americas at that moment?

L.E. – Something very unusual happened in the United States with the election of the first Bush,[5] who knew something about international affairs and was handed a situation in Central America out of the [Ronald] Reagan[6] administration that was simply unsustainable. So, what Bush did was to ask James Baker to fix it and he gave Baker a very broad freehand within I think only very general guidelines... I have a lot of regard for the first Bush. And Baker chose Aronson because he knew that he needed bipartisan support. The situation in Congress was simply out of control. He needed an active democrat with labor ties to be his assistant secretary for Latin America. And it was a very unusual situation in that Baker was absolutely Bush's man, so there was never any doubt that Baker spoke for Bush. And that put the State Department in a strong position, but that didn't guarantee anything. What happened next was that for the first time in recent times, the US built a first-class team for Latin America: we had Aronson, we had Carla Hills[7] as USTR [US trade representative]. And Carla Hills was somebody who I got to know and have a lot of respect for and her chief assistant for Latin America was a friend of mine – a Foreign Service officer, Myles Frechette,[8] who later was ambassador to Colombia among other things. So we had the USTR, we had State and we had in the Central American crisis something that assured attention and priority and even ambition. One of the interesting things looking at the people who worked on Central America, they tended to be the most ambitious and hungry people and none of them are now working on Central America –

---

[4] "The End of Conventional War in Latin America: The Peru-Ecuador War and Its Impact" – available at http://www.cornell.edu/video/ambassador-luigi-einaudi-peru-ecuador-war-impact.

[5] George Herbert Walker Bush was the 41st president of the United States, from 1989 to 1993.

[6] Ronald Wilson Reagan was governor of California from 1967 to 1975 and president of the United States from 1981 to 1989.

[7] Carla Anderson Hills is an American lawyer and public official. She served as United States secretary of Housing and Urban Development from 1975 to 1977, under the Gerald Ford administration, and as US trade representative from 1989 to 1993, under the George H. W. Bush administration.

[8] Myles Frechette was an American career diplomat, who, by request of Carla Hills, served as assistant US trade representative, for Latin America the Caribbean and Africa from 1989 to 1993. He was also ambassador to Colombia from 1994 to 1997.

none of them are now working on Latin America, for that matter. But in those days the difficulties of the time, the complexities, the challenges the United States was facing... There was attention and resources, there was a chain of command from the White House straight down, and it was organized. Unlike the Reagan period, when, in effect, my friend George Shultz,[9] as secretary of State, had to spent his time putting out fires and trying to control crazy people – like Oliver North[10] and Constantine Menges[11] and others – Bush and Baker developed a team that had attention, priority, high-level people and rapidly a solid working approach based on the need to resolve the Central American situation politically rather than militarily. And there, interestingly, Brazil played two important roles, together with Mexico: the first role is the known one: support for non-intervention with a twist of "non-US" activity. When Baena Soares was the secretary general of the OAS, he was in a sense, a guarantee for everybody: with a Brazilian secretary general, a man of the professionalism and independence of Baena Soares, the OAS is not going to be abused as easily as it was in the past. A small footnote on Baena Soares: I strongly believe in the importance of teamwork and that organizations need good leaders – I was happy to play a leadership role in opening US policy to views from Latin America, but I am even happier to give credit to Baena for playing a leadership role in response. Baena came to the OAS with a team. It is very interesting to notice that when I became the US ambassador there, many of the other ambassadors – the Chilean, the Mexican, others as well – had been ambassadors to Brazil in Brasília when Baena Soares had been secretary general of Itamaraty.

O.S. – I had not been aware of that. That's interesting.

L.E. – So he had a group of people who understood him, who knew they could work with him, who knew they could trust him. So Baena is the first Brazilian dimension linked to non-intervention. The second Brazilian dimension is that Brazil had been working with – and earning the dislike of the Americans over – the Rio Group.[12] And the Rio Group was seen in the American bureaucracy as sort of the opposition.

O.S. – Because it excluded the United States.

L.E. – Seen as the opposition really of the worst kind, because you couldn't claim they were communists, so they were harder to discredit. I had become known within the State Department as the defender of the Rio Group and had several times arranged meetings and other occasions that enabled the Rio Group – ministers, ambassadors – to present their case, etc. One of my roles not terribly well-known outside – although inside it was quite well known – is that I had survived all of these political changes and problems because I had really been, first, the member of the policy planning staff, the central staff, of the State Department under [Henry] Kissinger.[13] Then [I] had become the planning director for the Latin American Bureau. The State Department rotates its people every two or three years

[9] George Shultz is an American economist and businessman, who served as secretary of State from 1982 to 1989.

[10] Oliver Laurence North is a retired US Marine Corps Lieutenant Colonel, military historian and political commentator. He was convicted in the Iran-Contra Affair in the lates 1980's, but all charges against him were dismissed in 1991.

[11] Constantine Menges worked for the CIA as national intelligence officer for Latin America from 1981 to 1983 and as special assistant for President Ronald Reagan from 1983 to 1986. During this time, he took part in the planning of the US military intervention in Grenada, known as Operation Urgent Fury.

[12] The Rio Group (G-Rio) is a permanent association of Latin American countries for political consultation. It was formed in 1986.

[13] Henry Alfred Kissinger is an American statesman and political scientist. He served as US secretary of State from 1973 to 1977 and National Security advisor from 1969 to 1975, concurrently.

and policy planning is not appreciated at the lower levels, and because it requires an enormous amount of work nobody wants it. So I actually survived as the director of the policy planning staff of the Bureau for many years and developed a role as bureaucratic coordinator and institutional memory.

O.S. – Would you say that this is still the case today?

L.E. – No. They returned to a rotational system after I left. Look, there are some extraordinarily able people in the Foreign Service and, since we're speaking of the Brazilian context, I would say that one of the best ones is Thomas Shannon.[14]

O.S. – That's right, he will be missed in Brazil.

L.E. – Oh, my heavens! Well, he was very badly treated at the end of his period in Brazil.

O.S. – That's right, but he will still be missed, I think.

L.E. – Also a good person – but this is an example of what happens – take an officer who had agreed to become my Deputy in the policy planning operation: Donna Hrinak.[15]

O.S. – Yes.

L.E. – She was a competent and gifted person, that's why I wanted her – but being my deputy, particularly after I left, didn't seem very good and she avoided that, because the career people avoid those kinds of position. It's too much work and they don't go anywhere. In any case, I was very aware of Brazil and Brazil's views. The Rio Group had many people associated with it. The other country that was very important in this was, of course, Mexico and it's particularly important in terms of the OAS. Mexico had an ambassador for several years at the OAS, whose name I can't remember off the top of my head right now, but who was basically known as "Doctor No".

O.S. – [Laughter].

L.E. – His job was to say "no" to anything that the US said "yes" to. That was intended to keep a check on what was seen as US interventionism. And it generally worked well for that objective for its times. But now you had a Brazilian secretary general [Baena Soares] who knew how to get things done and a Mexican successor to "Doctor No" as ambassador – Icaza[16]. And Icaza, by the way, has written a very good memoir of his whole career that is called *"La Alegría de Servir"*, and he understood cooperation was under the right terms. One of the reasons I was good at what I did is that I liked the people I was working with, I certainly liked the Americans, and I also liked the Brazilians, the Mexicans and the Latin Americans and Caribbeans generally. I was particularly close to Peru. I understood their culture, and worked with them. Quite a few of my colleagues in the Foreign Service don't particularly like Latin America and Latin Americans, that made it hard to enjoy their work or to develop trust, and the kinds of understandings that are part of life, if it is going to be successfull.

O.S. – Right.

---

[14] Thomas Alfred Shannon Jr. is an American diplomat, who served as under secretary of State for Political Affairs from 2016 to 2018. He was also assistant secretary of State for Western Hemisphere Affairs from 2005 to 2009 and US ambassador to Brazil from 2010 to 2013.
[15] Donna Jean Hrinak is an American businesswoman and diplomat. She was US ambassador to Venezuela from 2000 to 2002, and Brazil, from 2002 to 2004. She is now president of Boeing Latin America.
[16] Eusebio Antonio de Icaza González is a Mexican diplomat. He was the Mexican ambassador to the OAS from 1986 to 1991.

567

L.E. – So in any case you have now, here, you have the Americans suddenly moving to a position, with the Bush Administration, where they clearly are going to try to resolve the Central American wars diplomatically. The Cold War was winding down. So in a sense, the fear is beginning to dissipate and what is also dissipating is a whole period of the military domination in the hemisphere. And that created an opportunity for commonality and here you have to take one's hat off to the Chileans, who, having got rid of Pinochet,[17] were eager to demonstrate the importance of democracy and what they had achieved. And so that was part of the setting for Resolution 1080[18] in Santiago. Now, let me make a couple of comments about all of this, though. In the first place, it took an enormous skill to put that through because the traditional position of most of Latin American countries, I think, including Brazil, was still the non-intervention posture. In fact it was a Brazilian diplomat who, at the key moment of the negotiations, came up with the formula that enabled 1080 to pass. It was Bernardo Pericás.

O.S. – We conducted an oral history interview with him, particularly about his role as Brazilian ambassador to Paraguay in 1999, and later on in Cuba.[19] Whenever things go wrong in Brazilian foreign policy these days, we say that we no longer have the likes of Bernardo Pericás. He was a great diplomat.

L.E. – Well, it's true. An extraordinarily able man.

O.S. – That's right. He had a key role in Central America.

L.E. – Specific role, very specific on developing democratic solidarity that reduced fears of intervention. American policy, led by Aronson, wanted to have a declaration against coups d'État and against military intervention – and I mention this in my most recent talks without identifying Bernardo – but the key phrase "the sudden or irregular interruption of a democratic political process," which got rid of the idea of coup, got rid of military opposition, got rid of everything and focused on what it was that we were trying to oppose, that was Pericás's language. He's the one that came up with that. But [in] the background, the real father of the success was, as I think I implied – I didn't say explicitly, but I'm telling you now – was Carlos Andrés Pérez.[20] And the reason was very simple: he was appalled – the way so many other people were – at the fact that the Inter-American System had been so weak and incompetent that it had been unable to deal with the [Manuel] Noriega[21] phenomenon in Panama.

O.S. – Of course.

---

[17] Augusto José Ramón Pinochet Ugarte was the leader of the military junta that overthrew the government of Chilean President Salvador Allende in 1973. He then became the head of the military dictatorship which ruled Chile until 1990.
[18] The OAS General Assembly Resolution AG/RES. 1080 (XXI-O/91) had the goal of promoting and protecting representative democracy in the Americas. It is considered as a predecessor of the Inter-American Democratic Charter, which was approved in 2001. The full text is available at: http://www.oas.org/juridico/english/agres1080.htm
[19] Bernardo Pericás Neto served as Brazilian ambassador to the OAS from 1989 to 1992 and to Paraguay from 1998 to 2000. Professors Oliver Stuenkel and Marcos Tourinho conducted an oral history interview with Pericás, which is available at: http://www.fgv.br/cpdoc/acervo/historia oral/entrevista-tematica/bernardo-pericas-neto-].
[20] The president of Venezuela from 1974 to 1979 and from 1989 to 1993.
[21] Manuel Antonio Noriega Moreno was a Panamanian military and the de facto leader of the country from 1983 to 1989. Despite not being an official head of state, he was part of the military junta that exerced actual control over Panama and appointed the nominal president, who had little power.

L.E. – And so it was that Carlos Andres Perez decided we could reinvent the old Venezuelan idea of non-recognition in the case of a coup, and he got the South American presidents to sign on to it. And then, once the presidents had signed on to it, the Foreign Ministries couldn't very well oppose it. They could try to keep it from being too bad, but... [laughter].

O.S. –That's right.

L.E. – But here, you know, I have to tell you my American colleagues almost blew it, because they didn't want to accept that there would just be a meeting, they wanted to go straight for the jugular, break relations and all kinds of things. It didn't make any sense. It couldn't be done; they didn't understand the environment. But Aronson, who was, in fact, my boss – all ambassadors work for the assistant secretary, in practice – did not want to settle for a meeting and we had an argument. It was an extraordinary argument, most of which happened in a stuck elevator in Santiago.

O.S. – [Laughter].

L.E. – In that elevator I convinced our delegation head, Larry Eagleburger[22] – who was was a clever and experienced career diplomat – that I was right and Aronson was wrong and I got his support to go through with that and we got the resolution 1080, accepting that it wasn't calling for automatic break of relations, but to support the draft we had worked out in the committee, which was to call for an automatic meeting of the Permanent Council. Now, let me say a couple of things there: again, Resolution 1080 instructs the secretary general to call the meeting. So, first of all, it doesn't say "instructs Baena Soares to act," but everybody accepted that language knowing that it was Baena Soares who was there, that Baena Soares was a cautious oldline diplomat, who wasn't going to do anything crazy, who wasn't going to jump just if the Americans told him to jump. So, again, it's another reason why Baena was so important. But it was also important procedurely, just as Bernardo Pericás' language on the sudden or irregular interruption of a democratic government avoided raising hackles on coups. The idea that it was an automatic convocation meant that you didn't have to wait the way they normally did in the Permanent Council for a government to ask for a meeting – no, this is going to be automatic. And that was a strong development and it put in the hands of the secretary general legal automaticity together with personal trust. That's what made that possible, and that's why I think that we were at the peak in the early, mid-1990's, in terms of the possibilities of regional solidarity and democracy. And the reason is very simple: it was new, and therefore we still had illusion on our side.

O.S. – [Laughter].

L.E. – And illusion in life is very important. Hope in life is very important. We also had the sense that maybe something could happen on the economic side. Remember that we were moving toward the acceptance – for the first time – of a summit process, the acceptance of ideas of free trade area. Now, you know, Brazil was not in the lead on that. The doctrine of [João Augusto de] Araújo Castro[23] was much too strong, the idea that the US was bent on trying to freeze world power in ways that would keep Brazil and others down. But, as I say, this was a period of illusion and of movement and Brazil was too smart to stand in the way

---

[22] Lawrence Sidney Eagleburger was an American career diplomat and statesman. He served as US deputy secretary of State from 1989 to 1992 and as secretary of State for a brief period between 1992 and 1993.

[23] João Augusto de Araújo Castro was a Brazilian diplomat. He served as Brazilian ambassador to the United Natons from 1968 to 1971 and to the US from 1971 to 1975. He was also the minister of Foreign Affairs from 1963 to 1964, under the João Goulart administration.

of illusion and movement. And other countries were pushing: as I said, the Chileans, the Peruvians... Peruvians in the post-Fujimori[24] period became extremely eager to support democratic procedures and Peru has had some very good diplomats. Carlos Garcia Bedoya,[25] who, unfortunately, died too soon, had been Foreign minister and ambassador to the United States, who was a major figure and understood both the importance of a global perspective – like Brazil – but also the importance of democracy, even though he was Foreign minister during the military regime. But Peru's was a military regime that was not of the order of some of the others elsewhere.

O.S. – Yes.

L.E. – So all these things came together. There was something that the Bush people called the "Enterprise for the Americas Initiative," which was an early version of what later became the proposal for a Free Trade Area [of the Americas].[26] And Carla Hills came as the representative of President Bush to the General Assembly in Paraguay, in 1990. So there was this political illusion, some sense of solidarity, some sense of relief from the past. A sense that things were moving, in the United States, in a positive direction. Unfortunately, the Americans kept blasting away at the need for democracy – but without putting anything behind it. As I said in my lecture, and I have to underscore the importance of this: you can't support democracy if you are just doing it rhetorically. You have to be willing to put some resources into it, to have some training, to establish a school, to enable electoral authorities to get together and so forth. And all of that takes money, and it takes time and it takes patience and it takes building cadres. The OAS never was given the support to do that.

O.S. – Do you think that elites across Latin America lacked a Latin American conscience or that there was a sense that there was no domestic incentive to invest in the OAS? Or that supporting the OAS would allow strengthening nationalist elements in the opposition? Or do you think that in the early 1990's there was little more than a tool for US interests? I mean, you still hear that today with the old school nationalist view that the OAS needed to be limited and Baena Soares actually said in his interview that he was so surprised that the only country that did not invite him to visit as secretary general of the OAS was actually Brazil. So he suddenly felt that he had lots of difficulties to gain access to Itamaraty. To him it was a surprise, in a sense, that being in that position, he suddenly realized that. There is an expression in Brazil which is called "vestir a camisa"[27] – so he really "dressed up as," he was the "OAS man." Actually, there is a photo that is quite famous, which shows him wearing an OAS T-shirt. And I think he embraced this so much, no longer being the representative of Brazil, and he regretted how much he thought his country was unhelpful in many of these processes.

What was your impression at the time about this phenomenon? You've written in a piece, also for Cornell, I think, a couple years back that this is a non-cooperative region, Latin America, and there is not a sufficient sense of the importance of working together in order

---

[24] Alberto Fujimori was the president of Peru from 1990 to 2000. In 1992, he dissolved Congress and concentrated power in what became known as *autogolpe* (self-coup).
[25] Carlos Garcia Bedoya was a Peruvian diplomat and academic. He was the Peruvian ambassador to the US from 1976 to 1979 and Foreign minister from February to November 1979.
[26] The Free Trade Area of the Americas (FTAA) was a proposed agreement intending to the elimination or reduction of trade tariffs between all members of the Americas, except for Cuba. Its origins come from the George H.W. Bush administration's Enterprise for the Americas Initiative and it was renewed by the Clinton administration at the 1994 Summit of the Americas. Negotiations, however, ended in failure as no final agreement was reached by the deadline of January 2005.
[27] Literally, "to wear the jersey"; figuratively, "to take up a cause." This expression is used when somebody embraces a function or a cause with great dedication, as its representative.

to deal with policy challenges that are domestic. Is that something that is a constant? Do you think that this was an issue, that this was an impediment during your time as ambassador at the OAS?

L.E. –I don't remember the context in which I may have said that, but my reaction now is to say that many of these problems are absolutely universal, they are not regional phenomena and they don't just affect Latin America or the United States. Look at the condition of the European Union today over migration – for that matter, over terrorism: they still don't have adequate exchanges of information on terrorism and on migration. They are leaving the border countries up in the air without any kind of support, and you have conversely this nationalist reaction against it. So, when one says that there is a lack of a regional vision, well, it depends on the time that we are discussing. In the 1950's, the European leaders had a vision that they needed to unite forces in order to avoid World War III and being destroyed the way they were the last time and today they are beginning to lose that. So these things do have to be tied in to the specific historical moment. And, as I say, I think in the early 1990's, you had the illusion of progress and the ability to recreate things, but it takes time, it takes a lot of time to establish that kind of thing and to overcome previous bad judgements. And one of the problems is that the OAS has been seen more as a tool of US interests than it is. You know, the last time the OAS acted as a US tool, Brazil was right in there, in the lead.

O.S. – That's right.

L.E. – And led the troops into the Dominican Republic. So Brazilians should feel bad about that.

O.S. – That's important to remember.

L.E. – But although that experience was a bit of a mistake, the Americans simply forgot about all of this to concentrate on other matters and not worry about the OAS. When I became ambassador, the mission wasn't and probably still today is not fully integrated into the State Department.

O.S. – Is it physically in the same building?

L.E. – Yes. It was not in a separate structure, in fact when I became OAS ambassador I had the old hide away office of John Foster Dulles[28] – not exactly a brilliant man from a Latin American perspective, but certainly a key figure who had commanded a beautiful second office. But being in the same building did not matter. The US ambassador before me,[29] was a man who didn't speak Spanish, who had been a congressional aide, whose way of communicating with the secretary of State was to write him letters.

O.S. – Right [laughter].

L.E. – There was no integration into the system. The main problem is this: the Foreign Service and the American way of working things is not multilateral, it is bilateral. Because if you do things bilaterally, you can bring to bear your power against one country at a time, not subjecting yourself to a voting situation where – as one of my colleagues once described it – the situation became like a dumbbell: the United States with its weight is on one side and everybody else is over on the other side, countering the weight. If you are the United

---

[28] John Foster Dulles was the US secretary of State from 1953 to 1959.
*Note from the interviewee:* The brother of Allen Dulles, director of the CIA from 1952 until he was forced to resign after the failed Bay of Pigs invasion against Castro, John Foster Dulles celebrated the 1954 coup in Guatemala as a "glorious victory."
[29] Richard Thomas McCormack was the US ambassador to the OAS from 1985 to 1989.

States, you don't want to be exposed to the trade unionism of the weaker states: the other side might get more weight than you have. You don't want to be caught in that situation. So if you have a policy that matters you pass it to our ambassador in Brasilia, or our ambassador in Asunción or in Buenos Aires. You don't pass it to our ambassador to the OAS. I was able to change some of that during the period that I was there, but it didn't last.

O.S. – You were speaking about that moment of illusion... When do you think that changed? After the illusion, usually comes a sad realization that...

L.E. – It's very hard to know, but in my instinct... You know, when one is working very hard – and I unfortunately spent my life working very, very, hard – one sometimes doesn't have time to see things that are right in front of one's nose. But my instinct was that the very negotiation of the Inter-American Democratic Charter[30] revealed the passing of the illusions. If you look at the Charter now – and some people have done very nice jobs with it, and the current OAS Secretary General Almagro[31] is desperately trying to find ways to restrain Venezuela – has gotten some interesting interpretations and so forth. But my view of that Charter always was that it was a retreat, not an advance.

O.S. – Interesting.

L.E. – Because it took away the automatic convening of a meeting: without automaticity you had to have all kinds of situations before you could act ... It restored the primacy of sovereignty in a way, that was clear... And it also codified the primacy of the governments with regard to elections. So, in a strange way, when you get a Charter and you spell everything out, you open the door to all of the traditional fears, concerns, limitations and legalisms that people who don't want any action can work to block action. And the final break came with the 2002 coup attempt against Chavez in Venezuela. In the discussions at the OAS, Brazil again showed it had good intelligence. The Brazilian ambassador, Valter Pecly Moreira,[32] said their reports suggested there was a good deal of popular turmoil and warned that this was not a good situation to invoke the Charter. That moment in Venezuela was the beginning of showing that abstractly beautiful democratic solidarity without engagement really wasn't going to work. I would be hard put to justify that. An instinct, an impression.

O.S. – Now, two questions about countries that are a bit peculiar: one is Suriname and the other one is Haiti. In both cases there was a democratic rupture while you were US ambassador to the OAS. Both countries aren't really seen by the rest of Latin America as part of Latin America, actually. I mean, Suriname is so far in the Brazilian imaginary and Haiti is distant too. They don't speak Spanish or Portuguese, you know, those countries don't really play a role there. Did you feel that, in the case of Haiti, the US policy was made easier by the fact that this was a country which most Latin Americans would not be able to locate on the map? Because it's really quite interesting that until 2004 there was no discernible policy by, basically, any Latin American country towards Haiti, except perhaps Chile.

---

[30] The Inter-American Democratic Charter was adopted in September 11, 2011, during a special session of the General Assembly of the OAS held in Lima with the objective of protecting democratic rule in the hemisphere. It also extended the notion of democracy: it should not be understood strictly as a form of government by an electoral majority, but also associated to a set of rights and values. The full text is available at: http://www.oas.org/charter/docs/resolution1_en_p4.htm.

[31] Luis Leonardo Almagro Lemes is a Uruguayan lawyer, diplomat, and politician, currently serving as the secretary general of the Organization of American States (OAS) since 2015. He was also the Uruguyana minister of Foreign Affairs from 2010 to 2015.

[32] Valter Pecly Moreira was the Brazilian ambassador to the OAS from 2000 to 2004.

L.E. – With regard to that, early on, I think you're right. What happened in Haiti, though, has been that there was an enormous effort by the United States to support [Jean-Bertrand] Aristide[33] after his election. And when that fell apart the first time with the [Joseph Raoul] Cédras[34] coup, I think the US policy and attitudes were very strong and they were domestically impelled also by the [Congressional] Black Caucus[35] and they were, in a sense, personal, in the sense that there had been a tremendous effort to support Aristide. So that all coincided with the ideology and with the idea that we were committed to democracy, so we should try to reverse that and so forth, you know, to the point that ultimately the United States actually intervened militarily a few years later.

O.S. – So Latin America didn't play much of an important role?

L.E. – No. If there was a supporting role that I can still remember in a clear fashion, it was Canada. Of course, Canada – like the United States – has a strong Haitian colony within it, and strong commitments. The situation was very different in 2004. I was at the OAS, not in the US government, but the primary driver in all these things often is the local situation. And unfortunately Aristide was one of the very few cases in the world where a man has a second chance to be president and has learned all the wrong lessons and ends up being outmaneuvered and outorganized by civilians with no government authority or power. I mean it was a very, very sad situation and the US ultimately... Well, I felt betrayed by the US. At that point, when all of this was happening I was the acting secretary general of the OAS and I attempted not to support Aristide as Aristide, but to support a procedure that could preserve democratic forms.

O.S. – Yes.

L.E. – And, again, that would have cost resources, it would have cost some money. And as Aristide lost, within Haiti, the illusion of power that he had had, his internal opponents became emboldened and it didn't really take that much to blow him over again. It was really very sad and it was not even the military who did it because the military had been disbanded jointly by Aristide and the US after 1994. Brazil taking control of MINUSTAH was probably very good for all concerned, and one reason it was good for the United States is that it enabled the US to wash its hands of the problem. Those are very strong words – and sure, the US continued to give money and make pronouncements. But notice: they gave no participation or troops to MINUSTAH.

O.S. – Right.

L.E. – And, in other words, they assumed no responsibility whatsoever and learned nothing for themselves. Brazil learned something: I think that probably Brazil's military ability, to the extent that it is asked to help maintain order, has improved. They've got domestic action in urban areas, they probably learned a little bit from being in Haiti.

---

[33] Jean-Bertrand Aristide is a Haitian politician and priest, he was Haiti's first democratically elected president. His first term as president, which started in 1991, was interrupted by a military coup. In 1994, a US military intervention reestablished Aristide as president and he governed until 1996. He was elected once again in 2000 and governed from 2001 until 2004, when he fled the country due to a military coup.

[34] Joseph Raoul Cédras was the *de facto* ruler of Haiti after leading a military coup against Jean-Bertrand Aristide in 1991. He governed from 1991 to 1994.

[35] The Congressional Black Caucus is a non-partisan American political organization made up of the African-American members of the US Congress. It was founded in 1971 with the intent of empowering and achieving greater equity for African Americans and other minorities.

O.S. – Yes, yes, absolutely, this is recognized. Haiti, from a military learning perspective, was clearly seen as a positive experience.

I wanted to ask you about a broader issue before moving to the case of 1995. There are two competing narratives in Brazil about the role of the United States in Latin America. There is the traditional one, which has a lot of support in the public opinion, by people like Luiz Alberto Moniz Bandeira,[36] who is a historian, that basically believes the United States has an active interest in undermining Brazil's rise. According to this view – and this is very widespread – there is a lot of effort in making sure that Brazil keeps stuck with its internal problems. And you've made a lot of references to this in your writings: that there is sort of an excessive obsession with the US role, which is actually not as influential as a lot of Latin Americans believe. And then, you have younger historians such as Matias Spektor, also from FGV,[37] who wrote the book "Kissinger and Brazil."[38]

L.E. – He talked to me about it, quoted me in it.

O.S. – Yeah, he is my colleague.

L.E. – Yes. You get along? I hope!

O.S. – Very much so. Actually, I spoke to him yesterday on the phone.

L.E. – Well, say hello to him.

O.S. – Wonderful. And he says that that perspective is wrong and that Kissinger actually worked actively to possibly have Brazil assuming more responsibility in the region.

L.E. – Of course.

O.S. – So some of the things could be delegated to Brazil. In fact, this is a recurrent theme among so many other elements that also show that when Brazil was strong, the bilateral relations was good. And during the key moments of the early 21st century when Brazil was beginning to articulate a more proactive role, the United States was actually quite happy with that. I personally believe this is a more adequate description. Now, what do you make of those narratives? Did you have to address those concerns constantly at the OAS? Did you feel that there was a lingering concern not only in Brazil, but perhaps in other countries, of the suspicions of the goals of the United States? Or do you think that Brazil began to understand, particularly in the case of the war between Ecuador and Peru, that the US was okay with Brazil taking the lead on these issues? Because Clinton was thinking about Rwanda and Kosovo and Somalia... I mean, getting bogged down in some negotiations in South America was perhaps not what the White House wanted, right? Do you think that Brazil began to understand that there was no US opposition towards Brazil taking the lead in those kinds of issues?

L.E. – Well, somebody once said, rather nastily, that American foreign policy has a lot of carpenters and no architects. Carpenters just work on one issue at a time, one day at a time, without any vision with no particular idea of where they are going with it. Now Kissinger actually was an architect, had a vision. He asked me to discuss the possibility of Brazil's

---

[36] Luiz Alberto Moniz Bandeira was a Brazilian political scientist and historian. He was an important exponent of Brazilian nationalist perspectives on international relations and an avid critic of US foreign policy.

[37] *Fundação Getulio Vargas* (Getulio Vargas Foundation), a private higher education institution in Brazil.

[38] *Kissinger e o Brasil* (Kissinger and Brazil) by Matias Spektor. Zahar, 2008. 234 pages.

assuming a broader international role, and asked me to speak to [Azeredo da] Silveira[39] about the possibility. Silveira's answer was a very wise one: that the United States was big enough and rich enough to survive accidents which there inevitably would be if one assumed broader responsibilities, whereas Brazil was not in a position to do at that point. Maybe it would have been better if, more recently, Brazil's leaders had realized that.

O.S. – [Laughter].

L.E. –I think, in general, the United States understands that it is better served when other countries are strong and prosperous and able to take care of their own problems. Now, in recent years, there has been a sharp conditioning element brought into all of that, because of the feeling that has grown in American politics – and it's now expressed by Trump – that even when they are strong and prosperous, these countries – foreigners – are successful because they're cheating us. So, in a sense, the United States is less comfortable with strong effective countries elsewhere than it was in the past or than it should be, in my view.

O.S. – Interesting. And how do you think this will affect Brazil, specifically?

L.E. – Now, generally speaking, you know, nobody knows anything about Brazil here and nobody knows anything about Latin America here. I have often tried to suggest to people that it is better for American policy to think of Brazil as a country in the world rather than a country in Latin America. Even though I also believe that they should be aware of Latin America as part of the world and not just Latin America. Because, implicitly, the American assumption is that Latin America doesn't matter and is too weak to make a difference.

O.S. – Yes.

L.E. – When Brazil... And I think is the only real time that Brazil has seriously crossed American strategic sense, is in the so-called nuclear deal with Iran.[40]

O.S. – That's right.

L.E. – That undid, at one fell swoop, all of the positive vibrations that had started to build. I don't know, it all depends how you look at things. The difficulty is also that Brazil's neighbors aren't very pro-Brazil either, most of them. They see Brazil doing well as a new horse in town to which you can hitch your economy and your ride, so it's a good thing. But, on the other hand, there's lots of resentment at what is seen as Brazilian arrogance.

O.S. – That's right. I think that there is a notion that Brazil is excessively concerned about its global status, particularly under Lula, and not paying enough attention to the task of consolidating its capacity to provide global public goods in the region. But that was in a later period. Do you think this notion about Brazil perhaps being potentially too proactive, that was already present in the 1990's?

L.E. – No, I don't think so, not at all. As I say, the only time that Brazil came across as a strategic problem was the Iran nuclear thing.

---

[39] Antônio Francisco Azeredo da Silveira was a Brazilian diplomat. He was Foreign minister from 1974 to 1979 and Brazilian ambassador to Argentina (1969-19740, the US (1974-1979) and Portugal (1983-1985).

[40] In 2010, amid tension regarding Iran's nuclear programme and the possibility of a new round of sanctions proposed by the United States, Brazil and Turkey proposed an agreement to avert the intensification of the conflict. The agreement implied that Iran would ship its stockpile of enriched Uranium to Turkey for further processing – its goal was to reduce international suspicion towards Iran's nuclear programme. However, the agreement was rejected by the US and the other permanent members of the U.N. Security Council.

O.S. – Yes, I remember that was 2010.

L.E. – For everything else, you know, Brazil is perceived in the United States much as any foreign country is, which is not much. Araújo Castro once told me the following story: when he went to present his credentials to Richard Nixon[41] they had five minutes. It was four minutes and Nixon was already getting restless, so Araújo said: "Who is next? Who are you seeing after me?" and Nixon said: "I don't know" and he went to his desk and he looked: "Oh, the new ambassador of France." One foreigner is like any another. As you know, my grandfather was president of Italy, I still have strong Italian connections and ties, and I have spent years explaining to Italian diplomats here [in the US] that Italy is no worse off than anybody else: if they are not being paid attention to, that's because no one's being paid attention to.

O.S. – Right and I think that is particularly difficult for Latin Americans to understand, because the US is so close and so influential.

L.E. – Yes, maybe it will be easier for your generation to understand as increased Chinese trade, and European trade, etc. develops different perceptions. Again, you see the importance of illusion. The US was seen – again, I see this so clearly from my Italian perspective – as super powerful: the US was the key force in the defeat of fascism and then the US came through with the Marshall Plan. Already at the end of the nineteenth century, also, the US was the recipient of hordes of hungry Italians, starving Italians, who were fleeing for a new world – and who were actually finding it! Although it was a difficult world, and, in those days, communications weren't very good, so they didn't know how hard it was, and they kept coming for years. But the illusion of American democracy, American prosperity – "money grows on trees in the United States..."

O.S. – Right, that's very interesting. In fact, I think Chinese influence will be good, so people contextualize and look at the US influence in a more realistic way, perhaps. Now, regarding the 1995 case – again, you talked a lot about this –, one of the interpretations that I've briefly summarized in my book project is that this is the beginning of a more active Brazilian role. After 1995, Fernando Henrique Cardoso[42] is becoming more proactive. Did you feel that this is actually the case or do you think this was more in Brazil's mind? A year later, when you were still US special envoy, Brazil avoids a coup in Paraguay and it sort of begins to really embrace its role. It was only in the 1980's that a sitting Brazilian president first visited Colombia and Peru. So in 1995, to many, Brazil is waking up, it is beginning to articulate a strategy, Cardoso is well respected in the region. Do you think that mattered to South American dynamics? And particularly to the bilateral relationship, did that, to your mind, make Brazil a useful interlocutor to Washington when potential crisis came up, or was this more something that happened in the minds of a couple Brazilian scholars on foreign policy makers? Putting it in another way, was the conflict between Ecuador and Peru really that difficult to solve? Or did the US look at that and say: "Oh, great, let's let the Brazilians take the lead on this role and we'll help a bit along the way"?

L.E. – The American establishment didn't think the conflict would be solved. But one of my initial conditions before accepting to become the special envoy was that I didn't want just a cease fire, but that we should stay at it until we got rid of the problem permanently. They said yes, and by that time in my career I knew how to make the American government work, which most of them didn't. We stuck at it, but it took a long time, it wore out the

---

[41] Richard Milhous Nixon was the US president from 1969 to 1974, when he resigned while facing an impeachment process.
[42] Fernando Henrique Cardoso is a Brazilian politician and sociologist. He was president of Brazil from 1995 until Janueary 1, 2003.

patience of many people in the US administration, but they let it continue... Brazil's role as chair of the guarantors of the 1942 Rio Protocol was critical. I may have had then a higher opinion then than I do now, perhaps, of Brazilian diplomacy. I have long argued that Brazilian diplomats are pound for pound the best diplomats in the world. And I've had some smart Brazilians say to me: "You're not so right in how well you think of us." But, still... Look, if I'm representing the United States and I'm in the middle of a situation where my associates are filled with good instincts and goodwill, but know very little, I am going to be desperate to find people who know something.

O.S. – That's right.

L.E. – [Laughter] and the Brazilians always knew something, so I was working closely with Brazil and Brazilian diplomats. I was the acting deputy head of the Policy Planning staff at that point, but I was not particularly politically favoured. Politically, I had some power but I was not, it was not political as such. It was bureaucratic, it was knowledge, a different kind of thing. So I was free to devote a great deal of my time to the Peru-Ecuador problem, whereas my Brazilian counterpart, Ivan Cannabrava,[43] had to worry about all Brazil's foreign policy and there was no way he could spend a lot of time on Peru-Euador. And the same thing was true for our Argentinian and Chilean counterparts, who were vice ministers with many other responsibilities. In fact, the Chilean sometimes seemed more interested in making sure that we didn't come up with a solution that would make life harder for Chile with Bolivia. So, you know, they had different levels of interest. Behind it all, I felt that I had the support and the trust of Fernando Henrique Cardoso, whom I also liked for other reasons. So I felt that I was in good shape with Brazil – sometimes even in better shape with Brazil than with my own government. What we did in Peru and Ecuador was affecting things in Brazil itself. For example, when folks at the US National Security Council became too frustrated, too tired and too bored to want to continue the helicopter support for the military mission...

O.S. – ... Brazil bought helicopters.

L.E. – Yeah, yeah. The Blackhawks were the first time that Brazil's army managed to buy helicopters rather than the airforce. So, all of this was affecting things... [It was] fairly obvious to me that Itamaraty and the Defence people weren't talking, and they weren't in a good shape. But Peru-Ecuador forced communication among them.

O.S. – It only changed, I would say, under Nelson Jobim.[44]

L.E. – Yes, Nelson Jobim is a great man! And he was very effective, he probably saved the Brazilian military – it would be my guess, restoring some sense of strategic sense and political respectability [laughter].

O.S. – He was also important to establish and institutionalize civilian control of the armed forces.

L.E. – Of course!

O.S. – After all, the Defense Ministry was only created in 1999.[45]

---

[43] Ivan Oliveira Cannabrava is a Brazilian diplomat. He was chief negotiator for Brazil during the Peru-Ecuador peace talks.
[44] Nelson Azeredo Jobim is a Brazilian politician and jurist. He was Defense minister from 2007 and 2011 and the president of the Brazilian Supreme Court (Supremo Tribunal Federal) from 2004 to 2006. In 2013, professors Oliver Stuenkel and Marcos Tourinho conducted an oral history interview with minister Jobim, which is available at: http://www.fgv.br/cpdoc/acervo/historia-oral/entrevista-tematica/nelson-jobim-iv.

L.E. – That's right.

O.S. – So, do you think that, in a sense, 1995 is seen as a moment in which Brazil suddenly sensed that there was an opportunity to play a more proactive role?

L.E. – Well, I think that may be true.

O.S. – But you would say that the US was still essential in overcoming the many obstacles and conflicts that 1995 produced, right?

L.E. – Oh, I think so.

O.S. – This is not part of the Brazilian narrative about this period of time. That is quite interesting. I kind of sensed that listening to the Argentines and the Peruvians, but it's important to hear about this from you.

L.E. – You know, for example, let's talk about illusion, another aspect of illusion. First of all, there is one area... The reason I jumped immediately in praise of Nelson Jobim is that during Peru-Ecuador he was in the Brazilian Supreme Court. He was, I believe, Chief Justice. And one of the things that we needed to do in the negotiation was to dot every "i" and cross every "t" also legally, particularly because Foreign Ministries, particularly in small countries and Latin countries, are the curators of boundary disputes and legalisms. You know, Brazil has a much more pragmatic tradition of a lot of things, and as a more powerful country, to some extent, it settled its boundaries more than a 100 years ago with the, what's his name?

O.S. – The Baron of Rio Branco.

L.E. – Exactly. Well, so we needed to get legal opinions on certain aspects of the boundary and Nelson Jobim was "the man," he chaired that group and rendered a vitally important legal decision. Now, there, absolutely, we could have done nothing without Brazil and Brazil's role. Fernando Henrique's support for a relationship with Fujimori was very important also. I sometimes felt I was the only American who got along with Fujimori.

O.S. – Personally?

L.E. – Personally.

O.S. – Okay. Interesting. We spoke a lot to Luis Felipe Lampreia,[46] who said what made dealing with Fujimori not easy was that he had a whole *mise-en-scène*. He used to sit higher than his interlocutors – perhaps not with a US interlocutor, however.

L.E. – In the ante-room of the presidential office in Lima, he had a *big* piece of melted down Nagasaki on a pedestal.

O.S. – Really?

L.E. – Yes. To keep the Americans in their place. He was a very interesting man.

O.S. – A very interesting character actually and very little understood in Latin America, by the way.

---

[45] In 1999, the creation of the Defense Ministry absorbed the former Ministries of the Army, the Air Force and the Navy, which became Commands under the authority of the new Ministry.
[46] Luis Felipe Lampreia was the Brazilian minister of Foreign Affairs from 1995 to 2001, during the presidency of Fernando Henrique Cardoso. Professors Oliver Stuenkel and Marcos Tourinho have conducted an interview with Lampreia, which is available at:
http://www.fgv.br/cpdoc/acervo/historia-oral/entrevista-tematica/luiz-felipe-lampreia

L.E. – Yes, oh, yes! You know, he won the election against [Mario] Vargas Llosa.[47] [Fernando] Belaúnde[48] had told Vargas Llosa: "You must run [for president], you are the only Peruvian known in the outside world." What Belaúnde and Vargas Llosa didn't understand until later was ...

O.S. – These people outside don't vote [laughter].

L.E. – Most Peruvians did not know who he was!

O.S. – Right, of course.

L.E. – And exactly at that moment people forget Fujimori is an agronomist. He was at the University of La Molina.[49] Everybody now associates him with assasinations at la Molina for which [Vladimiro] Montesinos[50] was primarily responsible.

O.S. – Yes.

L.E. – But the point is that Fujimori won in part because he ran a campaign ad that had a green plant shooting up. It was a simple ad that simply conveyed a key emotion: "Hey, I may be a 'chino,'[51] but I'm brown like you and I know that what you need is things to grow."

O.S. – That's right, that's right.

L.E. – You know, there was no contest and he was a man who kept things going, did many things and, at the bottom, he also wanted peace, but he had a real problem. His problem was that the Peruvian elite was of the opinion – that my friend former President Belaúnde shared: Belaúnde was the one who first told me that Fujimori wasn't born in Peru. Belaúnde said: "He was born in a tramp steamer I took when I was returning to Peru from getting my Master's degree in Architecture in Texas. He was on that ship out of Galveston, or wherever it was, filled with Japanese and his parents came in. He was a stow-away on board of that [ship] and therefore he has never buried anyone of his own blood in our soil, he will not understand or be capable of defending Peru." And that was a common view in the elite, a view that missed both the terrible nature of war and the gulf between them and the common people. Fujimori said to me: "I look at these dead boys" – because he went up to the border – "I had to look at the uniforms to figure out who is Peruvian and who is Ecuadorian." Peru's old elite sometimes did not identify with most Peruvians.

O.S. – Yes, that's right.

L.E. – I mean, those were brothers who were killing each other. This is one of the sad things about politics and internal problems within governments: Fujimori had gone up to visit Quito and he had seen the president of Ecuador [Sixto Durán-Ballén][52] and told him he was withdrawing the Peruvian troops from the border because he needed them to fight

---

[47] Peruvian novelist, professor and politician. He was the presidential candidate for the center-right coalition Frente Democrático (FREDEMO) in 1990, but lost the election to Alberto Fujimori.

[48] Fernando Belaúnde Terry was the president of Peru from 1963 to 1968, when he was overthrown by the military coup led by Juan Velasco. In 1980, he became the first civilian president after the military rule, governing until 1985.

[49] *Universidad Nacional Agraria La Molina* (UNALM) – the National Agrarian University.

[50] Vladimiro Montesinos Torres was a cashiered military officer who became the head of Peru's intelligence service in the the Fujimori government. He gained considerable control over government and the media through bribery, blackmail and coercion.

[51] The term is associated to Asian populations in Peru. Alberto Fujimori himself is also known as "*el Chino*," even though he is of Japanese extraction.

[52] Sixto Afonso Durán-Ballén Cordovez was the president of Peru from 1992 to 1996.

*Sendero [Luminoso]*[53] and, of course, when he said that, the military aides of the president of Ecuador heard that and it basically told them they had a free hand to move and do things to right what they felt were historic wrongs.

O.S. – Right.

L.E. – There were lots of things Fujimori didn't understand, he was in some senses an accident. One of the previous presidents of Ecuador, Osvaldo Hurtado,[54] became President when his predecessor was killed in a plane crash asked the then Venezuelan president, who was [Jaime] Lusinchi:[55] "Why do we have to face such hard times as president?" And Lusinchi looked at him and said: "Because that's the only chance we had to become presidents, the only time!" [laughter].

O.S. – [Laughter]

L.E. – In that sense, if it hadn't been for the violence of *Sendero* and the problems of the overly rigid Peruvian elite, Fujimori would never have been elected in Peru, but these things happen in funny ways, complicated ways. And the fact that he had neither governing experience or a party behind him made a sitting duck for the immoral and supremely ambitious Vladimiro Montesinos.

O.S. – It's interesting what you were saying that Cannabrava had to deal with other things and that becomes very obvious in the interview that the way they remember this is something they had to do on the sides…They committed several mistakes: one of the agreements was leaked accidentally to the press, there were procedural mistakes. Did you, at any point, sense that a stronger US role was needed otherwise this would not work? Because you were quite discrete throughout, right?

L.E. – Of course.

O.S. – This is why perhaps other groups are claiming credit for this. I mean, the photo of Cardoso with the presidents shaking hands, it's quite prominent in several books that I've used to teach Brazilian foreign policy. It suggests, in a sense, that Brazil solved a security challenge. Do you think that the way that this played out was good to help Brazil gain confidence and take a more proactive role? What I hear from you is that this picture is an interesting picture, but it doesn't give you the whole story… Because the US still had to play a role and make sure that…

L.E. – Yes, of course. You know, I have never tried to look at the problem this way, because, in fact, we made certain basic rules among ourselves and one of them was that we were to be the only legitimate source of public statements by our governments and we would only say [something] when we were together and had agreed on what it was: Cannabrava, the Argentine, the Chilean and myself, the four guarantor representatives.

O.S. – OK.

---

[53] The *Sendero Luminoso* (Shining Path) is a Peruvian maoist guerilla group founded in the late 1960's. Its terrorist activity went from 1980 until 1992, when its leader, Abimael Guzmán Reynoso, was captured. Since then, it has acted sporadically.

[54] Osvaldo Hurtado was vice president of Ecuador from 1979 until 1981, when he became president after the death of Jaime Roldós Aguilera.

[55] Jaime Ramón Lusinchi was the president of Venezuela from 1984 to 1989. His time in office was marked by economic crisis, rising inflation and corruption, which aggravated the crisis of the political system established in 1958.

L.E. – I'll give you another example, then I'll give you the generalization. The other example is that we met many times [and] I think never did the position we came out with in the end reflect the position that any one of us had come in with in the beginning and this, to me, was the purest expression of multilateral cooperation. It was respectful, it was willing to adjust positions, to allow for the positions of the others, and it was absolutely a team effort. You will remember that earlier I said: "I believe in teams." Well, I talked about the American team that was created under Bush 1 for Latin America; than we had the team that Baena Soares had at the OAS; and then we had the team among the guarantors during Peru-Ecuador. What the United States provided to the Peru-Ecuador negotiation in addition to diplomacy was the logistical tail, the helicopter support and the myth of US power. That was absolutely critical.

O.S. – Right.

L.E. – One other thing: Brazil provided, absolutely critically, the General who commanded MOMEP, the Military Observation Mission, Ecuador-Peru. Getting US agreement for that caused me a lot of difficulties with the Pentagon and the National Security Council, but they finally accepted it. There were other cases of key Brazilian leadership, like the role of Jobim we have already mentioned. But I would have to say that, below the presidential level, my role was more important than that of the other guarantor representatives. But not because I was the American, but because – unlike them – I was not so important to my government, I could spend more time on the negotiation, developing the elements of a solution.

O.S. – I see.

L.E. – I spent time, once I went and lived in Quito for ten days, getting the Ecuadorian Military Foreign Service to talk to each other and to trust me and then at one point I went back to the guarantors and I gave them an Ecuadorean position as my own, to avoid rejection of it just because it came from one of the parties. I had the time and patience to work to develop trust and maintain trust on all sides. And that is why I was chosen by my government for this role. When the shooting in the Cenepa broke out in January 1995 there were a lot of urgent meetings, it was taken very seriously by a lot of people in a lot of levels, but very fast it became clear this wasn't going to be solved easily and it was going to take a lot of work. And so, key officials in the American government said: "Let Einaudi take care of it, because he likes these people and he has the patience, because he was at the OAS."

O.S. – Right.

L.E. – So you have to understand that there are individual problems and idiosyncrasies here that have to be seen at the same time that one is building these gigantic phantasmagoric possibilities and theories. You know, I will tell you something – and you should check this again with [Osmar Vladimir] Chohfi:[56] I frankly believe that, except for Chohfi and a few others, most Brazilians – even in the diplomatic world – did not understand what was going on, how important this was to Ecuador, what its real roots were or how it could be solved.

O.S. – Yes. I would agree with that.

L.E. – And you know, changing to a different time, 2004: I was the acting secretary general of the OAS and I was worried that there was going to be a coup in Ecuador. I went to

---

[56] Osmar Vladimir Chohfi was the Brazilian ambassador to Ecuador from 1994 to 1999 and to the OAS from 2005 to 2008. Professors Oliver Stuenkel and Marcos Tourinho have conducted an interview with Chohfi, which is available at: http://www.fgv.br/cpdoc/acervo/historia-oral/entrevista-tematica/osmar-vladimir-chohfi

Brazil [and] the Foreign minister, your friend and mine – Celso Amorim – made me wait for two hours and then he said: "Stay out of it, don't worry about it, we will take care of it."

O.S. – How do you think that... What happened then?

L.E. – Of course there was a coup, but Amorim didn't know. He was busy building a global reach [laughter].

O.S. – Ambassador, thank you very much for your time.

# APPENDIX SEVEN

*Annals of the Fondazione Luigi Einaudi*
Volume LIV, December 2020: 35-44

## CONFLICT BETWEEN THEORY AND PRACTICE:
## THE ORGANIZATION OF AMERICAN STATES

LUIGI R. EINAUDI *

─────── ABSTRACT ───────

The Organization of American States (OAS) is a regional multilateral organization made up of the sovereign states of the Western Hemisphere. The author describes its charter, organization and history, then focuses on pathbreaking efforts to
support democracy that were subsequently severely hampered by lack of resources,
political conflicts, and the disengagement of key members, especially the United
States. He then analyzes the three organizing concepts of the OAS and of international organization more generally: multilateralism, geography and sovereignty,
and finds each of them challenged by contemporary developments. He concludes
that *multilateralism* remains essential and that *geography* and *neighborhood* still matter, but that *sovereignty* should be understood as setting the terms for working with
others, rather than as a basis for rejecting cooperation. To maintain sovereignty,
countries must deal with the outside world, their neighbors perhaps most of all.
And all – small and large, large and small – must contribute their share.

**Keywords**: Democracy, Multilateralism, Organization of American States, Regionalism,
Sovereignty.
JEL Codes: F5, H7, N4.

The OAS is made up of the sovereign countries of the Western Hemisphere. It is the world's oldest regional organization, dating to 1889-1890,
when eighteen States of the Western Hemisphere founded the Interna-

───────

* Luigi R. Einaudi is a retired U.S. diplomat and educator. He earned A.B. and Ph.D.
degrees at Harvard, taught at Harvard and Wesleyan before joining the RAND Corporation
in 1962, teaching also at UCLA. In 1974, he joined the Policy Planning Council at the State
Department. He was named Ambassador to the OAS in 1989. In 2000, he was elected Assistant
Secretary General of the OAS and served as Acting Secretary General in 2004-2005. Since retirement, he has lectured at Georgetown, Cornell, the National Defense University, the Smithsonian and in Italy. Address for correspondence: leinaudi@outlook.com.

ISSN: 2532-4969
doi: 10.26331/1114

tional Union of American Republics to exchange commercial information. This initial technical mandate gradually expanded, aided by Franklin D. Roosevelt's Good Neighbor policy, which accepted the sovereign equality of states and non-intervention in their internal affairs. In the aftermath of the Second World War, a new OAS Charter was adopted, whose preamble declared, rather grandiloquently, but capturing an ideal dating from the European discovery of the Western Hemisphere, that "the historic mission of America is to offer to man a land of liberty". The founding states of the OAS were twenty-one: the countries of Central and South America plus Cuba, the Dominican Republic, Haiti, Mexico and the United States. Canada and the newly independent countries of the Commonwealth Caribbean gradually joined between 1967 and 1991, bringing the total to thirty-five. OAS headquarters are in Washington, D.C., in a beautiful building donated primarily by Andrew Carnegie. Sixty-eight states from outside the hemisphere, the Vatican and the European Union are permanent observers. Spain, France, and Italy maintain observer missions headed by Ambassadors.

In keeping with the Charter's emphasis on the sovereign equality of states, all OAS members have the same formal powers. Like the United Nations, every state has one vote. Unlike the United Nations, there is no Security Council and no veto. Policies are set by an annual General Assembly of foreign ministers. Between Assemblies, policies are set by a Permanent Council made up of national representatives with the rank of Ambassador. Agreement is facilitated by relatively small numbers (35 compared to 193 at the U.N.). Nonetheless, the absence of veto provisions and extreme member diversity put a premium on consultation, traditionally managed through sub-regional coordination. A Secretary General and an Assistant Secretary General from different sub-regions are each elected for five-year terms to administer a General Secretariat whose functions are described as "promoting democracy, defending human rights, ensuring a multidimensional approach to security, fostering integral development and prosperity, and supporting Inter-American legal cooperation".

An "Inter-American System" loosely coordinated by the OAS includes the Pan American Health Organization, the Inter-American Juridical Committee, the Pan American Institute of Geography and History and the Inter-American Commission of Women, the first international body dedicated to the advancement of women, all of which had come into being before the second World War. The Inter-American Defense Board and the Inter-American Institute for Cooperation in Agriculture came in 1942. 1959 saw the formation of the Inter-American Commission on Human Rights and the Inter-American Development Bank. The Inter-American Drug Abuse Control Commission was founded in 1986. Since the 1990s, ministers for domestic affairs – education, justice, labor, trade, science and technology, security – also meet under OAS auspices. Set forth this way, the Inter-American System seems a true *engranaje*, a set of gears that meshes countries and interests, from democracy and human rights to development and security.

The OAS, however, is an organization of governments, and – despite the substantive and institutional variety of its numerous entities and activities – of governments represented through their foreign ministries. This has important consequences. One is that the capacity of foreign ministries to represent their entire government varies greatly from country to country and issue to issue. And since foreign ministries are part of the executive branch, they naturally tend to influence OAS bodies to side with executive authorities when they come into conflict with legislatures and courts. Importantly also, non-governmental actors and other civil society representatives participate only to the extent each member state allows.

The Inter-American Commission on Human Rights is an important exception. Unlike the United Nations, whose Human Rights Council is made up of governments, Inter-American Commission members are elected individually and serve in their own right rather than as representatives of their countries. The Commission helped keep liberal democratic values alive during the quarter century of authoritarian governments that dominated Latin America from the 1960s to the 1980s.

The place of military institutions in the Inter-American System is also unique – partly because it has never been fully clarified. Unlike Chapter VII of the U.N. Charter, the OAS Charter conveys no coercive authority. Indeed, the 1948 OAS Charter did not explicitly incorporate the 1947 Inter-American Treaty of Reciprocal Assistance (the Rio Treaty), which served as the precedent for NATO and its Article 5 commitment to mutual defense. The Inter-American Defense Board was recognized as an OAS entity only in 2006, and its most important activity is educational, the Inter-American Defense College. As happened in Haiti after 2004, peace-keeping operations in the Americas go to the U.N. by default.

From the 1950s through the 1980s, OAS activities were marked by tension between U.S. fears about Communist penetration and Latin American fears of U.S. intervention and desires for economic support. The 1954 covert intervention by the United States in Guatemala went largely unchallenged at the OAS but pressures arising from the intervention led the United States to agree to the creation of the Inter-American Development Bank. Fear of the Cuban revolution provided the impetus for the Alliance for Progress, facilitating a 1962 resolution excluding the then government of Cuba from the OAS. The Alliance for Progress, however, gradually foundered on differing perceptions and lack of resources. In 1965, the OAS supported the U.S. invasion of the Dominican Republic after the fact, but this became the last time the OAS would approve any form of military intervention. In 1979, OAS Ministers rejected a U.S. proposal for a peace force in Nicaragua, and the OAS was largely marginalized from the Central American conflicts that followed, with peace efforts falling to *ad hoc* sub-regional groups. U.S. failure to back Argentina against the United Kingdom in the 1982 Falklands/Malvinas war was interpreted regionally as a repudiation by the United States of its Article 5 obligations under the Rio Treaty. The OAS was again sidelined when the U.S. invaded Grenada in 1983 and Panama in 1989, and yielded to Brazil, Argentina, Chile and the United States in the settlement of the Ecuador-Peru war of 1994-1995. Despite these setbacks, the OAS did play an important role in resolving other disputes, including the fighting between El Salvador and Honduras in 1969 and gathering the hemisphere's heads of state in Washington to act as guarantors for the Panama Canal treaties in 1977.

The 1990s brought what at first seemed like an ideal reset for the OAS. The Old World's negative influences declined as the authoritarian example of Franco's Spain came to an end and the Soviet Union collapsed. The United States called for a new world order. In Latin America, the Central American conflicts came to an exhausted end and de facto military regimes everywhere were yielding to democratic processes. By 1991, when the General Assembly met in Santiago, Chile, all of the governments represented there could claim some form of democratic legitimacy. General Assembly Resolution 1080 authorized collective response to "sudden or irregular interruption" of democratic processes. Haiti, Peru and Guatemala, among others, subsequently felt the sting of regional disapproval. In 1993, the OAS Charter was amended to allow the suspension of a member whose democratically constituted government had been overthrown by force. Electoral observation and concern for human rights, often driven by NGOs, became the core of the organization's activities and public image. In 1994, heads of state and government met at a summit in Miami and agreed to negotiate a Free Trade Area for the Americas. 2001 brought the adoption of a new region-wide "Democratic Charter".

Article 3 of this Charter stipulates that the

essential elements of representative democracy include, inter alia, respect for human rights and fundamental freedoms, access to and the exercise of power in accordance with the rule of law, the holding of periodic, free, and fair elections based on secret balloting and universal suffrage [...] the pluralistic system of political parties and organizations, and the separation of powers and independence of the branches of government.

This provision is powerful, even unique, in its specificity. The United Nations charter, for example, does not contain even the word "democracy". Without the OAS, the development of common ground to advance democratic practices could never have taken place.

But principles, however noble, must still be put into practice.

Innumerable crises and five summits later, positive expectations have not been realized. Venezuela's evolution has split OAS membership into intractable camps. There is controversy over the meaning of democracy, the value of free trade, and the future of the OAS. The Inter-American System is becoming skeletal, fragmented by lack of common purpose and crippling reductions in resources from member states. In 1991, Resolution 1080 called for pressure against undemocratic actions, but it also called for "incentives to preserve and strengthen democratic systems, based on international solidarity and cooperation". What actually happened, however, however, is that resources available to the OAS regular fund have been cut in real terms by more than 25% since it was given the mandate to support democracy.

Today, almost a generation since the adoption of the Democratic Charter, there are few shared definitions, little solidarity, and no resources for institutional support and development. The underpinnings of democracy must include effective public administration, public education, and other human and organizational underpinnings of democracy, such as independent and transparent electoral and judicial systems and a free press. Domestic arrangements cannot as a rule be determined from the outside without violent intervention, but I am convinced that the Venezuelan tragedy would have developed differently had Resolution 1080 and the Inter-American Democratic Charter led to an effective multilateral support system with incentives as well as sanctions – as intended when adopted.

So, where next?

Gaps between theory and practice, between promise and performance, have many sources.

This is of course a bad time for international organizations everywhere. Throughout the world, national governments are hampered by nationalist angers, information overloads, and mass migrations that challenge social identities. Changes in technology and in the elements and loci of power add to the disruption.

These difficulties have also led to the decay of the fundamental organizing concepts of international cooperation.

The OAS is an excellent example. The OAS is a multilateral organization of the sovereign states of the Western Hemisphere.

This simple definition combines *three concepts*.

- *Multilateralism*, which means "generalized principles of conduct" – the creation of predictable universal or at least regionally common rules rather than a temporary coalition of a few countries on a specific problem.
- *Geography*, as in the proposition that "the peoples of this [Western] Hemisphere (or any other region) stand in a special relationship to one another which sets them apart from the rest of the world".
- *Sovereignty*, the sovereign equality of states, the organizing principle of the international system since the 1648 Peace of Westphalia.

Today, in 2019, all three concepts are operationally challenged.

*Multilateralism* is associated with inefficiency more than order. International law has been weakened by repeated failures to ratify treaties or abide by their obligations. A cynic might argue that *multilateralism is now just an idealistic illusion in an increasingly Hobbesian dog eat dog world*.

Does *geography* still matter in the age of the jet and the internet? In 1889-1890, many in the Americas felt they were building a New World, removed from the Old. Today it is not an exaggeration to say that regional pride has been victimized by the new technologies of globalization. Even at local levels, it seems, fragmentation has often replaced integration and community.

Most critically, *Sovereignty* has long meant that individual states are to be inviolate from outside intervention and free to decide whether or not to participate in any particular activity. This is particularly important in the Americas, where the great and asymmetric power of the United States in relation to its neighbors has a long and sometimes bitter history.

That multilateralism and geography still matter is evident in the fact that climate change, illegal drugs, migration and arms trafficking – to take just a few examples -- cannot be addressed by any one state alone. Such problems do, of course, also create domestic pressures and these can in turn make international cooperation more difficult. The rise of non-governmental actors, the organizational and informational impact of new technologies and the expression of previously suppressed grievances, the decline of programmatic political parties, the risks of terrorism and opportunities for foreign meddling – all increase the difficulties governments face in making decisions. But these difficulties do not make multilateral understandings any less relevant. If anything, they make multilateralism even more important than in the past.

For the OAS, a critical question is how will the United States pull its weight? U.S. gross domestic product is more than double that of the other thirty-four OAS members combined. This overwhelming concentration

of wealth in the United States is an unspoken obstacle to regional cooperation. Many in the hemisphere see the United States as self-interested
and unreliable, a Gulliver focused on extending and legitimizing its power.
U.S. leaders tend to see their neighbors as Lilliputians using multilateralism as a form of trade unionism of the weak. Such great asymmetries in
power and perception breed distrust, in the United States as well as in its
neighbors. Recent U.S. inaction – not ratifying treaties and often being an
absentee in regional discussions, can be as debilitating as the more overt
interventions of the past. Still, the OAS is the only forum that brings the
United States together with the rest of the hemisphere in a setting dedicated to the harmonization of national practices into international law.
But will the U.S. listen?

Returning to basic concepts, the most important is to rethink sovereignty.

Europe suffered through two world wars fought in the name of sovereignty, nationalism, even autarchy. As the first World War ended, my
grandfather, Luigi Einaudi, wrote:

> We must abolish the dogma of perfect sovereignty. [...] The interdependence
> of free peoples, not their absolute independence, is the truth. [...] A state isolated
> and sovereign that can survive on its own is a fiction, it cannot be reality. Reality
> is that states can be equal and independent among themselves only when they
> realize that their life and development will be impossible if they are not ready to
> help each other.[1]

Clearly, however, sovereignty cannot be reduced to an obsolete aspiration from a predigital age. Yet in today's globalized and interdependent
world, sovereignty's first line of defense should not be understood as non-
intervention, but as cooperation, working with others, best expressed as
mutual engagement or *engranaje*, a meshing of gears to make the world
turn better than it would otherwise.

So here is my final point: *The world needs laws and relationship-building,
not walls or nation-building.* Armies and barriers are important, but are less
effective under most circumstances than relationships built on respect and
shared rules. Relationships need to be developed, and rules need to be negotiated. In this, people, as well as resources, are critical.

Governments often lack personnel with the expertise to reconcile national interests that differ. A multilateral Academy of Public Administration, with students nominated by the member states to study a broad curriculum, would over time produce a network of professionals who know

---

[1] "Il dogma della sovranità e l'idea della Società delle nazioni", *Corriere della Sera*, 28 dicembre 1918.

how to work together to contain issues that might otherwise degenerate into quagmires of missed opportunities or even escalate into conflict. Having officials that understand how to cooperate without sacrificing sovereignty would be an insurance policy for progress and peace, providing a unique foundation for a safe neighborhood.

Times have changed, but some old truths still apply. *Geography* and *neighborhood* remain key cultural references. *Multilateralism* is a prerequisite to develop the frameworks for cooperation needed on the increasing number of matters affecting daily life. *Sovereignty* still expresses national pride. The new truth, however, is that, unlike the past, individual states can no longer retreat, like Voltaire, to cultivate their separate gardens. To take care of ourselves and advance our national interests, we must also deal with the outside world, our neighbors perhaps most of all. And all – small as well as large, large as well as small -- must contribute their share. Or, to quote Luigi Einaudi again, writing this time as President of Italy,

> The necessity of unifying Europe is obvious: states as they exist are but smoke without fire [...] The choice is not between independence or unification but between existing united or vanishing.[2]

REFERENCES

The OAS Charter and texts of regional treaties and key resolutions may be found at www.oas.org, the critical source for OAS activities.

The Columbus Memorial Library is the institutional memory of the OAS and the Inter-American System. Its extensive holdings include important hemispheric collections as well as official documentation.

ARRIGHI J.M. 2012, *L'organisation des états américains et le droit international*, Leiden and Boston: Martinus Nijhoff [Reprint from *Recueil des cours*, Académie de Droit International, The Hague, vol. 355, 2011, pp. 239-437]. The OAS Secretary for Legal Affairs lays out the legal foundations and contributions of the OAS to international law.

HERZ M. 2011, *The Organization of American States (OAS): Global Governance away from the Media*, London and New York, Routledge. A Brazilian professor evaluates the OAS on security, democracy and the rise of sub-regional institutions since the end of the Cold War.

*The Inter-American Agenda and Multilateral Governance: The Organization of American States.* A Report of the Inter-American Dialogue Study Group on Western Hemisphere Governance. Washington, D.C., April 1997. Prepared at a peak of optimism about the OAS. Available at: http://archive.thedialogue.org/PublicationFiles/The%20Inter%20

---

[2] L. EINAUDI 1956, *Lo Scrittoio del Presidente (1948-1955)*, Torino: Einaudi: 89.

American%20Agenda%20and%20multilateral%20Governance%20the%20OAS.pdf (accessed September 30, 2020).

WHITAKER A.P. 1954, *The Western Hemisphere Idea: Its Rise and Decline*, Ithaca, N.Y.: Cornell University Press. The classic history of the "proposition that the peoples of this Hemisphere stand in a special relationship to one another which sets them apart from the rest of the world".

# APPENDIX EIGHT

The Americas in the World
Luigi R. Einaudi
Text used for remarks for WIFA Webinar, October 27, 2020

Thank you, Tom Pickering, for that generous introduction; Connie Morella for presiding with your usual grace; and Philip Hughes, for originating the invitation.

As I get along in years, I realize that a lot has changed in our lifetimes and I wonder what the future will bring. That is the subject of these remarks, focusing on Latin America and the future of the Americas in the world.

- In the 1950s, when I was in college, fewer than 10 million persons in the US were foreign-born; Persons born in Italy, Germany, Canada and UK, Poland and even Russia outnumbered those born in Mexico; My first trip in 1955 came about because the NSA could not find a single student activist at Harvard who spoke Spanish; "send E: he at least speaks Italian!"; I went, and my Italian did prove useful because few of the people I met in Chile, Argentina and Uruguay spoke any English.

- Today, according to the latest census figures, 44 million foreign-born persons live in the United States, of whom 12 million were born in Mexico, followed by India and China. No European country is in the top ten. At the same time, even in deepest South America it is rare to find people in leadership groups who don't speak some English. Meanwhile, back at Harvard, I read that 13 percent of the student body is Hispanic and English proficiency is not tested for admission.

Clearly, to quote Yogi Berra, "The future ain't what it used to be." At the same time, I am reminded that Jean Jaures once said we should never talk about the future because the present is hard enough to predict. And, I would add, the present is hard to predict because we often see it through the lenses of the past.

- What we perceive about our neighbors to the south often starts with exploration and discovery followed by armed conquest blessed by the Church overwhelming noble savages with disease and gold-seeking greed followed by mercantilist colonialism leading to caudillos and human rights violations all melded into a Black Legend of Spanish rule;
- Add to that Portuguese, French, and British colonialism adding African slaves to the exploitation of Indian populations, the whole creating poor unstable countries, portrayed as banana republics dependent on natural resources in the hands of local elites in bed with US corporate power built on the backs of both black and native Americans.

Even contemporary images can add to the confusion: consider the impact of videos of gigantic expanses of Amazon jungles, empty it appears save for a few primitive peoples, now being televised out of concern for the effects of development. Yet the image of Brazil they project is at best incomplete: Brazil is as urban and geographically diverse as the United States and its indigenous populations total less than half of one per cent of Brazil's more than 200 million Afro-European population.

My friend Tom Shannon, a distinguished Foreign Service Officer who was Ambassador to Brazil and knows the hemisphere well, has described Latin America as trending from authoritarianism with closed economies based on import substitution towards democratic governments with open economies based on regional integration; and from exclusive to inclusive societies moving from isolation to global engagement. Tom, like me is an idealist and something of an optimist, but I believe he is spot on about where things are going.

- 80% of Latin America's people are now urban. In what Marx inaccurately called the idiocy of rural life, children are valuable assets on the farm. Why send children to school, if teachers make them work on THEIR garden instead of yours? In urban settings, people have fewer children. In our times, population growth rates have dropped to less than half of what they were. Brazil Mexico Argentina are all at non replacement levels.
- Primary school attendance is now pretty much universal and universities are sometimes topnotch, but secondary education lags badly, as does science. Only Brazil invests more than 1% of GNP in research and development.

- The emergence of middle and professional classes has undone the traditional ruling triad of big landowners, church, and the military. After a conservative spasm to repress social change in the wake of the Cuban revolution, military governments fell into disrepute and have been out for a quarter century. Modern societies are too complicated to rule with bayonets. The 1990s brought a surge of transitions to civilian governments and a proclamation of regional democratic solidarity.

- But Democracy has not proved a panacea. Underlying tensions, social injustice and the scars of history breed corruption, political confrontations and populism. This century has seen a noxious trend toward reelection and authoritarianism as well as presidential impeachments.

- Castro and Chavez still evoke headlines, particularly in Florida, but they are both dead, their countries depressed and their regional followers in decline.

- From Brazil to Mexico and Peru entire political classes have been tarred by corruption. Odebrecht, the Brazil-based *multilatina* construction company reached its tentacles from the Andes to Mexico. And illegal drugs, corruption, and uncontrolled migration have demoralized and alienated far too many. Even so, civil society, judges and press have placed a spotlight on corruption, even producing dramatic presidential impeachments.

- Consumption by previously marginalized groups has driven domestic economic growth, but the COVID pandemic is now accentuating deep inequalities everywhere. Major economic convulsions are predicted, with downturns on the order of 10% of GDP expected in many countries.

These complicated patterns can take dramatically different forms in each of the 35 very different countries that make up the Americas.

- Brazil has long seen itself a separate from its Spanish-speaking neighbors. When the Portuguese court moved to Brazil to escape Napoleon, Brazil became a seat of Empire, with possessions in Africa and Asia that conveyed a sense of global reach that lasts today. With a sense of the frontier and national destiny that rivals that of the United States, Brazil has become a major global exporter of agricultural products as well as raw materials.

- The Andean countries along South America's spine are Chile, Bolivia, Perú, Ecuador, Colombia. Their large Indian populations are a living memory of the Inca Empire and explain why some have argued their region should be called "Indoamerica" instead of the conqueror's Latin America. Like California, their shores are lapped by the Pacific, which creates an increasingly manageable link to China.

- Venezuela, half Andean, half Caribbean, has been ruined by black gold and its sense of nationhood warped by its early history and later closeness to the United States.

- The Caribbean is our third border. Its small island states stress that security must be understood as multidimensional – including health and climate as well as policing. Rising waters like those now affecting the US from Florida to New York are nothing new to them. 80% of The Bahamas is 3 feet or less above sea level. The hurricanes that have been lashing our gulf coast and Puerto Rico with increasing regularity make landfall there first. At the time of the US revolution of independence from Britain, the value of exports from St Domingue, today's Haiti and DR, was greater than the combined exports of our 13 colonies. They included 60% of the world's coffee, and 40% of sugar consumed in Britain and France. Meanwhile, the economies of the Commonwealth Caribbean, which were still colonies when I was in college, are vulnerable and dependent on tourism, thus devastated by the travel restrictions of the coronavirus pandemic.

- Haiti in 1804 became the world's first independent black republic. Today Haiti is the poorest country in the Americas, its situation a mockery of Western civilization's pretensions.

- Central America. A century ago its countries put C.A. on their stamps to make sure foreigners would understand where they were. But go there, and each country is a separate universe. They survived domestic civil wars aggravated by the Cold War, but today still face the pains of modernization amid the ravages of climate change. The environment has driven migrations since the beginnings of time; the extinction by drought of the Mayan civilization may be finding its modern equivalent in "El corridor seco" in Guatemala and Honduras that has become a driver of migration to the US.

## And then there is Mexico

Mexico is our biggest partner in trade in goods, and is, like Canada, increasingly integrated with us -- and not just through the new U.S.-Mexico-Canada Agreement that updated NAFTA. The land border between us is almost precisely 2,000 miles. More than 40 million current US citizens, 90% of them born here, are of Mexican origin. But Mexico remains unique in spirit and culture.

Next year will mark the 500$^{th}$ anniversary of the Spanish Conquest and the 200$^{th}$ anniversary of Mexico's independence from Spain. And it is just more than a hundred years since the Mexican Revolution, which led to an explosion of cultural creativity, one particular part of which has always impressed me: the concept of the need to forge a new race of mankind by melding indigenous and immigrant Americans into a *"Raza Cósmica."* All this said, the Mexican government knows it is closer to the United States than to God, and this fact sets the table for its official calculations. I will return to Mexico in my conclusion.

This has been a highly selective overview, and I have left out some important countries entirely. If we have time and you wish we can discuss individual counties more during our discussion, but first I want to turn to the regional and global context.

**Let me start with the Americas.**

The Preamble to the Charter of the Organization of American States asserts that "the historic mission of America is to offer to man a land of liberty." This lofty evocation of the ideal of the New World in contrast to Old Europe has never managed to be brought to earth.

The closest we came was perhaps in 1991 when, seeking to consolidate the wave of democratic transitions that ended dictatorships from Argentina and Brazil to Chile and Central America, OAS Resolution 1080 called for collective pressure against undemocratic actions. That resolution also called for "incentives to preserve and strengthen democratic systems, based on international solidarity and cooperation." What actually happened after that, however, is that resources available to the

OAS regular fund were cut by more than 25% in real terms since it was given the mandate to support democracy.

Today, a generation since the adoption of the Democratic Charter in 2001, there are few shared definitions, little solidarity, and no multilateral resources for institutional support and development. Democracy requires underpinnings of effective public administration, public education, human resources and organizational forms such as the separation of powers and independent and transparent electoral and judicial systems and a free press. Domestic arrangements cannot as a rule be determined from the outside without violent intervention, but nonpartisan international support can help deter violations and strengthen institutions. I am convinced that Venezuela's slide into tragedy would have developed differently had Resolution 1080 and the Inter-American Democratic Charter led to an effective multilateral support system with incentives as well as sanctions – as intended when adopted. Venezuela's evolution has split OAS membership into intractable camps. There is controversy over both the meaning of democracy and the future of the OAS. The Inter-American System has become skeletal, fragmented by lack of common purpose and crippling reductions in resources from member states.

Perhaps the biggest problem goes back to independence from colonialism. The Americas account for almost 30 per cent of the globe's land area and cover virtually every geography and climate. The thirteen former British colonies in North America came together and have managed to stay together as the United States. To their south, a smaller number of Spanish territories fragmented into even more independent states. A century later, one thinker wrote that "Independence has been a disappointment," because "it has turned the history of each of our countries into the anti-history of its neighbors."

Believers in Indo-America questioned whether Latin America existed. And it is certainly true that visions for a common future have not prospered. Pan Americanism including the United States is relegated to libraries; the OAS is finding breathing difficult, and the various alternatives ballyhooed twenty years ago are now blips in even worse shape. Outside of North America, Central America's electricity grid is one of the few positive signs of regional or subregional integration.

As a U.S. citizen and a strong believer in our greatness, I hate to say this, but I suspect the single biggest reason for the decline of the Western Hemisphere ideal is the United States. The US accounts of 80% of the hemisphere's economy. The overwhelming concentration of wealth and success in the United States is an unspoken obstacle to regional cooperation. Many of our neighbors view the United States as self-interested and unreliable, a Gulliver focused on extending and legitimizing its power. U.S. leaders tend to see their neighbors as Lilliputians using multilateralism as a form of trade unionism of the weak.

Asymmetries in power and perception make cooperation difficult. Henry Kissinger went to Tlatelolco in 1974 preaching community. The Foreign Minister of Guyana responded, "but sir, have you forgotten Aristotle's teaching that community among unequals is impossible?" We in the US often dismiss distrust among our neighbors as the irrelevant product of things that happened long ago. But asymmetry is sowing distrust as we speak. A staffer who served in the current White House said matter-of-factly a month ago that our neighbors have learned that you "Go against Trump at your own peril."

## The World

Latin America was long described as part of the US back yard. The history of US foreign policy before WWII was largely the history of hemispheric relations. Except for occasional cringe-worthy references to the Monroe Doctrine, those glories immortalized by the Yale Historian Samuel Flagg Bemis (who was known as American Flag Bemis) are long forgotten. Certainly, few today even remember that the precedent for NATO was the Rio Treaty.

But it is not by chance that the Pope comes from Argentina. Almost 40% of the world's Catholics are today in LAC. Three years ago, when the lady President of Argentina emerged from the Vatican after meeting with the pope and said triumphantly the Pope is Argentine, the lady President of Brazil answered just as triumphantly, yes, but God is Brazilian. Earlier this month the President of Mexico took Mexico's Catholic Bishops to task during his morning press conference saying it was not heeding Pope Francis' encyclical 'Fratelli tutti' which criticized inequality and the "dogma of neoliberal faith". He has also asked Pope Francis to mark next year's 500th anniversary of the arrival of the Spanish conquistadors by issuing an apology for the role the Catholic Church played in atrocities committed during the conquest.

But if Latin America can still identify with the West, questions have certainly arisen. When I was a student, elites complained that "the US treats us as if we were the Third World." Guevara answered "we are the third world." Yet it has become apparent that the Third World does not exist. After the Nonaligned Movement, the *Brics* and *South-south* ties were touted as new forces. But for all the talk of the "rise of the rest," trying to place countries in a new global order is increasingly difficult, and Latin America's place has declined. When the UN was founded in 1945, the Americas accounted for 20 of 50 member states. With the independence of the Commonwealth Caribbean that number grew to 34, but the UN now has 193 members. Brazil's global rise proved a flash in the pan when it attempted to broker a nuclear deal with Iran; since then economic troubles and corruption have turned the country inward.

China is now Latin America's second-largest trade partner. For Brazil, Chile and Peru, China is probably the largest market, buying raw materials and food and making major infrastructure investments: electricity in Brazil, a multi-billion dollar megaport at Chancay in Peru. With 20 years of experience, China is learning to operate in the hemisphere. Importantly, it is also taking advantage of multilateral instruments like the WHO at a time when the US is seen as in retreat multilaterally. China's Covid mask diplomacy includes donations of PPE: masks, hazmat and ventilators have, in the words of the Inter-American Dialogue's Margaret Meyers, been "extensive and continuous" at a time when several countries in the region feel they were cut off by US purchases of such equipment for the US and victimized by the scandalous US treatment of the Pan American Health Organization reported in today's *New York Times*. Could Chinese ai diagnostic platforms prove the wave of the future?

**The future**

The coronavirus pandemic is just the latest in a perfect storm of global stresses (demographics, environment, inequality, cultural and racial identities) that are bringing global disorder and huge uncertainty about the future. The risk now that the cleavage between OECD and developing countries will grow, even as more mass migrations are stimulated by climate change and ambitions for a better life as well as localized wars and violence.

We in WIFA heard Dr. Pannenborg tell us last month about the dominance of India, China in production of active pharmaceutical ingredients, a fact that fits the reweighting toward Asia expected by many economists.

And then there is the simultaneous crisis of globalization. Closing of borders and travel limits reflect a weakening of global leadership and of international organizations, US - China tensions, increasing confrontations generally, national firstism and sovereignty defined as zero sum to not lose -- without realizing that winning the game now requires cooperation to build and solve. Everyone is too busy domestically to deal with crises elsewhere, bad actors getting away with things.

So where next? Some economic decoupling seems likely, but the genie of globalization will not go back into the bottle. At the same time, some increased regionalism seems likely, in Asia, with China's Silk Road and the Asian investment Bank; in Europe, with the EU recovery fund; perhaps in Africa. Most certainly regional potential is there in the Americas as well, from North America, to the Caribbean Basin, to the Americas as a whole. There may be a post-covid opportunity to take advantage of eagerness to rebuild, renew, try new approaches. Even so, we will need to simultaneously evaluate what functions and interests we want to support, how and where, and no longer assume we are the indispensable universal nation that others will follow regardless of their interests, and perhaps out of fear. We will need to participate, listen, share.

More than verbiage will be required on all sides. The US will not be able to just "build back." Must in fact "Build back better". Not just reactivate memberships, whether it be WHO or Paris Accord. Or give lip service to UN, OAS, etc. World has changed. The US has changed. The Americas have changed.

The US presidential campaign's focus on Venezuela and Cuba overlooks the vital importance of Mexico to the future of the United States. The principal planks of President Trump's 2016 campaign were migration, trade, security. Mexico, the single most important US trade partner, was the most affected. And the most slandered. The talk of "Disease-bearing" murderers and rapists the middle ages. And talk of the beautiful Wall obscured the fact that the big wall-building push had already was more than ten years ago and that Mexican migration to US was actually on the way down. In fact, since 2007-9 financial crisis and recession, more Mexicans have returned to Mexico than have come to the United States. Since 2016, more non-Mexicans than Mexicans, mainly but not exclusively Central Americans, have hit our border with Mexico, And to the surprise of many, radical populist President Lopez Obrador has supported US restrictions -- perhaps a calculation more of necessity than choice, but a fact nonetheless. Mexico is doing its part at the border, holding back Central American migrants.

Missed in all this is that our desire to reduce dependence on China underscores that North America can be a key. Like the US, Mexico has lost thousands of jobs and hundreds of factories to

China. And it is time to stop thinking of Canada as just another state to our North.

Which brings me to Security. Peace on our borders has long been fundamental to US capacity to project power in the world. We are rediscovering that consolidation and control of sensitive supply chains is important to security. The US done little to control illegal money flows and nothing to stop the iron river of weapons that fuel drug violence, many of which come from China through US middlemen in California and Texas. Yet since NAFTA and 9/11, Mexico's cooperation with the United States has been so close as to be embarrassing to Mexican nationalists.

The US is scheduled to host the next Summit of the Americas in 2021. Eric Farnsworth has suggested a new hemispheric pact on trade. A report from the Wilson Center and the US-Mexico Foundation suggests that "The partial decoupling of China from the North American economy will bring both challenges and opportunities, each of which are best faced with the United States, Mexico and Canada united and working together as a region."

I believe Canada, Mexico, Central America, the Caribbean, even perhaps northern South America are part of the sphere created by the wealth and dynamism of the United States. The Caribbean Basin, broadly defined to include the Caribbean islands (including Cuba, Haiti and the Dominican Republic as well as the Commonwealth Caribbean), plus Mexico, Central America, Colombia, Venezuela, Guyana and Suriname, should be engaged, both multilaterally and bilaterally, with a focus on institutional support for democracy as well as on economic development and migration. But a renewed Caribbean Basin Initiative will not be enough. In the Americas as a whole, the bilateral trade arrangements just negotiated with

Brazil should be expanded, with perhaps a rethinking of the TPP, and a focus on better defining where China is an adversary to be resisted, but also where it is just a competitor to be met.

I don't believe the US or any of the other countries of the Americas should be forced to choose between regionalism and globalism. I was the Ambassador to the OAS when one of the early NAFTA agreements was signed there. As inevitably happens when an Ambassador accompanies his president, I became something of a protocol officer, and spent much of the time escorting US businessmen invited to the ceremony. I well remember two them complaining unhappily to each other that they did not want to be limited to North America, that their interests were global. I believe that is a false choice, for all concerned. Power starts at home and builds outward. The best regionalism is compatible with universalism.

To make the future work for us, I think the most important idea is to rethink sovereignty. Of course our interests come first, but the parading of sovereignty and "me first-ism" is really just vitamins for bad politicians.

Sovereignty's first line of defense in today's interdependent world should not be understood as nonintervention, keeping others out, and attacking foreigners, but as cooperation and working with others to get the best deal possible under real circumstances. I think this is best expressed as mutual engagement or *engranaje*, a meshing of gears to make the world turn better than it would otherwise.

*Sovereignty* still expresses national pride. The new truth, however, is that, unlike the past, individual states can no longer retreat, like Voltaire's *Candide*, to cultivate their separate gardens. To take care of ourselves and advance our national interests, we must also deal with the outside world, our neighbors perhaps most of all. And our neighbors, all countries -- small as well as large, large as well as small -- must contribute their share. The Americas, starting with North America, then extending to the Caribbean Basin and beyond, are a logical foundation for a common prosperity.

The starting point was best articulated 150 years ago by a Mexican, Benito Juarez: "El respeto al derecho ajeno es la paz." Peace is respect for the rights of others. *The world needs laws and relationship-building, not walls or nation-building.* Armies and barriers are important, but are less effective under most circumstances than relationships built on respect and shared rules. Relationships need to be developed, and rules need to be negotiated. Corruption and bullying need to be fought by all parties and are best fought together. Learning how to cooperate without sacrificing sovereignty would be an insurance policy for progress and peace, providing a unique foundation for a safe neighborhood.

# APPENDIX NINE

March 17, 2009

Senator John F. Kerry
Chairman
Senate Foreign Relations Committee
439 Dirksen Senate Office Building
Washington, DC  20510

Dear Chairman Kerry,

We -- diplomats, military leaders, and senior officials who have been responsible for US relations with Latin America and the Caribbean over the past 30 years -- write to urge bipartisan support for Senate ratification of a treaty that creates a framework to combat illegal trafficking in the kinds of weapons used by the drug gangs and criminal enterprises in Mexico.   Ninety per cent of these weapons are illegally shipped into Mexico from the United States.  This treaty creates a foundation for cooperation without requiring any changes to US gun laws.

The Inter-American Convention against the Illicit Manufacturing of and Trafficking in Firearms, Ammunition, Explosives, and Other Related Materials (known as CIFTA from its Spanish acronym), calls for marking firearms, licensing gun exports, criminalizing illicit trafficking and strengthening international information exchange and law enforcement cooperation.  Operating specifics are left up to individual countries to determine in accordance with their own laws, programs and sovereignty.  The treaty makes clear that "enhancing international cooperation to eradicate illicit transnational trafficking in firearms is not intended to discourage or diminish lawful leisure or recreational activities such as travel or tourism for sport shooting, hunting, and other forms of lawful ownership and use."

CIFTA has been signed by 33 countries and ratified by 29.  The US was an original signer in 1997, and although ratification is still pending, Executive Agencies make the Bureau of Alcohol, Tobacco, Firearms and Explosives (ATF)'s E-Trace system available to Central America and Mexico, assist efforts to manage firearms under the Merida Initiative, and provide some modest training for customs and border authorities through the Organization of American States (OAS), which staffs CIFTA's Consultative Committee.

With the recent spillovers of drug violence into the United States, our ratification of CIFTA is now urgently needed to help protect the domestic safety and security of the United States itself.   Ratification would also respond to the security concerns of our Mexican and other hemispheric partners about the upsurge in violence and criminality caused by the transnational cartels that produce, ship, and sell illegal drugs in our neighborhoods.

The Summit of the Americas in April and the OAS General Assembly in June will be good opportunities to convey the clear and irrefutable message that, with CIFTA ratification, the United States is part of critical efforts to reduce the illegal flows of weapons that threaten hemispheric stability.

We appreciate your attention to this urgent issue.

Sincerely,

Cc:  Senator Richard G. Lugar, all Members of the Foreign Relations Committee

Hon. Elliott Abrams
Assistant Secretary of State for Inter-American Affairs, 1985-1989

Hon. Bernard Aronson
Assistant Secretary of State for Inter-American Affairs, 1989-1993

Hon. Harriet C. Babbitt
U.S. Ambassador to the OAS, 1993-1997

Hon. William G. Bowdler
Assistant Secretary of State for Inter-American Affairs, 1979-1981

Carl H. Freeman
Major General, US Army (Ret.)
Chairman, Inter-American Defense Board, 2000-2004

Hon. Luigi R. Einaudi
U.S. Ambassador to the OAS, 1989-1993
Assistant Secretary General, OAS, 2000-2005
Acting Secretary General, OAS, 2004-2005

John C. Ellerson
Major General, US Army (Ret.)
Chairman, Inter-American Defense Board, 1995-1996

John R. Galvin
General, US Army (Ret.)
Commander in Chief, U. S. Southern Command, 1985-1987

Paul F. Gorman
General, US Army (Ret.)
Commander in Chief, U. S. Southern Command, 1983-1985

James R. Harding
Major General, US Army (Ret.)
Chairman, Inter-American Defense Board, 1992-1995

James T. Hill
General, US Army (Ret.)
Combatant Commander, U. S. Southern Command, 2002-2004

Hon. Carla A. Hills
United States Trade Representative, 1989-1993

George A. Joulwan
General, US Army (Ret.)
Commander in Chief, U.S. Southern Command, 1990-1993

Bernard Loeffke
Major General, US Army (Ret.)
President, Inter-American Defense Board, 1989-1992

Hon. John F. Maisto
U.S. Ambassador to the OAS, 2003-2007

Hon. Victor Marrero
U.S. Ambassador to the OAS, 1997-1999

Barry R. McCaffrey
General, US Army (Ret.)
Commander in Chief, U.S. Southern Command, 1994-1996
Director, White House Office of National Drug Policy, 1996-2001

Hon. Langhorne A. Motley
Assistant Secretary of State for Inter-American Affairs, 1983-1985

Hon. Roger F. Noriega
U.S. Ambassador to the OAS, 2001-2003
Assistant Secretary of State for Western Hemisphere Affairs, 2003-2005

Hon. Otto J. Reich
Assistant Secretary of State for Western Hemisphere Affairs, 2002

Hon. Peter F. Romero
Assistant Secretary of State for Western Hemisphere Affairs, 1999-2001

Hon. Harry W. Shlaudeman
Assistant Secretary of State for Inter-American Affairs, 1976-1977

John Thompson
Major General, US Army (Ret.)
Chairman, Inter-American Defense Board, 1996-2000

Hon. Terence A. Todman
Assistant Secretary of State for Inter-American Affairs, 1977-1978

Hon. Viron P. Vaky
Assistant Secretary of State for Inter-American Affairs, 1978-1979

Hon. Alexander F. Watson
Assistant Secretary of State for Inter-American Affairs, 1993-1996

Fred F. Woerner
General, US Army (Ret.)
Commander in Chief, U. S. Southern Command, 1987-1989

# APPENDIX TEN

Our Italian American Heritage Today
Luigi R. Einaudi
Casa Italiana Sociocultural Center
Washington, D.C.
April 24, 2022

Preparing this lecture was something of an adventure. Sometimes it filled me with pride. Other times it was painful. Migration is usually not entirely voluntary, and the consequences can be ambiguous. So please bear with me.

In the 1840s, Giuseppe Mazzini, the prophet of Italian unification, wrote a friend "I dare not tell you that I have found parts of London chock full of Italians living in a state of absolute barbarism. They were illiterate and they did not know how to speak. They tried to communicate with me in an incomprehensible gibberish of their local dialects mixed with pidgin English. Italy to them was a foreign country."

Of course, Italy was not to be fully united for another twenty years, and mass migration across the ocean to the Americas would begin even later. But by the early 1900s, Italian migrants and their descendants would account for half the population of Argentina and almost ten per cent of that of both Brazil and the United States. In fact, for fifty years, from 1920 to 1971, Italians were the largest single foreign-born group in the United States.

Italy's census for 1911 revealed that more than one out of every six Italians had emigrated. The impact of this exodus was enormous. Both of my grandfathers wrote books about it. My mother's father, Roberto Michels, wrote *L'Imperialismo Italiano* [Italian Imperialism, 1914] arguing that Italy's emigration was a form of colonial expansion, by which Italian artisans, peasants and workers were bringing progress to Africa and the Americas. For this analysis he drew the ire of Lenin who reviewed the book and called him a "servile bourgeois" for suggesting that imperialism could be anything other than the inevitable byproduct of capitalism. My father's father, Luigi Einaudi, did not waste time on labels. He wrote that the exodus showed that Italy lacked *"the environment to allow the development of individual courage and initiative. Only when the laborers of northern Italy and the farmers of the mezzogiorno fled Italy's inhospitable soil and its starvation wages, and flooded the empty lands of the New World did they unleash their treasures of energy and tireless work."* (*Un principe mercante* [A Merchant Prince],1900, p. 160)

When in 2003 the then President of Italy Carlo Azeglio Ciampi visited Washington, I was Acting Secretary General of the Organization of American States and had the enormous privilege of hosting him. I said then that of Italy's many contributions to the Americas, *"perhaps the most important has been the men and women who have themselves become part of this New World. . . . At the start of the twentieth century, migrants with less than modest means and little formal education were the driving force; fifty years later, center stage was occupied by engineers, entrepreneurs and technical specialists who were building with their American peers the infrastructure and institutions of modernity."*

That was almost a generation ago. What is our Italian American heritage today?

We are not Italians, and many of us have never been to Italy. We are Americans. But we are also not the original Americans, and we are not like our forebears who first came to these shores. We are Italian Americans, one of the many peoples who immigrated to this New World in search of freedom and a better life.

We have indeed built a new life. But we are not easy to label or describe. We came from different parts of Italy and started at different times. And in the building of that new life, we changed ourselves and changed the world around us. What do we remember of our old life? What did those who came before us contribute? The answers usually come in disconnected flashes. Snippets of family history. Bits of popular culture. Grand exaggerations. Moments of shame best forgotten.

Are these fragmented images and memories of things past tied somehow together? Do they have meaning for our future? What is it that our schools don't teach, but should?

Let me start with some snippets and bits.

The Einaudis were originally shepherds and mountain folk in the Val Maira, one of the poorest valleys of the Maritime Alps, a valley so desolate that when winter comes the population dwindles to a few hundred. My grandfather said that there, above Dronero, Einaudis were as common as stones. In the 1860s, his father, my great grandfather Lorenzo, migrated down from those beautiful but harsh mountains into one of the rich valleys of Italy's Piedmont, where Dogliani is now our family home. His descendants are now spread all over Italy, the United States and Argentina. Other Einaudis fled over the mountains to France, instead of down toward the plains -- I know some who went that way wound up in Mexico.

Nothing unusual here. Italians have always been on the move. It is no accident that the Western Hemisphere is identified with Italian explorers, Cristoforo Colombo claimed it for Spain; Giovanni Caboto (better known to us as John Cabot) was the first European to set foot on North America since Leif Erikson; Giovanni da Verrazzano charted the coast of North America; and Amerigo Vespucci gave his name to the New World.

Dogliani, my family's home town of 5000 souls, also produced an explorer adventurer: Celso Cesare Moreno, soldier, steamship Captain, adventurer in China, foreign minister of Hawaii for a week in 1880, briefly member of the chamber of deputies in Italy. In 1886, a front-page article in the *National Republican* newspaper of Washington, D.C. entitled "End of Italian Slavery" reported that *"a very strong and stringent bill was introduced yesterday in the House of Representatives for the purpose of abolishing Italian slaves and laborers under contract by the cruel Italian padroni."* The article said the bill was introduced by a Congressman from Massachusetts "at the request of Mr. C.C. Moreno." Now incorporated into **18 USC 1584: Sale into involuntary servitude,** the Padrone Act is a landmark in legislation against human trafficking. In keeping with the maxim that no good deed goes unpunished, Moreno was later indicted for libel against the Italian Ambassador, whom he had accused of collusion in the slave trade of Italians.

Were any of you struck by this reference to Italian "slaves"? I was born here of parents who came in search of freedom from Mussolini's Italy. I grew up here. My formal schooling is entirely American. I always thought "slaves" referred to Black people. It was not until I was an adult and found an old poster in my grandfather's library about the ransoming of Italian Christian slaves in North Africa that I realized that I could have once been a slave, too.

The migrants who traveled to America did not leave behind their class differences. Mazzini's disturbed but also disdainful description of the migrants in London shows a trace of that: they were illiterate, could speak neither Italian nor English, and knew nothing of Italy. He seemed ashamed. And of course, there were exploiters among the exploited. Children were sometimes sold by parents to make ends meet. Some migrants were so poor they obtained passage to America by contracting themselves to unscrupulous go-betweens like the "Padroni" Moreno denounced. And there was probably more than a touch of class and regional antagonism in the relations between Moreno, an adventurer from Piedmont, and the Italian Ambassador, a Baron from Naples.

To further complicate matters, in coming to America the new migrants were dropped into a new culture. The United States was divided, like Italy, between urban and rural, and between North and South. The Union had won the Civil War, but the country remained in formation. The original Indian inhabitants had largely been conquered when not exterminated, but in a nation of immigrants the English, the Spanish, the Germans, Swedes and Irish had all gotten there before the Italians. Someone said the Irish came green but soon became white in order to compete with freed former black slaves. Many Italian immigrants were darker than the Irish and had experienced discrimination before they came. Neither white nor black, they clung together in "little Italys" and tried to avoid issues of race. There were some famous lynchings, but Italians were treated better that Black Americans and better also than the Chinese who became the objects of the Chinese Exclusion Act of 1888.

And there were other differences among the various waves of immigrants. Only some 5% of the Irish and Swedes went home, but 49% -- almost half -- of the Italians who arrived in the United States between 1905 and 1920 returned to Italy after a few years. I do not know how many left after Senator Henry Cabot Lodge declared in 1896 that Italians and other recent immigrants belonged to *"races with whom the English-speaking people have never assimilated, and who are alien to the great body of people in the United States."* Lodge's disrespect may have instilled in some a feeling of inferiority and even shame, but it also fueled a burning desire to excel and prove him wrong. Some spent their whole lives denying their Italian origin while being secretly fiercely proud of it.

Migration is a loss for the family who loses a member who emigrates. Repeated enough times, the loss can become an open wound for the sending country and a source of controversy in the receiving country. Such emotions have led to sharply conflicting mythologies. French elites referred to emigrants as the *canaille*, the rabble or dregs of society -- good riddance. In America some argued the opposite, that migrants were the best and the brightest, those with the initiative to leave and the talent to make it here. Official Italy for years focused on emigrants as potential markets and sources of remittances. More recently, trying to cope with globalization and its impacts, Piero Bassetti has come up with the concept of "Italics", which he defined as native Italians, plus Italian speakers, plus descendants of Italians plus Italophiles. He estimated their number, scattered throughout the world, at 200 million, three times Italy's population. According to Bassetti, Kobe Bryant was an "Italic" because Kobe lived in Italy from the age of six to that of thirteen, spoke Italian, and owned shares in an Italian basketball team.

And while debates raged over who they were, the Italians who lived in Boston's North End, New York's Five Points and similar neighborhoods worked like hell and sent everything they could back to family in the old country. Most of them survived and raised new families in America despite the disrespect, low pay, miserable housing, disease and lack of support from the authorities of their new country. One thing was clear: they had no safety net but themselves and their families.

We are now more than a century away from the World War I peak of arrivals. That is four or five generations. More than enough time for the revolt of the second generation against their parents to peter out. More than time enough for the migrants to evolve from Italians to Italian-Americans to American-Italians to just plain Americans. More than enough time for even oral histories to begin to dry up.

Still, there is a lot we can say about our immigrant heritage.

We believe in hard work. That is certainly not unique, as an overwhelming majority of those who come to America come because they do not want to be deprived of the fruits of their labors. But first-generation Italians typically brought with them skills that set them apart: pride in work of their hands, and the knowhow to plant a little *orto* [kitchen garden] to grow vegetables.

We appreciate food and wine. This is one area in which Americans can proudly draft off Italy's success. Take pizza. When my grandmother cooked pizza in Piedmont, she pronounced it a Neapolitan dish – and her square, thick but light crusts had little in common with the round, cheese tomato and everything else piled on pizza Italy reimported from the United States after the war. Italy's ingredients are fantastic, fresh and brought to market respectfully. But today it is the American version of pizza that is now everywhere in Italy and much of the world. Sometimes, of course, the best of Italy can be grossly misinterpreted, even in food. When the billionaire entrepreneur Gianni Agnelli visited President Kennedy at the White House, he brought as a gift one of Piedmont's greatest delicacies, a very valuable giant white truffle. That night, at dinner, his hosts served the truffle, boiled, like a giant potato.

We value family. A strong family is a source of joy, but it is also a primal need, protection, an insurance policy against prejudice and the difficulties of dealing with others in a new environment whose leaders and authorities are not to be trusted.

And most of us are Catholic, comfortable with its saints and festivities and sensitive to the universalism of the Vatican. It is not by chance that the Pope comes from Argentina. More than 40% of the world's Catholics today are in Latin America. Six or seven years ago, when the lady President of Argentina emerged from the Vatican after meeting with the Pope and said triumphantly the Pope is Argentine, the lady President of Brazil answered just as triumphantly, yes, but God is Brazilian. We of Italian descent could all sit back and smile, knowing Pope Francis is really one of us (his father, Mario Bergoglio, emigrated from Asti, the next county over from ours in Piedmont, and for the same reasons as my father, to escape fascism).

Growing up in upstate New York, I was a fan of the New York Yankees. In 1948, I was thrilled when I saw Joe DiMaggio in a hotel bar. He was as elegant in a suit as in his movements rounding third base after a home run. I could not get enough of those Yankees. They had Frankie Crosetti, Yogi Berra, Phil Rizzuto, and Vic Raschi. I was no good at baseball, but they made me proud.

When I visited Italy, my sporting heroes were different. Gianni Cucelli, the tennis champion whose prime years were stolen by the war. Fausto Coppi and Gino Bartali, the fantastic cyclists who helped restore Italy's pride by winning the Tour de France. We don't know these names over here, not even that of Gerlando Bordin, the only person in history to win both the Boston Marathon and the Olympic Marathon, and whose brother sells the best rabbit livers in Dogliani. When he won the Boston marathon, Bordin toasted his victory by opening a bottle of Dolcetto di Dogliani wine.

We may not know those names, but the mainstream of American culture has been influenced – dare I say improved -- by Americans of Italian origin and qualities thought to be Italian. Nor is it just work, food and family. Music, fashion, opera, movies, art, crime, soccer, even physics, banking and medicine. Most of the time, however, the specific form or shape is American. Consider Frank Sinatra's phrasing: his diction is exquisitely pure American English.

There are downsides. The Italian-born Lucky Luciano personified organized crime – and then the movie the Godfather was built on the insulting stereotype that Italian Americans send people to sleep with the fish. No one stops to think that there are far more Italian Americans in law enforcement than in crime. How many people know there is a bust of anti-mafia judge Giovanni Falcone at the FBI Academy at Quantico? Or that we might learn from the division of labor between Italy's militarized Carabinieri and the *Polizia municipale,* its essentially unarmed local police? People don't die at traffic stops in Italy.

**Italians and our Founding Fathers**

The internet and the cell phone have created a culture of immediacy disguised as universal but that is fragmented and unanchored, without the strength of neighborhood or community. Economic history is virtually no longer taught in universities. The teaching of political history is in decline. Black history is controversial. Italian American history is simply absent.

The Italian American Museum of DC challenges this loss of history with a focus on the contributions of Italian-Americans to Washington. Entering, the first display includes tools used by artisans who contributed much beauty to this city, from the Capitol to the Lincoln statue, Union Station, the Washington Cathedral, even the marble for the Vietnam Memorial. L'Enfant planned the District with Rome as well as Paris in mind, sketching an equestrian statue inspired by the statue of Marcus Aurelius on Rome's Campidoglio to stand where the Washington Monument now stands. That statue, to have been of George Washington, was never built, but Giuseppe Franzoni's nine-foot sculpture of Liberty, unveiled in 1807, dominated the rostrum of the Speaker of House. It was destroyed when invading British troops burned the House Chamber in 1814.

A replica of one of Franzoni's corn cob capitals is at the IAMDC. But the visitor will also get a glimpse of something less widely known: How Italian thinkers shaped the basic principles on which the United States was built. Filippo Mazzei and Gaetano Filangieri influenced the drafting of the Declaration of Independence and the US Constitution through correspondence with Thomas Jefferson and Benjamin Franklin. Filangieri, a Neapolitan nobleman turned revolutionary, believed that natural rights were "the dictates of universal reason and of the moral code which the Author of Nature has imprinted on the heart of every individual of the human race." Mazzei, a peripatetic surgeon, businessman and pamphleteer, who briefly ran an experimental farm near Monticello, wrote in a Virginia newspaper in 1774, that "*Tutti gli uomini sono per natura egualmente liberi e indipendenti. Quest'eguaglianza è necessaria per costruire un governo libero. [Bisogna che ognuno sia uguale all'altro nel diritto naturale.]*" Jefferson translated Mazzei into English, then used his concepts to challenge the British King, writing in the Declaration of Independence that "all men are created equal" and "endowed by their Creator with certain unalienable Rights." A recent book, *The Birth of American Law: An Italian Philosopher and the American Revolution* [John Bessler, 2015] analyzes the influence of another Italian, Cesare Beccaria. Beccaria's treatise *Dei delitti e delle pene* [On Crimes and Punishments, 1764] argued that punishments should be preventive, proportionate, swift, and publicly arrived at without the use of torture or capital punishment.

John F. Kennedy said in his '*Ich bin ein Berliner*' speech [1963] that "*Two thousand years ago, the proudest boast was 'Civis romanus sum'.*" For me, the ascent of civilization takes a direct path from Roman citizenship to the U.S. Bill of Rights. There is no Italian Kosciuszko or Lafayette. But ideas do not rust like the sword.

In my mind, the rights to which all now aspire began with *Civis romanus sum*: I am a citizen of Rome. I have rights.

**What my Italian background gave me.**

My family made me aware there were different ways of looking at things. My Italian background gave me skills my purely American friends did not have.

This is not a matter of politics or of ideology or even of culture. It is a matter of experience. Take language. How could Americans know how to pronounce other languages if they had never heard foreign tongues spoken?

How could Americans know and feel the full pain of war? The Civil War was long ago, and until 9/11 American soil had been inviolate from foreign action or invasion for nearly two centuries. Without having suffered wars and foreign occupation, how could Americans understand, let alone appreciate, the value of having neighbors like Canada and Mexico, with whom we are at peace and who share our dreams?

And some Americans don't know the pain of discrimination, because they have never experienced it. I grew up lucky. In the 1930s and 40s, when the Home Owner's Loan Corporation was red-lining Black housing in Chicago, it considered Italians fit for "Blue" areas -- not "Green", not the best, but still "Desirable". And in the university town of Ithaca, New York, where my father taught, I did not face much personal prejudice.

It was not until I went to Harvard that I discovered that some important stereotypes had come with the original colonists from England. The line "The Englishman Italianate is the Devil incarnate" is by John Lyly in 1578 [Hawkwood the mercenary in *Euphues*]. Shakespeare asks "Am I politic? Am I subtle? Am I a Machiavel?" [*Merry Wives of Windsor (1602)*, Act III, scene 1]. I had so absorbed the idea that Machiavelli was an unprincipled and amoral manipulator that I was totally unprepared when my professor in a political theory class asked me if I thought Machiavelli was the first Protestant? I had to learn that Machiavelli was also a believer in virtue, who thought citizens could also distinguish truths from the lies of false prophets. Most people see the world mainly as they would like it to be rather than as it is – and accuse those who see its flaws as having evil intent. Machiavelli was one of the first to understand the world as it was without losing sight of what he wanted it to be.

As I was growing up in mid-century United States, there were enough successful Italian Americans in politics to make it unnecessary to cower to the Cabots and the Lodges. After secretly meeting Winston Churchill on a battleship off Newfoundland in 1941, Franklin Delano Roosevelt wrote his cousin Daisy that "Churchill is a tremendously vital person and in many ways is an English Mayor LaGuardia". Then he added "Don't say I said so," revealing that a shadow of prejudice probably still lingered. But Fiorello LaGuardia, a former Congressman and Mayor of New York City was not alone. Thomas D'Alessandro, father of our current Speaker of the House, Nancy Pelosi, was himself a Congressman and Mayor of Baltimore. There was no shortage of Italian American political role models, even before Geraldine Ferraro.

In my own career, the suggestion Jeane Kirkpatrick made that I be fired as the "wop down the hall" was offset by James Baker's decision to "not hold your italianness against you" in nominating me to be an ambassador. And when I was sworn in as a U.S. Ambassador, perhaps the most touching sight for me was my formerly stateless mother tightly clutching and waving a tiny American flag.

Put simply, my experience is that our Italian American heritage today makes us distinctive, but that it is no longer degrading or handicapping. Some people still anglicize their name to avoid seeming foreign, but we still have enough national leaders named Panetta and Giuliani, Pelosi and Pompeo, Cuomo and Garcetti to know that we are accepted as real Americans without needing to worry that we will be considered aliens or even anarchists if we do not hide behind an anglicized name.

Against that background, let me address two issues of current importance, issues that our Italian heritage gives us voice to address.

**The challenge of immigration policy**

Our experience as Italian Americans has taught us that immigration is a win-win proposition, not a zero-sum game. Both Italy and the United States have benefitted. Our heritage also teaches that the greatness of the United States is closely tied to the fact that, despite some still glaring faults, our national utopia consists of a rule of law that accepts the rights of *all* individuals, in which all lives matter, and in which all should have equal opportunities regardless of gender, race, class, religion or nationality.

Even so, migration policy has become an emotional problem. For some years now, countless men and women have entered the United States who daily exert relentless energies to better themselves in ways impossible in their countries of origin. Their sheer numbers are again bringing growing controversy. I say "again" because today's immigrants have brought the foreign born to about 13 per cent of those living in the United States. That is close to the 15 percent of 1910, at the peak of Italian and other European migration to America. In the 1950s, when I was in college, fewer than 10 million persons in the U.S. were foreign-born; Persons born in Italy, Germany, Canada and the UK, Poland and even Russia outnumbered those born in Mexico. Today, 44 million foreign-born persons live in the United States, of whom 12 million were born in Mexico, followed by India and China. I remember meeting with Gianni Agnelli in New York in the 1980s, and hearing him worry that U.S. ties to Italy would be weakened by the new arrivals, especially those from Asia. Clearly, to quote Yogi Berra, "The future ain't what it used to be."

And there is another problem. Migrants from Mexico and Central America are not crossing an ocean. Land borders obviously make it easier to go back and forth. They also make it easier to replenish and preserve their culture rather than integrate into ours. But to say that our civilization is at threat misses the point. *They* are now part of *us*. Lashing out and repeating the mass expulsions of Mexicans in the 1930s will uselessly compound the pain. We already send repatriation flights daily to Mexico and countries in Central America and the Caribbean -- with effects that are strategically ineffective, locally destabilizing and regionally demoralizing.

What is needed is a return to the spirit of equality before the law that made America great. My friend, the University of California's Caesar Donato Sereseres, once commented wistfully that Native Americans had a lot of experience with what happens if you lose control of immigration. We need immigrants. But we do not need shadow communities that live in the dark, ghettoized, fearful, and at the margin of the law. That is not the American way. We need to control immigration. There is nothing wrong with walls. But walls need gates if they are not to imprison those they are meant to protect. So the real issue is, what are the rules for going in and out of the gates? Today there seem to be few enforceable rules. Uncertainties and visa delays are preventing many highly qualified persons -- engineers, doctors, IT specialists -- from coming to the United States.

As Italian Americans, our heritage makes clear we should not want to shut others out just because we are already here. To regain control in a way that is worthy of our civilization, we need to develop immigration laws that will shape an open system, with dignity and responsibility for all. The controls should define the qualifications and rights of guest-workers, distinguish between migrants and refugees, specify requirements for citizenship, and identify national security and health concerns. To make sure our rules are respected by other countries, their provisions should be approved multilaterally. And then those laws should be enforced, cooperatively and rigorously. As the old Roman saying goes, *Dura lex sed lex*. The law is hard but it is the law.

As a footnote, let me say that immigration is today also a problem for Italy. Since the 1960s, many more people enter Italy than leave it. Something like seven per cent of persons living in Italy today are foreign born. The United States has announced it will accept 100,000 Ukrainian refugees. Last week, more than 100,000 Ukrainians refugees were already in Italy. Since Putin's aggression, Europe faces crises in both migration and defense.

Which brings me to a second issue we need to face, **the Riddle of Sovereignty**.

*Sovereignty*, the sovereign equality of states, has been the organizing principle of the international system since the 1648 Peace of Westphalia.

*Sovereignty* has long meant that individual states are to be inviolate from outside intervention and free to decide whether or not to participate in any particular activity. The problem is that our times *require* cooperation. I have just argued that is the case with migration, but it also applies to cyberspace, illegal drugs, weapons from small arms to drones and nukes, terrorism, disease, climate change – even most economic activity. No longer can any of these problems be controlled by any one state acting alone. Unfortunately, however, efforts to manage these issues stimulate nationalist recoils.

When sovereignty is linked to nationalism it can easily lead to war. Europe suffered through two world wars fought in the name of sovereignty and nationalism. As the first World War ended, my grandfather Einaudi wrote: *"We must abolish the dogma of perfect sovereignty. The truth, reality, is the interdependence of free peoples, not their absolute independence ... A state isolated and sovereign that can survive on its own is a fiction, it cannot be reality. Reality is that states can be equal and independent among themselves only when they realize that their life and development will be impossible if they are not ready to help each other."* ["Il dogma della sovranità e l'idea della Società delle nazioni," Corriere della Sera, 28 Dicembre 1918.]

Clearly, however, sovereignty cannot be reduced to an obsolete aspiration from a predigital age. Sovereignty is as vital to the protection of a country's rights as privacy is to individual rights. Yet in today's world, with so many problems escaping national boundaries and control, sovereignty's first line of defense should be understood – not as doing whatever we want, not as nonintervention -- but as **international cooperation.** The best words I have found in English to express this way of working with others is mutual engagement. The words *engranaje* in Spanish or *ingranaggio* in Italian, a meshing of different gears, may express what I mean more clearly: Gears do not break, but work together to make things turn better. The idea is to cooperate with others in ways that advance our interests without abandoning them. *The world needs laws and relationship-building, more than it needs walls or nation-building.*

My former Treasury and IDB colleague Ciro de Falco suggests developing such understandings may come more naturally to persons brought up in smaller countries that are exposed to neighbors with different languages and cultures. For example, the inhabitants of divided preunification Italy had to adjust to so many occupying powers over so many centuries, that they had to learn flexibility just to survive. This, he suggests, may teach humility, the ability to see the other side's position, and help develop social skills like listening, admitting mistakes, looking for allies, and giving credit to others.

Not too surprisingly, Ciro calls this the Italian "modo di fare." Go to Palermo or Siracusa and you will see why Sicily was once the center of civilization. It has been said that "Norman Sicily stood forth in Europe—and indeed in the whole bigoted medieval world—as an example of tolerance and enlightenment, a lesson in the respect that every man should feel for those whose blood and beliefs happen to differ from his own." [John Julius Norwich].

A good friend of mine and Ciro's, the late Paolo Janni, an Italian diplomat who long lived in the United States, wrote a book in 2008 [*L'occidente plurale*, the West is more than one] in which he argued that the United States and Europe had drifted apart from common origins. Since the end of the Cold War, Europe was turning inward and fragmenting, the United States, also turning inward, was militarizing foreign relations and even to some extent its police. Even so, in a later book on President Obama [*L'uomo venuto da ogni dove*, The Man from Everywhere 2010] Janni caught something else: the spirit of universalism. In the steps of Filangieri and Mazzei, we are neither Italians nor Americans, "*in questo mondo c'è una sola razza - la razza umana.*" In this world there is only one race, the human race, and we had better learn to respect all of its members, however different they may be.

I turn again to my grandfather, this time to his appeal for Italy to ratify the peace treaty ending World War II: "*The Europe Italy hopes for, and for whose realization it must fight, is not a Europe closed against anyone, it is a Europe open to all, it is a Europe in which men and women are able to freely advance their different ideals and in which the majorities respect the minorities . . . And to create such a Europe, Italy must be ready to sacrifice part of its sovereignty.*" [*La Guerra e l'unità europea, 1947*]:

Today, 75 years later, in the midst of the desperate conflict in Ukraine, I would reformulate that to say that everyone, including the United States, must be ready, not so much to sacrifice sovereignty as to redefine it to include cooperation with other countries on issues whose management requires common action. In the name of sovereignty, the United States Senate has for the last quarter century refused to ratify international treaties, from the Rights of the Child to the Law of the Sea. The United States of America does not belong to the International Criminal Court. Beccaria would not agree. Jefferson, who in our Declaration of Independence called for "a decent respect to the opinions of mankind" would not agree.

## Conclusion

In conclusion, as Italian Americans, we have a heritage of which we should be proud. We have much to be proud about, in Italy, in America, and in what we have produced together.

Looking to the future, I see two sharp, even dramatic alternatives. One is to say, we have come far -- it is time to stop and enjoy what we have. The other is to say, we have indeed come far -- and in coming far we learned we must build on our principles to carry us further, and by God, we will not stop.

If we allow ourselves and America to stop and drift in the glorification of the past, to wall ourselves in to defend where we think we are, we will be giving up on the ideals that made America the world's magnet. Italian Americans will then become just one of many morally impoverished fragments of a world in retreat.

If, on the other hand, we continue to build on our immigrant dream of a society open to all and united in freedom, then Italian Americans will be an essential force in building the new civilization we seek, both as descendants of the *civis romanus* and as shapers of the new America and ultimately of the destiny of the universe, as Filangieri put it when commenting on our Constitution. This second choice builds on our culture, food, and religious traditions, **and** reaches beyond them to extend the path from Rome to America to becoming citizens of the world.

Whichever way it goes, whether we become fragments of a country in decline or part of a new civilization, the result will depend to a large measure on understanding our Italian American heritage. For that reason, I want to again thank our hosts, Ciro and Francesco, Father Dall'Agnese, and all who support the IAMDC, beginning with Robert Facchina. To live up to our heritage, we have to appreciate how we got here, and to do that, we have to write our own history. No one will do that for us.

Thank you very much.

# INDEX

Bunker, Ellsworth, 121, 490

Bureau of Inter-American Affairs (ARA), 85, 89, 113, 194, 216, 260, 289–90, 470

Bureau of Alcohol, Tobacco, Firearms, and Explosives (ATF), 507

Bureau of Intelligence a n d Research (INR), 22, 70

bureaucracy, 70, 82, 109, 111, 125-6, 151, 184, 196-7, 225, 281, 318, 323, 360, 477, 484, 496, 502, 539, 542, 543

Buridan's ass, 156, 502, 543

Burlando, Everett J. "Buck", 68

Burns, Robert, 503

Bush, George Herbert Walker, 21, 162, 221–22, 224–26, 229, 245, 260–3, 271–3, 276, 280, 299, 319, 329, 534, 537, 565, 566, 570

Bush, George W., 22, 226, 250, 371, 403, 414, 422-4, 429, 433, 443, 453, 537

Bush, Jeb, 467

Bushnell, John, 145, 247

Bustamante y Rivero, José Luis, 381

Butcher, Suzanne, 119, 286

# C

C-21 aircraft, 309, 333, 340, 341, 361

Cabot, John, 616

Caboto, Giovanni. See Cabot, John

Cabranes, José, 489

Cabrera, Dalcy, 377

CAEM (Peru war college), 70

Caldera, Rafael, 347

Calero, Adolfo, 186

Calle Calle, Carlos Rafael, 342

Calley, William, 192

Canabrava, Ivan, 313, 337, 355, 577, 580

Canada, 191, 229, 240, 248-9, 261, 271, 316, 378, 413, 424, 434, 447, 462, 492, 552, 543, 598, 606, 624, 629

Caramagna, Sergio, 186, 256, 378, 393

Carbaugh, Jim, 227, 576, 577

Cardoso, Fernando Henrique, 311, 313, 347, 350, 352, 355

Cardozo sisters, 449

*Caretas*, 321

Caribbean Community and Common Market (CARICOM), 238, 420, 427, 432, 439, 450, 507; CARICOM membership, 552n15

Caribbean, 14, 88, 114–15, 193, 216, 223, 234, 273, 292, 370–71, 393, 430, 451,479, 481, 487, 513-6, 541, 597, 604, 608, 627; Caribbean Basin Initiative (CBI), 158–59, 193, 606

Carnegie Endowment for International Peace, 3, 480
Carter administration, 111-115, 139, 153, 166–67, 199, 490
Carter, Jimmy, 77, 92, 95, 120, 126, 130, 133, 139, 167, 252-3, 464, 484, 495, 529-531
Carter, Rosalynn, 222–23
Carville, James, 349
Casey, Bill, 180
Casey, Ed, x, 285, 289, 499
Casey, Ellen, x
Casimir, Jean, 424
Castaneda, Ricardo, 171, 177
Castellanos, Miguel, 138
Castor, Suzy, 425
Castrillón Hoyos, Dario, 355
Castro, Fidel, 56, 57, 59, 65, 96, 99, 121, 145, 251, 257, 411, 431, 495, 504, 596; "The Incredible Shrinking Fidel," 283
Catholic Church, 32, 68, 143, 174, 390, 602; in Central America, 152-4; in Haiti, 425; Jesuits, 8, 123, 137, 143
Cavero Calixto, Arturo, 70, 73
Cawley, Carolyn, 272
Cedras, Raoul, 270, 573
Cenepa, 302, 304-5, 311, 317, 319, 333, 367
Center for Inter-American Relations. See Americas Society
Center for Strategic and International Studies (CSIS), 484
Central America, 22–23, 31, 98, 109–11, 115, 119–20, 122, 132-67 *passim*, 179–82, 184–85, 198, 212–13, 215–17, 238, 240, 245, 250-1, 273, 371, 376, 458, 493–95, 506–7, 598, 605–6; Appendix One, 513-6. *See also* El Salvador, Guatemala, Honduras, Nicaragua; border conflicts
Central American Free Trade Agreement (CAFTA), 388, 458
Central American Integration System (SICA), 238, 391
Central Intelligence Agency (CIA), 37, 73, 84, 86, 100, 150, 152, 202, 206, 212, 483–84, 492; Cuba estimate, 282
Cerezo, Vinicio, 187–89, 191
Chamorro, Pedro Joaquín, 177
Chamorro, Violeta, 119, 252
Charles, Eugenia, 216, 423
Chase, James, 197
Chatten, Bob, 130, 470
Chatten, Pat, 130, 470
Chávez Mena, Fidel, 175
Chávez, Hugo, 103, 173, 257, 405, 408–9, 411, 572, 596
Cheek, Jim, 109, 160

Chen, Sylvia "Madame Wu", 69
Chevalier, Gerardo, 449
Chewning, Lawrence, 376
Chiaradia, Alfredo, 313, 348, 355
Chile, 28-31, 76, 84–86, 88, 201, 229, 324, 366, 376, 406, 460, 603; Chilean Communist Party, 99; Pinochet coup, 96-102; influence on military academy in El Salvador, 169; support for democracy, 266-9
China, 603, 607
Chohfi, Osmar, 341, 581
Chrétien, Jean, 423
Christian Democratic International, 212
Christian Democrats, 52, 101, 165, 169, 172, 211
Christie, Perry, 429
Christopher, Warren, 125-6, 280–82, 284-5, 305, 313, 335, 529
Churchill, Winston, 625
Ciampi, Carlo Azeglio, 458, 614
CICAD. See Inter-American System
CIFTA. See Inter-American System
Clark, Bill, 180, 199
Clark, Jerry, 120
Clark, Wesley, 332, 343
Clarridge, Dewey, 152
Clinton, Hillary, 279
Clinton, William Jefferson "Bill," 21, 51, 226, 279–82, 291-2,

314, 336, 339, 352-3, 358, 421, 431, 444, 494, 507, 535
Coffee, Bobby, 42–43
Cohen, Hank, 152
Colby, Bill, 490
Cold War, 31, 64, 144, 149, 179, 202, 210, 217, 280, 458, 477, 494, 499, 505, 546, 552, 598, 631
Colombia, 32, 76, 109, 121, 185, 190, 236, 256, 262, 356, 378, 388, 390, 407, 410, 460, 489–90, 559, 597, 606
Columbus Memorial Library, 66, 272, 418, 511, 559
Columbus, Christopher, 284, 616
Comisión Internacional contra la Impunidad en Guatemala (CICIG), 190–91, 193
Comisión Internacional de Apoyo y Verificación (International Commission of Support and Verification) (CIAV–OEA), 186, 219, 255
Commonwealth Caribbean, 267, 445, 450, 552, 598, 603, 606
communism, 7, 158, 210, 243, 276, 287, 475, 495, 542
Communists, 29, 32, 47, 56–57, 59, 65, 85, 98, 133, 137, 152, 167, 179, 211, 231
Condor. See Operation Condor; Cordillera del Condor
Congress for Cultural Freedom, 28
Congressional Black Caucus, 414

496, 509; "Marxism in Latin America, from Aprismo to Fidelismo," 55; "El sistema no funciona," 74; eulogy for Napoleon Duarte, 172-5; "The End of Conventional War in Latin America: The Peru-Ecuador War and Its Impact -CornellCast," 299; *News Hour* interview on Haiti, 439-445; on Public Service, Appendix Four; on Italian Americans, Appendix Ten

Einaudi, Marco T. (brother), 8, 28, 44, 66

Einaudi, Maria (daughter), ix, 27, 53, 158, 231

Einaudi, Mario (father), 3, 9–11, 13, 16, 20, 28, 53-4, 231, 510

Einaudi, Mario (son) ix, 231

Einaudi, Paula Ferris (wife of cousin), xvii

Einaudi, Peter (son) ix, 231

Einaudi, Roberto (uncle), 8, 373

Einaudi, Roberto M. (brother), 8, 28, 45

Eisenhower, Dwight, 57, 94, 206, 207, 542

El Mozote, 163

El Salvador, 115, 119, 133-200 *passim*, 243, 245, 375, 380-388, 397–98, 479, 507. *See also* border conflicts

elections, 201, 251, 2666, 378, 402, 406-7, 556; El Salvador, 136, 142, 148-50, 165, 176; Nicaragua, 178-85 *passim*, 236; Guatemala, 186-9; Panama, 246; Peru, 271, 340, 413; Haiti, 419-21, 424, 426, 447; OAS, 376, 466

electoral observation, 402; Nicaragua, 237, 249, 252, 255, 258; Peru, 340, 413; Paraguay, 459-60; Dominican Republic, 460

Ellacuría, Ignacio, 138, 176

Ellerson, John C., 610

Elliott, William Yandell, 37

Ellsberg, Daniel, 63, 66–67

Emerson, Alla, 26, 38

Emerson, Rupert, 26, 36, 38

Enders, Tom, 98, 146–51, 180, 199, 245, 533, 534

*Engranaje* (gear, or mutual engagement), 264, 370, 607, 630. *See also* Sovereignty

Erikson, Leif, 616

Estrada Doctrine, 265, 267

Evangelista, Matthew, ix, 474

Exeter, see Phillips Exeter Academy

**F**

Facchina, Robert, 633

Facio, Gonzalo, 107–8

Fainsod, Merle, 38

López Obrador, Andrés Manuel, 605

López Trigoso, Vladimiro, 343

Lopez, Johnny, 150

Lord, Winston, 79, 81, 93, 102, 197, 281–82

*Louisville Courier Journal*, 45

Love, Joseph L., 60

Lovshin, Ralph, 25

Lowenthal, Abe, x, 60, 120

Lucas García, Romeo, 188

Lucas, Stanley, 431–32, 435

Luciano, Salvatore "Lucky," 621

Lugar, Richard, 497, 609

Lula da Silva, Luiz Inácio, 101, 410–11

Luna, Ricardo, 311, 342

Lusinchi, Jaime, 580

Lyly, John, 625

# M

Machiavelli, Niccolò, 34, 625

Mack, Jim, 305

Maduro, Nicolás, 410, 456

Magaña, Álvaro, 169–71

Maguire, Robert, x

Mahuad, Jamil, 313, 349–57, 361, 371-2

Mailliard, Bill, 107

Maisto, John, 259, 269, 435, 453, 455, 467, 611

Majano, Adolfo, 164–65

Managua, 109, 166, 389, 392

Manatt, Michele, x, 339

Mandela, Nelson, 291

Manning, Patrick, 429

Maradiaga Rodriguez, Oscar, 390

Marchionatti, Roberto, x

Marcona Corporation, 105-7

Marrero, Victor, 611

*marrons*, 428

Marshall, George Catlett, 80, 116, 206, 281

Martabit, Juan, 313, 349, 352, 355

Martelly, Michel, 449

Marx, Karl, 472, 503

Marxism, 37, 55-7, 138, 503

Mathias, Charles "Mac", 497-8

Matos Mar, José, 75

Matthewman, Robin, viii, ix

Maullin, Richard, 67

Maw, Carlyle, 106

Mayorga, Silvio, 33, 179

Mazzei, Filippo, 623, 631

Mazzini, Giuseppe, 613, 617

McBride, George McCutcheon, 337

McCaffrey, Barry R., 51, 307–10, 317–19, 327, 330–31, 359, 363, 549, 611

McCarron, Bernadette, 259, 476

McCarry, Caleb, 431

McCarthy, Joseph, 21, 37, 47, 210, 242-3

McComie, Val, 493

McCormack, Dick, 232, 571

McCurdy, Bill, 25

McFarland, Stephen, ix, 305

McFarlane, Robert, 469

McGarity, Bob, 120

Neumann, Sigmund, 60

New Deal, 7, 20, 47, 284, 293, 505

New Dialogue, 85, 92, 102

Nicaragua, 109, 119, 132–35, 140–42, 155, 160, 166, 178–81,183-88, 198–99, 213, 237, 244–46, 250–53, 255, 257–58, 378, 388–89, 392–93, 460, 473

Nixon, Richard M., 54-5, 66, 68, 76, 86, 89, 105, 206, 226, 273, 281, 529, 539, 576

*No More Vietnams? The War and the Future of U.S. Foreign Policy* (Adlai Stevenson Institute), 66

Noriega, Manuel, 231, 244–48, 259, 264, 376, 568

Noriega, Roger F., 21, 339, 434, 435, 437, 439, 453, 466, 490, 611

North American Free Trade Agreement (NAFTA), 131, 159, 272–73, 285, 598, 607

North, Oliver "Ollie," 152, 161, 180–85, 566

Norway, 190, 447

nuncios, 8, 153, 390, 422, 435, 448

# O

O'Brien, Ana Colomar, 378

O'Connor, Sandra Day, 555

O'Hara, Harry, 285

O'Meara, Andrew P., 121

O'Scannlain, Diarmuid, 30

Oakley, Phyllis, 118, 122

OAS. *See* Organization of American States; Inter-American System

Obama, Barack, 273, 477, 631

Obando y Bravo, Miguel, 390

Occam's razor, 156,

Odebrecht, 201, 596

Odria, Manuel A., 32, 73

Oduber, Daniel, 121

Office of National Drug Control Policy (ONDCP), 331

Office of the Secretary of Defense for International Security Affairs (OSD/ISA), 68, 71

Oil, 76, 103, 131, 248, 301, 324, 346, 350, 405, 410, 476

Operation Condor, 95, 100

Orfila, Alejandro, 375, 461

Organization of American States (OAS): structure, 237, 462-4, Appendix Seven, 583-591; 213, 219, 221–22, 227–28, 232, 234–37, 240–49, 252–53, 255–56, 258–62, 264, 266, 270–74, 291, 373–74, 380, 397–98, 403–4, 412–13, 422, 453–57, 459–60, 462–64, 467, 507–8, 547; budget, 143, 461, 599-600; Charter, 236, 255, 265, 379, 393, 402, 434, 455–56, 548, 559; General Assembly, 91, 174, 263–64, 406, 419, 423. See Inter-American System

Suriname, 114, 266, 270, 552, 606

Sussman, Colleen, 198

Swigert, Jim, 119

Switzerland, 3, 7, 447

Szulc, Tad, 196

# T

Talbott, Strobe, 286, 287, 291, 308

Talmon, J. L., 257

Tambs, Lewis, 185

Temple Black, Shirley, 214

Terán, Edgar, 342, 346

terrorism, 95, 214, 403, 475, 505, 542, 547, 621

Terry, Lisa, ix

Thatcher, Margaret, 217

Thayer, Yvonne, 286

the centre cannot hold, 168

*The New York Times*, 58, 81, 196, 239, 445

Theodore, René, 401

theory: complexities of, vii; gaps between theory, practice, and history, 35, 500, 502-3; must account for facts, 49, 292, 541-2; at Harvard, 34, 37, 88, 625; "freezing of power," 105; "popular will," 257; totalitarianism, 149, 257; "national security state," 203; bureaucratic models of decision-making, 502

Thomas, Christopher, 373

Thompson, John, 611

Thompson, Margery, ix

Tingley, Tyler C., 537

Tiwintza. *See* Tiwintza

Tiwintza, 303, 305, 312, 319, 322, 326, 347–48, 354, 356, 360

Tocqueville, Alexis de, 15, 134

Todd, Jim, 243

Todman, Terence A. "Terry," 77, 98, 124–30, 160, 214–16, 430, 506; 1978 speech on human rights, 127-29; *See also* Appendix Three

Tohá, José, 84

Toledo, Alejandro, 413

Tomassoni, Cristina, 377, 393

Tonton Macoutes and Chimères, 426

Tordesillas, 299

Torrijos, Omar, 121–22

torture, 32–33, 189, 204, 484, 623

tradecraft (diplomatic), 295; trust, 88, 122, 163, 292, 324, 337, 339, 364, 382, 387, 485-6; patience, 361–62; memorandum of conversation, 94-5; UNODIR, 504-5, 543; A-100 course, 117; leading from behind, 273-4;

Tragen, Irving, 463

training: leadership development, 209; *see* education

transfers, of arms, 78, 203, 214, 494, 507, 509; of property, 356; of technology, 89, 262-3 transitions between U.S. Administrations: Ford-Carter, 111-12; Carter-Reagan, 139, 145, 159; Reagan-Bush, 245; Bush-Clinton, 21, 279-80; impact on foreign policy, 134, 139, 144, 280

Trazegnies, Fernando de, 342, 348, 366

Trinidad and Tobago, 248, 373, 377, 445, 508

Trujillo, Rafael, 108

Trump, Donald, 575, 605

Tuccari, Francesco, x

Tudela, Francisco, 329, 335, 339, 342, 413

Turner, Delancey, 476

Tuttle, Rick, 61

# U

U.S. Air Force, 63, 64, 68, 70-1, 216, 301, 403

U.S. Army, 5, 41-52, 70, 125, 139, 150, 243, 317, 333

U.S. interests under resourced: viii; lack of resources for diplomacy compared to Defense Department, 117, 471-2; lack of resources for democratic objectives, 166, 271, 438, 464, 600

U.S. Marines, 50, 106-7, 132, 166, 218, 278

U.S. Southern Command (SOUTHCOM), 119–20, 247, 308–9, 318, 329, 331, 508

UCLA, 54, 63, 70, 112, 337, 478

Ukraine, 365-6, 628, 631

Ulam, Adam, 55, 56

Ungo, Guillermo "Meme," 165

United Fruit Company, 31, 103

United Nations: Security Council, 229, 240, 381-2, 446-7; Human Rights Commission, 465–66; Observer Group in Central America (ONUCA), 255; Stabilization Mission in Haiti (MINUSTAH), 377, 448-50

Univisión, 272

Uranga, José Manuel, 313

Urbankiewicz, Edmund, 46, 459

Urbankiewicz, Paulina, 46

Utopia, 527-28 538-40, 543

# V

Vaky, Viron Peter, 9, 22, 73, 75–76, 81, 86, 98, 100, 110, 130, 132–33, 141, 160, 164, 264, 307, 325, 469, 475–76, 480, 484, 490, 549, 611

Valdés, Juan Gabriel, 446

Valdez, Jorge, 347

van Halen, Juan, 306–7, 360

Vance, Cyrus, 127, 130, 178, 307

World War II, 3, 14, 46, 63–64,
68, 210, 213, 236, 470, 505,
546, 553, 631
writing, 10, 67, 69, 94, 542

## Y

Yaqui Indians, 407
Yeats, W. B., 168
Yeats, W. B., 168
*Yenan Way, The* (Ravines), 65
Young, Andrew "Andy," 113–15,
222, 223, 531
Young, Arthur, 134

## Z

Zamora, Oscar, 32
Zamora, Ruben, 165
Zartman, William, 344
Zimmerman, Warren, 92

# Association for Diplomatic Studies & Training
*Capturing, Preserving, and Sharing the Experiences of America's Diplomats*

If you enjoyed this oral history, go to ADST.org where you can access thousands more.

ADST has the world's largest collection of U.S. diplomatic oral history. But that's not all we do:

- Our diplomatic oral histories cover over 80 years, including histories of **pioneering African American, Hispanic, and women diplomats**.
- Our web series of **850 "Moments in Diplomatic History"** captures key historical events—and humorous aspects of diplomatic life.
- ADST.org attracts over **one million visits annually**— everyone from journalists to practicing diplomats, distinguished academics, and students from around the planet.
- We create and share high school and university **lesson plans on diplomatic history** and other educational materials, directly and through a range of local and national partners.
- Our **70+ podcasts** are available through iTunes and PodBean, with 10,000+ downloads.
- ADST has facilitated the **publication of over 100 books** by members of the Foreign Service and others.
- We also support the work of the **Foreign Service Institute**, providing material for those who are training today's diplomats—and tomorrow's.

*Please visit ADST.org to make a donation to support this work and to sign-up to receive our newsletter.*

***If you are interested in ordering additional copies of this oral history (or others from our collection), please email OHBook@adst.org.***